MUSICAL MORPHOLOGY

Musical Morphology

A Discourse and a Dictionary

SIEGMUND LEVARIE *and* ERNST LEVY

THE KENT STATE UNIVERSITY PRESS

An earlier edition of this work was published by the Institute of Mediaeval Music, Binningen, Switzerland, despite the objections of the authors, who took the position that it was unauthorized, incorrect, and not truly representative of their work. The present edition is fully authorized.

Arnold Schönberg, *Sechs Kleine Klavierstücke*, op. 19, Universal Edition No. 5069. Copyright © 1913 by Universal Edition, renewed 1940 by Arnold Schönberg. Used by permission of European American Music Distributors Corporation, sole U.S. agent for Universal Edition and Belmont Music Publishers, Los Angeles, California 90049.

Copyright © 1983 by The Kent State University Press, Kent, Ohio 44242
All rights reserved.
Library of Congress Catalog Card Number 82-21274
ISBN 0-87338-286-2
Manufactured in the United States of America

Library of Congress Cataloging in Publication Data

Levarie, Siegmund, 1914—
    Musical morphology.

    Bibliography: p.
    Includes index.
    1. Music—Terminology. I. Levy, Ernst, 1895–
II. Title.
ML108.L48   1983   781'.5   82-21274
ISBN 0-87338-286-2

Le cose tutte e quante
hann'ordine tra loro; e questo è forma
che l'universo a Dio fa simigliante.

(Paradiso i. 103–5)

Contents

Pitch Designations

Throughout this book, octave ranges are named according to the following system:

Capital letters (C, D, E, etc.) are reserved for general pitch names without regard to a specific octave range.

Preface

The first part of the book, a systematic Discourse, is based on six specific musical compositions. Like all examples, they were chosen to make a point. As a help in analysis and above all for the systematization of phenomena, induction is indispensable.

The second part of the book, arranged as a *dictionnaire raisonné*, investigates and explains concepts and terms necessary for coping with musical morphology. Here attention moves from the more general toward the more specific. The different topical approaches, comparable to a variety of comments on a central theme, complement each other.

Like any dictionary, this one is not meant to be read in alphabetical order; but unlike most dictionaries, it should be perused *in toto*. Overlapping of some ideas and items, inevitable in this kind of arrangement, answers a useful purpose whenever preserving the clarity of a continued discourse. Cross references are marked by an asterisk. They should lead the reader casually but necessarily from one item to another: the entries are part of a dictionary and not independent essays. For the same reason, some concepts (Tone, Triad, Consonance-Dissonance, and others) have been given relatively little space; they have been exhaustively treated elsewhere.[1] All translations, unless otherwise identified, are by the authors. All footnote references are shortened; the complete titles can be found in the Bibliography (pp. 336 ff.).

The purpose of the whole book is to serve our understanding of phenomena in relation to principles. A basic premise underlying all considerations is the correspondence of outer phenomena and inner experiences. This psycho-physical parallelism, implied or stated, may refer to the composer and his work, or to the work and the listener—it is always assumed to be present. Every examination of a musical object presupposes that only the analogy of processes in our mind with processes in nature and art permits us to apprehend the outside world. Whatever bias emerges from our approach (idea over realization, *ontic over gignetic) is a symptom of our tellurian shortcoming. Regardless of the human tendency to favor one side of a *polarity over the other, we know that theoretically both sides are equally valid.

Hugo Kauder, with his special insight and understanding, made decisive suggestions for the shape of the book. Suzanne Levy created a most favorable atmosphere for the production of the manuscript by providing support in many tangible ways. The Research Foundation of the City University of New

[1]See particularly the authors' *Tone*.

Preface

York gave money. Our friends and colleagues Ernest McClain and Robert L. Sanders encouraged our efforts all along and finally went to the enormous trouble of reading the manuscript cover to cover. Their criticisms and suggestions have helped mold the text of this book. We wish to record our affectionate gratitude.

Brooklyn-Morges

Ernst Levy died on Easter Sunday 1981. By that time, the manuscript of our book was completed. As printed here, it fully accords with his thoughts and words. He did not live to see the published copy.

DISCOURSE

I. Fundamentals and Methods

There exist countless musical forms but only a few musical formal principles. Together they supply the contents for a musical morphology.

Morphology is the study of form. The concept *form* points to something assumed to be stable—an entity, a type. One might object that there is no such thing, for everything changes continuously. This view is particularly popular today. In all fields the dynamic aspect of the world is stressed, and the paradox that "change is the only permanent state" has acquired near-official status. Yet nobody is really capable of negating form. What then is the relationship between fluidity and shape, becoming and being, change and type?

Absolute and universal change means absolute and universal absence of order, in short, chaos. Under such conditions, there would be no phenomenalization at all. The world would be unknowable and besides there would be no subject present to state the fact. Chaos is nonbeing. At the other extreme stands a manifestation of absolute being. Such a world of types and forever fixed patterns would know neither birth nor death. The world in which we actually live differs from either extreme. It appears to us first as a world of forms. It is also a world of change, but the change takes place between remembered forms. When the physicist tells us that most matter exists in the form of energy, the term *form* is here a technical expression that contradicts its real meaning. One had better say that most matter exists in an unphenomenalized state. It is the phenomenalized part that makes the world, including the physicist.

The changing, gignetic aspect is thus tied to its opposite, the *ontic aspect, without which it makes no sense. Thinking in terms of types, of forms, is the necessary precondition for the observation of change. States of being are as real as states of becoming. The young boy is as truly an entity as the old man into whom he will eventually grow; and both, although transitory, are individuals and types. Man as a species has changed and may expect to change further, but each stage is the realization of a form tendency growing out of principles that are themselves not subject to change. Stars come and go, but all heavenly bodies approach the form of a sphere. A cubic star will never be found, for the form would be contrary to the mechanical laws valid in our universe. Many such principles have been isolated and recognized. Spiral tendency may be observed in nebulae as well as in plants. Polarity permeates the inorganic and organic realms as well as the spiritual one. Change is thus understood as based on the unchanging. To our way of thinking, the statement is not reversible; for change presupposes something that changes, and that entity is exactly "some thing," an ontic phenomenon.

Musical morphology is consonant with these general premises. Some people think that music is the fluid art par excellence, following motions and emotions of the soul and bound to no formal rules or at best to superimposed rules which are of secondary importance. Other people, on the contrary, hold that music is a purely formal art, much akin to architecture, in which motions and emotions are inevitable by-products. Both opinions err through one-sidedness. Without delving into general aesthetics at this moment (for instance, whether there exists a specific aesthetic emotion or whether music is capable of eliciting specific feelings), we need only point out that nothing received through the senses is free of accompanying feelings. Music is certainly not a purely formal art. Even if we imagined it to be so, its very formality would possess stirring components inseparable from any form, let alone from an acoustical form. Music, however, is just as clearly not a gelatinous art (if such a one could possible exist) but primarily an art of forms. The very paths of our emotions are not devoid of form. Aside from chaotic moments experienced by everybody, the unfolding of feelings and the course of emotions, though far removed from the formalism of thought patterns, are not shapeless. Emotional shapes derive from underlying principles such as action-reaction, activity-repose, gathering and losing of speed and power, and others. Nothing produced by an organism, like the human body and mind, can be completely shapeless. The unconscious and subconscious seem less clearly ordered places; but their products, when brought to light as in an opus or in a dream, instantly crystallize. Nobody can possibly observe a product of his unconscious or subconscious mind without at the same time shaping it to some degree.

Thus music must be granted both a formal and an affective character. The distinction is that between *musica musicans and *musica musicata*, terms intended to characterize two trends standing to each other in a relation of polarity. *Musica musicans* identifies music unfolding according to its own immanent principles. *Musica musicata* is the kind of music at the service of affects and, in a way, shaped by them. As in all manifestations of polarity, one is likely to rate one pole "positive." *Musica musicans* appears as the fount of rejuvenation to which music turns periodically for fresh energy. The two trends alternate, of course, throughout history; but the "negative" *musica musicata*, far from offering replenishment, usually appears as a slightly corrupt expansion of the preceding period, whereas *musica musicans* indicates a renewal and revival. In this sense, *musica musicata* summarizes tendencies otherwise diversely known as subjectivism, romanticism, baroque, and the like. On the most general and abstract level, it is identical with Nietzsche's "dionysian." *Musica musicans*, depending on principles immanent in music, is "apollonian."

What is the meaning of "principles immanent in music"? The answer cannot be simple, because objective and subjective components are not neatly separable. Tone, no doubt, is objectively structured. This fact would be irrelevant to the art, however, were it not that we respond to the structure in a particular way suggesting a psycho-physical parallelism. The situation is further complicated by the observation that not only our psyche responds to the physical structure of tone but that inversely tone is also to be imagined as responding to psychical impulses. The most obvious example is the leading-tone tension resulting from psychic currents induced in tone (cf. *Alteration). Structure and induction are paradigms of, respectively, *musica musicans* and *musica musicata*. Their intertwinement at the very roots reinforces the thesis of psycho-physical correspondence. Not only subjective principles but objective ones as well can be considered expressions of structural principles of our psyche projected into music. The principles inhere in both music and the soul.

A subtle yet fundamental relationship exists between a composition and the listener. It is based on the projection of energies from the music to the listener. Music is not an object existing independently of our psyche. The locus of the composition we hear is inside us, not out there on the printed page or the concert stage. Yet musicians who have to talk and write about music consistently refer to it in terms that objectify the notes and materialize the events. Consider as an example the statement that the leading tone moves up into the tonic. What moves? Is something being done to the tone or does the tone do it? Is it pushed or does it move? Does it expend energy or does it create energy? The example is typical rather than isolated. The vocabulary in the service of music seems totally materialistic: what else are terms like alteration, attraction, up and down, interval, distance, skip, volume, texture, fabric, tonal center, tonal space, and all the rest? One must concede that this kind of language is factually wrong, and yet it is psychologically correct. As long as we bear in mind that tone and music are purely psychic events, the conventional language remains meaningful. The musical "matter handled" by the composer is infused with his inner energies. A note acquires material quality which is imaginary but which helps explain tonal behavior. It is a quality different from that possessed by real matter. For in music the primary event is the composer's inner subjective force (and later, in an ideal sense, the listener's) which induces psychic energy in tones as if they were objects. What makes it even possible to talk about musical structures and forms is this relationship between us and music.

Musical morphology thus emerges as a psycho-physical study. Musical forms reveal much of ourselves. In this sense, one may refer to music as a language. There are people who restrict thought to verbal expression, but the musician is clearly aware of thinking in music. In the light of this broader definition of thinking, the grammars of music seem no more arbitrary than those of language. They are, in fact, less arbitrary inasmuch as, being purely formal, they give a large role to the objective component whereas linguistic grammars are determined by convention. Hence there are many languages. In this respect, thinking in music is rather comparable to that in logic and mathematics, although the comparison will not bear being pressed very strongly. The various thinking processes in our enlarged definition are indeed each *sui generis*.

Specifically musical thinking, manifesting itself in and through time, is of an energetic essence as are all time forms. They are created through movement. The question how movement can be perceived both as a fluxion and as a whole points to the coexistence of two mental faculties. One is memory functioning as a tool that draws the successive instants together into one image. The other is the irrepressible and irresistible teleological urge toward a gestalt.

5

In this respect, music is not different from any other time shape. What sets music apart is that time constitutes its very element. Just as empathy with space is a precondition for understanding architecture, so empathy with time is essential for understanding music. Human measures set the limits. Rhythms, when of time-shapes that lie beyond the psycho-physical parallelism, are musically inoperative. We do not resonate to rhythms that are too large, or too small, or purely mechanical. The cosmic is musically operative only to the extent that it is reflected and symbolized in the human microcosm.

The scientific quest for principles is itself a gestalt urge. Our ways of thinking, which are processes of change, are themselves obedient to form principles that give rise to forms. Both the principles and the resulting forms are the subject matter of pure mathematics and symbolic logic. The mathematically oriented reader might therefore be disappointed by the unmathematical treatment of the matter on hand. We remind him that the significance of the contacts between music and mathematics diminishes the farther one moves away from fundamentals toward the artistic. To be sure, number is in everything, and a logico-mathematical model can capture many aspects; but all that has to do with feeling and volition escapes number. Life in its essence is not amenable to mathematical treatment. Though not life, an artifact is yet a life product. Art products vary greatly as to the components that may be significantly explained by number. A piece of pottery is indebted to geometry far more than a painting or a piece of music. Hence mathematical analysis is revealing in the first case while bypassing the essentials in the two other cases. We may go one step farther. Suppose a piece of music produced by a mathematical model. If it is judged musically valuable, we may safely assume that the values put into the model were taken from music in the first place. Hence a reference back to the model is worthless. A mathematical model may parallel an aesthetic one but never explains it.

We perceive the wealth of forms as a function of form principles or, musically speaking, as variations on principles. The discrepancy between abstract formal schemes and actually experienced forms is of basic interest, for in morphology it is precisely the variation that matters. To say of a composer that he has "permitted himself some liberties" does not do justice to the musical reality. We prefer to admit right away the immense morphological variety and to consider it as resulting from a play of formative forces. At the same time, terminology gains clarity. Musical form principles are few although we cannot be sure that they have all been recognized and stated. Principles unite in groups which in turn may be reduced to some grand or first principle. Because expressiveness, that is, aesthetic significance, decreases with the increasing generality of principles, a first principle is of little practical importance to our investigation. We are not even certain what it is, although many factors point to *polarity as the prime mover that causes the musical cell to proliferate and to induce the musical monad to become a dyad.

The diminishing importance in the perspective of principles has considerable aesthetic-theoretical and philosophical implications. Musical analysis proceeds at first inductively, starting with the single phenomenon and then progressing toward ever more unifying principles. But there are limits to the fertility of this method; for continued induction can reduce any composition, through a series of perfectly licit and logical operations, to one cadence and eventually to one tone, to the monad. In the process, the composition has disappeared. A musical work exists and lives in what has been called the foreground. The value of the piece lies in its individuality, not in what it has in common with other pieces (which concerns style criticism). To remain significant and helpful, analysis need therefore penetrate no further than that layer of which the degree of generality is still close enough to the individual aspect to illuminate it profitably. Against the background of a more or less immediate generality, individual characteristics show in a particular relief; but a generality too far removed and cut off from the individual blurs the insight. The all too great number of filiations implicit in a remote generality precludes a meaningful choice among possible explanations. The distant principle explains everything and nothing.

Each piece of music is an individual form, and the statement is in a sense correct that there are as many musical forms as there are compositions. Individual pieces can be grouped into categories for the sake of convenience. When we use a word like *rondo*, we think not so much of a particular composition as of certain characteristics shared by a multitude of similar pieces. The grouping is thus the result of an abstraction. A category successfully characterizes the place of a composition in the continuum of history, that is, it says something about the period and style to which it belongs. If we find that a composition adheres to sonata form, it is not likely to have been written before the eighteenth century; we can relate its style to other such pieces. But this convenient grouping is inadequate for the understanding of an individual composition. The similarities between the finales of two Beethoven symphonies tell us less about the work than the particular differences. The pointing-out of a second theme or of a development section remains an external description and begs the more significant morphological questions: how is the new theme reached? why does it stand where it does? how does the middle section relate to the whole? why is its shape what it is? The point may be further illustrated by reference to the type of work called *theme and variations*, if we liken the theme to a principle, and a variation to an individual piece. The value of the variation is that of the extreme foreground. Each variation is unique and distinguished as an individual from the species. Its descent from the theme can shed light on both the variation and the theme; but the individual value of the variation is not explained by our reducing it back to the theme, for both possess their intrinsic, irreducible value. Once the insight has been gained that the art of variation is based on a gestalt underlying both theme and variations, further analysis operates for the most part on the variations themselves.

Yet formal abstraction, at first merely convenient by facilitating organization, eventually leads to fruitful thoughts. If pursued far enough it reveals primary principles. In the process leading to principles we have thus distinguished three stages. In the first, we merely describe a composition by isolating keys and themes and other noteworthy features. By uncovering relationships among these features within the same work we initiate musical analysis. In the second stage, we establish relationships among similar and analogous qualities shared by a multitude of compositions. Here abstraction sets in, which produces the conventional catalogue of forms. In the third stage, the appearance of primary principles admits the construction of a musical morphology. There have been some isolated attempts and successes in the past, and we shall gratefully utilize any such prior discovery. Established pairs of concepts like "growth and limitation" or "matter and form" reveal a dialectic truth about structure that relates music to universal polarity. One wonders whether such principles are reached by systematic abstraction or whether they are preconceived ideas guiding the entire process. The very nature of an idea keeps it operative in both directions. An idea springs up to explain a given fact; but the fact, once seen in the light of a new interpretation, then acquires varying meanings by virtue of being inserted in a fresh web of thought. In a morphological inquiry the term *form* may hardly be employed except to connote the *idea* of form, as if holding fast for a moment what in our experience—musical and otherwise—is never fixed and at rest but always fleeting and moving.

If, in contrast to the situation in the natural sciences, the usefulness of the inductive method in musical morphology is thus seen to reach early limits, the reason lies in the unavoidable introduction of the term *value*, particularly as applied to individualization. The word has no place in science. To the physicist, free energy and phenomenalized energy are of equal importance. Not so in musical morphology which is essentially concerned with individualization, with the particular piece of music, with the value peculiar to the piece. Value, like any complex notion, is difficult to define. Everybody takes the "value of the individual" for granted but cannot state just what it is. Life is valued, but nobody can say why. In some cases such as intervals or chords, the concept of value may be replaced by that of specific quality, but again we are at a loss to explain why "specific quality" should be valuable. Yet value is the central concept in the morphology of art, the very existence of which hangs on it. Music does not consist in an application of general principles found inductively. The absurd expression "applied art" encountered in college catalogues betrays the deep misunderstanding brought about by a scientific twist of the mind inappropriately employed. There is no "unapplied art." The individual is what really exists; the species is an abstraction useful in many instances but precisely not in the arts. Moreover, current scientific methods cannot successfully treat the innermost problems even of general morphology. The situation is concisely described by Francis Warrain: "To every scientific problem reducing the diversity of the real to an original unity ought to correspond another scientific question accounting for the selection of the existing realities among the possibilities admitted by the generality of the law."[1] A science satisfying this postulate does not exist today. If it did, its scientific character would be widely denied on the grounds that it is value-directed, that is, teleological.

The inherent methodological difficulties are of old standing not only in music. The intelligent observer whose senses help him reach acute discriminations is likely to consider a preconceived idea as a burden. The prophet

---

[1]" . . . qu'à tout problème scientifique ramenant la diversité du réel à une unité d'origine devait correspondre une autre question scientifique rendant compte de la sélection des réalités existantes entre les possibilités admises par la généralité de la loi." Warrain, pp. 5 f.

needs no theological studies. The intensely musical person needs no system. He is at home in his labyrinth (to use Goethe's language) without worrying about a thread that might lead him through it more rapidly; whereas the investigator standing on a platform assumes the risk of easy contempt for the single case and of deadly generalizations for phenomena that have life only as separate individuals.[1]

In practice, induction and deduction constantly alternate. The oscillation is the result of obvious virtues and vices inherent in both methods. Historical musicology at its best made good use of the virtues of both methods. August Wilhelm Ambros, pioneering just about one hundred years ago in the history of the Netherlands schools, reached valuable stylistic generalizations on the basis of the available music. By the inverse method, a scholar coming across an unknown musical manuscript in some library will be able to place it in the proper historical context by relating it to general criteria. On the other hand, the pitfalls of induction often trap program annotators who pretend to offer an analysis whereas they actually transfer the music into words by rendering a "blow-by-blow" account of the events. The vices of deduction have been widely spread by textbooks that explain musical forms as static "patterns," thus causing unending distress to students who rightly fail to fit an individual composition into the offered scheme. Another example of this kind is Schindler's suggestion to Beethoven that the last piano sonata is incomplete because it lacks the expected number of movements.

Amidst these difficulties we submit that the danger of the analytic method is greater when not preceded by a synthetic idea. One can reduce a living organism, like a work of art, into its elements but cannot revive it by putting these elements together again. Therefore we shall yield to the tendency known to scientists and artists alike and well formulated by Goethe in the course of his own morphological studies: "To recognize organic formations, to comprehend their external sensible features within a context, to interpret them as indications of an inner structure, and thus to achieve an understanding of the whole."[2]

Thinking in music cannot be elucidated by thinking in other terms; hence, talking about music is difficult. A study in musical morphology aims at sensitizing us to specifically musical shapes. To this end, all means may be used. Ultimately, however, the world of music—a world entirely *sui generis*—has to be comprehended in its own terms. Musical thinking is the goal.

---

[1]Goethe, "Zur Morphologie," pp. 53 f.

[2]"Es hat sich daher auch in dem wissenschaftlichen Menschen zu allen Zeiten ein Trieb hervorgetan, die lebendigen Bildungen als solche zu erkennen, ihre aüssern sichtbaren, greiflichen Teile im Zusammenhange zu erfassen, sie als Andeutungen des Innern aufzunehmen und so das Ganze in der Anschauung gewissermassen zu beherrschen." Ibid., p. 55.

II. Growth and Limitation

Any form, in music or elsewhere, is the product of two basic forces: one generating, and the other limiting. The interplay of both forces is essential. Growth without limitation leads to a kind of universal cancer, an annihilation of form, whereas limitation without a generative counterforce remains an empty concept, a denial of matter. Neither process alone is capable of yielding a morphology. As a first step toward understanding the morphé of any phenomenon, musical or other, we must recognize, isolate, and interrelate those elements that produce growth and those that counteract it.

For this purpose, we shall investigate six pieces, arbitrarily chosen except for their stylistic spread and readily exchangeable for any other comparable set:[1]

(1)   Gregorian Kyrie I from Missa III (In Festis Solemnibus. 2.).
(2)   Organum "Benedicamus" from the school of Compostela.
(3)   Josquin des Prez, Kyrie II from *Missa Pange lingua*.
(4)   Bach, closing chorale from Cantata 78.
(5)   Beethoven, *Marcia funebre* from Symphony no. 3.
(6)   Schönberg, fourth piece from *Sechs kleine Klavierstücke* op. 19.

We shall first point out certain characteristics of the music and then proceed from them to the formulation of principles.

GROWTH: SIX CASES

For our immediate purpose, we restrict ourselves to two questions: what initiates growth in a musical composition? How does growth continue? Forces limiting the growing power will be discussed afterwards.

(1)   Gregorian Kyrie I from Missa III (In Festis Solemnibus. 2.).

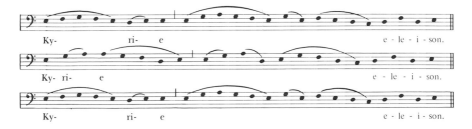

[1]The source of (1) is the *Liber usualis*, p. 22. The Compostela organum (2), preserved in the Codex Calixtinus, f. 190, has been reprinted by Anglès, *Huelgas*, 3:47. Our remaining examples are too popular to require source references.

The chant of the Gregorian Kyrie is set off by an oscillation around the opening tone e_1. The vital force here is the thrust upward from the given tonal level. This disturbance of the neutral condition—an arbitrary artistic act at the moment—comes in conflict with the tendency to restore it. The melody drops back to the original position, but inertia drives it beyond the goal, where the process and direction become reversed. As if following a law of oscillation, the amplitude of the secondary curve below the position of rest is slightly smaller than that of the initial curve above. The energy temporarily spends itself on reaffirming the regained tonic e_1.

The continuation of the first Kyrie exclamation after the incision grows out of this oscillation. The amplitude around the central point e_1 increases by one whole step in each direction. The wider swing accounts for the greater length of the second phrase and also for the ripple in the descending wave. Continuing the established up-and-down rhythm, the second wave shows the same general behavior as the first, but it is more complex. It requires a deeper breath, metaphorically and actually, appropriate for the wider and longer oscillation and for the variations within the descent. The result is an intensification of the movement. The cadential "eleison," ending the wave, reestablishes the tonal and melodic balance. Taking in the growth of the entire Kyrie I—as one might try to comprise in one glance the total shape of a tree without at first being distracted by leaves and twigs—we are quickly aware of the identity of the third and first exclamations, the main structural feature of the whole. The middle Kyrie is ostensibly different, most strikingly so in the central fall of a fifth. Yet one soon recognizes many details that have grown out of the movement of the first exclamation. There are again two main oscillations, both in the same up-down direction, of which the second one is longer, wider, and more ruffled than the first. The overall length and ambitus are the same. One hears similar intervallic and rhythmic motives. Most noticeably, the final balancing cadences are identical. The whole second exclamation sounds like a contrasting variation activated by the intensified breathing energy of the first.

(2) Organum "Benedicamus" from the school of Compostela.

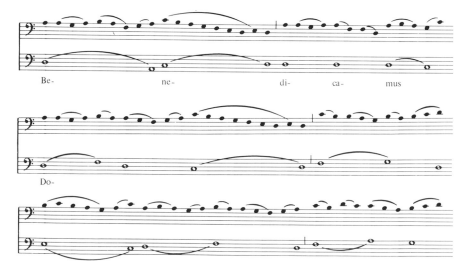

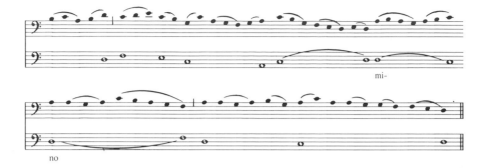

mi-

no

The Compostela organum would produce similar insights if we concentrated on the tenor chant alone, which forms the backbone.[1] Thus we can isolate in the tenor the decisive phenomenalization of energy in the initial skip of a fourth and the consequent push back toward the temporary reestablishment of balance on d_1. The second member after the incision continues the oscillation; and the result, here as in the Gregorian example, is a longer, wider, and more complex wave. Both members come to rest with the same cadence. But these characteristics concern us less than the new, specifically polyphonic, morphological forces. The fresh source of energy springs from the parting of the lines and subsequent interplay of divergence and attraction. The duplum, which stylistically could begin on unison or octave, in this case has split off from the tenor by directly materializing the inherent tonal potential of the fifth. The oscillation around a_1 contains a tendency to move away from the tenor; but the effort of the ascent to c makes the melody snap back, like a stretched rubber band, all the way to the tenor finalis. While thus each separate line possesses its own growing power, the energy gained from the relationship of the two melodies toward each other—in short, from the new concept of polyphony—is more than just the sum of its components. The lower voice in the Hypodorian mode and the upper voice in the Dorian mode are complementary; each covers part of the area on either side of the given finalis.

The splitting of the starting tone in two directions, which initiates growth, also carries within itself the germ of a desired reunification, which is temporarily accomplished on the octaves a_2–a_1 and c_1–c, and more definitively on the unison d_1 at the end of the phrase and eventually of the piece. The stretching of the tenor serves well the growth of both the discant line and the whole. Each chant note becomes identified with a *Klang* on which the fluid discant elaborates. In this busy activity of unfolding in time an otherwise momentary chant tone, the discant, proceeding with considerable liberty, submits to the cohesion of the polyphonic fabric whenever the *Klang* changes, particularly so in cadences. Those are the moments of consonance, that is, of more or less strong reconciliation of the two otherwise divided voices. In addition to this basic and morphologically understandable rule of early polyphony, the musicians around the year 1100 knew very well the concomitant need for independence arising out of the initial split. John Cotton prescribed:

---

[1] *Liber usualis*, p. 124.

"Ubi in recta modulatione est elevatio, ibi in organica fiat depositio & e converso" ("When the tenor rises, the organum should fall, and the other way around").[1] Even if this sentence was hardly so stringently obeyed as expressed, it conveys a very early formulation of a basic polyphonic principle contributing to growth. Safeguarded by this double relationship to the given chant—consonance and contrary motion—the discant can freely indulge in its own up-down and forward movements which produce extended ornamentations and melismas around otherwise tight cells.

(3)   Josquin des Prez, Kyrie II from *Missa Pange lingua.*

[1]*De musica.* Reprinted in Gerbert, 2:264.

A highly developed polyphonic composition, such as the second Kyrie from Josquin des Prez's *Missa Pange lingua,* is energized by the technical demands of imitation. One can, if one wishes, isolate, in this as in any other case, the growing power of each individual line. Thus the lead-off voice of the soprano comes to life through the rhythmic articulation of the opening tone *g* (3/4) and gathers momentum in the rhythmic acceleration and intensification (3/8 + 4/8 + 5/8) of the subsequent rise and fall. But what concerns us here primarily is the growth of this composition as a polyphonic whole. Imitation is the given condition of the particular style. The answer of the second voice, although on a different pitch, is tantamount to a splitting in two of the initial cell. The splitting then continues with the entrance of each new voice. The trend of polyphony is thus congenitally toward an indefinite multiplicity. The desire for reunification—so obvious in the example of early polyphony— is here repeatedly thwarted by the rhythmic independence and hence incongruity of the parts. When one voice has apparently recovered a state of balance, the other voice pushes forward. Even before soprano and alto become reconciled, tenor and bass have begun their activities in turn; and the growth continues—ad infinitum, one is tempted to say.

Rhythm seems to be the strongest of the expansive forces. Much can be learned from the first soprano phrase (of which the first half, one remembers, gained life from the rhythmic articulation of the opening tone and the subsequent rhythmic intensification of the melodic curve). The melody of the second half (mm. 4–6) repeats the curve with a wider amplitude—similar to the technique observed in our Gregorian example—and even marks the indebtedness to the first wave by the employment of a similar four-note motive at the top. But what really determines the morphological growth of the entire phrase is the rhythmic relationship of the two halves. They mirror each other around the central incision:

$$3 \, \flat \mid 3 \, \flat + 4 \, \flat + 5 \, \flat \parallel 5 \, \flat + 4 \, \flat + 3 \, \flat \mid 3 \, \flat$$

The simultaneous counterrhythm of the alto complicates and intensifies the situation considerably:

$$3 \, \flat \mid 3 \, \flat + 4 \, \flat + 5 \, \flat + 6 \, \flat \mid 3 \, \flat$$

We spoke of a "congenital trend of polyphony toward an indefinite multiplicity." The course of this composition makes us increasingly aware of a kind of arbitrariness in its continuation. One notices the obviously new section as marked by rests in all voices but the tenor; but why just this continuation which seems inherently neither cogent nor necessary? It may be best explained as a completion of "unfinished business" although there may be many ways of winding up the loose ends. The most urgent is the unification of all participating voices into a full sonority; they do not move simultaneously in a four-part polyphonic texture before the second section is well under way. The soprano, leading off in both sections, attracts attention to its own curve and ambitus: breaking off on *c*¹ in a Phrygian setting, it demands a continuation to sink back to the tonic, whereby the climactic *d*¹ of the total line is rounded off by its lower octave just one note before the last. The prominence of the soprano (not a rare phenomenon after 1500 and even more understandable in the absence of a cantus firmus as in this Kyrie) is further underscored by parallel tenths first in the tenor and then in the bass. Apart from the general outline and the initial rhythmic reminiscence ($\downarrow$. $\downarrow$ $\downarrow$), the new theme sounds arbitrarily invented. Yet it serves the principle of imitation. The bass alone carries it out, as if forming against the soprano an outside frame for the unified texture; the missing two sequential units are accounted for in the closing cadence. If alto and bass are the voices that spill over in a double cadenza after their partners have already come to rest (characteristic of a typical device of Josquin's), one accepts their role as compensatory for each having been a follower in the exposition.

(4) Bach, closing chorale from Cantata 78.

Homophony adds a life force of its own, most organically when it accords with that of the melody it serves. The first tone d^1 of the closing chorale tune in Bach's Cantata "Jesu, der du meine Seele" receives a special charge from its position as a fifth of the underlying G minor triad. The balance of the harmony is disturbed—a point that becomes noticeably clear if one compares the layout of the opening chord with that of the final chord, which is perfectly poised in its conformation to the harmonic series. The tendency of the melody to descend from the fifth to the tonic, inherent in its overall structure, is thus immediately elucidated by the harmonization. The curve begins at its peak— explosively when contrasted to the rise and fall of our Gregorian example. The melodic descent here utilizes the interval of a fourth as a motivic cell. The generative power of the fourth issues from its conspicuously not being the fifth which the harmony has prefigured. The motive appears pure in the first measure, and then in two sequences filled out by step progressions (mm. 2 and, respectively, 3–4). At the end of the entire opening four-measure phrase, the melody has thus descended one fourth, each measure accounting for one step. This melodic motive and span are nourished by the simultaneous move of the bass down a fourth from tonic to dominant. The growing power of this seed extends through the entire chorale; for not until the very last phrase does the melodically incomplete fourth stretch to a fifth which rounds off the descending scale, and the harmonic half cadence is answered by the definitive dominant-tonic progression.

In the given homophonic-metric style, the structure unfolds as if there were no other way. Just as the opening two-measure phrase in the tonic is answered by a two-measure phrase in the dominant, so this entire strophe is now answered by its repetition; and the symmetry of this eight-measure group now demands a balancing unit of equal length. Any deviation from this metric growth, though possible, would be perceived as an anomaly, like a knot on a branch. The arrangement does not originate in the given text; rather, the eight-line form of the literary stanza also follows musical principles. The harmonic structure of the second half underlines and mirrors the metric symmetry: it flows back from dominant to tonic in two-measure phrases, first in the relative chords (mm. 10 and 12) and then in the authentic chords (mm. 14 and 16).

Throughout, the melody pursues its task of completing the descending scale from the fifth to the tonic, utilizing as a unifying motive the characteristically incomplete fourth. Having supplied the initial momentum in the opening four-measure strophe, the force of this drive and of the motive asserts itself in a literal repetition or counterstatement, doubling, as it were, the available energy. In the continuation of the second half, the melody overshoots the goal in the descending fourth b-flat to f; or, taking this phrase as a whole, we can think of the desired descending fifth completed but on a wrong part of the scale (c^1 to f). The melodic climax of the whole chorale (e^1-flat) is reached by an inversion of the motivic fourth piled on top of itself so that the climax is moreover experienced as the peak of a seventh. After this detour, the initial situation and melodic level are regained: within the next two measures, d^1 occupies five beats and is at last harmonized as the top of a D major dominant chord. Then the closing phrase spends all accumulated energy on the one complete descending scale from fifth to unison—contained in the seed of the beginning, unfolded in the continuation, and now finally accomplished. By appearing in doubled time values, even in this last descent the motivic fourth d^1 to a displays its vital role within the whole composition.

(5) Beethoven, *Marcia funebre* from Symphony no. 3.

The masters of the Vienna classical school combine the polyphonic and harmonic accomplishments of their immediate predecessors; but the new distinguishing element in their ripe style stems from meter. Organization by multiplication of a steady time unit—familiar from dance music—indeed characterizes the music of the entire period and not only an avowed march like the second movement of Beethoven's Eroica Symphony.[1] Repetition of an initial unit creates a phrase; repetition of the phrase, a period; of the period, a section; and so all through the movement. Any modification of, or substitution for, the repetition does not invalidate the basic process. This element of metric repetition accounts for the growth of cell units by multiples of 2. The eight-measure phrase at the beginning of the *Marcia funebre* shows this organization very clearly. The unfolding of the harmonic cadence and the rise and fall of the melody are shaped by the metric process. The metric-harmonic style sets up a framework of high structural probability. But whereas the Bach chorale grows out of the inherent potential, the Beethoven march is energized by a series of willfully imposed interferences. Within the given regularity of the opening phrase, one signal disturbing event (Beethoven's "idea" or "invention") acts as a particularly strong generative irritant, like a grain of sand inside an oyster shell. The melodic compass of the determinate octave g_1 to g (around the centric c) is transgressed by a climactic dissonant ninth (m. 6). The triadic flow of both the melodic outline and the harmonic progression is simultaneously stalled on the tense ambivalence of a diminished seventh chord. As if the sudden suspension of the arsis in the group rhythm were not enough of a metrical upheaval in a march, the whole event (anticipated melodically, harmonically, and metrically by the heterophony of the bass) explodes dynamically (*sf*) in an otherwise weak measure.

The generative power of this tone A-flat pervades the whole composition, charging and recharging the march until it assumes unprecedented dimensions. This kind of manifestation of energy, by continued upheaval, is singularly effective within the ostensible framework of a rather rigid meter and set form. In the very first repetition, the melody is deflected precisely on the crucial pitch (m. 14, crescendo). We recognize the force of A-flat again in the shaping of the episode theme (mm. 17 ff., see particularly mm. 19, 21, 22, 27, 29); the modulation of the restatement (mm. 31 ff.); and the modulation to the trio (mm. 65 ff.). The metrically established structure traditionally calls for the symmetry of march-trio-march. Yet the section after the return of Minore is

[1]The full score is too long to warrant reproduction at this spot. A reader of this book is likely to have easy access to a copy of the music.

about twice the length of its earlier counterpart and longer than the first Minore and Maggiore sections together. The willful detour begins precisely on the critical tone *a*-flat in the sixth measure (m. 110) and lasts for about the same length as the main section before finding the real recapitulation (m. 173). The entire detour—the big event of the whole march—can be morphologically understood as an exploration of the disturbing agent A-flat, harmonically as well as melodically. The detour ends when all energy bestowed on the exploration has been spent so that nothing but the bare A-flat remains (mm. 157 ff.). Because the ensuing real recapitulation is considerably more concise than the opening Minore section—the need for an explicit exposition of the critical A-flat having disappeared—a coda (mm. 209 ff.) compensates for the apparent lack of symmetry. The organic relationship of this closing section to the whole movement is clearly marked, not just by the length which reestablishes the violated metric proportions, but by the final utilization of the genetic force A-flat. Thus one understands the harmonic deceptive cadence toward A-flat major; the melodic last flickering in the expressive oboe and clarinet voices (particularly mm. 215 ff., 225 ff., 232 ff.); and the cadenza-like breaking-up of the first violin (particularly mm. 236, 242). The growing power, that is, the disturbance outside the tonic triad, literally does not come to rest until the dynamically pronounced penultimate measure. The principle of metric disturbances and restorations of balance, made audible by the concurrence of harmonic disturbances, governs the smaller structural units as much as the whole. Without having to identify for our immediate purpose all such occurrences, we need merely point to the metric and harmonic caesuras organizing the exposition. One hears a structure in which the main march motive, after the opening eight-measure phrase and its immediate repetition, returns twice more, the intermittent separations clearly setting up their own but related morphological properties and proportions.

(6) Schönberg, fourth piece from *Sechs kleine Klavierstücke* op. 19.

In the Piano Piece by Schönberg one discerns three sections of about equal length, clearly separated from each other by a cessation of movement (mm. 5 and 9); but at first hearing, these sections hardly seem to relate to each other. Elements once encountered—such as the initial dotted rhythm or the figuration in sixteenth notes—never recur. Harmony is denied. The main impulse comes from rhythm. The three sections can be interpreted as variations on a rhythm emerging from the relation of the first two measures to each other.[1] Anticipated in character by the brisk initial anacrusis, the result, contained within the opening phrasing slur, is an anapaest with an appended afterbeat: ◡ ◡ | — ◡. This rhythm generates the movement and also ties the subsequent sections to the first. At its initial appearance, the rhythmic figure coincides with a melodic motive:

[1]Cooper and Meyer in *Rhythmic Structure*, pp. 174–77, use this piece to illustrate "rhythmic transformation."

20

In the course of the composition, the melodic motive undergoes transformations which detach it in varying degrees from the initial anapest.

The immediate answer at the beginning, in the tradition of a classic metric consequent, is dominated by the same rhythm (mm. 3–4). The upbeat makes the point clearly, notwithstanding the increased internal movements and the slight extension due to a shift of the second anapaestic syllable (from the third to the fourth eighth of m. 3). Each phrase spans an octave—the first from a^1 to a, the second from e^1 to e. The resulting correspondence, though not translucent, derives in this respect from the traditional imitation at the fifth. The statement-answer relationship of the two phrases is thus reinforced. The melodic motive contributes by appearing, although in variants, in the consequent. Ignoring the spelling (which is justified in this borderline style between tonality and atonality) and hearing the accented sixteenth notes (m. 3) as appoggiaturas, one is left with a B-flat minor scale prepared by its proper dominant triad F. A disturbing and for the moment unexplainable element is the sharply accented interval outside the phrase (m. 2). The corresponding spot in the consequent, although a chord conglomeration (m. 4), reestablishes a relation to the whole by accepting the low dynamic level and spanning another octave, d_2–d. The particular pitches of the three octave events—A, E, and D—are unexpectedly conventional within the externally experimental context.

The fundamental anapaest with an afterbeat, already heard in two versions in the opening section, fills the second section in further transformations of varying extension. From the current of the rhythm, the A-octave arises for a fleeting moment with an intimation of the opening melodic motive. One wonders whether the two other octave events, on E and D, determine, now reduced to a hint, the very pronounced last two pitches of this section. The third section develops the anapaest on several levels. In diminution one hears it in each of the two groups that rush from *forte* to *fortissimo*; and in augmentation, in the unit of the closing three measures. Taken together, these three transformations form an overall anapaest which, in turn, provides the accent of a still larger similar rhythm that spans the three sections of the entire composition.

The rhythmic development is occasionally attended by that of the melodic motive. Initially identified with the rhythm, the motive splits in three at the first repetition (mm. 3–4); this behavior might have some bearing on the three-section morphé. Motive and rhythm are farthest apart in the middle section (cf. m. 7), whereas they show some reconciliation at the end (m. 10).

INITIAL GROWTH: PRINCIPLES

These six cases each display an individual vitality. We shall investigate first those forces that initiate growth, and those that provide for continued growth, before turning to examples and principles of limitation. The question arises whether these compositions might all be offsprings of a genetic force that lies beyond and above all musical styles. Examining our findings, as it were, naïvely—a difficult but fruitful attitude—we notice an event that we may describe as a splitting of a given unit or element. The opening tone of the Gregorian Kyrie seems to be pushed in two opposite directions; it moves up and it moves down. The Compostela organum makes the initial split more obvious by letting two separate voices act out the polar tendencies. Imitation, as perfected by the Franco-Flemish composers, shows the same phenomenalization in a higher degree of musical complexity. Statement and answer form a complementary whole. The common fifteenth-century notation "Two in One" or "Three in One"—in these or similar words—bears witness to the procreation of several voices out of one. In a homophonic style, the symptoms indicative of a split are necessarily different; but the underlying principle of polarization remains discernible. In the very first chord of the Bach chorale, the unity of the triad is disrupted by the prominent position of the melodic fifth, which seems to break out of it and for the rest of the piece strives to return to it. In the very first phrase of the chorale, the tonic chord opens up into its two extreme harmonic potentials, the subdominant and dominant, and finds its tonal definition in a full perfect cadence. If Beethoven has been called "forceful" or "violent," the example from the Eroica serves to prove the point. Technically the procedure is closely related to that of the chorale: a melody pulling out of a given triad, and the triad unfolding in a cadence that reaches to both poles of the tonality. But here the disruptive element in the melody lies outside the normative span, both melodically and harmonically. Moreover, the marked dynamism within the regular metric arrangement heightens the urgency of the event. Schönberg departs from tradition but not from the necessity of initiating growth. As is not the case in the earlier examples, rhythm almost alone defines the main event. Against the duple norm of two-times-two measures, the initial distinct anacrustic behavior and the subsequent dissolution and shift set up their own countercurrents. The disruption is intensified by the two sounds outside the line—the first shockingly loud at a rhythmically very weak moment, and the second suspending the rhythm altogether by a fermata across the barline. The melodic motive initially identified with the basic anapaest splinters away from it. Moreover, without imputing traditional tonal intentions to the composer, we cannot help but hear the three octave events as symmetrical pulls away from the opening statement.

The concept derived from all these examples, that a given unit splits in order to initiate growth, is familiar to us not only through music. Biology offers an immediate analogy. The mere language of biologists suggests the same possibilities, and difficulties, we encounter in musical inquiry. The term *growth*—as many other terms—implies both a process and a force. In referring to the oscillation around the opening tone of the Gregorian chant, we described the process of up-and-down as much as the force causing it; and therein we differed little from the scientist describing growth. Nor need the musician assume that the biologist's insight into what produces growth is any more precise than his own. The best scientists are the first to recognize the common handicap. D'Arcy Thompson, in his classic study *On Growth and Form*, warns that although the forces and the effects of forces operating in the phenomenon of cell division seem to have a close analogy with known physical phenomena (such as attractions or repulsions), "neither the forms produced nor the forces at work can yet be satisfactorily and simply explained."[1] He concedes that there are actions taking place within cells which may or may not yield in time to the methods of physical investigation. "Whether they do or no, it is plain that we have no clear rule or guidance as to what is 'vital' and what is not." The method he suggests is to analyze meanwhile, bit by bit, those parts of the whole to which ordinary established laws more or less obviously apply. The musician is pleased to find his own approach thus shared by an eminent scientist. It takes the full authority of Thompson to declare that "there is a certain fascination in such ignorance" and to limit the destiny of Science to studying rather than knowing, to searching rather than finding truth. He summarizes his initial discussion of growth through cell division with a warning against a preponderantly materialistic explanation of morphological phenomena. If such a warning should be heeded by biologists, how much more so by musicians! "Morphology is not only a study of material things and of the forms of material things, but has its dynamical aspect, under which we deal with the interpretation, in terms of force, of the operations of Energy. . . . Matter as such produces nothing, changes nothing, does nothing; and however convenient it may afterwards be to abbreviate our nomenclature and our descriptions, we must most carefully realize in the outset that the spermatozoon, the nucleus, the chromosomes or the germ-plasma can never act as matter alone, but only as seats of energy and as centres of force." This is the same concern we have voiced from the beginning. Whatever the conveniences of language, to the musician concepts like tone, motive, phrase, chord, or texture are carriers of energy and only therefore can be treated as objects.

Beyond the empirical evidence supplied by separate disciplines, such as music and biology, the idea of genesis by division is a transcendental heritage of mankind. It dominates the first chapter of the Bible. God separates the earth from heaven. He divides the light from the darkness, the waters under the firmament from the waters above the firmament, the dry land from the seas, the day from the night, Eve from Adam. The same idea determines Plato's explanations of creation. In the *Symposium*, the story is told as a fable.[2] Zeus cuts in half a globular being with four arms and legs and with two faces in order to create man and woman. The mutual attraction of the sexes becomes thus intelligible as a desire for reunification. In the same dialogue, Plato quite specifically states that music is created by a division and subsequent reconciliation of high and low, and of fast and slow.[3] *Timaeus* develops the same idea in more esoteric and also mathematical terms.[4] God creates by dividing the whole; and the process of division is then carefully elaborated in precise numbers that have musical and symbolic significance. For this explanation of the principle of any genesis, Plato was indebted to Pythagoras, whose experiments on the monochord taught a general truth about the universe. Just as division of a string creates individual tones and leads to the discovery and

[1] Pp. 13 f.
[2] 190–91.
[3] 187.
[4] 28 ff., in particular 35–36.

23

establishment of basic musical laws such as consonance and dissonance or major and minor, so the whole world can be understood as a multiplicity of phenomena derived from one process and governed by polarity. The Pythagorean tradition is not only old but continuous. Pushed into the background by the rationalism of the eighteenth century and the materialism of the nineteenth, it has found vigorous modern articulation in the works of Alfred North Whitehead, who wound up his famous lecture on "Objects and Subjects" with the blunt statement: "Throughout the universe there reigns the union of opposites."[1] With all his enormous interests, Whitehead gave little attention to music; but his explicit principles are applicable to our topic as much as to the ones he tested and interpreted himself.

Growth is initiated by the division of something. The truth of this statement is found in our musical sampling and in the testimonies of the biologist and the philosopher. In these and other fields, the initial split of a given unit creates a particular morphé, thus providing the basis for any morphology. We resist the temptation to elaborate upon a possible parallelism between the musical situation just described and the release of energy resulting from the splitting of a physical atom. The "given unit," to which we have repeatedly referred, in music is tone. It is the smallest unit, in any case.

Now, musical tone has a morphology of its own that bears on musical composition.[2] What the ear perceives as tone originates in the outside world as vibration. To produce this vibration, the instrumentalist or singer disturbs a neutral state of balance or rest: the violinist plucks or bows his string, the wind player agitates the air column contained by his instrument, the percussionist hits his kettledrum, and the singer presses air through his vocal cords. In all these cases, an oscillation has to be generated for a tone to come to life. One can speculate on the striking similarity between the initiation of movement in the cases of both a single tone and a musical event. The underlying basic principles are the same, to wit, the disturbance of a position of rest, the division of a given unit, and the symptom of elasticity, that is, of a force trying to restore the deformation by a return to the original state. This moment of initial energizing defines both the juncture and also the separation of the physical and psychological happenings. It determines the parting point of nature and art. The material of music, it is true, is largely shaped by the unfolding of tone in an acoustical, physical sense; but the further creation of music is subject to musical, psychological laws. In this sense, we can understand art as being both related to nature (because man is part of nature) and yet distinct from it (because man is a creator in his own right).

The play of energies recognizable as natural in a single tone and as artistic in the man-made explorations and variants within a whole composition, each are symptomatic of some kind of oscillation. Hence the event in both cases is rhythmic and (to use an expression of Whitehead's) "life-bearing." If there is a morphological archetype, it is rhythm. The smallest musical cell as well as the largest musical composition are born and shaped by rhythm.

Here we can do no better than quote Whitehead at length:

[1]Published, among other places, in *Adventures of Ideas*, p. 190.
[2]For more details, see the authors' *Tone*.

Wherever there is some rhythm, there is some life, only perceptible to us when the analogies are sufficiently close. The rhythm is then the life, in the sense in which it can be said to be included within nature.

Now a rhythm is recognisable and is so far an object. But it is more than an object; for it is an object formed of other objects interwoven upon the background of essential change. A rhythm involves a pattern and to that extent is always self-identical. But no rhythm can be mere pattern; for the rhythmic quality depends equally upon the differences involved in each exhibition of the pattern. The essence of rhythm is the fusion of sameness and novelty; so that the whole never loses the essential unity of the pattern, while the parts exhibit the contrast arising from the novelty of their detail. A mere recurrence kills rhythm as surely as does a mere confusion of differences. A crystal lacks rhythm from excess of pattern, while a fog is unrhythmic in that it exhibits a patternless confusion of detail. Again there are gradations of rhythm. The more perfect rhythm is built upon component rhythms. A subordinate part with crystalline excess of pattern or with foggy confusion weakens the rhythm. Thus every great rhythm presupposes lesser rhythms without which it could not be. No rhythm can be founded upon mere confusion or mere sameness.

An event, considered as gaining its unity from the continuity of extension and its unique novelty from its inherent character of "passage," contributes one factor to life; and the pattern exhibited within the event, which as self-identical should be a rigid recurrence, contributes the other factor to life.[1]

FURTHER GROWTH: PRINCIPLES

In our investigation of forces that initiate growth, several morphological concepts, and basic ones at that, have already come to the fore: disturbance and restoration of balance, energy, polarity of forces, recurrence and novelty, rhythm. We shall keep them in mind as we examine—as naïvely as we attempted to do before—the continuing growing power of a musical composition while temporarily ignoring the limiting counterforce. When a musical cell splits in two, it yields either a twin, that is, an identical repetition; or a modified counterpart, that is, a variation in the widest sense; or a related but contrasting organism.

Among the three possibilities, exact repetition is the simplest and hence the most accessible. In our six examples, repetition supplies the cadential refrains and the outside frame of the three Kyrie exclamations; some opening and closing formulas in the Compostela organum; imitation of head themes and of voice pairs, as well as prolongation of a situation (mm. 13 ff.) in the Franco-Flemish Mass movement; the antistrophe in the Bach chorale; and metric pyramiding of phrases as much as of sections in the course of the Beethoven march. Characteristically, there is no exact repetition in the twentieth-century piece, except for the pure rhythm of the two *fortissimo* measures. But in all these and other instances of exact repetition one must distinguish between the technical device and the morphological result. The repetition of any musical unit cannot possibly be "exactly the same," for it always contains the new element of a relation to the first statement. We concede the occurrence of mechanical repetition, but we deny its contribution to anything organic and

[1]*Natural Knowledge*, pp. 197 f.

vital. Henri Bergson expands on this thought in *An Introduction to Meta-physics* by a multitude of analogies from which the best, namely music, is unfortunately missing:

> There are no two identical moments in the life of the same conscious being. Take the simplest sensation, suppose it constant, absorb in it the entire personality: the consciousness which will accompany this sensation cannot remain identical with itself for two consecutive moments, because the second moment always contains, over and above the first, the memory that the first has bequeathed to it. A consciousness which could experience two identical moments would be a consciousness without memory. It would die and be born again continually.[1]

For our purposes, then, the distinction between exact and modified repetition might profitably be replaced by the recognition that morphologically no musical repetition can be exact and that we rather deal with a wide spectrum of different kinds of repetition. At one end of the spectrum lies indeed the apparent identity of the units which, however, lose their actual identity in the musical process of time. Within the spectrum, at varying degrees, lie all those technical devices which are more or less indebted to the principle of repetition. We think of them as modifications or as "variations" in the widest sense.

Our six pieces supply ample illustrations of modified repetition. The technical device of *imitation*, introduced in medieval polyphony, has remained a main morphological force in all Western music, even in homophonic styles. The imitation in our Josquin movement is technically not different from that in later Bach fugues, Haydn sonatas, and Bartók concertos. In a monophonic or purely homophonic piece, which by definition excludes the possibility of imitation, a single voice can perform the whole task alone by such technical devices as a melodic *sequence* (in the modern meaning of this term) or a metrical arrangement suggesting *antecedent-consequent*. Our Bach and Beethoven pieces supply illustrations of these techniques throughout, and the Schönberg piece gives hints. In all these cases of generally audible but somehow varied repetition, a *motive* fulfills the useful function of acting as a clarifying carrier of a morphological force. Repetition also appears in far less obvious shapes. The Gregorian chant among our examples, as also the first soprano line in Josquin's Kyrie, repeats an initial oscillation with *increased amplitude* and thereby gains momentum in a manner that differs only in external features but not in principle from the block-building repetition by metrical units such as antecedent and consequent. Similarly, the Compostela organum indulges in playful *figurations—extensions* and *contractions—*of characteristic scale passages. The discant of this early polyphonic composition, in particular, places the vague repetitions of its movement moreover in the service of the *unfolding of a sound* as defined by each individual tenor note. The variations that produce growth are here not so much concerned with their own internal cogency as with the transformation of a tone locus, a single pitch, into a temporal process. Vastly different in appearance, the enormous *detour* caused by the tone A-flat in the Eroica march can be morphologically understood as a manifestation of a very similar principle. The piece by *Schönberg* is chiefly built on *transformations* of an initial rhythm, incidentally attended by those of a melodic motive.

[1]P. 26.

All these, and more, modified forms of repetition show the process of growth by variation. What they share is the derivation of the total material from the same parentage. Any development or unfolding or continuation in these cases derives from prior material. We can speak of *idiogenesis* (from Greek *idios*, 'same') if the material of a new section stems from that of its antecedent. The outcome is more or less modified repetition.

There exists, however, the possibility of growth by contrast rather than variation. We can speak of *heterogenesis* (from Greek *heteros*, 'other') if the material of a new section is different from that of its antecedent. The outcome here is juxtaposition. The main distinction between growth by repetition or by juxtaposition pertains to the genesis; but in both cases, the antecedent particular imposes itself on the novel particular.

Among our examples, the middle sections of two compositions lying far apart in time—the Gregorian second Kyrie exclamation and the Maggiore section of the Eroica movement—supply clear and sufficient evidence of heterogenesis. One could think equally of the second halves, respectively, of the Josquin composition and the Bach chorale as gaining justification by sheer contrast to whatever has preceded them.[1] Yet these latter two cases reveal the hairline that sometimes separates variation from contrast. Exactly at what point does a real metamorphosis occur? It all depends on whether we favor the relationship or the contrast, the sameness or the novelty. In any case, the new section must maintain some relation to the given situation, or the unity and hence organic intelligibility of the work of art would be fatally jeopardized. The contrast, with all its differences and new characteristics, cannot stand alone without losing its role as contrast. In this sense, we might as well place this particular kind of growing process into the same spectrum, as we called it before, at the other end from exact repetition. Between the almost identity and the maximum contrast lie all the many forms of modified repetition.

This morphological explanation of contrast as correspondence has a strong advocate in Alfred Lorenz, whose reasoning is worth following in support of ours.[2] Using Richard Wagner's music dramas as the material for his investigations, Lorenz quickly concedes that the return of a section—recapitulation or antistrophe—cannot possibly be identical with its first occurrence, musically as little as dramatically. Every return is a variation, and Wagner's technical devices are basically the same as those of classical and preclassical musicians: figuration; modification of harmony, rhythm, melody, dynamics, or timbre; addition of polyphonic voices; rearrangement of motives; etc. Just as traditional harmony has long recognized the substitution of some chords for others, so Wagner often operates with a substitution of motives. Lorenz here speaks of "free symmetry" and "symmetry by contrast" (*Gegensatzsymmetrie*), leaning thereby slightly on Max Dessoir's concept of "isodynamics."[3] The history of art supplies him with convincing witnesses, as the almost rigid identity of parts in early paintings gradually yields to free and contrasting correspondences. The figures arranged in adoration of a central

---

[1]Cooper and Meyer, *Rhythmic Structure*, defend the Schönberg piece against being interpreted as "a merely whimsical juxtaposition of moods."

[2]*Ring*, pp. 121–24; *Tristan*, pp. 5 f.

[3]*Aesthetik*, pp. 121 ff.

Madonna approach mirror images in many medieval representations. Ghirlandaio's angels, in such a situation, appear in identical colors while the lateral figures vary the colors although still maintaining repetition of position and shape. Rubens frames the central portion of the *Battle of the Amazons* left and right by falling horses which do not repeat but correspond. In his *Bethlehem Slaughter of the Children* the corresponding groups are connected by the contrasting motives of "fanatic murder" and "fanatic defense" of the children. In the same master's *Last Judgment* the left ascent to heavenly salvation is totally different in mood from the right descent into hellish despair; yet the correspondence is so great that the painting appears symmetrical. Jacob Burckhardt operates with similar insights when noting, for instance, that Andrea de Sarto's exact architectonic structure is mostly "symmetry hidden by contrasts."[1] Lorenz provides a musical example by noting two motives in *Die Walküre* of which their related meanings admit their use as equivalents: Siegmund's "flight" music which leads to love, and the real "love" music.

Our inquiry into the tendencies that favor continued musical growth has left us with repetition and juxtaposition. But either one is a rhythmic event; and thus we find ourselves again led back to the elementary force of rhythm. Rhythm assures continued growth; for as each cycle in the round of experiences provides the conditions for its own repetition, it is also self-repairing. "The end of a completed cycle is the proper antecedent stage for the beginning of another such cycle."[2] As the repeats become elaborated, energy is not so much spent as refreshed. Rhythm, in Whitehead's amusing terminology, counteracts fatigue. As a composition moves along, it is constantly recharged.

LIMITATION: SIX CASES

It is now time to investigate the forces that limit the form of a musical composition. To avoid misunderstandings, one must sharply distinguish between two kinds of limitation. One is that force that checks the growth of a particular work of art. The other, in a much wider sense, differentiates altogether art from nature. Only the former is under consideration for our present purpose. The latter deserves a separate inquiry. It concerns that quality that distinguishes the real King Henry VIII, for instance, from his histrionic counterpart as presented by Shakespeare or from his portrait as painted by Holbein. From the indefinite continuum of the king's life, the artists selected, as the case may be, events and situations limited by a definite beginning and end. Our immediate question, however, deals only with the artistic limitation counteracting the growing power within a particular work of art. This limitation in a narrower sense poses its own difficulties; for being a distillate gained from processes of a unified whole, it cannot always be shown pure without admixture of elements equally capable of contributing to growth. We have encountered symmetry, for instance, as a principle favoring growth; and we shall encounter it again as limiting it. Yet after these avowed qualifications, enough of the forces and processes primarily responsible for restraining extension can be isolated by way of our six specific cases.

[1]*Cicerone*, p. 837.
[2]Whitehead, *Function of Reason*, pp. 21 f.

(1)   The shape of the entire Kyrie is most obviously determined by the symmetric frame set up by the two outside exclamations around the contrasting center. We note that the concept of "symmetry" can here be understood only in reference to the total unit of each of the framing sections; for according to the precise concept of common bilateral symmetry, the third exclamation would have to proceed backward from the last note to the first (as happens, for instance, in the third movement of Alban Berg's *Lyrische Suite*). The repetition of the first exclamation by the third certainly limits the growth but it cannot do so alone. True, the resulting symmetry is satisfactory but it need not be final. Repetition could continue to recur unless it were further limited by number. In this case, the number of units involved is 3—two repetitions around a center. This number shows its strength even more clearly in its application to the "eleison" refrain. Although recognized by character, position, and recurrence as a cadential formula, that is, as an element defining an end, the refrain, too, by itself could be made to serve further growth, as, for instance, in a baroque rondeau. The power of number coordinating all these forces—repetition, contrast, symmetry, refrain—checks the further growth of this Kyrie I. Besides these factors which limit the unfolding of the composition in time, there are others which pertain to the "tonal space" in which the action takes place. There is limitation in time and there is limitation in space. To the latter refer the conditions imposed by the given mode, in this case the Hypophrygian. There is strict adherence to the tonal material of the mode, and the ambitus is held to a hexachord.

(2)   The—literally—underlying limitation of the Compostela organum is the given tenor. To the composer the advantage of a *res prius facta* is great, for the whole responsibility for artistic restraint is thus taken from his shoulders. No wonder that reliance on a given cantus firmus accompanies the advance of polyphony for centuries. This employment of a ready-made outside force differs in kind somewhat from the utilization of forces inherent in a composition. The restraint is arbitrarily imposed even before the piece begins to run its course. The limitation is borrowed "at second hand." For the hearer to acknowledge this limitation, he must know the melody beforehand, as was doubtless the case throughout the centuries in which a cantus firmus was employed. The morphology of the tenor by itself, of course, follows its own laws of genesis, continuation, and arrest; one can isolate them, if one wishes, in the manner we have outlined for our other example of Gregorian chant. The specific limitations imposed by polyphony interest us here. Those pertaining to the tonal space come first to mind. The maximum distance of an octave between the two voices prescribes a strict boundary within which the music has to move. The insistence on perfect intervals at junctures as marked by the movement of the tenor further restricts the free play of the polyphonic forces. Contrary motion, moreover, although not so strictly obeyed as the theorists would have it (one remembers John Cotton's explicit prescription spelled out around the year 1100), circumscribes the formative activity permitted within the specifically polyphonic space. Much more difficult to seize is that morphological aspect of this organum that derives from the passing of time. The points of the cantus firmus are well defined and clearly spaced, it is true, but the motion of the discant against it sounds playful to a degree suggestive of arbitrariness within each circumscribed tonal field. In this particular

29

rather early organum, the breath holding together the tenor melody still renders it intelligible as a sensible unit and thus somewhat limits the play of the discant. But already in the organa of the next generation, such consideration would not in the least influence the morphology of the whole. Consequently, with all the limitations we have described, the form of this piece seems open at the end. Taken as a polyphonic morphé, it continues like one of those Chinese pictures of bamboos and rushes drawn on a scroll that unrolls indefinitely. This kind of freedom is only possible on the basis of a rather rigid restriction such as the given tenor in our case.

(3)   Number furnishes the most obvious limitation, but for the composer more so than for any inevitable morphé of the piece. In advance he has decided on four voices, which prescribe the exact process, though not form, of imitation. In advance he has decided on two main sections (beginning, respectively, in mm. 1 and 9), in line with the sectioning demanded by the given text and the technical tradition of his style. But these limitations do not grow out of the music itself. Again one is struck by the tendency of a really polyphonic piece toward indefinite continuation. To counteract it, the composition contains built-in signposts to indicate the approaching end. Foremost is the dissolution of the established polyphonic texture by the homorhythmic rapprochement of all participating voices. The turning point is the strong cadence on the tonic of the Phrygian mode at the beginning of measure 12— the first one of its kind in the whole piece. It is followed by abandonment of imitation and independence of the voices in favor of a rhythmic adjustment and cooperation that actually results in homophony. The cadential reiterations (seven times c_1–d_1–e_1 in the bass beginning with the last ♩ in m. 11) signal the end with an insistency that can only be understood as a willful attempt to stem the otherwise unrestrained current of imitation. The seventh and last of these bass repetitions is slowed down and then interrupted by two cadenza measures (16 and 17). The delay acts as a ritardando, applying the final brake, just as the reduction of the soprano ambitus from the initial octave to a mere three tones around the tonic signals the imminent cessation of movement.

In his editions of two Obrecht Masses, the Netherlands musicologist Max Van Crevel has disclosed the discovery of another limiting factor.[1] His complex but convincing arguments point again to number, not as a cardinal quantity, but as a value capable of forming organisms by its inherent qualitative and morphological power. Without letting ourselves become distracted at this moment by the underlying theory, we note in the Kyrie by Josquin the presence of the number 18 as a morphologically shaping and limiting force. The opening soprano melody consists of 18 ♩ —more precisely, of 18 ♪ (3♩ + 3♪ + 4♪ + 5♪) rhythmically mirrored around a central axis. Passages in the other voices are similarly oriented, to wit: the first alto and tenor imitations (3♪ + 4♪ + 5♪ + 6♪ after the static head motive); the entire first wave of the bass (3♩ + 3♪ + 4♪ + 5♪); the melodic sequences initiating the second section (3×3 ♩ in the soprano, 3×6 ♪ in the alto, and 3 ♩ + 3♩ in the tenor); the three closing cadenza measures (subdivided by the bass into 1♪ + 5♪ + 1♪ + 5♪ + 3♩); and probably others. The entire movement is 18 measures long. Very remarkable is the shaping of these 18 measures into two sections of 8 measures each (not to be con-

---

[1]Obrecht, *Opera*, vols. 6 and 7.

fused with the appearance of similar units in metric music) which are then rounded up to 18 by the coda. The coda thus appears not as an arbitrary cadenza but as an inner morphological necessity.

(4)   In contrast to the Josquin composition which, although "measured," is not shaped by meter but rather by a rhythmic organization governed by number, the morphology of the Bach chorale is determined by meter. The varied groupings within a Josquin line, even when perceptibly projecting a rhythmic value, are likely to be obliterated by the polyphonic texture; for the counterpoints mostly follow different groupings at the same time. The metric organization of the Bach chorale subjugates everything including rhythm. In the service of meter, rhythm here relates the smallest as well as the largest groups toward each other and as a result creates a shape that is spontaneously intelligible because it seems inevitable. The epode (mm. 9–16) must match the weight of the first half, just as the antistrophe (mm. 5–8) balances the strophe, and the second phrase of the strophe (mm. 3–4) balances the opening statement. The limiting principle is again related to symmetry though of a different kind from that in the Gregorian Kyrie; for symmetry in this piece, like all other elements, is also under the power of meter. Melodically relevant to limitation is the completion of unfinished business: only the very last phrase leads the opening tone d^1 straight down a fifth to the abiding tonic g, satisfying a natural tendency that had been artistically disrupted throughout the chorale by the characteristically incomplete fourth. But this final solution could have been offered earlier or postponed until later, were it not for the exact restriction prescribed by meter. Similarly, the harmonic wave, while following a cogency of its own, gains shape and dimension only through meter; for the crucial points exactly coincide with the metric punctuation as signified by the fermatas: t-D: ‖ dR-tR-D-T.

(5)   The metric principle ruling the Bach chorale also pervades the Beethoven march. But whereas it appears pure and supreme in the former, it is persistently violated in the latter. The violations and subsequent restorations here signify the main morphological process. Because the Beethoven movement, as we have shown, proceeds from a headstrong and voluntary generative power, the limitations checking its growth may be expected to be closely tied to the conventions of the style. Each modification or variation presupposes a model, and the willfulness of an artistic form can increase only with the clarity of the archetype. The characteristic "Beethoven touch" is possible only against the firm framework of a tremendous moral restraint. The huge detour of the march is understood in relation to the surrounding conventions. The spatial extension is controlled by a unifying tonality; the temporal extension, by the assumption of a metrically established march pattern.

Tonality is phenomenalized by *cadence stretching across the entire piece. The harmonic cadence of a simple march would be tonic-nontonic-tonic paralleling the ternary form march-trio-march. This overall cadence is clearly audible in the *Marcia funebre* as t-T-t before the gigantic detour widens it to t-T-s-t. The inserted exploration of the subdominant region (be it F minor or A-flat major) was carefully prepared by such smaller turns in the exposition (cf. mm. 31 ff., 51 ff.) and, of course, by the all-pervading A-flat. The expectation of the final return to the tonic C minor is so strongly embedded in the tonal style of the work that the long and unsettling detour can-

31

not possibly go astray forever. The primary function of the recapitulation is to restore the tonal balance by "getting rid" of the irritant A-flat and the concomitant subdominant region. The resurgence of A-flat in the coda is mainly a reminiscing summary. The spatial, cadential limitation remains tied to meter. We note the purely metric proportions (expressed in measures) of the four sections that spell out the cadence: t(68)-T(36)-s(68)-t(36 + 39). The length of the coda (mm. 209 ff.) compensates for the abbreviated return of the exposition after the detour. It restores the violently disturbed balance.

(6)   The Piano Piece by Schönberg, one suspects, could go on. Being a set of variations on a rhythm, it has no inherent form; for variations, like beads on a string, need an extrinsic device for organization and grouping. The three sections leave the piece open at the end. There is no discernible tonal center; and if the last b_1-flat sounds like a leading tone to the given finalis, too many other chromatic progressions throughout the piece might simulate a comparable claim. The melodic motive gives only the faintest morphological hint of closing the form by rejoining the original rhythm in the last section (m. 10). It is the overall rhythm supported by dynamics that sets the effective limitation. The anapaestic idea, which is the underlying "theme" of all detailed transformations, relates the three main sections to each other. The double anacrusis represented by the first two sections leads to the accent represented by the dynamic plateau of the last section. The anapaest is completed with the piece. Dynamically, at least, very little could follow the triple-forte of the last note. The cogency of this limitation is somewhat weakened by the initial shape of the fundamental rhythm which contains a weak afterbeat, so that one might rightly expect an analogous feminine ending of the whole piece. Moreover, nothing within the composition (save perhaps its placement within a set of short pieces) need prevent this large anapaest from becoming the anacrusis to a still larger structure. The conciseness of the piece heard against the ambivalence of the open ending might well be an intended style characteristic.

LIMITATION: PRINCIPLES

Our six cases have yielded varied musical symptoms of morphological generation and growth, all of which ultimately relate to the elemental life-force of rhythm. What limiting counterforces can be abstracted from the same cases? Although a musical composition unfolds in time and thus must be limited by a *temporal* process, it also fills a musical space—the playing field, so to say, of the participating forces—and thus demands *spatial* containment. These two kinds of limitation should be profitably separated, although their manifestations sometimes overlap.

The elemental boundary of musical space derives from the concept of *tonality* in the widest definition of this term. Tonality supplies all the tonal material used by a composition and—most important—the center of gravity around which it may be grouped. Tonality determines the hierarchy among the diverse processes pulling toward and away from this center. All our examples earlier than the twentieth century show themselves bound by tonality, be it under the name of medieval mode or modern key. In each of these compositions, the center of attraction is unmistakable. It is the point at which all movement eventually terminates. The early works never transgress the basic tonal material. The symphonic movement of the nineteenth century, by going far beyond the immediate boundaries of the key, shows the gravitational attraction to the final tonic all the more dramatically. The argument is irrelevant that five out of our six cases are chosen to illustrate tonality, for we strongly believe in the universal force of a tonality, however defined, in music of all civilizations and periods. If Arnold Schönberg considered tonality a mere convenience,[1] we submit that, on the contrary, even his atonal music recognizes some aspect of tonal hierarchy, to wit, the unique treatment of the octave and the ordered (though perhaps tedious) repetition of the tone row. All other modern experiments, short of the totally chaotic ones which do not repay consideration, contain some symptom of hierarchy that relates them to the general idea of tonality.

The specific devices phenomenalizing tonality are manifold. Melodically the clearest and strongest are *scale, ambitus,* and *finalis.* Directly perceptible in our early examples, they set equally forceful limits to all but the twentieth-century piece. In a twelve-tone composition, their functions would be taken over by the row. *Counterpoint laws* stake off the space that two voices can occupy (as most ostensibly demonstrated in the Compostela organum); but they also apply to questions of temporal growth and limitation. Harmonic definition of tonality derives from the primary force of the *triad,* which is the standard for the behavior of all harmonies generated by a mode. Melody and harmony join in setting a boundary to the flow of a composition by the force of *cadence.* This term should be understood not only as a formula signaling the approaching end (as found in all compositions with varying conventions allowing for differences of style) but as a morphological determinant of tonality and, particularly in its harmonic manifestation, of the structured outline of a whole piece.

The example of cadence has definitively pushed our discussion across the threshold separating spatial from temporal limitations. The line, as we initially stated, is helpful but cannot be sharply drawn. Unambivalently belonging to the latter are devices such as the given tenor found in our example of early polyphony. It is a "secondhand," extrinsic device, as we called it before, because it is introduced from the outside instead of organically arising from the piece it serves. It furnishes a ready-made, prefabricated structure. The limitation is set before growth sets in. In the same category belong techniques such as the *isorhythm* of the fourteenth century, obviously all organa and conductus, as well as the entire *cantus firmus* literature. Here belongs further the imprint of the given theme upon the form of each individual variation (although by no means on the morphé of the whole set) in the classical "theme and variations" setup. We do not hesitate to identify this whole category as being limited by a *res prius facta,* well aware of the usual restricted application of this term to polyphonic parody compositions of the sixteenth century. The same category, in its widest sense, also comprises many twentieth-century techniques which proceed from preconceived conditions such as *twelve-tone*

[1]*Harmonielehre*, pp. 28 ff. 145, et al.

rows, serial arrangements, and extramusical *parameters*. The foreordained limitation apparently characterizes styles that, for one reason or another, are insecure about the genuine morphological process. (A cantus firmus—other than a straight setting of a chorale—in the hands of Bach hardly ever acts as a primary shaping factor but rather as a counterpoint which does not determine the length of the piece.) In the "childhood" centuries of polyphony, that is, until about the maturity shown by Josquin des Prez, the technical demands of counterpoint absorbed all creative attention. The composers from Perotinus to Machaut and Obrecht (to name only the very best) must have gratefully accepted the support offered by a ready-made tenor. Significantly enough the *res prius facta* disappears with the sixteenth century when the technical problems of counterpoint cease to pose undue difficulties. Spontaneous musical forms rather than techniques begin to challenge the imagination of composers and to fill the literature. The rise of instrumental music with its manifold forms, unhampered by predetermining texts, is one of the concomitant symptoms. In much of the prefigured music of our day, the *res prius facta* is a (not always musical) device to lend some support to compositions in their search for a style. It is, to say the least, a reassuring handrail amidst uncertainties.

Of primary morphological importance, on the other hand, are the limitations arising directly from the current of a composition, as we encountered them in the investigation of our six examples. The limiting force of *number* asserted itself in most cases. Counteracting the principle of repetition in the Gregorian Kyrie, it closes the process of extension. Supplying an abstract value to the otherwise free behavior of the voices in Josquin's Kyrie, it organizes the parts and the whole. It restricts the growth of the Bach chorale by evidencing a power of 2. It permits violent disruption of the Beethoven march by serving as an insistent background reminder of desired proportions. In the Piano Piece by Schönberg, it gives equal length to the three groups of transformations of a rhythm. These manifestations of number must not be thrown into the same hamper, nor can we obtain a comprehensively meaningful result by taking each case separately. Number is too general a concept to be appropriated by a special purpose. It is the final abstraction from everything; and therefore we run the danger of ending up with empty hands when trying to reduce all musical phenomena to it. Precisely because number is an all-pervading concept covering both quantities and values in all fields, special care must be taken to isolate and separate for our purpose only those aspects that are directly relevant to musical morphology.

Foremost among our examples, and of a distinct kind, is the phenomenalization of number in the hands of Josquin (and, as future musicological studies are likely to show, of most Netherlands composers). The quality and value of 18—whatever its symbolic significance of which Josquin was doubtless aware—immediately and forcefully join the other musical elements in shaping the piece. There is no question here of "counting" 18, for the number relates to shorter as well as longer note values, to varied groupings and different phrases, to tactus divisions, and to the whole. The number is here hardly audible yet morphologically autonomous. Different in both kind and efficiency is the appearance of number in the Gregorian Kyrie. It limits the possible recurrences of a statement without any further claim to formative interference. The three sections are easily heard as 3. One can count them. The same principle would apply to a rondo where the theoretically endless repetitions of the ritornello are limited only by the counteraction of a perceptible number, such as 5 in R-x-R-y-R or 7 in R-x-R-y-R-z-R. We note that in order to close the procedure, the number must be odd. In a more complex yet analogous manner, number shapes the form of Bach's Goldberg Variations where groups of 3 numbers each culminate in a canon, and the canons themselves relate to each other in an arithmetic progression from the unison to the ninth. In the tenth group the chain is broken by the substitution of the Quodlibet for a further canon.

The relation of number to *meter* is so obvious that one has to guard oneself against abstracting to a point where one is left, like Euphorion's parents, holding an empty garment instead of the desired shape. Meter is a main characteristic of homophonic music. Our three more recent examples are consequently strongly bound by it. The rhythm of the Bach chorale, its life force, is so subjugated by meter that the form of the piece can be measured in powers of 2. The willfulness and the distortions of the Beethoven march can be heard for what they are only because of the implicit regularity of the underlying meter. The "theme" of the Schönberg piece is a metrical foot. Meter means order. It does not simply measure time but rather calls upon our faculty of sensing time and of modifying its speed of flow. The regularity of meter is connected with our pulse (of which we are usually not conscious) and with walking. Hence its proper number is 2. The left-right sensation of rhythmicized meter is strongly understood and not only in march music. It underlies Bach fugues, Mozart sonatas, and Haydn quartets. On a lower level, powers of 2 reaching units of 16 or 32 measures determine the shape of almost all dance music. The writer of modern popular songs and dances is on his guard to observe this boundary as if it were a sacred law.

The mere word *meter* lies at the root of the word *symmetry* (from Greek *syn*, 'together with', and *metron*, 'measure'). The dictionary definitions stress balanced proportions, also the "beauty of form arising from balanced proportions." Correspondence of parts is the minimal condition. In our examples, symmetry, "together with meter," sets many limits. The correspondence is around a central section in the Gregorian Kyrie and the Beethoven march so that the resulting form is ternary. It is around a central axis in the Josquin and Bach movements so that the result is binary. The correspondence among the three sections of the Schönberg piece is such that the effect becomes cumulative. Moreover, symmetry in all these examples also affects the smallest parts, setting off against each other such units as two successive waves in the plainchant, two successive pairs of imitation in the Netherlands piece, strophe and antistrophe in the chorale, antecedent and consequent in the march, and one small anapaest against the next in Schönberg's Piano Piece. In all these instances we must be wary of intepreting symmetry in the common visual sense. Notation, it is true, often suggests a visual symmetry by such signs as double bars or da capo indications, and by the general visual arrangement of notes on a page; but such signs are not audible, and different notations have existed and can be constructed which in no way visualize the existing musical symmetry. Actually even the visual arts, such as painting and architecture, must treat symmetry not as a static appearance but only as a dynamic movement, thus paradoxically profiting from the true musical condition (to which, as Walter Pater claims, all arts aspire). Mathematical terminology is here very precise and revealing. It treats symmetry exclusively as an operation: "A body, a spatial configuration is symmetric with respect to a given plane E if it is carried into itself by reflection in E."[1] The emphasis rests, not at all on a given situation, but on the carrying of a unit to another place in space or time according to a certain procedure. If one should thus consider the symmetry of a picture or building as the outcome of a dynamic operation, how much more so the symmetry of a musical composition! The symmetry of the three Kyrie exclamations, for example, is not an arrangement of two repetitions around a contrasting section. It is the morphological event of carrying a musical unit across a barrier in time and thereby both shaping and terminating the movement. The symmetry of the Bach chorale is not a static property but rather the product of various motions which convert one element into another. The resulting transmutations tell us more about the genesis of the form than about its static appearance.

The aesthetic implications of symmetry admit of one more morphological operation encountered in our samples and elsewhere: the *completion of unfinished business*. This phrase connotes a task of which the process and completion define the form. If some musicians have rightly identified the task with the contents of a composition, we have here reached the morphological event in which content and form coincide, in which the action of the former determines the shape of the latter.[2] Among our illustrations, the Beethoven march dramatizes the play of forces most audibly. The generative power springs from a disruption. The continuation is driven by the consequences of the disruption. The end "gets rid of it" and restores the initial state of balance. All disparities within the movement, be they melodic, harmonic, or rhythmic, have become unified as task and piece are completed. The Bach chorale, less dramatically but more immediately, begins with a top-heavy triad which pushes by its inherent tension the entire movement down to its final chord. Continuation is not fruitful, for all dissonances have become resolved. Even the undramatic music by Josquin gives evidence of the fruitfulness of this technique. One need only remember the interrupted and finally completed bass cadence at the end or the requirement inherent in polyphony to lead all voices together after some initial splintering. The change of texture from polyphony to homophony (mm. 12 ff.) is a concomitant signal pointing toward the end. Outside our sample cases, works by Haydn often show the insistent interruption of a theme by some unexpected event until the task of eventually completing the theme correctly leads the movement to its own conclusion (cf. the first movement of the "Surprise" Symphony,[3] the finale of the Piano Sonata in C major, Hoboken no. XVI:50, and others). Compositions of the eighteenth and nineteenth centuries abound in examples, whereby the missing completion can pertain to melody, harmony, rhythm, or any other con-

---

[1] Weyl, *Symmetry*, p. 4.

[2] Cf. the writings by Heinrich Schenker. A particular case is well analyzed by Marco, "Musical Task."

[3] Marco, "Musical Task."

ceivable element.[1] The device, though genuinely musical, is "dramatic" in the sense that it invites an analogy with the art of poetics. A play or story starts with a neutral situation, disturbs it by the inappropriate or unexpected behavior of an agent, and pursues the consequences to the final resolution. Typically our illustrations of this technique all come from style periods exposed to the influence of opera. If the resolution is explicit within the work (as in any Tolstoy story or Beethoven symphony), we characterize it as classic; if it is left to the reader's or listener's imagination (think of a Kafka story or Schumann's "Warum?"), as romantic. In either case, the limit is set by the principle of balance, that is, by proportion and symmetry in the widest possible sense. Empedocles speaks of the "concord of discords" as the essence of all life and creation. "According to him the universe is alternately in motion and at rest— in motion, when love (*philia*) is making One out of many, or strife is making many out of One, and at rest in the intermediate periods of time."[2] In the same spirit, Christian Huygens, formulating his wave theory of light in the seventeenth century, explained the propagation of light as the tendency toward restitution of a continuously disrupted balance.[3] This physical explanation has an artistically valid counterpart. The path of music is the tendency to restore a disturbed state of balance. The forces at work to bring about the disturbance as well as to countervail it produce all musical morphology.

---

[1]For detailed analysis, see Levarie, *Figaro*, particularly the Sinfonia and nos. 4, 11, 19, 24 and 27.

[2]Aristotle *Physics* viii. 1. 250 b.

[3]*Treatise.*

III. Multiplicity and Unity

Multiplicity is given. Unity is an idea. Multiplicity as such is never postulated; it simply happens. Unity, however, being essentially an idea, becomes a postulate. We hardly ever criticize a work for lack of multiplicity, but we sometimes complain that a work lacks unity.

When we say "a work," we mean that there are not several works but one. Now the work may be *one*—that is, something effectively delimited in space and time—and yet lack unity. Again a work may consist of separate parts—thus appearing less definitely limited in space and time—and yet show unity. In fact, unity is not describable in mathematical terms. Mathematical analogies may be found for each particular case, but they are of no immediate interest to the musician and may therefore here be ignored.

In an artistic sense, unity means the wholeness of individuation, the indivisibility ("in-dividual") of something thought of as a whole. Unity in its essence is always nonmaterial, nonhaptical, and thus intangible. The demonstrability of materially unifying elements, as in a Czerny étude, points to a superficial kind of unity. The purpose of studying each and every perceivable material factor of unity in the masterworks is purely anagogical. As we refine our outer and inner senses, the scrutinizing and listing of technical factors stand only at the beginning of a perceptive process leading from material to intangible signs of wholeness.

Because of its character as a time art devoid of external models, music is peculiarly suited to convey the truth, valid in all the arts, that the ultimate *locus where the work "happens" is the psyche of the individual. The faculty enabling us to compose or recompose a time sequence is memory. Without memory, the perception of a work of music is impossible. Specifically, the experience of unity depends on our remembering a sequence of moods, a line of development, a flow of energetic processes, an inner cadence—all of which give meaning to the concomitant material signs.

While bearing in mind that the ultimate kind of unity is formed by the individual in his own psyche, we might yet conveniently distinguish between a principle of subjective unity and a principle of objective unity. These abstractions designate extreme states which clarify actual tendencies. A schematic image like the following tries to show what happens in each case:

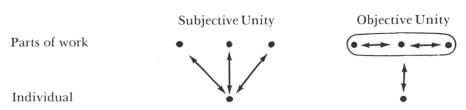

Subjective unity is achieved solely in the mind regardless of the degree of unification in the object. The parts of the work may here be exemplified by motivically unrelated movements of a suite. There is nothing to connect the movements materially. The listener's cooperation is indispensable for bringing the whole to life. The interaction between the parts of the work and the individual is reciprocal. The movements beamed at the listener as separate entities converge in him and gain unity when reflected through his focus. The listener's participation is, of course, also required in the case of objective unity. Here, however, a degree of material unity can be isolated regardless of the final "happening" in the individual. Think of a set of variations on the same theme or of a sonata in which the separate movements are thematically interconnected.[1] Objective unification is materially preformed. It is built into the work.

The two concepts apply equally to *multipartite and *manifold compositions. Although the former consist of several movements and the latter of only one, external appearance has little to do with essential unity. Mozart's *Die Zauberflöte* with almost two dozen numbers is indeed a highly unified multipartite, whereas Strauss's *Alpensinfonie* in one uninterrupted movement remains a somewhat disjunct manifold. Because it is good practice to start music analysis with phenomena and discriminations that are readily grasped—grand distinctions come first, finer ones later—our initial investigation will concentrate on multipartites. The principles here more easily isolated can subsequently be readily tested on manifolds. We shall progress from externally unifying factors (incidental groupings, expected groupings, text, and style) to intrinsically musical elements (key, substance).

Incidental groupings of diverse pieces brought about by an occasion like a musicale at home or a concert in a hall should not be underestimated in their contribution to unity. The circumstances are obviously "terrestrial" rather than musical but cannot fail to affect the hearer. The creation of a good *concert program depends on the unification of an otherwise incidental grouping.

Expected groupings as provided by an eighteenth-century dance suite or a Viennese sonata are also externally unifying. An expected number and order of pieces structures a series and also limits it. Ideally its effectiveness presupposes a great deal of awareness and artistic insight on the part of the audience. Even so, the cohesion and limitation of multipartite sets like Bach's Partitas always remains uncertain to a degree. The best informed listener need not expect the Chaconne after the preceding standard movements of the D minor Partita for Unaccompanied Violin. The only function of detailed movement and tempo indications on printed concert programs is to alert the listener to "what he is in for." If the audience misses such gross distinctions as end and beginning of movements, the fault can lie in either inadequate advance information or the composition itself.

Text is doubtless the first agent of unity in vast vocal works like oratorios and operas. It is what the composer knows as a unified gestalt before writing a

---

[1] A cogent illustration is Mozart's G minor Symphony of which all movements are preoccupied with an upward leap of the sixth, in three of them on the same pitches. A subtler example is Beethoven's Opus 111.

note. In some works of this kind, text might remain the main agent of unity. It certainly dominates the overall form of, for instance, Bach's *Passion According to St. Matthew* in which neither the succession of keys nor any other interrelation of movements yields significant signs of unity. In this respect, later composers are musically more careful. Mozart's master operas are held together, not just by the plot, but rather by an all-embracing structure. Of Schubert's two song cycles, *Die schöne Müllerin* is strongly unified by both the story and the music whereas *Winterreise* dispenses with the structural contribution of a plot. Just as romantic temper and romantic philosophy blur the borderlines between the different arts, so they envelop the several parts of a work in an all-embracing sweeping motion. Tangible signs of unity become more frequent and obvious. Berlioz employs the same melodic theme in all movements of his *Symphonie fantastique*, and the technique is no longer that of obvious rhetorical quotation as in the finale of Beethoven's Ninth Symphony. Above it all looms Wagner's idea of a "totally comprehensive work of art" (*Gesamtkunstwerk*). The primarily musical unity of even his most complex operas has been detected and recognized.[1]

Style itself is a powerful cohesive factor particularly if the composition belongs to a strong, generally accepted style. When we think of plainsong, the individual chants appear to us like cutouts from a larger whole. Even if historic remoteness here contributes, it is not a decisive element in giving a unified impression. Common style unifies. The more a style becomes a matter of personal achievement, the more the individuality not only of the composer but of the work itself reaches prominence; and the projection of unity shifts from the style to the individual case. The point can be illustrated by a comparison of the situations surrounding, respectively, Bach and Beethoven. The established style of the figured-bass period made a multipartite or manifold by Bach in a way self-unifying. The experimental style of dissolving classicism made unity in a comparable work by Beethoven a major problem. In the first case, unity could be taken for granted; it was there to begin with. In the other case, unity was something to be striven for. Bach's devices grow out of the unity of style. Beethoven's devices act as safeguard against the threat of disparity. Actually none of the unifying devices used by Beethoven is new, but the significance of the use changes. Bach and Handel could lightheartedly borrow movements from other works and even from other composers without jeopardizing the stylistic unity of a multipartite. Beethoven welded each work into a strong unity by itself so that it appears differentiated from, rather than united with, other pieces of his total opus. This trend initiated by him has persisted into the twentieth century. (Bruckner's unified style is a noteworthy exception: his symphonies all phenomenalize the same *eidos*.) Characteristic is the extreme importance ascribed by contemporary schools of composing to purely structural cohesion. The complex and partly impalpable notion of style becomes here completely haptified as well as reduced in practice to only the technical component.

Key (or, in a wider sense, tonality) is a materially uniting element of a specifically musical nature. Key permanence throughout a multipartite can

---

[1]Cf. the various volumes by Lorenz on Richard Wagner.

be replaced by key relationship without impairment of the inherent unity. Permanence of key is a more primitive device than permanence of substance because it exhibits a unity that is very little specific. Specific unity is one proper to the material on hand. The greater the dependence on the material on hand, the greater the degree of intrinsic unity. In this value scale, absolute key does not rate high. Music, particularly of a structural kind, is fairly independent of the specific character of the various keys. Inversely, the same key can serve different works. A piece can, so to speak, be easily "peeled off" the key without losing its essentials. Transposition alters little whereas a change of substance would destroy the identity. Key permanence appears thus as an extrinsic unity of lesser significance, at least for all music until the middle of the nineteenth century when, together with the new attention for sonority and timbre, key consciousness gains ground as a relevant aesthetic factor.

Key permanence, as a unifying factor, remains below the hearer's consciousness; for on a conscious level it could only be felt as, quite literally, monotony. The only moments when it demands awareness are those in which its underlying uniformity is broken by a contrast. In the keyboard multipartites by Bach, such is never the case in the Italian Partitas and French Suites, and only occasionally in the English Suites (no. 3, Gavotte II; no. 4, Menuet II; no. 5, Passepied II). The brief spans of contrast in these latter, obtained by a change of mode on either the established tonic or the tonic relative, are actually effective only against the much stronger key permanence and therefore have little bearing on the whole. Shape and unity in the eighteenth-century dance *suite thus nearly always derive from the standard succession of the component pieces; and deviations from the norm gain appreciation by our relating them to the expected outline.

Key relationship develops when the principle of a grand cadence, as it shapes a single piece, is applied to a group of pieces. Unlike the dance suites, most other multipartites by Bach gain unity by cadential organization. In his concertos, the fast-slow-fast arrangement of the usual three movements is generally strengthened by a parallel tonal arch of related keys. His Cantata 78—as one example for many—uses different interpretations of the same key signature of two flats as a bind across seven movements; the grand *cadence centering on G creates symmetry besides cohesion:

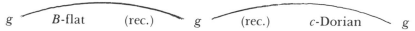

$$g \quad \textit{B}\text{-flat} \quad (rec.) \quad g \quad (rec.) \quad \textit{c}\text{-Dorian} \quad g$$

A cadence, by nature, unites two principles: that of a process and that of positional hierarchy. Both produce a feeling of tension and release but of different kinds. The first, more easily described, corresponds exactly to the experience of inhaling and exhaling. The second, by analogy, corresponds somewhat to the tension and relief felt when one leaves for a trip and returns. A gravitational center is experienced, and the position of distant points is appreciated in relation to the center. The first kind of feeling prevails in short cadences; the second, in grand cadences. Both are natural consequences of tonality.

The nature of grand cadences that generally unify classical multipartites can be demonstrated by the key relationships in the nine symphonies by Beethoven:

Number	1st mov't	2nd mov't	3rd mov't		4th mov't
I	C	F	C		C
II	D	A	D		D
III	E♭	c	E♭		E♭
IV	B♭	E♭	B♭		B♭
V	c	A♭	c		C
VI	F	B.♭	F	f	F
VII	A	a	F		A
VIII	F	B♭	F		F
IX	d	d	B♭		D

Except for the Second Symphony in which the cadence moves to the dominant, all keys, when not directly within the tonic realm, relate to the subdominant. This "downward" tendency of the grand cadence is noteworthy, for it counterbalances and prepares the exuberant and almost profusely strong dominant cadences at the end of each symphony. The contrasting key thus appears incorporated into the tonal flow of the other movements and contributes to unity in a way one does not suspect at first hearing. Haydn and Mozart prepared this technique of favoring the subdominant for the slow movement of a sonata.

Key relationships, important as they are, can hardly be appreciated spontaneously in a lengthy multipartite. The fineness of the web shows only after careful study. The ear may be affected by the unifying force of a grand cadence across the twenty songs that form Schubert's *Die schöne Müllerin* but will not immediately perceive the subtle romantic interrelations. The cycle begins in B-flat major and ends in E major. The tonality, however, is G major, stretching from the second to the penultimate song and reaching an appropriate dominant climax in the central "Mein!" In retrospect, the two outside songs appear as a symmetric frame. The key relations of the other songs to the tonic underlie the architecture of the whole.[1]

Musical substance, like key, can create unity by virtue of substance permanence and, at a later stage, of substance relationship. The notion is complex, because music in even its simplest manifestation as monody consists of an integration of at least two elements, melody and rhythm. The substance of later music is an integral entity of harmony in addition to melody and rhythm. Music is indeed born whole. Unless warranted by a special purpose, the notion of musical substance should not be disintegrated by separate treatment of the several ingredients.

Substance permanence is readily evidenced in the kind of multipartite commonly called *theme and variations*, although the techniques which here appear in sharp outline can obviously occur in any piece of music. The theme

---

[1]See Appendix A, pp. 311 ff., for a detailed analysis.

is always well defined and delimited. The degree of permanence carried through the work is not fixed but changes from variation to variation. Modifications of permanence are innumerable, and systematization therefore difficult. The following schema which attempts to carve out the relevant principles is necessarily imperfect and somewhat arbitrary like all classifications, but it might serve as a barrier against a flood of an otherwise endless variety of phenomena:

Elements of Permanence	*Means of Variation*
(a) Melodic structure (incl. rhythm)	Ornamentation
(b) Harmonic structure	Melody
(c) Metric structure	Harmony
(d) Motives	Transformation
(e) Raga	Transformation

The elements are arranged from the most particular (the given theme) to the most general. Because that which is being varied becomes successively the permanence, the elements of melody and harmony (a and b) reappear necessarily as means for the next degree of variation (b and c). The extreme cases of variation where the permanent element grows ever more general involve transformation (d and e). The next stage after *raga would indeed be the scale; but in the sense that all music consists of variations on a scale, the technical meaning of the variation concept recedes into anonymity. By way of the suggested schema, we shall attempt to trace and illustrate the role of substance permanence as a factor of unity behind multiple appearances:

(a) With the theme as a given entity, permanence is high in the kind of variation that keeps the melodic structure clearly recognizable while modifying it through ornamentation. None of the other elements need be touched. There are many degrees of ornamentation, from simple ornaments expressed by conventional signs to a more or less total liquefaction of the melody. Bach can offer examples: at one extreme, the embellished versions of some of his three-part *Sinfonie* (nos. 4, 5, 7, 9, and 11); at the other, the complete kinetic dissolution by a Double of each of the four movements of his First Partita for Unaccompanied Violin. Such variations are perceived as modifications of the melody, which thereby provides the underlying substance permanence.

(b) When the harmonic structure is preserved, we can hear new melodies built on the given progression. Of this very common technique, Beethoven's Eroica Variations for Piano give a particularly pointed example by introducing and establishing the harmonic bass in isolation long before the *Tema*. The intrinsic interdependence of harmony and meter often preserves the metric structure along with the harmonic. Bach's Goldberg Variations, in which the melody of the initial Aria immediately disappears, are unified not only by the harmonic scheme but by a permanent overall metric organization, notwithstanding the enormous variety of tempo and specific meter. All thirty-one movements of this multipartite show two halves of equal length. The norm of sixteen measures for each half remains intact throughout; the modification to eight measures in some relatively slow variations (nos. 3, 9, 21, and 30) and to thirty-two measures in the fast second half of the Ouverture (no. 16) is merely one of notation and, if anything, emphasizes the metric, in addition to the harmonic, permanence.

(c) If the metric structure alone remains, the basis for variation becomes so general that one actually experiences new pieces all along. In this category belong most of Beethoven's "Veränderungen," 'changes', on a waltz by Diabelli. Within the safe framework of metric organization, the composer can quote *Don Giovanni*, write fugues, and indulge in almost any kind of fantasy without jeopardizing overall unity.

(d) Motives alone can supply substance permanence after melody, harmony, and metric structure have given up their identity. We deal here with "free" variations, which are actually pieces built on motives taken from the theme. The Diabelli Variations, particularly the big Fuga, point in this direction as do many chorale variations by Bach, although in such works some higher elements of permanence—meter, harmony, and even melody—seldom leave the motivic operations entirely alone. Good examples of this technique are the motivic "working-out" sections that tie the development section of a classical sonata to both the preceding exposition and the following recapitulation.

(e) In this type where the elements of permanence are minimally specific, only a succession of unrhythmicized tones remains. New entities can be formed out of various combinations of these tones. Good examples are Franco-Flemish polyphonic pieces employing a given chant, not straight as a cantus firmus, but rather as an outline of melodic behavior. In some modern editions, these free-floating tones are marked by asterisks or small crosses as a guide to the reader.[1] Traditional twelve-tone technique transforms an initial series of tones through various rhythmic and harmonic combinations. Raga occasionally assists Bartók in building a melody (witness the beginning of *Mikrokosmos* no. 125). It underlies a type of writing Stravinsky favored in various works (for example, *L'histoire du soldat*).

The ideas and techniques derived from substance permanence that we have traced through our schema are not confined to any one type of music. Although variations on a theme, of which the very object is the manifestation of multiplicity and unity, show them in relatively pure state, they enter all kinds of composition and readily associate with monodic, polyphonic, or homophonic idioms.

Substance relationship arises in a gradual transition from substance permanence to otherness by transformation. Unity gained from musical substance actually always implies relationship, for total permanence (unlike in the case of key) would result in nothing but identical reiterations. Substance relationship does not lend itself to treatment in categorical terms. It is a concept that comes to life only through the accumulation of experiences, both aural and intellectual. For the limited end of conveying musical experience, we turn to our six specific compositions. We may expect less exclusive evidence on multiplicity and unity than we have found in multipartites. Yet, like

[1] Cf. the volume of the Trent Codices published in *Denkmäler der Tonkunst in Oesterreich*, vol. 61.

every work of art, even the shortest and smallest, each copes in its own way with the postulate of internal cohesion.

(1) The Gregorian Kyrie III presents no particular difficulties in projecting unity. It is very short, though (as the Schönberg piece will show) brevity alone is not necessarily a unifying factor. The key—in this case, Phrygian on E—is so unambiguous that the whole melody sounds as if it were solely in the service of the underlying scale. The separate phrases of the melody all behave in the same way, as oscillations around the central finalis e_1. The variants among the three curves remain related to each other by the two intervallic events and profiles of third and fourth. Mainly, however, the style appears so unified to us—be it because of the distance in time or the editorial accomplishment of Saint Gregory—that the piece, even without some of the technical details listed, would sound like "one."

(2) The Organum demands cohesion, or at least interrelation, of the two participating voices. The unity of each voice by itself could be discussed in terms of the preceding example. What concerns us here, however, is the unity of the new polyphonic texture. It arises exclusively from the quality of the intervals at crucial points. The organum voice possesses considerable liberty in unfolding its own movement but is tied to the foundation of the stronger chant whenever the latter asserts itself. Perfect consonances prevail. Their very nature indicates that the organum voice at the unison, octave, and fifth merely spells out what is inherently contained in the fundamental tone. The few less consonant intervals (only seven out of thirty-eight) do no harm. Two sixths immediately move to a perfect consonance, and the two fourths are readily absorbed by the surrounding thirds. Cohesion is greatest at cadential points. Among them, five unisons are heard; the relatively small number helps avoid the interpretation of unity as premature termination of the movement altogether. Each of the unisons lies at the end of a copula, a descending scale passage in quick notes; and all but one are on the Dorian finalis.[1]

(3) Whereas in early polyphony, such as the Compostela organum, the newly gained independence of the second voice is barely tamed by the consonance of intervals, in late polyphony, such as the Kyrie by Josquin, the perfected contrapuntal technique can afford to strive for interdependence among the participants. The central issue is to render cohesive different voices, each of which yet insists on maintaining individuality. Substance relationship dominates the first half by virtue of almost literal imitation in all four voices. In addition, the second half offers a great deal of parallel movement. Throughout, the independent rhythms of the separate voices supplement each other to fuse into a whole. One has the feeling that the composer's complete mastery of the situation permitted him to concentrate on the dominating idea of rapprochement of the four parts without having to worry about impairing any other quality.

(4) Bach's homophonic setting of the chorale subordinates everything to the cohesive force and harmonic implications of the melody. The main idea is

---

[1] The exceptional unison on the third degree of the scale (four chant notes from the end) must have puzzled the editors of the *Historical Anthology of Music* sufficiently to adjust it in their printed version to a fifth. Cf. Davison and Apel, p. 24, no. 28b.

the uninterrupted scale movement from the opening fifth d^1 down to the tonic g—attempted over and over again but fully accomplished only in the very last phrase. At the opening, chord and melody contradict each other; at the end, they do not. The conclusion is the only one on G reached directly via a fifth and on a strong beat. The harmony realized out of the potential of the melody unifies the whole chorale by the span of a large cadence: t-D:‖ dR-tR-D-T. The open end of the strophes is answered, first by the respective relatives, and only at the very end, corresponding to the finally completed descending scale, by the main functional progression dominant-tonic. The melody uses all seven scale tones. The span of a fourth assumes the role of characterizing the incomplete fifth. The metric arrangement by powers of 2 contributes to the clarity of the cohesive process.

(5) The Funeral March from the Eroica Symphony by Beethoven—the longest of our examples—is built on the assumption of a known and expected unity so that the piece, as its main task, may dramatically disrupt it. A march is a common form. The bow around a central trio must seem to guarantee at least structural unity to any halfway knowledgeable listener. Against the safeguard of a standard structure, Beethoven permits himself, not only the melodic and harmonic disturbance discussed at length in our inquiry of growth and limitation, but also a detour (mm. 114–72) that under other circumstances might wreck cohesion. This extra section, which bulges asymmetrically after the Maggiore in the middle, does to the whole what the tone A-flat has done to the opening eight-measure period. The relation becomes even clearer if one hears the long detour as an unfolding in time of the critical pitch—from the interruption of the melody in the false recapitulation on exactly a-flat (m. 110) through the relative key of F minor (mm. 114 ff.) to the stark return (mm. 157 ff.) ushering in the real recapitulation (m. 173). The metrical orientation of this, as of any, march helps recuperate the lost balance:

Exposition	Maggiore	Detour	Recapitulation	Coda
68 mm.	36 mm.	68 mm.	36 mm.	39 mm.

The detour compensates by relating in length exactly to the exposition. The recapitulation, reduced in weight because of the preceding false turn and deviation, not only suggests a structural correspondence in length to the Maggiore section but regains full emphasis in relation to the exposition when heard together with the coda. This balancing function justifies the considerable extension of the coda which, taken as a unit by itself, is moreover needed to close the overall form.

(6) Schönberg's Piano Piece, short as it is, offers the greatest resistance to being heard as a unit. Neither tonality nor style is of any help; for the former is all but abandoned, and the latter is radical. Nor do melodic motives or harmonic progressions suggest any but the most tenuous substance relationships. Yet there is an underlying rhythmic behavior which, supported by dynamic levels, ties the details of the piece to the form of the whole and thus proffers itself as a unifying force. The piece readily falls into three sections of equal length, the caesuras clearly marked by a fermata (m. 5) and a full rest (m. 9).

Discourse

The paramount idea is a rhythmic unit stated by the first little phrase and subsequently reiterated in various transformations.[1] The "fundamental rhythm" is anapaestic with two upbeats and an afterbeat:

The immediate repeat introduces a small shift as the result of overlapping. The second and third sections are similarly organized although the rhythmic transformations are far from obvious. In the second section, the fundamental rhythm appears first condensed and then stretched. In the third section "there is first an extremely intense and rapid review" (m. 10). It prepares the last three measures which, each by itself and taken together, project the final transformations of the fundamental rhythm. The loudness levels of the piece as a whole obey the idea of an anapaest: a two-unit anacrusis terminates in the dynamic plateau of the third section.

On the level of highest synthesis, multiplicity grows out of Oneness and tends back toward it. The transition from multiplicity to unity, according to Heinrich Wölfflin, consists in "the dissolution of the independent function of the form of the members and the emergence of a dominant overall motif."[2] The effect of the dominance is that all elements—melody, harmony, rhythm, detail, etc.—begin to serve the same end. In Martin Buber's words: "The polarity that man experiences in himself wants unity. Unity is never 'being'. Unity is eternally 'becoming'. Unity comes not from the world but from our doing. The poet finds it in his work."[3] From a viewpoint at which experience and idea meet, Nicolaus Cusanus speaks: "He who considers that each unity has a multiplicity joined to it, and that each multiplicity is held together by a unity appropriate to it, sees simultaneously in unity the One and the Many, and in multiplicity the Many and the One, without which there would be no order and species but confusion and deformity."[4]

---

[1]We here follow, with some modifications, the analysis suggested by Cooper and Meyer, *Rhythmic Structure*, pp. 174–77.

[2]*Grundbegriffe*, p. 166.

[3]*Daniel*, p. 122.

[4]*De principio* in *Schriften*, 2:246.

DICTIONARY

List of Entries

ACCENT

Although since the seventeenth century the term has been readily applied to general situations of the most divers kinds, etymology ties accent to music. *Ad cantus* (a literal translation of the Greek *prosodia*) specifies something that happens 'to songs'. From here the concept has entered language as well as all types of music. Generally, accent connotes a device which lends special prominence and importance to a sound or, by analogy, to some other event.

In music, one can give prominence to a tone within a melodic line by making it louder, higher, or longer. Thus we distinguish three kinds of musical accent: dynamic, tonic, and agogic. Each of these three accents can also appear in its "negative" form: the softest, lowest, or shortest tone of a melody may demand our attention as much as its "positive" prototype. The negative form succeeds because, like the positive, it denotes an extreme.

All accents are essentially rhythmic. Rhythm is the mode by which time becomes phenomenalized. It is an artistic means to fashion time. Among the three musical accents, the dynamic and agogic are submodes of pure rhythm. The agogic accent becomes metric when the durations are established on the basis of a common measure or—differently said—when they are rational. Written out by relatively larger notes, the agogic accent thus becomes part of the structure, whereas the dynamic accent appears rather as a human contribution "ad cantum." (Even in the ostensibly mechanical act of walking, we place one foot, usually the left, more strongly than the other.) The tonic accent, apart from its contribution to rhythm, is created by pitch; it is a melodic accent.

Given the ubiquity of rhythm, one can also apply the notion of accent—beyond the three kinds of which the primary connection with chant and words is evident—to harmony and timbre. In the harmonic structure of a composition, one can easily find intensifications which have primarily the rhythmic function of accenting a point in time. Very characteristic and obvious in this respect is an organ point on the dominant. A specific example is the sole diminished seventh chord in the opening theme of the *Marcia funebre* from Beethoven's Eroica Symphony (m. 6); but here the powerful influence which meter exerts on the meaning of chords causes practical difficulties in separating the harmonic from the metric accent.

Play of sonorities can also produce effects which result in an accent of timbre. Anton Webern's orchestration of the Ricercare from Bach's *Musikalisches Opfer* distributes the opening theme among three solo brass instruments. For the last two notes before the answer, the harp, marked *pianissimo*, doubles the solo trumpet. The clear intent is intensification of the cadence. The intensification produced by the two harp tones affects not dynamics, for the trumpet is hardly reinforced, but timbre. This technique stems from Ar-

54

nold Schönberg's concept of *Klangfarbenmelodie*, to which he first referred in his *Harmonielehre* (p. 471) after conscious experiments in his slightly earlier *Fünf Orchesterstücke*.

Considering that each vowel sound represents a particular timbre, one may raise the question of timbre accents in vocal music. Thus far only initial and inconclusive studies exist concerning the extent to which composers of all periods have purposefully used and placed the given vowels for accentuation.

Although normally the different kinds of accents do not act in isolation, their relative importance varies with style. Tonic and agogic accents characterize Gregorian psalmody and plainsong in general; here the dynamic accent, though found, is not essential for the clarification of a phrase. In numerous passages by Bartók and Stravinsky, on the other hand, dynamic accent often structures phrases that would remain incomprehensible without it. In plainsong, dynamic accent plays a subordinate role; in many modern works, it fulfills a basic structural function.

In metric music, the interpreter must beware of adding the dynamic to the agogic accent. The barline establishes by position a kind of hidden dynamic and agogic accent which ideally acts only implicitly and in our subconscious. A simple-minded performer puts a dynamic accent on every downbeat; children often play in such a manner. In the rhythm|♩ ♩ ♩| the accent on the half note is purely agogic and should not be disturbed by the addition of a dynamic accent. The interpreter can leave the agogic accent alone (for instance, in the first allegro theme of Beethoven's *Leonore* Overture No. 3), unless the composer prescribes a disturbance by a sforzato (as in the modulation to the second theme later in the same composition). If we pull out the positional accent from the subconscious by force of dynamic accentuation, the phrasing deteriorates badly by the subordination of rhythm to meter.

In the widest musical sense, accent is an integral part of rhythm, including meter. Accent is the device that brings to the fore a time lapse.

AESTHETIC STANDARDS

The question of standards hinges on one's interpretation of the concept of value. To relativists, value does not reside in the object but presupposes an evaluating subject whose appetite determines the degree of value he assigns to the object. The more common an appetite, the more general the recognition of value. Some values seem to be universal, because they correspond to desires shared by many; others are recognized only by few. Relativism is a foreground phenomenon—hence its power to produce evidence and its popularity. It is located at the inception of a dialectic process, accepting the relation between subject and object as primary and given. Because the relation changes with the substitution of another subject, evaluation remains on the descriptive level of *de gustibus non disputandum*.

Contrary to this attitude which considers value as extrinsic to the object, one may search for intrinsic aesthetic norms that exist without the postulation of a knowing subject. Common denominators can be reached from the premises that there is such a thing as the outside world, that it is orderly, and that there is correspondence between the structure of this outer world and that of our mind. Whether spiritual appetites are prompted by spiritual absolutes or, as the relativist would claim, by physico-chemical processes within us, a teleological assumption cannot be avoided, were it only that of "serving life." Teleology, in any case, is a metaphysical, not a material, notion. The only really open question is whether the epistemological assumption of correspondence between the structures of inner and outer worlds extends to the value concept.

Craftsmanship is generally admitted to be a concept bearing on the worth of a work of art such as a musical composition. While being a necessary condition, craftsmanship alone does not suffice to define aesthetic standards of a higher order. Historical periods exhibiting an established, universally recognized musical *style—the early eighteenth century, for example—teem with well-made but otherwise unremarkable works, or with well-made works more remarkable than others but still far from outstanding. What places Bach above Telemann? Originality (in the generally accepted sense) cannot be the criterion, for in a stylistically powerful period all composers write by and large in the same style which guarantees the internal and external musical grammar (cf. *Matter and Form). In the eyes of the guild, a piece showing excellence in both respects is a masterpiece, and its maker is a master; yet we know that the most impeccable craftsmanship can produce a dull and commonplace piece.

The difference between such a composition and a truly great work lies in what it signifies. To inquire into the meaning of music is to stir up a hornet's nest. Actually opinions diverge only when dealing with the specific contents of music, which does not concern us here. They all stipulate that any object, let alone a man-made thing like a work of art, signifies something to man. We may reject at one extreme the explicit theory that music takes its meaning from the outer world. The theory at the other extreme claiming that music is nothing but a design in tones yet implicitly concedes, were it only for the pleasure with which we behold an arabesque, that music means more than the mere perception of tones. If neither craftsmanship nor originality provides the ultimate standards for distinguishing between a trite and an outstanding composition, what in the contents of a piece of music can produce differences in overall quality? The meaning we are looking for cannot lie in one detail or another. It must lie hidden behind all details in the point of unity, in the source, from which the totality of the contents flows. We should like to call this locus of the meaning of the work the *eidos*. The reconstitution of the eidos—originally in the composer's mind and subsequently in the hearer's— is the ultimate purpose of the work. In Aristotelian terms, the eidos is the final cause of a composition.

We submit that the value of a work depends on (a) the scope of the eidos and (b) the adequacy of the phenomenalization of the eidos, that is, craftsmanship in a higher sense. These statements are universal enough to apply to all styles. They clarify notions even without constituting a body of precise standards. Eidos must not be confused with *beauty. Whereas beauty is bound to a dialectic process of absorbing the ugly in ever higher syntheses, eidos does not exclude the ugly a priori and is thus the more general concept. As a practical implementation of these abstract notions, we shall attempt to search for the relevant aesthetic norms in two kinds of examples.

The operetta *Die Fledermaus* by Johann Strauss is a delightful masterpiece in every respect. Craftsmanship in both the higher and the lower senses of the term is superb: the eidos of the work is perfectly realized, and technical proficiency is uncontested. The opera *Parsifal* by Richard Wagner is another masterpiece. Both *Die Fledermaus* and *Parsifal* are outstanding works. In this respect they are equal. Yet there remains a difference. Somehow one feels that *Parsifal* is more "important," more "weighty" than *Die Fledermaus*. The reason lies in the greater scope of the eidos. Again, if we were put in the unfortunate position of having to save from destruction either *Parsifal* or Bach's B minor Mass, the best connoisseurs would probably decide in favor of the latter. The scope of its eidos is even wider, and not because of the religious content actually present in both works. If we now pair *Die Fledermaus* and the B minor Mass, the distance separating them seems enormous—greater even than that separating *Die Fledermaus* from *Parsifal*. Certain limitations inherent in opera affect the eidos. A purely choral or instrumental piece, by being less restrictive, offers more favorable preconditions for the permeation of the work by the eidos.

Our second kind of example permits us to be more specific. The theme of Bach's Organ Passacaglia is an enlargement of a theme by the slightly older French organ master André Raison:

Bach's theme is twice as long as Raison's; but the vast superiority of Bach's theme does not reside in this quantitative modification, for we can easily produce a version that puts the longer theme on the musical level of the shorter:

Greater length by itself does not guarantee superiority. It is rather a consequence of the scope of the eidos. It is not an essential symptom but a concomitant. We can inversely increase the significance of Raison's theme without stretching it:

Of these two versions, (1) sounds slightly superior to (2); but the point cannot be proven by any quality discovered in the musical foreground phenomenon. Version (2) exhibits less rhythmic variety, it is true, than version (1), but so does Bach's consistently better theme. Version (1), on the other hand, stays within the narrowest melodic compass. The qualitative difference between the themes by Bach and Raison, in short, cannot be explained by length, rhythm, range, or any other surface characteristic. The eidos alone, from which all meaning flows, helps us rate one above the other. For this reason, comparatively small changes in the music suffice to trigger a disproportionately great effect. Once the eidos is taken into account, the musical body can then be studied as a means of expressing the eidos. The *Harvard Dictionary of Music* quotes the Talmud as a head motto and also in the entry on "Aesthetics": "If you want to understand the invisible, look carefully at the visible." The precept is valid only if one presupposes the invisible. Foreground music phenomena become meaningful by being studied in the light of that invisible. Otherwise the study remains merely descriptive.

Aesthetic standards may gain clarity by our producing further transformations of Raison's theme:

These are four modifications of our earlier version (1) brought about by different combinations of accidentals. The differences can be described as transitional changes from a maximum hierarchical stability of the tones in (1a) to a maximum of leading-tone tension in (1d)—in short, from greater onticism to greater gigneticism. The versions may be characterized as follows:

(1a).   Phrygian. Hierarchical quality, especially as the ontic function of d_1-flat as a leading tone downward is immediately cancelled by the motion upward to e_1-flat. The tone d_1-natural in the last measure introduces an internal *modulation.

(1b).   Mixture of Phrygian and harmonic minor. Internal modulation occurs earlier, on b_2-natural. The ontic quality of the flat seventh degree is thus cancelled in favor of melodic movement.

(1c).   Aeolian. Same change as in (1b) but in inverted succession.

(1d).   Harmonic minor. Leading-tone quality at both points, d_1-natural and b_2-natural. The most facile version, lacking the severity of the other extreme (1a).

The hearer must decide for himself to the eidos of which of these versions to assign the greatest scope, and he may then call it the most "beautiful." His subjective judgment will approach objective value the wider his own scope. A contemporary of Bach's—living in an artistically strong period of an established style—would have admitted as "normal" only (1d) and rejected as "archaic" all other versions. In a stylistically undefined period like ours, one adjusts more readily to past as well as current conditions. An effect experienced at one time as unusual and surprising may become at another time a normal part of the vocabulary with a parallel change in value judgment from "daring" to "usual." Effect is indeed inseparable from *context of which *style is the most general aspect. Fortunately our adjustment to styles of the past permits us to react with undiminished force to a musical event then considered adventurous—witness the perennial extraordinary impression on most hearers made by the C major chord on the word "Light" in Haydn's *Die Schöpfung.*

Although the concept of eidos, as we have tried to show, permeates even a short stretch of music such as the themes by Bach and Raison, it reveals its total scope only in the whole work. The manner in which pieces continue shows most patently the differences in scope of the particular eidos or, in unfortunate cases, the absence of an eidos. The strength of the eidos permits a composer to use a standard theme for unsuspected possiblities. Such is the case in Bach's *Kunst der Fuge* but also in almost any rondo by Mozart.

Pinpointing the value of a musical work is as hazardous as catching the eidos. In the mind of the listener (and sometimes even of the composer), the eidos forms slowly through a perpetual oscillation between the perception of the music and a referral of the ever newly resulting situation back to the "invisible" and inaudible source. After innumerable repetitions of this process, the accumulating deposits will have built up an eidos. Often such an accomplishment needs more than a single hearer or even a single generation, but true eidos values have generally always been recognized, albeit after a considerable lapse of time.

AGOGICS

The term, introduced by Hugo Riemann,[1] means literally a "leading away," "carrying away," "leading towards." In music, it denotes nuances of tempo. Agogics has the same relationship to time as dynamics has to loudness. The primary musical implications are therefore rhythmic and metric, and the only possible indications pertain to faster, slower, or fluctuating tempo.

Rhythmic agogics is reflected in terms such as *accelerando* (speeding up) and *ritardando* (slowing down) for gradual tempo changes; *accelerato* (usually replaced by *più mosso*, *più vivo*, etc.) and *ritenuto* for sudden tempo changes; and *rubato* ('robbed') for subtle tempo variations toward both fast and slow.

Rubato may affect the whole of the musical texture or only part of it; an example of the latter is a free melody against a steady accompaniment. Rubato is often applied deliberately and consciously but is actually inseparable,

[1] *Dynamik und Agogik.*

59

whether one is aware of it or not, from any music-making. Anybody who has ever tried to play in time with a metronome has quickly realized that tempo, except when associated with grossly metrical body motions such as marching or sawing, is never constant in a strict, mechanical sense. The tempo of physiological processes—breathing, blood pressure, etc.—varies continuously and naturally imposes accelerandos, ritardandos, and rubatos. In turn, these physiological processes vary under the influence of music and music-making. A tempo indication, and be it metronomic, is only a prescribed norm around which the actual speed oscillates.

There exists a natural relationship between agogics and dynamics. An increase of energy entails both accelerando and crescendo; a decrease of energy, both ritardando and decrescendo. The urge to couple crescendo to accelerando and diminuendo to ritardando corresponds to the natural effects of increasing and decreasing energy and is therefore wholly instinctive. Counteracting this natural trend achieves special effects. Crescendo coupled with ritardando or even with a steady tempo suggests an accumulation of energy felt to be present potentially instead of kinetically. The orchestra scores by Brahms and Bruckner yield many characteristic examples of this kind; moreover, all forceful endings with a written-out or spontaneous ritardando belong in this category. Exceptional is the use of diminuendo coupled with accelerando, expressive of evaporating energy, of diminution or cessation of all resistance.

Metric agogics is reflected directly in musical notation rather than in signifying words. It pertains to any changes resulting from the metric-rhythmic build of measures and groups. The morphological value of agogics, which has appeared to match that of dynamics, here has a direct bearing on structure. Any change in the meter of a piece, because of the nature of meter, is necessarily discrete. In the scherzo of Beethoven's Ninth Symphony, the grouping by three measures (*Ritmo di tre battute*) after the established four is a metric accelerato (mm. 178 ff.); the return from three to four measures, a metric ritenuto (mm. 233 ff.). The shift from 3/4 to ¢ at the end of the same movement is part of an even more drastic stringendo (mm. 547 ff.). We deal here actually with tempo variations; but what matters morphologically is that these variations in the metric-rhythmic build of measures or groups result in an increase or decrease in the density of time production.

We may also speak of melodic and harmonic agogics but shall find them difficult, if not impossible, to isolate from rhythmic and metric agogics. They may belong to either. Melodic agogics is rhythmic in nonmetric music such as Gregorian chant and most Oriental monody. An example is the ictus recommended by the Benedictine editors on the second syllable of the word *eleison* in our given Kyrie. In metrical music, the changes produced by melodic agogics become identical with *augmentation and diminution. The difficulty of isolating harmonic agogics from meter is evinced by the dearth of actual cases we can quote from the literature. Harmonized Gregorian chant—a musical self-contradiction—might serve to illustrate the possibility. Perhaps the opening measures of the *Tristan* Prelude by Richard Wagner can be interpreted in terms of harmonic agogics if one is willing to accept as given a deliberate metric indeterminateness. In metrical music, on the other hand, harmonic agogics is a common phenomenon. It follows the melody and is generally governed by the barlines.

Metric agogics is possible because of our expectation of regularity of an established pattern—an assumed inertia, so to speak. The understanding of a change in structure as a tempo variation is often a delicate matter because of the uncertainty as to how to interpret the abnormality of a group. Agogics and particularly metric agogics thus belong to the general field of *phrasing. The questions that arise, often caused by inherent or notational ambiguities, are important not only theoretically but also practically because they have an immediate bearing on performance. The following examples are meant to clarify some cases:

(1)   Codex Montpellier, H 196, folio 93 verso and 94 recto, Ave beatissima—Ave Maria—Johanne. This motet runs throughout in triple meter; more precisely, it is governed by the second rhythmic mode. Just before the finalis—in modern terms, in the penultimate measure—we find an extra beat (a common occurrence in the motets of this codex). One modern editor has transcribed this feature as a 4/4 measure leading from the established 3/4 pattern to the cessation of tonal movement on the finalis.[1] Another modern editor retains the 3/4 notation but marks the spot *ritardando*.[2] Either interpretation recognizes the rhythmic slowing-down before the end, although the transcription as 4/4 measure shifts the solution to metric agogics.

(2)   Bach, French Suite no. 4, Menuet I, mm. 14–15. This is a typical example from among countless baroque movements in triple meter where a hemiola in the cadence, produced by a shift in agogic accents, effectuates a slowing-down, although the underlying beat remains unchanged. These two measures form a 3/2 unit against the surrounding 3/4 pattern.

(3)   Mozart, Piano Sonata no. 13, B-flat major, K. 333, beginning. The first period is 4 measures long and regular; the second period, however, extends over 6 measures. The music leaves no doubt about the interpretation. Whereas the first period is binary (2×2), the second period is ternary (3×2). The result is a metric ritenuto.

(4)   Mozart, Piano Sonata no. 11, A major, K. 331, Menuetto, beginning. The first two periods have 5 measures each. There is no difficulty of interpretation, for the fifth measure in each case is a prolongation. Against the expected four-measure pattern of a minuet, the effect is that of a metric ritenuto. Afterwards the periods become ordinary, 4 + 4. In these shorter periods, the music is suddenly vivacious: the change in structure corresponds to the change of attitude.

(5)   Beethoven, Piano Sonata no. 6, F major, op. 10 no. 2, second movement. The six measures before the recapitulation (119–24) may admit of two opposing interpretations, between which one can choose only after careful examination of the context and not according to any general rules. Until the spot in question, one has heard only regular periods of 2×4 measures. The critical six measures appear as 4 + 2. Probably they should be interpreted as 3×2, producing a metric ritenuto. One could argue that the preceding measures

[1]Apel, *Notation*, p. 300.
[2]Rokseth, *Polyphonies*, 2:130.

(117–18) are an elision, the ambiguity intensified by the long rest. If so, the six irregular measures belong to a period of eight, and the result would be an acceleration.

(6)   Beethoven, Piano Sonata no. 13, E-flat major, op. 27 no. 1, second movement, mm. 42 ff. The situation is comparable to that in the preceding example: two regular four-measure phrases are followed by six measures. If we hear these six as 3×2, a slowing-down would be implied. In this case, however, an elision with the last two measures of the preceding phrase (mm. 48–49) seems plausible, and an agogic accelerato eventuates.

In examples (3) through (5), we have described the agogic change as ritenuto, and in example (6) as accelerato, because the notation indicates a sudden shift. Yet the effect seems to be, respectively, that of ritardando and accelerando, for the elongation or shortening, as the case may be, is perceived but gradually.

ALTERATION

Altering a note means lowering or raising it by a semitone in order to create a tendency of that note toward the neighbor note. The alteration has the purpose of sensitizing a note which is not naturally sensitive. In the diatonic scale, the reciprocal attraction of the notes of a semitone exists by force of the given position. Characteristically, the note succumbing to the attraction is called *note sensible* in French and *nota sensitiva* in Italian (whereas the parallel terms *leading tone* in English and *Leitton* in German suggest not a state but an activity). Whether the sensitivity results from alteration or position, we deal in principle with the same phenomenon. We shall discuss it by way of the example of alteration in which it manifests itself most clearly.

One must ask oneself how it is possible that a tone can be raised or lowered—a procedure that actually results in the production of a different tone—all the while preserving its identity. From an ontic point of view, the operation is evidently impossible. A tone, a harmony, are what they are. The musical phenomenon, thus viewed, is in a state of rest, of "being." It is an entity. Neither tone nor harmony can abandon its actual state without eventuating in a different tone or harmony that has no genetic relation to the former. In this conception, there is no place for alteration.

Alteration stems from the domain of melody. It is accomplished under the influence of a melodic current which forces a note either up or down while conserving its identity. In the analogous case of the leading tone, this tendency of one note toward its neighbor is a quality inherent in the normal position of the leading tone in the diatonic scale. In the case of a melodically altered note, however, we must consider the additional tension that binds the altered note to the note that has suffered the alteration. In the first Molto allegro theme of Mozart's *Don Giovanni* Overture, for instance, the altered note d^1-sharp is both fastened to d^1-natural and pushing toward e^1:

Now the reason for the imagined resistance by the main note against a displacement (the affinity of a note with its altered state) and for the tendency of a note toward another note (the "sensitive" quality of the altered note) cannot be imagined as residing in the notes themselves. It must be looked for in a milieu assumed to surround the tones. To understand only the alteration, the conferring of a quality of elasticity on that milieu would suffice. Elasticity would explain the resistance against the displacement of a note as well as the conservation of its identity during the deformation. But elasticity alone would not explain the tendency or sensitivity of a note. We must therefore suppose the presence of other forces acting upon the tones.

We are thus led to think of the milieu as a kind of "field of forces." This hypothesis clarifies the phenomena of both resistance and tendency. It also leads to a first understanding of the concept of "tonal space" with which we are free to identify the milieu. This space is a notion rather uneasy to seize or define. Nonetheless we are obliged to acknowledge that it possesses a character of interior reality (cf. *Time and Space). We need only remind ourselves that without this imagined space, tones would find themselves devoid of the attribute of pitch; the spatial array of tones (*échelle sonore*) would not exist. The sensitization of a note is thus an operation performed not on the note itself but on the tonal space. Thus understood, music is a manifestation of a play of spatial forces.

We have posed this principle of a musical space by suggesting that it is structured by a configuration of forces germane to melody. There exists still another factor which acts in the creation of the spatial structure.

Whereas melody, by definition, is essentially gignetic, harmony (as also an isolated tone) is essentially ontic. This ontic conception can comprise an ensemble of harmonies (or tones) because of the notion of hierarchy, which is inherent in the deployment of tone in harmonic perspective. The hierarchy is well demonstrated by the *Pythagorean Table. It is a hierarchy of position. Spatial morphology must therefore be understood as the result of a concourse of forces that are ontic-harmonic as well as gignetic-melodic.

Strictly speaking, the term *alteration* does not belong in a treatise on harmony, which has the task of analyzing and elucidating harmonies from their purely harmonic, that is, primarily positional, aspect. The harmonic hierarchy, however, is capable of producing tendencies of its own kind. In melodic gigneticism, these tendencies arise from the play of live forces in the tonal space. Consider, as an example, the motivic progression in C major from a^2 to g^2 via a^2-flat on the climax of Beethoven's *Leonore* Overture No. 3 (mm. 606 ff.). Hierarchic gigneticism, on the other hand, is first of all a formal force, a force of position. It explains, for example, the cogency of the progression T-S-D-T (I-IV-V-I). Harmonic tendencies may eventually assimilate themselves to melodic; we can think of voice-leading as a consequence of position. In all these cases, we are in the presence of forces which produce spatial configurations and create the structure of the tonal space.

It is important to think of each of these configurations, such as a scale, as ensembles, as a whole. The changes occurring from moment to moment will always affect the ensemble of the configuration. The possible variations submit themselves to the grammar of style which fixes the hierarchic structure and imprints its particularities on the gignetic gestures. The hierarchic elements will, of course, offer more resistance to the deformations and changes of all sorts than the gignetic elements, be these latter melodic or gignetically used harmonic forces. Indeed the inertia of hierarchic factors is the quality that permits a style to lend a definite character to a whole epoch without thereby impeding the free play of individual composers. A cadence, let us not forget, is not only a chord succession triggered by a harmonic drive but first of all a chord succession based on preestablished hierarchy. A Landini cadence is very convincing although lacking leading-tone tension, because it is built on a preestablished configuration of forces, different from ours, which defines its field. Similarly, a scale is not just a melody but an ensemble of tones previously fixed. It is, moreover, an ensemble of harmonic origin and hence also of hierarchic nature. The melodic tensions of plainchant are entirely positional. In early polyphonic compositions in which a Gregorian melody appears as the tenor, as in a Perotinus organum, the hierarchic attitude becomes obvious when one long-held note moves to the next.

Alteration, in its widest implication, emerges as a style criterion, for different periods have significantly shown different attitudes toward it. The historic role is sketched in the article *Ontic-Gignetic.

AMBITUS

The term defines a limit. To a Latin, the *ambitus muri*, literally the 'walking around the wall', signified the circumference, and hence the restricting boundary, of the enclosed city. The ambitus of the human *voice is a confining musical feature prescribed by nature—normally less than two octaves for each voice, and a total of not more than four octaves, from c_2 to c^2, for the combined ranges. This given and fixed circumscription has influenced our concept of melody and also of ensemble throughout the ages. However one may define melody, the unifying factor of a human ambitus remains essential. Instruments can mechanically extend the vocal range at either end; but a melody played in the extreme octaves on a solo piccolo or solo tuba, by distortion of a normal condition, sounds funny (the "Vivat Bacchus" duet from Mozart's *Entführung*) or eerie (Sparafucile's first appearance) or both (Monostatos's aria).

A similar situation exists in an ensemble. In all vocal music and in the early instrumental transcriptions of vocal models, the ambitus is naturally set. But also in all later instrumental compositions, the main "playground" of music lies within the four octaves symmetrically arranged around middle *c*. Extensions of this ambitus, easily accomplished by the mechanics of an instrument, are either doublings at the octave (which are really modifications of timbre) or virtuoso excursions (which dazzle precisely by their leaving the middle ground). The theoretically unlimited ambitus of electronic instruments can become serviceable when practically restrained by some morphological consideration; otherwise it contributes to the unintelligibility of a constructed language.

In Gregorian chant, ambitus is a decisive factor in distinguishing authentic from plagal modes. In the former, the tones of the mode are confined by the octave span of the finalis; in the latter, they encircle the finalis. The defining quality of ambitus here has consequences that reach into scale and melody construction.[1] In the original authentic modes, as we know them from Greek theorists, scales were constructed by the juxtaposition of two tetrachords of the same pattern which thus spanned an octave. The three possible placements of the semitone within any tetrachord admit of three scales:

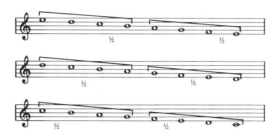

In the first, the semitone lies at the bottom of the tetrachord; the resulting (Greek) Dorian scale has a descending tendency. The second, Phrygian, with the semitone in the middle, is neutral. In the third, the semitone lies at the top of the tetrachord; the resulting Lydian scale has an ascending tendency. These three authentic scales each present the beginning of a row that can be continued throughout the entire tonal realm. They are *open* scales.

In the plagal modes, on the other hand, the scales were constructed by the joining of two parallel tetrachords at a tone they share. This point of juncture becomes a center (a kind of *mese*) around which the tones of the scale rise and fall:

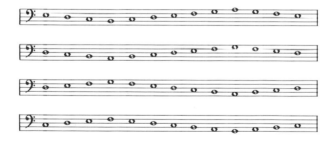

The central attraction of the finalis does not let the tones stray beyond the given ambitus. These plagal scales are *closed* forms. In their equilibrium of rise and fall, closed scales appear as prototypes of melody.

Ambitus in polyphonic music manifests itself in two different ways. We can illustrate the difference by comparing a motet of the thirteenth century with—to choose another three-part composition—a classical string trio. In the first case, the three voices have about the same ambitus. As a result, they cross, overlap, and produce for the composition a total ambitus that is no larger than that of each individual voice. In the second case, violin, viola, and violoncello each occupy their own specific tonal area. Crossing and overlap-

[1]Cf. Kauder, *Counterpoint*, pp. 1–16.

ping is now neither necessary nor normal, and the total ambitus far surpasses the individual potential. These two general stylistic attitudes carry significant morphological consequences. The early polyphonic example can be thought of as starting with a given ambitus which is subsequently shared by the participating voices. The motet proceeds as if a unified total sound were divided, as if a given structured circumference were now populated with life. The later polyphonic composition, quite on the contrary, creates a new ambitus of its own by the independent and dynamic behavior of the voices by themselves and toward each other. The three parts jointly construct an outer circumference for a given population. Whereas the thirteenth-century motet takes apart a predetermined ambitus, the classical trio brings one into being before our ears. The distinction is not chronological. We rather deal with two polar functions of ambitus that relate to the concepts of ontism and gigneticism.

ARCHETYPES

We consider archetypes innate and inescapable forms of our mind. Whereas the philosophic interpretation of archetypes is subject to opinion, their reality is not. One may hold the opinion that archetypes are anchored in nature, or are determined by our bodily constitution, or are a priori structural elements of our soul, or that archetypes, nature, body, and soul are all manifestations of universal principles. In any case, archetypes permeate our conceptual as well as our intuitive thinking.

We use the term *idea* in a more general and abstract sense than the term *archetype*. We would say that order is an idea but that modes of order are archetypes. Tonality is an idea; major-minor are forms determined by archetypes, as are all form concepts. Our urge to interpret reality in terms of archetypes is strikingly revealed by our search for an underlying form wherever we meet with apparent lack of formal determination. In this search, we all show a latent disposition to certain identical reactions. Characteristic in this respect is the quest in many fields for cycles or the tendency toward geometric abstractions. The emerging images are evidently forms of a shared psychic attitude or they would not appear in divers civilizations and periods. Examples are plentiful: circle, square, cross, mandorla, world egg, world tree, trinity, symmetry, etc. In every such case, we hope to find a mode of order.

In music, archetypes govern all areas. The entries of this dictionary testify to their prevalence. Melodic modes of order are given by the basic intervals, such as octave and fifth, and by all scales. There are certain melodic motives that seem to belong in this category, such as the Dorian repercussion

, the balanced figure ,

and others which recur independently of style. They are to be understood as fragmentary scale variations, in which an archetype has become a gesture. The triad is a harmonic archetype. The six rhythmic modes of the thirteenth century are more or less conscious attempts to deduce archetypes.

Archetypes and ideas, being essentially metaphysical, cannot ordinarily be apprehended directly. They can only be found empirically. They are known only indirectly through variations in phenomena that approximate them.

This allowance for approximation defines archetypes as norms. Norms are enunciated not in terms of law but of principle. Laws do not allow for either approximations or exceptions. Norms do, and this quality makes them the presiding concepts of the organic, of life. Because life is characterized by movement, by oscillation, by tension between two poles, variation is not a makeshift but an essential quality of life. Variation, in the broad as well as the specific meaning of the word, therefore elucidates the value of the individual in life and in art. We are freshly aware of the necessity of separating form principles from the forms themselves. We are also warned that any reduction of musical phenomena to underlying, simpler shapes destroys the uniqueness of a musical utterance while leaving that utterance unexplained. Uniqueness will always remain inexplicable; but by starting from principles we can at least create a feeling for its genesis, whereas by pushing reduction to its far limit and bypassing the normative principles we shall always end up at the motionless One. Archetypes are at the least a reference point, at the best an ideal toward which one strives. They give teleological direction.

ARIA

The concept refers to the Neapolitan da capo type which dominated the international opera scene throughout the eighteenth century. It is the only aria type with a definite morphology; for neither has the name *aria* other formal connotations, nor are other operatic solos, whatever their title, bound to a prescribed and expected structure. *Aria*, one often forgets, is the Italian word for *air*. The French word, identical with the English, designates a general kind of song. The physiological connection with a vocal piece is obvious; the sensitive Italian nomenclature may well give recognition to *breathing form.

There is a good reason that da capo form, the least dramatic of all, became an operatic favorite. In a drama, as in life, no earlier situation is ever exactly retrieved. (When it is, as in George S. Kaufman's *The Man Who Came To Dinner* or Joseph Kesselring's *Arsenic and Old Lace*, the contrived effect is deliberately and successfully burlesque.) But the role of an aria is not to propel the drama but rather to exhaust the lyrical, emotional potential of a particular moment. In terms of the drama, an aria stops the action, as if the running of a movie were arrested on one frame. At the end of an aria the action resumes at the point at which it had been left at the beginning. The invited applause at that moment contributes to the morphologic isolation of the musical piece from the dramatic play.

In the Neapolitan opera style, the closed form of a da capo aria makes sense. As composers became increasingly concerned with dramatic development within a musical number, they strove to reconcile the need for a musically open-ended aria with the conventional da capo form. An early solution was a piece in which a complete lyrical da capo structure is followed by a new dramatic section, usually faster and always open. Mozart, who understand-ably favored this form, portrays by it in *Le nozze di Figaro*, for instance, the psychological change in the Countess's attitude (no. 19, "Dove sono"). When in the same opera he abandons the ternary arrangement altogether, he some-times employs new terms (*Cavatina* for the barforms of nos. 10 and 23) but also retains the conventional title (for instance, for the basically binary nos. 12 and 26).

Composers later in the nineteenth century, prompted by the drive to adapt music to drama, continued experiments in this direction. An instructive example in this respect is Weber's *Der Freischütz*, of 1821. The opera contains seven solo pieces, of which four are called aria—one for each protagonist— and three by other names. Of the latter, Kaspar's *Lied* (no. 4) is a song in three strophes; Aennchen's *Ariette* (no. 7), a comic number with a real da capo; and Agathe's *Kavatine* (no. 12), a brief unified number that suggests an abbre-viated da capo. In a sense, all three numbers still lean on ternary organization. Of the four arias, those of the two lovers (nos. 3 and 8) are similar in structure: there is a return, in greatly increased tempo, to the main key (in Max's aria to the tonic relative) but not to the first theme, the middle section contrasting to the extent of admixing recitative passages. Aennchen's aria (no. 13) is a straightforward da capo, in line with her uncomplicated character. The vil-lain Kaspar's aria (no. 5), on the other hand, is the least conventional, perhaps suggestive of a rondo idea but hardly of the Neapolitan prototype.

One generation later, in 1853, Verdi in *Il Trovatore* characteristically combines tradition and innovation by incorporating arias in longer units which he entitles *scena*. The word *aria* itself occurs only three times out of fourteen vocal numbers. As in *Der Freischütz*, the leading roles are each given one aria. All three are open-ended by virtue of the now well-established ap-pearance of a new, fast second part. A da capo forms the slower first part of only Count Luna's aria (no. 7); but in the other two cases (nos. 11 and 12), elements of recapitulation survive unexpectedly in the respective allegro sections—almost as if to justify the old and almost superseded name. The traditional structure is further loosened by the insertion of other voices at various points.

By the end of the nineteenth century, the requirement of theatrical ex-citement and continuity was making arias obsolete. In Bizet's *Carmen* (1875), one single *air* remains (no. 22) with a complete da capo arrangement as old-fashioned as Micaela herself who sings it. The realistic operas of the period necessarily favor open structures which push the action forward. Mussorg-sky's *Boris Godunov*, for example, which was first performed in 1874, con-tains songs and monologues but no arias. The morphological contribution of the term *aria* has been spent. Where numbers remain at all, noncommittal names take over, such as cavatina, romanza, Lied, chanson, canzone, scena, and others.

In the changing relationship of music to text, aria is an extreme case of literary subordination. *Arioso* is an example of rapprochement. It combines in one piece elements of both recitative and aria. Syllabic treatment and ab-sence of text repetition represent the former; melodic invention and richer texture, the latter.

The influence of da capo aria on classical sonata and symphony should be duly recognized. The popularity of da capo aria doubtless contributed to the evolution of sonata form from a binary to a ternary structure. Many slow movements, moreover, are clearly instrumental transcriptions and elaborations of the vocal model. One could, of course, claim that the inherent strength of bowform did not depend on an opera aria to gain recognition; but the chronological coincidence and internal evidence are too manifest to be ignored. The supremacy of vocal over instrumental music, obvious in the early history of music, asserts itself, unexpectedly, in a fruitful and healthy manner.

ATONALITY

Tonality, in the widest sense of the word, denotes a system of reference, of audible coordinates. The center of the system may be either a single pitch (as in monophony) or a group of pitches (as in harmony). Tonality is essentially a harmonic phenomenon, because it involves a single pitch or a complex of pitches retained through time by memory. Polyphony pertains to tonality only inasmuch as it includes the experience of harmony or of "sounding together." After being weakened for a long time by the progressive infiltration, and eventual eruption, of chromaticism, tonality was completely overpowered by it in the present century. Atonality ensued. Among the divergent developments within the atonal style, we shall focus on the so-called twelve-tone school, an invention of Josef Matthias Hauer and Arnold Schönberg.

The immediate advantages of the dodecaphonic system are evident, persuasive, and reassuring. The theory is articulate. The rules are unequivocal without excluding individual interpretation. The grammar can be taught and learned. Yet a principle of which the name begins with the negative prefix *a-* can hardly be a constructive one.

The fundamental assumption of dodecaphony is that the relation among the twelve tones is not natural but arbitrary. The listener is asked to perceive only the difference in interval size, in the purely spatial sense. Consequently, the concepts of consonance and dissonance have disappeared from dodecaphonic theory. At the same time, the dodecaphonist fully respects the identity aspect of the octave. Now to recognize the octave as a harmonic entity while denying the harmonic nature of other intervals is a lapse of logic. In what way are we supposed to hear the other intervals? One cannot suspend an irrepressible evaluation which one is still required to apply to the octave.

The tone row, or series, as well, does not increase the morphological wealth. It is one of the many possible configurations of the twelve pitches. To say configuration is to say gestalt. Hence the interval between any two consecutive pitches is not perceived in isolation but actually with reference to the gestalt of the entire series. The latter thus constitutes a frame of reference which conforms to our initial definition of tonality. Because this frame is identical with its content, it is also identical with the tonic. In other words, dodecaphony is not entirely atonal; rather, it makes use of only one tonal function—the tonic. It is a monotone of twelve pitches. A tone row may be transposed; but in the intentional absence of a line of reference, transposition becomes merely a change of altitude. But then what precisely can the meaning of altitude be? Higher or lower than what? Some presupposition of a median or normal altitude would again reintroduce the tonality concept.

Fear of tonality, a-tonality, robs music of the essential characteristic of respiration—the alternation of tension and release. Dodecaphony reflects this lack in its grammar while trying to provide for compensation. Melodic progressions are replaced by a succession of disjunct tones, meaning large intervals, so that no preponderance of one pitch over another is established. Dissonance is searched out to prevent the evocation of the triad, the natural and mortal enemy of dodecaphony, as being the primordial and omnipotent creator of tonality. Dynamics and sonority are favored in this basically anti-vocal and even anti-instrumental style. Complicated rhythms take over, often abstractly worked out on paper or tape.

Atonality is a general contemporary phenomenon. Obsessive fear of tonality reveals a deep aversion to the concept of hierarchy or rank. The "individuals" (pitches) are put on equal footing; none must outrank another. Can we avoid being reminded of the leveling tendencies of our epoch? The revolt against tonality—including all distinction between consonance and dissonance—is an egalitarian revolution. Bach could still declare that the laws of counterpoint by themselves prove the existence of God. Atonality denies this statement.

AUGMENTATION-DIMINUTION

These devices are generally thought of as modifications of melody. One may raise the question whether they cannot under circumstances be heard as modifications of time. All depends on what one accepts as established, so that in relation to it the augmentation or diminution may be properly interpreted.

A melody, whether in long or short note values, will not be understood as an augmentation or diminution unless preceded by a normative statement against which it may be measured. The first statement of a fugue theme, for instance, be it slow or fast, establishes our sense of time for that particular piece. Introducing augmentation or diminution in the first exposition— never encountered in the *Well-tempered Keyboard*—would only muddle the barely launched movement of time. Once the tempo is set, it provides a frame of reference for all subsequent events. On this premise, we hear the theme played in doubled note values as slow because it takes twice as long as the normal theme.

There is the other possibility, however, that we accept the melodic entity, not our stop watch, as the given measuring rod. The more musical happenings we hear within a given clock time, the longer that chronological time span appears to us subjectively. In this case, augmentation makes subjective time flow faster; diminution, more slowly. In the confrontation of tempo against melody, we can readily experience melody as the stable element, tempo as the fluctuating stream on which it floats—particularly when we deal with something as clearly defined as a fugue theme. Musical time is not identical with clock time. It is produced, not by the regular ticking of a pendulum, but by the density of musical events. The whole original theme takes as long as only half of the augmented version. Instead of having heard the entire theme after a certain lapse of time, in the augmentation we have heard only half of it. Less has happened within the same number of seconds. The musical density is reduced by half.

The paradox resolves itself when we ask ourselves what we consider as constant—the tempo or the melody. If we assume that augmentation never occurs out of context with an established time flow, then it slows the composition objectively. If we accept the melodic entity, not our stop watch, as the measuring rod, then we experience the augmented event as going by faster subjectively. The two solutions are not mutually exclusive. Probably we hear polychronally.

Diminution reverses the phenomenon. The interpretation hinges on the attachment of our inertia to tempo or to melody. In the first case, diminution speeds the music. In the second, it increases the density, and we feel slowed down.

The situation becomes complex when the countersubject to the fugue theme, or any fixed counterpoint, does not participate in the augmentation but keeps its original shape. The polyphony here pertains to the simultaneous flow of different time experiences. Because the main theme is usually the more memorable of the two, one is likely to be led by its appearance, although in augmentation, and measure the countersubject against it, that is, to hear the countersubject, although in normal size, accelerated.

An extreme but still frequent consequence of this technical intricacy is a contrapuntal combination in which the same theme occurs simultaneously in different sizes—normal, augmented, diminished, and even double-diminished (as in the finale of Beethoven's Piano Sonata op. 110). Bach's *Die Kunst der Fuge* systematically explores the increasingly intensified possibilities. A famous example is the Agnus II from Josquin des Prez's *Missa Hercules Dux Ferrariae* in which all three participating voices sing the same melody simultaneously at the measured ratios of 1 : 1/2 : 1/3.

BALANCE

Although the etymology evokes a physical tool (*bi* + *lanx*, 'having two scales'), the term denotes an archetype. Functioning as a norm, it suggests a desirable state: there are positive implications in a "balanced budget" or a "balanced diet." Actually equilibrium need not be a virtue in all circumstances. We may profitably restrict our inquiry to the balance between opposing and equally worthy qualities, in short, to concept pairs derived from polarity. A tentative and by no means complete list of such musical concepts follows:

up	—	down
step	—	skip
major	—	minor
dominant	—	subdominant
high	—	low

loud	—	soft
fast	—	slow
short	—	long
arsis	—	thesis
inhaling	—	exhaling

There is no necessary connection among all members of the left column, or all members of the right, although some relationships exist. The main characteristic of each pair is that the two members represent opposing and complementary forces. We expect them to balance each other in the course of a good composition; for being an archetype, balance establishes a norm toward which the forces strive. The strong dominant tension in a Beethoven symphony, for example, is stabilized by the subdominant orientation of most slow middle movements. Fugue themes by Bach exemplify melodic equilibrium by balancing rise and fall, skip and step:

The normative quality of balance must be understood in terms of musical behavior or, for that matter, of the behavior of any living organism. Life is oscillation. Total equilibrium means death. If all forces acting on or in a system are equalized, all motion comes to a standstill. Contrary forces have canceled each other. The system becomes inert. The physical term for this permanent state in which no observable events occur is *maximum entropy*. How living organisms avoid the decay leading to entropy, has been a topic diversely treated and answered by scientists and philosophers. In any case, an exchange of contrary forces must take place. The Nobel Prize winner Erwin Schrödinger makes the point that "the device by which an organism maintains itself stationary at a fairly high level of orderliness (= fairly low level of entropy) really consists in continually sucking orderliness from its environment."[1]

In music, where balance is as essential as in nature, all these speculations apply. When all participating opposing forces have neutralized each other, when all the ups and downs, and subdominants and dominants, have canceled each other, the piece is finished. Such a process is not mathematically precise, and should not be. Nor are the theoretic conditions ever exactly met in practice. But the principle contains a musical truth. A composition keeps moving, continues its life, in an effort to cope with entropy. The balancing of high by low is, among other comparable factors, the contents of a piece. The need to follow a subdominant by a dominant, or an inhaling by an exhaling, maintains the musical motion. The "orderliness sucked from the environment" is the composer's contribution.

Attainment of balance is a classical concept. There are many instances

---

[1] "Heredity," *The World of Mathematics*, 2:295.

where, in order to produce a special effect, the ideal of balance is deliberately not phenomenalized. The archetypal quality of balance is present here as well, or the effect would not be understood as a violation or exception. Without the norm behind it, the effect would have to be taken at its face value and thus lose its "effectiveness."

Examples are particularly common in styles that are basically "romantic"—not only in the nineteenth century but in other "romantically" inclined periods such as the *ars nova* and the baroque. Bach, in his Cantata no. 105, writes a movement for soprano, oboe, two violins, and viola. Obviously, there is no balance of range. The soaring quality of the high texture gains its desired effect by our tacitly comparing it, balancing it, against the normal equilibrium from top to bottom. Bach is "classical" enough to establish an overall balance by following this particular movement with a lengthy accompanied recitative for bass.

Analysis of small or large structures yields endless examples of balance, maintenance of motion, and the fight against entropy. All composing begins with a disturbance of an implied indifferent state. The disturbance is the impetus of the work.

BARBARIANISM

Music begins with an artifact: *tone and *scale, the basic building materials, are complex end products of a highly artistic selection process. From the unformed world of sound, such unordered phenomena as noise, continuous pitch variation, and asystematic chance relations have been eliminated to reach the threshold of music.

We call barbarian any music that deliberately returns to a precivilized, premusical state in which the unformed, the undistilled, the inarticulate are placed on the throne as supreme values. Thus the main characteristics of barbarian music are reliance on noise, on glissando, and on asystematic interval relations.

The art of music, of course, makes use of these premusical phenomena, but it does not permit them to prevail. In a civilized context, tamed wilderness is a welcome spectacle. The noise producers of the orchestra—percussion instruments, particularly those without definite pitch—play a limited role in classical music, the antithesis of barbarian music. In the rare instances when Mozart and Haydn used cymbals (there is no instance in the music of Bach), the conscious purpose was to invoke the barbarian, witness the Turkish music in Mozart's *Die Entführung aus dem Serail*. Glissando is even rarer. Fast chromatic scales, as in the first movement of Beethoven's E-flat major Piano Concerto, or the notorious glissando octave runs in the finale of his Waldstein Sonata remain stylized and employ discrete pitches. A singer's or string player's portamento comes closest to continuous pitch variation. Classical style never prescribes it but rather leaves it, with considerable risks attached, to the discretion of the performer's taste. Asystematic chance relations of intervals, finally, remained totally excluded from the development of civilized Western music until the twentieth century. Even the most daring chromaticists of the sixteenth century always backed up their experiments by reference to some underlying harmonic rationale.

From recorded music history, barbarianisms—except when used purposefully and tamed within a musical context—are on the whole absent. The development of music (and of good art in general) is identical with that of civilized man. Occasional barbarian outbursts were revolts against a given attitude but not against the spirit of music itself. Pope John XXII, in his bull of 1324–25, condemned the secular uprising of the "new art" with such terms as depravity, wantonness, irregularity, and excess. A plaque on the Bardi palace in Florence honors the leader of the Camerata by crediting him with returning the art of music, barbarized [*sic*] by the foreign Flemings (such as Josquin des Prez and Adrian Willaert), to the sublimity of Greek melopoeia. Compositions of the kind advocated by Bardi and his followers were in turn heard by G. M. Artusi, a solid musician of the next generation, as "deformations of nature and propriety." To us, none of these originally revolutionary efforts sounds barbarian, not because we have "become used to it," but because each in its own way accepted as a basis for further operations the artistic accomplishment of discrete tone and some ordered scale.

Today the departure from traditional music is one of principle. One cannot brush off the revolt as an "interesting experiment" but must recognize the trends behind the experiment. For the first time in music history, proportion and the art of *bene modulandi* are openly declared without value by an irruption of the irrational. Noise, continuous pitch variation, and asystematic chance relations—the phenomena eliminated on the long path from chaotic sound to civilized music—are claimed to be essential. The inarticulate and the unformed have been elevated to aesthetic principles. Because electronic instruments are capable of producing any and all of these premusical sounds, they appear as the most typical representatives of modern barbarianism. (Theoretically they could be put to good use like any other instrument if treated as tools with defined limitations.) Their strong influence has created an ideal of sound which is now in turn painstakingly emulated by older, more customary instruments and by performing groups. Electronic music concerns itself with the becoming of phenomena out of chaos. It barely touches upon the phenomenon before sinking back into the unformed. It suggests the destruction of the existing. Tone appearances out of noise and shape appearances out of the inarticulated remain fugitive. The struggle of the uncreated toward phenomenalization is deliberately held back at the threshold where cultivated music, in becoming articulate, takes over. Electronic music is precreational, premusical, barbarian. One cannot even take it as a companion—not even as an inner companion—to the proverbial desert island. Traditional music exists in the mind, independently of physical realization. Electronic music exists only in performance: destroy the apparatus and nothing is left. It is a full surrender to matter and machine.

To the extent to which they do not contribute toward disintegration and dissolution of forms, these premusical products (one notices in passing) are cast in traditional forms. A style which renounces on principle articulated and ordered phenomenalization, that is, morphological limitation, appears to grasp helplessly though illogically at conventional structures. Some of the pieces actually sound like extreme cases of a preartistic verismo. The question deserves further investigation. In retrospect, many present products may turn out to be rather conservative.

The new barbarian music has been claimed to be "good" on the grounds that it is an expression of our time. As far as essence is concerned, art is always the same. The times change. It is the times that more or less approach art, not the other way around. In more rational and balanced periods than ours, the greater proximity of life and art has given rise to the misunderstanding of art as an expression of the times. In such periods, life—happily for the people who experience it—is to some extent an expression of art. In other periods, like ours, art can only maintain its own vision, its own norms. The new barbarianism, with its premusical worship of noise, glissando, and indistinct pitches, offers no vision and denies natural and artistic norms. It is like screaming during a catastrophe—an occupation that is neither musical nor artful.

BARFORM

The lasting popularity of barform across centuries and styles vouches for its inherent strength. The origin in Greek drama explains the basic behavior. Two half-choruses appeared symmetrically and made symmetrical statements. The words differed, of course, but followed parallel thoughts. Meter, rhythm, and length were identical. The melody, we assume, was also identical for both statements. Small variations of the elements involved would not invalidate the experience of symmetry. The two choral groups probably also danced—or at least certainly pantomimed—their respective parts. The Greek words *strophe* and *antistrophe*, which designate these sections of the drama, still reveal the inherent motion; for they literally mean 'turn' and 'counter-turn' (terms intelligently but unsuccessfully proposed by Ben Jonson).[1] The binary orientation demonstrated by strophe and antistrophe was raised to the second power, as it were, when the half-choruses stood still and, joining forces, contraposed to the combined strophes a balancing and often climactic *epode* (the 'stand', in Ben Jonson's word). The principle is dialectic and has often invited comparison of the three musical parts with, respectively, thesis, antithesis, and synthesis, Hans Sachs, explaining the form to Walther von Stolzing in the third act of *Die Meistersinger von Nürnberg*, compares the epode to a child issuing from a pair.

Besides equalling in importance, that is, often in musical duration, the two strophes together, the epode must be inherently new, if only to become distinguished from any possible misinterpretation as one more strophic repetition. The newness may be melodic (cf. *The Star-Spangled Banner*), harmonic (cf. "Trockne Blumen" by Schubert), rhythmic (cf. the opening chorus of Bach's Cantata no. 78), technical (cf. the strettos in the first fugue from the *Well-tempered Keyboard*), or of any other musical quality or combination of qualities appropriate to the task. In all cases, the decisive break between the

[1]See his poem "To the Immortall Memorie, and Friendship of that Noble Paire, Sir Lucius Cary, and Sir H. Morison."

two strophes on one side and the epode on the other serves as a lasting reminder of the original binary dance orientation.

By not returning to the beginning, the form sounds open at the end. It therefore conveys a tendency toward continuation. This is a virtue in all musical situations where continuation is desirable. Thus the form characteristically dominates the literature of strophic structures. From the songs of trouvères and minnesingers in the Middle Ages, when the name *barform* springs up, it finds its way into the majority of Protestant chorales (such as the Bach example in our Discourse), children's songs, folksongs, and subsequently themes of variation cycles. Richard Wagner favors it throughout his operas for the formation of musical units within the continuous flow of the drama. Compared to the closed organization of a da capo aria, which forces us back into an earlier situation, the dramatic advantage is immense.

The openness of barform makes one rightly wonder why the two halves, of which the second must bring new material, are heard as a whole. The unity is produced by *topology. The juxtaposition of two entities in clearly demonstrated balance outweighs the disparities. Hence some factors usually remain constant below the changing events of the epode. The continuation of meter and tempo from the strophes into the epode form the most common bond. Thus measured balance is very frequent, be it the familiar $4 + 4 + 8$ of simple structures or the immense $39 + 39 + 78$ of Brangäne's attempt to calm Isolde (first act, mm. 770–925). But weight and value count as much as meter: Isolde's lament and love death form a chronologically short but intensively equivalent epode to the two strophes that fill the whole preceding act.

The deserved popularity across centuries of barform is partly rooted in the balance of its parts, but partly in the manifold potential, which holds out promises by its ambivalence. Barform is binary according to contents (the epode differing from the strophes) but ternary according to structure (there are three units). The binary principle is unmistakable in the balance of strophe against antistrophe, and of the two strophes jointly against the epode. But a dialectical principle intervenes; for there are three terms involved, which act upon each other not unlike the two premises and conclusion of a syllogism.

The situation grows even more complex when the inherent risk of the open end becomes alleviated by a musical closing of the form that does not disturb the binary balance. One device to this end is the identical cadencing of all three terms. A good example is Martin Luther's "Ein' feste Burg" where the heavenly forces return at the end musically and literally to vanquish the adversary devil who had appeared with the epode. Strophes and epode become still further assimilated to each other when the head theme of the strophes returns at the end of the epode, creating a *recapitulation barform*. This recapitulation, though abbreviated, reinforces the impression of closing the form, to which the psychological acceleration of the time lapse contributes (a complete da capo, as in a Handel aria, always sounds longer than expected). The widespread popularity of this form attests to its efficiency. We hear it in children's songs ("Three blind mice," "Twinkle, twinkle," etc.), classical melodies (Beethoven's Ode to Joy, Brahms's variation theme borrowed from Haydn, etc.), and entire operas (Walther's successful prize song at the end of the third-act "epode" of the *Meistersinger* as compared to his unsuccessful attempt in the first-act "strophe"). While the recapitulation does not disturb the balance between the two halves, the push toward *bowform becomes audible. The stages of the process leading from *binary to ternary structure are well documented by the evolution of *sonata form. In a small way, "Twinkle, twinkle" is equally revealing. The original is an eighteenth-century popular song, "Ah, vous dirai-je, Maman," on which Mozart, among others, wrote a set of piano variations (K. 300e). In that form and in its early existence as a children's song, the melody is clearly binary, that is, a recapitulation barform with an abbreviated repeat of the head theme at the end. Only very recent generations have dropped the antistrophe so that the overall shape suddenly emerges in closed ternary proportions.

BASSO CONTINUO

Only the morphological contribution of basso continuo concerns us here, that is, neither the intricacies of the shorthand notation nor variants of realization. Basso continuo presents a reconciliation of polyphony and homophony—an urgent necessity after the triad was uncovered and established in the sixteenth century as an autonomous unit. Organ practice at the end of the high polyphonic period had shown the way toward an accommodation of both the old and new styles. The improvised *bassus pro organo* permitted the directing musician at the instrument to carry a polyphonic line if the singer was in need of support or altogether absent; or to play an obbligato; or to reduce the polyphonic complexity to a harmonic outline. As a help toward accomplishing the latter, and as a concomitant of the new figured-bass style, the modern score arrangement superseded the old choir books and part books.

An immediate result of the harmonic orientation within a polyphonic fabric is *heterophony. While the basso continuo player strikes a chord, the solo lines embellish it; or the basso continuo player may provide harmonic ornamentation against a clear melody. In either case, the audible product—not the written composition—is heterophonic. Heterophony becomes here incidentally a real mediator between polyphony and homophony, and not a preparatory step to either as in other cultures at other times.

A lasting contribution of basso continuo—outliving the performance practice by becoming an inherent characteristic of almost all later compositions—is the emphasis on a shaping bicinium. The bass against the melody now holds the behavior of all other voices in control. The basso continuo forms not only half of the outside frame but also determines the role of the inside parts. It sets harmonic limits to melodic activity.

What is the primary shaping power of a basso continuo—the line of the lowest voice or the chord progression it prescribes? The answer varies with the particular case. Both functions, of course, always participate, but the emphasis changes. Preference for one or the other is often indicated by the nature of the composition but may be influenced by performance practices. A violoncello playing along in the secco recitatives of a Bach cantata brings out the contrapuntal relation of the two prescribed voices, whereas in the same situation a harpsichord without doubling by another bass instrument suggests merely harmonic underpinning of the now sovereign monody.

The practice of basso continuo, though not the morphological gain, was abandoned in the second half of the eighteenth century as soon as the classical masters established and confirmed a new kind of polyphony and a fresh awareness of harmonic functionalism. The two are interconnected, for it was the security provided by the clear functions of chords that permitted composers to develop melodic individuality for all participants. The precise lines of the middle voices made the improvisatory support by a basso continuo superfluous, just as the chord progressions no longer needed a bass for definition. To a composer of the basso continuo period, a C major chord in first inversion, for instance, was still a chord on E in which the normally expected fifth was replaced, as indicated in the figured bass, by a sixth. To later composers, under the impact of Rameau's *Traité d'harmonie*, it was a function of its root, C, not of its bass, E. The change-over is clear in the works of Haydn. Practice of basso continuo led to the recognition of functional harmony, by which it was superseded.

BEAUTY

The notion of the "beautiful" resides in the aesthetic domain. As soon as one says "beautiful," one also says "ugly." Is the ugly equally at home in the aesthetic domain? Is one then permitted to speak of an ugly work of art? While feeling the absurdity of this last question, one knows that the representation of the ugly is not at all excluded from art. The concept pair "beautiful-ugly" bears witness to the universal principle of *polarity. The pair exists in diverse modes of incarnation. On the sensory and emotional planes, it appears under the terms "agreeable-disagreeable" or "pleasure-pain." On the moral plane, the proper terms are "right-wrong" or "just-unjust," but the archetype reveals its true character in the reference to "moral beauty."

Art exists among conditions that are not those of everyday life. The latter have generally preempted the attribute of "reality." Actually both art and life are intensely real, but each in its own way. Whether one takes the metaphysical or the materialistic approach, a clear distinction must be drawn in order to arrive at an answer to our initial question.

Movie critics have occasionally pointed out the conflict between the "reality" of the picture and the "unreality" of the accompanying film music. In a literal sense, the reverse is true: the auditory part is always a real sound, whereas the visual part remains a two-dimensional picture on a screen. The dilemma disappears if one remembers that art exists on a plane of reality entirely different from that of life. Artistic activity is related to that of "play." Children "playing war," for instance, are very serious about it; but if one of them actually gets a little hurt and cries, the others stand around him in amazement. Their play reality has dropped to life reality. Play realities can be very powerful in their momentary effects on us. Theater audiences have been known to shake their fists at the villain on the stage, and they generally applaud the virtuous hero. The attitude of such audiences is precisely naturalistic and not artistic. They bring the illusion of the play onto the plane of ordinary reality. When art moves too close to nature, the proximity becomes embarrassing. Compared to a plain marble statue, life-size wax figures, dressed in real clothes, adorned with real hair, and painted to give the illusion of life are not "art" even though their production requires considerable skill. Art is not intended to produce the illusion of ordinary life. Even in the imitative arts, which take their material from the world of everyday, there must always be elements suggesting something outside and above the actualities depicted. Music does not take even its material from "real life." Nevertheless, it is a "real happening" but on its own level.

In the process of transposition from life to play, from nature to art, the notions of ordinary reality change values. The beautiful and the ugly, the good and the bad, everything and its opposite, lose one kind of reality to acquire another. In the new artistic reality, the things of the former no longer exist except as symbols. A dialectical synthesis has been accomplished. Thus art becomes the symbol of a "better world" in the sense that the antithetic notions of this world shed their character of strict opposition by uniting in a superior value. Ordinary reality finds itself transfigured; a new "incarnation" of beauty arises.

With this distinction in mind, the notion of "an ugly work of art" becomes absurd. Such a thing does not exist, nor does a wicked or immoral work of art. The ugly, of course, can be represented. Iago is hideous, but his role in *Othello* does not impair the "good" quality of the play. If a composition by itself is ugly, it ceases to be a work of art. One might object that, this being the case, one should also refrain from calling a composition "beautiful"; for a thesis cannot exist without its antithesis. The polarity continues, it is true, but the conflict has lost its sting. The synthesis, identified with beauty, has superseded the antithesis out of which it has grown. The transposition from the plane of life to that of art intensifies the realization of the synthetic concept of beauty while correspondingly weakening that of the preceding polarity. There is an artistic way of living which consists in letting the apparition of artistic reality be reflected on the plane of ordinary reality. In such a condition, beauty begins to reign in ordinary life. The realization is very difficult. Some of us attain it at moments. Only saints succeed constantly and perfectly.

One can further pursue a possible antithesis to the artistic concept of beauty by transcending life itself. Death is the antithesis of life and so of art. We cannot experience the Infinite which embraces both life and death; but by creating the impression of beauty in art above the polarity of the beautiful and the ugly in daily life, we are led to at least a presentiment of the ultimate synthesis. It is this process that produces the ecstasy of artistic experience.

BEGINNING

"A beginning is that which is not itself necessarily after anything else, and which has naturally something else after it."[1] The first half of Aristotle's

[1] *Poetics* vii. 1450b.

definition reaches back to the supersedure of silence by music. The second half stipulates the initiation of growth. A position of rest has to be artistically defined before it can be artistically disrupted. To our morphological condition of an initial division, Aristotle gives the underpinning of an initial situation. The first musical event, whatever its kind, determines the particular microcosm which the remainder of the composition will occupy.

The beginning of a piece accordingly affects the total morphology in two ways. (1) It becomes a reference point which inevitably conditions the listener's reaction to everything that follows. (2) It generates a motivation for the piece to unfold.

(1) Two different but equally authentic beginnings of the same composition permit the musician to experience vividly the subsequent effect on the whole work. Verdi's *Don Carlos* illustrates the point. The original version begins with a big lyrical love scene between Don Carlos and Elisabetta in the park of Fontainebleau. It defines the basic mood against which the later scenes in Spain rise as somber disturbances. The duet of the lovers at their first meeting after Elisabetta's marriage to King Philip assumes a singularly sentimental tone because it harks back to their first duet in happier surroundings. In the reworked version, which is now commonly performed, the opera begins in the oppressive atmosphere of the Emperor's funeral chapel, which defines the point of reference for everything that happens afterwards. The Fontainebleau scene is missing. The same duet of the lovers, which sounded sentimental but affirmative before, now sounds like a desperate effort to break away from the relentless heaviness of the given climate. The music has not changed in a literal sense, but it has assumed a different morphological role because heard in relation to a different referral point established at the beginning.

This practical example has theoretic counterparts in all those rules of counterpoint that deal with a proper beginning. They are all obviously abstractions from musically valid experiences and insights. The beginning becomes directly identified with the point of reference, the tonal center, which we normally call the tonic. Even in atonal music, the twelve-tone row is usually stated at the onset. The establishing of the tonal center can be accomplished in various manners, depending on the individual composer or the style of the period. The simplest and most convincing manner is laid down in the old rule that the first note of a melody should be the tonic itself. So proclaims Philippe de Vitry in the fourteenth century ("Unisonus est vox per quem primo incipimus cantare")[1] and Heinrich Schenker in the twentieth ("Der Cantus firmus muss allezeit mit der Tonika der Tonart angefangen werden").[2] Medieval hymns ("Pange lingua") comply with his rule as naturally as Verdi arias ("Caro nome" from *Rigoletto*) or popular tunes ("God save the King"). Examples are legion. Development in style permits the substitution of a representative relative for the tonic as an opening note. The fifth and third, being closest in tonal hierarchy, gradually become vested with authority to open a piece ("Omnis inceptio naturalis armonica," that is, according to the thirteenth-century author, the unison, octave, fifth, fourth [*sic*],

[1] In Coussemaker, *Scriptorum*, 3:17.
[2] Schenker, *Kontrapunkt*, p. 51.

minor third, and major third).[1] The opening note of, for example, Schubert's "Der Lindenbaum" (fifth) or Beethoven's main theme in the finale of his Ninth Symphony (third) are clearly and sufficiently representative of the tonic to establish an undisputed tonal center. With varying style, simple chords can be used (Beethoven's Third Symphony) or long cadences (Beethoven's First Symphony).

The last example leads into the technique of the romantic school, where purpose is often intentionally veiled (but never, in a good composition, ignored or forgotten). Beethoven's last symphony, like his first, starts in the middle of a cadence; the ambivalence is clarified by the dynamic outburst at the moment the cadence reaches the tonic. The beginning of the same composer's Fifth Symphony produces deliberate uncertainty, and only our familiarity with the work has conditioned us to accept C minor as unchallenged tonality. The first choice upon hearing the major third G to E-flat is to interpret it as part of an E-flat major triad (only the descending direction raises a small suspicion of the real tonality). Analogously, the next two tones can be easily accepted as the dominant of this supposed key; the famous rhythmic irregularities of these measures intensify the uncertainty. Clarification occurs with the first sound of the tonic note C and the full triad above it (m. 7). Reinterpretation of a beginning by subsequent events is proffered by Wagner's *Tristan und Isolde* where the opening in A minor is only in retrospect (three acts and four hours later) understood as the subdominant in a huge IV-V (s-D) cadence that spans the entire opera to the final love-death in B major.[2] One can measure the romantic impact of these last cases by comparing them to the beginning of almost any Bach prelude where the first four harmonies carefully define the complete T-S-D-T cadence before this balance is disrupted by a moving and shaping force. In the first prelude of the *Well-tempered Keyboard*, for example, the event of the descending bass scale begins properly in the fifth measure, similarly so in the second prelude, etc. Modern composers have developed their own techniques of introducing and confirming a point of reference at the beginning in relation to which the subsequent events become meaningful.

(2) A beginning must also generate motivation for the piece to unfold. For this purpose, it creates tension, and in yielding to the inherent tendency toward crystallization, it creates time. The initial disturbance justifies its existence by finding its own forms. In the words of the mathematician Andreas Speiser: "Ein völlig gesetzloser Zustand wird völlig gesetzmässig durch die Zeit hindurchgetragen" ("A wholly lawless state is carried wholly lawfully through time").[3] The composer may be likened to the dramatist who early in the plot has to introduce a particular thought, or person, or action which will cause development and continuation of the story. Thus the promise of the witches to Macbeth in the first scene of the play begets the need for further development of action which will show how the promise is realized. The in-

[1]Anonymus 4, in Coussemaker, *Scriptorum*, 1:354.

[2]The tonic of E major is subtly suggested throughout the opera but reached and established only once, in the feverish climax of Tristan's hallucination (III, 893 ff.). Cf. Lorenz, *Tristan*, pp. 173 ff.

[3]"Ueber die Freiheit," p. 4.

troduction of the witches also begets the need for their reappearance for reasons of economy. In *The Brothers Karamazov*, to illustrate the point further, the first book, on "The History of a Family," establishes the setting, against which the second book, describing "An Unfortunate Gathering," introduces tensions within and among various people which drive the story by means of development toward a final release. The characters and tensions once introduced, besides contributing toward the central plot, also require individual treatment. Dostoevsky's skill shows by his utilizing every detail as part of the whole as well as an entity in itself, and forgetting none.

Similarly in music a composer will early introduce a tension, most commonly in the form of a dissonance, which will necessitate movement toward a final release. In short compositions, this dissonance may be mild to accomplish its purpose, as, for instance, the neighboring note to the dominant in the second measure of Schubert's "Der Lindenbaum." In long compositions, the dissonance must be strong to engender enough power to warrant an extended movement, as, for instance, the famous C-sharp in the seventh measure of Beethoven's Eroica Symphony. Having introduced it, Beethoven not only gains impetus for the rest of the movement but economically is also forced to use it again, as he does, for instance, in the analogous place in the recapitulation when the flute—surprisingly but logically—brings the first theme in D-flat major. "Das erste steht uns frei, beim zweiten sind wir Knechte," Mephistopheles says to Faust.[1] "We choose the first; we're governed by the second."

Goethe's thought is here identical with Speiser's quoted earlier (see p. 81). The underlying morphological principle applies whether shown dramatically by Mephistopheles' behavior, or experienced artistically and philosophically by creative minds, or demonstrated cosmogonically by the world we live in. God was as free as anyone in creating this particular world with its particular laws. He could have made another choice. The world could have been different. But once initiated, this creation is bound to continue on its prescribed course.

Cf. also *Beginning, Middle, and End. *End.

BEGINNING, MIDDLE, AND END

The first and last terms, strictly speaking, have no separate existence, for they are attributes of the middle term. Anything having reality in time shows an instant of appearing and another one of disappearing. In spatial terms, we would call these instants *limits*. Aristotle's famous formulation concerning the temporal conditions of tragedy fits equally well those of music. In either case, the work of art must be "complete in itself, as a whole of some *magnitude. . . .* Now a whole is that which has beginning, middle, and end. A beginning is that which is not necessarily after anything else, and which has naturally something else after it; an end is that which is naturally after something itself, either as its necessary or usual consequent, and with nothing else after it; and a middle, that which is by nature after one thing and has also another after it. A well-constructed piece, therefore, cannot either begin or end

[1]Goethe, *Faust*, part 1, line 1412.

at any point one likes; beginning and end in it must be of the forms just described."[1]

The condition that a composition be complete is too self-evident to require explanation at length. No morphology is possible without the presupposition that the object under discussion is complete. A fragment, such as the Venus of Milo, immediately raises the question of the missing parts and relates the given entity to the norms of the imagined whole. The aesthetic satisfaction offered by the statue in its present state depends doubtless on the beauty of the existing details but is "romantically" and significantly heightened by the suggestiveness of the total morphology.

Beginning, middle, and end are concepts reappearing throughout our investigation, though under different names. Whereas the Aristotelian terms connote positions, our primary analogies—initiation of growth, continuation of growth, and limitation—describe forces and processes. The three terms evoke an association with the cycle of breathing, presupposing a departure from zero, an accumulation of energy, and an arrival at a point of repose. Beginning, middle, and end are thus another manifestation of the ternary principle which appears in music as an archetype (cf. *Binary-Ternary).

*Beginning and *end are treated separately elsewhere in this Dictionary, but the middle of a composition defies theoretic abstraction. It is the soul and body of the composition, intelligible as an individualized particular but void of meaning when considered out of context. It lacks an underlying morphological principle short of the positional spelled out by Aristotle. Little can be gained outside specific analysis. Each middle possesses its own morphology. A development section of a sonata has its own beginning, middle, and end. The "how" of the development is the contents of the section. The question ceases to be morphological except in concrete particulars.

The worth of the Aristotelian concepts is the distinction they make possible between art and nature. It is a definitive and all-embracing distinction. The creative artist imposes upon himself laws which constitute the true object of the opus. Unless something possesses a definable beginning, middle, and end, it is not a work of art. A picture has a frame, a theater a curtain, and a story a plot. In writing an Odyssey, Aristotle comments, Homer did not make the poem cover all that ever befell his hero but he took an action forming a complete whole with a discernible beginning, middle, and end.[2] A historic biography, on the other hand, unless it lays claim also to being a work of art, will loosen these restrictions as much as possible, and the continuity of nature escapes them altogether. In Goethe's words:

> Das ist die Eigenschaft der Dinge:
> Natürlichem genügt das Weltall kaum;
> Was künstlich ist, verlangt geschlossnen Raum.[3]

> This is the property of things: the All
> Scarcely suffices for the natural;
> The artificial needs a bounded space.

[1]*Poetics* vii. 1450b.
[2]*Poetics* viii. 1451a.
[3]*Faust*, part 2, lines 6882–84.

BINARY-TERNARY

The importance of the prime numbers 2 and 3 surpasses that of all others in the production of musical forms. Whereas our harmonic vocabulary has long included the number 5 (the major third) and is pushing well beyond the senarius, in morphology we apparently encounter great difficulties in apprehending 5 directly as an undivided whole. In pentadic meter, we do not seem able to avoid interpreting the rhythm ♩ ♪ ♩ as either ♩ ♩ ♩ or ♩ ♪ ♩. This difficulty inhering in microforms, we may expect our need for subdivision to assert itself even more strongly in macroforms.

When dealing with numbers in music, one must always keep in mind their archetypal meaning, without which the morphological realities appear muddled, and analysis remains descriptive. The significant morphological distinction between binary and ternary is above all qualitative, not quantitative.

The number 2 emerges from unity as the basic principle of polarity. When Pythagoras divided the monochord string in 2, he produced musically the interval of the octave but philosophically the whole phenomenal world—the diapason which comprises and defines the totality of possible events. The force of 2 characterizes the story of creation as told by different civilizations. God in the first chapter of Genesis performs a series of divisions by 2. The Chinese see the world as an interplay of Yin and Yang. Plato splits a mythological total being to gain male and female. Duality in all cases indicates a generative process, which is associated with the earth, the chthonic. Thus 2 is also an eminently rational number, "down to earth," conveying reason and order in an almost mechanical way. We count oscillations, as of a pendulum, by the to-and-fro. We hear the ticking of a watch as tick-tock, not as tick-tick or tick-tock-tock. We graduate measuring units, such as weights and distances, into halves, quarters, and eighths. If we accentuate in walking every second step, not every third one, we recognize the strong association of 2 with the organization of our body. The pulsation of our heart, alternating between systole and diastole, supplies us with a built-in duple meter, that affects a wide variety of body motions, such as lifting-striking, pushing-pulling, or, in most general terms, tension-release.

The number 3, as against the archetypal meaning of the number 2, is confining rather than generative, and hence artistic rather than mechanical, spiritual rather than chthonic. The division of the string by 3 produces the interval of the fifth and thereby determines the musical field of action. Three points define a circle as clearly as the triple concept of *beginning-middle-end defines a work of art. Trinity is a spiritual force that we find at the root of most religions. Aeschylus's Prometheus places "the Fates triform" at "the helm of Necessity."[1] The Jewish Lord Zebaoth is "three times holy." The Hindu *trimurti* consists of Brahma, Shiva, and Vishnu. In the Roman Catholic Church, the Trinity is the substance of the Godhead. Against this triadic spirit, the dualism advocated by the Albigensians appears understandably as heresy.

The word *spirit* means 'breath', and 3 is the specific number of the breath-

[1]Lines 115–16.

ing process. In normal breathing, exhalation is followed by a rest. The total cycle—unlike the oscillation of systole and diastole—is a ternary "in-out-rest." We must not think of the relative duration of the three periods as strictly determined, particularly as the transition from the exhaling to rest periods blurs. Regardless, however, of whether the breathing-out stops completely during the rest period, the two together are always longer than the breathing-in period, usually at least twice as long. Only in abnormal breathing, as when we are "out of breath," the fundamental ternary rhythm turns into a panting in-out by skipping the rest period. Because the feeling of that period remains with us, a binary rhythm is always somewhat more hurried than a ternary. The effect of "cut" time relates to this fact. The presence of a phase of recovery distinguishes an organic wave from a mechanical process, the breath of life from the oscillation of a pendulum, the flux of rhythm from the order of meter.

The archetypal distinction between 2 and 3 has necessary morphological consequences. The binary left-right of dancing differs basically from the ternary *tempus perfectum* of mensural music. Goethe has suggested that all music lies between the extremes of dance and religion,[1] and we might parallel his qualitative discrimination by stating that all musical forms lie between the possibilities of binary and ternary organization. The distinction between instrumental and vocal music might appear as a corollary.

*Dance music, based on the alternation of left and right, and on the juxtaposition of male and female, couple and square, builds in powers of 2. It is responsible for the standard of a four-measure or eight-measure phrase, as it governs the music of the eighteenth and nineteenth centuries. The number 2 is form-producing only when the two parts produce a whole, which is the case when they are interdependent in a complementary sense. The concept of "two of the same" pertains not to morphological considerations but to the creation of matter. In music, this necessary interdependence is established by the principle of tension-release, normally in that order, occasionally in the reversed succession sinking-recovery. The medieval dances ductia and stantipes supply good examples. A unit called *punctus* is heard first with an "open" ending and then repeated with a "closed" ending.[2]

The two statements complement each other like the more familiar classical antecedent and consequent, which are probably derived from dance. The tension created by the half cadence of the first member is resolved by the full cadence of the second.

The variation theme of Beethoven's Piano Sonata op. 109 shows binary form in an idealized state. The first half still ends open, and the second half

[1]*Maximen und Reflexionen*, 1237–39.
[2]Davison and Apel, *Anthology*, p. 43.

closed. The metric balance of the two halves harks back to ancestral dance orientation. The melodic line, however, flows in a unified curve from beginning to end, and the harmonies unfold one extended cadence.

The interdependence of two sections producing a whole is very strong in the *barform, in which two parallel corresponding strophes forming the first half are balanced by a weighty and new epode forming the second half. The term *strophe* (= turn) concedes the indebtedness to dance. The overall form is open, for there is no return to the material of the beginning. It therefore lends itself well to the dramatic progression expected of a stage play, be it a Greek drama or an opera by Wagner. The succession of strophe and antistrophe is probably related to that of statement and echo, though the latter is not necessarily its formal cause. One can pursue the principle of binary parallelism through many similar musical phenomena, such as psalmodic antiphony, double choirs, and hence perhaps also the usual organization of vocal or instrumental bodies into four groups.

Binary form, whenever it is found associated with the metric principle, produces structural regularity and symmetry around an imagined time axis. This axis is a "neuralgic" point in the binary form: it tends to grow real, and when it does, the binarium dissolves into a ternarium. For this reason, binary forms are unstable and subsist only as long as their extension in time is not too great. The Bach chorale that has served us all along as an example (cf. p. 16) shows such symptoms of lability. The first section consists of strophe and antistrophe ending on the dominant. This open cadence exactly on the axis asserts strongly the necessity for the second section. The epode leads away in the first four-measure phrase after which the closing four-measure phrase is not a recapitulation but a correspondence, an answer to the very first four-measure phrase. The germ of a latent ternary orientation is recognizable.

Because of this inherent lability, the binarium, considered "incomplete" by the Pythagoreans and "imperfect" by medieval theoreticians, contains in itself an impulse toward repetition, toward the continuity of the pendulum motion. Hence we find that most strophic songs, hymns, chorale tunes, and themes of variation cycles are binary. The many repetitions seem to serve the necessary function of strengthening the precarious binary structure.

The process of morphological stabilization is best accomplished when the neuralgic point assumes, by growth, the reality of a middle section. The analogy of barform and syllogism has often been made. Out of two propositions, a new conclusion is reached. The crucial logical event is precisely what happens between the two halves, the jump from the given statements to the fresh achievement. As soon as this transition is spelled out in music, binary form becomes ternary.

The term *bowform* has been most commonly accepted for this musical structure in which a middle section is symmetrically framed as by an arch or bow. All da capo pieces, be they arias or minuets, fall into this category. The element that probably contributes most to the stability of the ternarium is symmetry in the ordinary meaning of the term, that is, identity, or at least equivalence, of the last part with the first. The repetition of the opening statement closes the structure. The symbol of a closed circle for *tempus perfectum* is appropriate in every respect.

This quality of perfection caused Hugo Riemann to state that all musical forms are ternary. We think to be morphologically more relevant by stating that all binary forms tend to become ternary. The evolution of *sonata form provides a well-known example, but the truth can be as easily demonstrated in miniature forms like the variation theme of Mozart's Piano Sonata in A major, K. 331. The piece has two parts, both to be repeated. Thus it preserves externally the binary form as we find it perfectly embodied in Beethoven's variation theme of the Piano Sonata op. 109. But in the Mozart example, the contents deviate from the external appearance. The first part is closed, beginning and ending on the tonic. The second part begins on the subdominant and leads to a recapitulation of the first part. Metrically the two repeated halves are of equal length (8 measures each); the two coda measures, admirably prepared, need not concern us here. Thus the external axis is still imaginary, lying on the repeat barline; but the internal axis is not, because it tends to lie on the middle part. What prevents it from actually lying there is the shortening of the opening eight measures to only four in the recapitulation, made possible by the double strophe of the first half. A true bowform evolves when the transition section (here the first phrase of the second half) becomes both the external and internal middle around which exposition and recapitulation form a symmetrical frame.

In this evolution from a binary to a ternary structure, the repeat of the second half loses its meaning as soon as it contradicts the overall symmetry. The repeat of the first part remains defensible from a purely metrical viewpoint to balance the now much longer and weightier second half. Such is still the case in the first movements of the first three Brahms symphonies, which thus maintain what has become "a fiction of binary structure." With the disappearance of also the first repeat sign in his last symphony, the ternary structure of the original binary form is acknowledged.

A comparison of a Neapolitan opera with one by Wagner is revealing. The former favors the ternary da capo aria, which is most undramatic, but compensates for it by an overall binary structure with a characteristically "open" theatrical situation at the first finale. The three great Italian operas by Mozart follow this division into two parts, the end of the first deliberately displaying dramatic confusion and uncertain outcome. Wagner, on the other hand, prefers barform in his operas, for they push the action forward. The overall structure of his operas, however, is almost always ternary. There are strong correspondences between the first and third acts of *Lohengrin*, *Tristan*, *Parsifal*, and others; the resulting bowform seems to close what the units within the acts ("periods," in Lorenz's terminology) have left open.

The following table, by no means complete, summarizes the antithesis:

2	3
Octave	Fifth
Splitting	Confining
Generative	Cadential
Chthonic	Spiritual
Mechanical	Artistic
Heart beat	Breathing

Meter	Rhythm
Dance	Religion
Instrumental	Vocal
Barform	Bowform
Open	Closed
Unstable	Stable
Imperfect	Perfect

BOWFORM

The alliance of symmetry and the ternary principle has rightly bestowed special strength and popularity on the ABA form. It can be found under many names and in varying dimensions in most countries and styles—be it Gregorian Kyrie, Neapolitan aria, classical scherzo, or simple folksong. The underlying principle is always identity or correspondence of the outer sections, governing a brief Mozart minuet as much as the whole of Wagner's *Parsifal* (where scenery and action visualize the inherent musical parallelism between the first and third acts).

The symmetry of bowform, which seems perfect to the eyes, is always significantly modified when perceived through the ears. Even when the closing section is identified by a literal da capo rather than being written out, it sounds different because we have heard it before. "Nobody can bathe twice in the same river," Heraclitus formulated this problem. *Topology matters greatly in music. The opening section of a bowform is a fresh experience. The repeat by the closing section is heard in relation to the earlier experience, by which it is inevitably qualified. Not only have we become older and musically richer, but the music, too, has a changed reference point. Topology justifies the conventional omission of internal repetitions in the da capo section of almost every classical minuet. While the repeats in the opening section are doubtless conveniences to acquaint the listener with new material, they are also important structural components which intensify the binary dance orientation. Hence the explanation that familiarity with the material demands the eventual omission of the repeats, though correct, is inadequate. The symmetry of the structure would be seriously endangered by the reduction of the closing section by half were it not for a kind of "acoustical perspective" created by topology. Actually one never fails to hear complete symmetry because of the shrinking in time of remembered events. Hence a full da capo with all repeats would impress us as a retardation and, by contradicting the flow of time, seriously impair the impression of symmetry.

The middle section of a bowform has a primary morphological obligation to provide separation and contrast. To this purpose, a variety of musical means may serve: new motives, modulation, change of mode, different rhythm and tempo, varied texture. Yet proportion asserts itself noticeably without apparent external necessity. Thus the middle section is almost without exception less important than the outside frame—exactly the opposite to the visual counterpart which usually focuses on the central panel of a triptych, or the central section of a building, or the central door of a cathedral, or the center of a picture. The human body, too, contains the vital parts in the center, surrounded by "branches." Musical topology again provides the explanation. The first "thing" we hear—a tone, chord, motive, series of tones, key—supplies per se the orientation, the reference, for all that follows. Music, creating time by moving from a beginning to an end, cannot do it otherwise. The one exception that comes to mind concerns certain improvisatory forms. Claudio Merulo's Venetian practice of harboring a ricercar in the middle of a toccata can still be recognized in Bach's Toccata et Fuga in D minor for organ. In this late example, however, the inevitable musical trend has reduced the improvisatory sections to the secondary roles of prelude and coda.

In classical compositions, proportion is often spelled out more precisely. The Maggiore middle sections of the funeral marches in Beethoven's Third and Seventh Symphonies are each almost exactly one half the length of the main section. In the Eroica, moreover, the same proportion determines the extent of the detour between the false and real recapitulations.

Bowform is by definition closed and hence undramatic. Handel must have known this fact as well as anyone; his da capo arias should be taken for the musical happening they are instead of being criticized as "operatically static."

The inherent strength of bowform often influences the subordinate as well as the main parts of a structure. Minuets by Haydn and scherzos by Bruckner usually shape both the main and trio sections by a complete internal recapitulation. The resulting scheme, ABA-CDC-ABA, approaches *rondo characteristics.

BREATHING FORM

Musical forms are phenomenalizations of the all-pervading principle of rhythm. The basic rhythmic experience of living man is breathing. In a deeply meaningful sense, any musical form is related to that of breathing. We are not referring here to breathing as the carrier of singing and hence of the most intimate musical experience, although the connection doubtless increases the relevance. What matters to our inquiry is the form breathing takes, for it becomes a criterion for all other forms.

Externally, breathing consists of two phases: inhaling and exhaling. Inhaling is the initial act, both of the newborn baby at the moment it begins its life, and of the singer or speaker who wishes to produce a sound. Inhaling creates pressure and induces us to push out the air. Exhaling causes relief and frees us to draw in fresh air.

> Im Atemholen sind zweierlei Gnaden:
> Die Luft einziehn, sich ihrer entladen.
> Jenes bedrängt, dieses erfrischt;
> So wunderbar ist das Leben gemischt.
> Du danke Gott, wenn er dich presst,
> Und dank' ihm, wenn er dich wieder entlässt.

> In drawing breath there are two kinds of blessing:
> The fetching of air and then the expressing.
> Strain and relax, hold and then give;
> Thus wondrously mixed in this life that we live.
> Thank God for crowding hard on you,
> And for His releasing thank Him anew.

> Goethe, *West-östlicher Divan*

The two phases thus exhibit a qualitative polarity which, in varying phenomenalizations, underlies all musical forms. The alternation of tension and relief is vital to musical continuity. One must not assume that breathing form is therefore fundamentally binary; for against the external appearance in two phases, an internal ternary organization of time makes itself felt. Exhaling takes about twice as long as inhaling, so that the total act of breathing consumes about three time units. The ternary orientation is further emphasized by the three points—beginning, middle, and end—that mark the contour of the two phases. The cycle needs the minimum of these three points before regenerating itself.

In the normal shape of this ternary morphological archetype, the accent coincides with the naturally long exhalation. It thus falls on the middle section: ĭn-ōut-rest, ĭn-ōut-rest, or ♪│ ♩ 𝄾 ♪│ ♩ 𝄾 . This emphasis throws light on the significance of all those events of a composition that lie between beginning and end. Within the total experience, the accent may shift. An abnormal situation places it on the inhalation: ĭn-ōut-rest, ĭn-ōut-rest, or│♩ ♩ 𝄾│♩ ♩ 𝄾│. Such is the case when we pant or sob. Note that in both instances exhaling retains its relative length compared to inhaling. All rhythms are modifications of these two fundamental breathing forms. The interrelations between breathing, accent, and length produce the different modes of *rhythm and meter, and influence phrasing. The length of the cycle is morphologically irrelevant. The principle is valid in short songs and entire operas.

Among our six cases illustrating the Discourse of this book, the contents of the Bach chorale illustrate well the inhalation by the strophes leading to the exhalation of the epode. The example is particularly revealing of morphological subtleties, for the metric organization of 8 + 8 is not exactly identical with the rhythmic breath of 12 + 4; relaxation does not set in before the last two phrases. The coincidence of both kinds of organization is more readily heard in the andante theme of Beethoven's Piano Sonata op. 109: the intensity rises toward the double bar in the middle and symmetrically falls back from it. Perhaps the implied "simplicity" makes this melody singularly suitable as the carrier of the following complex variations. The inverse breathing process with the accent on the inhalation is obviously rarer though dramatically very effective. The explosive beginnings of such works as Beethoven's Fifth Piano Concerto or Verdi's *Falstaff* admit of such an interpretation, although great care must be exercised in relating such details to the whole. The traditional three concerto movements fast-slow-fast probably belong in this category. Within the safer confines of our six particular cases, Josquin's Kyrie demonstrates this principle in the unrolling of both the shape of the head themes of the two sections and the overall relation of these sections to each other.

Is breathing form then binary or ternary? It contains both and hence is committed to neither. It is the idea behind all musical forms. The in-and-out, the alternation of tension and relaxation, governs all further manifestations. Binary and ternary archetypes, such as barform and bowform, both derive from it. Although they share the field, bowform seems to be musically preferred, if only because it parallels the concept of *beginning-middle-end and directly phenomenalizes the ternary organization of breathing. Binary form, like all musical forms, also shows three "external" points; but the central axis has no aural reality.

In this context, Hugo Riemann's suggestion that all musical rhythms and forms are ternary and anacrustic, though overstated, deserves some sympathy. He sensed the triple orientation of rhythm and the need for a preparatory gesture. But by attempting to construct a somewhat rigid system, he overlooked the wider possibilities inherent in breathing form. We can modify his view by asserting equivalence of *binary and ternary morphological forces while conceding the tendency of musical forms toward ternary structures. This tendency is not necessarily phenomenalized in every case; the discrepancy between an actual event and the underlying norm accounts for the individuation of the event and of the form it takes. As a by-product of this ternary preference, every musical form is ideally closed, that is, the cycle inhalation-exhalation-repose, or tension-relaxation-balance, implies a return to the neutral departure point from which alone any self-regeneration becomes possible. The idea of "closed" is inherent in that of "end," which we accept as an artistic necessity. The many open forms that exist are, properly understood, deviations from the tendency. We hear them as demanding some kind of closure; and if the piece remains open, it earns its aesthetic effect from this quality. The tendency of music to aspire to the ideal of ternary orientation is well demonstrated by the historic development of *sonata form.

CADENCE

A cadence defines. In a morphological inquiry, the thing defined is of less immediate concern than the manner in which the definition proceeds and the means it employs. The object of the definition may be any musical unit—a phrase, melody, key, tonal center, or other element of musical orientation.

The manner in which a cadence accomplishes a definition must not be expected to resemble the syntax of language or any kind of logic other than musical. Our habit of requiring a definition to be either verbally articulate or mathematically precise often stands in the way of our coping with musical events in purely musical terms. The means at the disposal of a musical cadence are exclusively musical, that is, the definition will be either melodic, or harmonic, or rhythmic, or any combination of these elements.

Consider the case of a single melody. As we hear the first tone, nothing is really defined except, if you wish, the disturbance of silence. The single tone may belong anywhere and do anything. It predates any musical process and hence knows nothing of cadence. A succession of two tones stakes out the field of an interval, but the discourse remains undefined. No hearer can tell whether the second tone leads away from the first or fulfills it, or whether jointly they are subservient to a yet unspecified force. The step from D to C, to illustrate the point, can just as well be the beginning of a descending Dorian scale as the end of a descending C major scale, not to mention numerous other possibilities in G major, G minor, F major, B-flat major, and others. With only two tones there is no definition and hence no cadence.

The situation changes drastically with the presence of three tones. Obviously there are many three-tone successions which do not define anything, either. The opening augmented-triad motive of Liszt's *Faust* Symphony, for example, sounds deliberately vague and uncommitted. But whereas an interval, free from harmonic or rhythmic help, is under all circumstances powerless to define a musical process, however small, a succession of three tones contains the potential of determination and thus of cadence. A melody, besides obeying the necessary movement forward in time, can move only up and down. Three tones, according to musical logic, are the minimum necessary for a complete movement in both directions and hence for a possible definition. A definition has to pinpoint; a center of reference may emerge through the preponderance of one of the tones by repetition:

It may also become audible as the resultant of two opposite and balanced pulls, although the tendency of the first tone always to be understood as tonic needs some rhythmic help for clarification:

The cadence becomes particularly clear when these possibilities combine, although such combination exceeds the minimum of only three musical events:

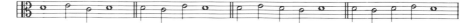

There is hardly a limit to further expansion. The morphological point made is the minimal presence of three tones for a melodic cadence. One is reminded of the definition of a circle by not less than three points, or of a syllogism by three elements.

The principles are the same in a harmonic cadence. One chord defines as little as one tone. Even a perfect triad is not really at rest if we recall the inherent dominant quality of every major triad, and the inherent subdominant quality of every minor triad. For similar reasons, the succession of the apparently clearest two triads cannot readily form a definitive cadence:

This progression is as readily heard as an arrival on F minor (V-I, or D-t) as it is heard as a departure from C major (I-IV, or T-s). There is no unambivalent halt, no definition, and no cadence. Three chords are the minimum needed for clarification. Upward and downward pulls can now be polarized, and repetition can add its own weight:

Thus understood, cadence emerges as a primary rhythmic event. It presupposes not only the existence of a departure point as much as that of an arrival point, but also an energetic process connecting the two. We recognize the manifestation of the Aristotelian principle that a poetic whole must have a *beginning, middle, and end. This formal definition acquires a vital sense in the musical cadence by reinterpretation as initial impulse, tension, and relaxation. The total event is that of the *breathing form. Breathing proceeds as a life impulse from zero, accumulates energy during the tension of inhaling, and spends it during the relaxation of exhaling. Breathing is in effect the physiological symbol of the primordial form of an energetic process. Music is essentially energetic; it manifests itself through movement. Thus cadence is the life form of music. It is its vital form. One finds it in the detail of a composition as much as in the whole, in a short melody as well as in a huge symphonic movement. A musical unit follows its own laws of morphology independently of the cadence; but the cadence, if successful and persuasive, will relate to the whole so that the two apparently separate morphological forces mutually reflect upon, and explain, each other. Breathing is an image of life: birth—unfolding of life—death. And just as life is made of ever longer "cadences" starting with the first breathing cadence, so also the musical work is made of superimposed cadences with ever longer breathing cycles.

Because of the rhythmic nature of every cadence, the concept of cadence cannot possibly be the property of a certain style or a given grammar. All music is forever cadential. Music which does not breathe cannot live.

CADENZA

In Italian (as also in French and German), the same word denotes both *cadence and cadenza. The common origin reveals a common function, but cadenza is by far the narrower concept. It applies primarily to the approaching conclusion of a composition or section. A cadence establishes this conclusion in the form of a musical definition. It is thus stricter in behavior than the preceding flow of the composition. A cadenza utilizes the alternative behavior: it relaxes the established technical conditions of the piece. Either behavior readily indicates the near halt; but whereas a cadence punctuates the musical movement by tightening the form, a cadenza does so by dissolving it.

A cadenza is occasionally placed at the beginning of a piece. Here the license of the cadenza precedes the definition established by the initial cadence. An opening cadenza preludes the genesis of a structure just as a closing cadenza heralds the dissolution. Examples of a cadenza introducing a work can be heard in Beethoven's Fifth Piano Concerto and Brahms's Double Concerto. Mozart likes to place a cadenza at the beginning of a sonata development section, as in the respective first movements of the Sinfonia Concertante for Violin and Viola or the String Quartet in G major, K. 387.

The particulars of a cadenza, as of a cadence, change with style, but the principle remains the same—a burst of almost reckless freedom. In all styles, the placement at the very end of a piece is the most common. The following references to final cadenzas, which can be easily multiplied, merely try to suggest the historic span.

In Gregorian melodies, the very last Kyrie exclamation usually contains a noticeable melismatic extension of the otherwise repetitive formula. Free melismas are also characteristic of the "Ite, missa est" at the very end of the Mass and of most "Amen" statements. The development of the latter into the typical "Amen" fugues in the Gloria and Credo movements of later Masses is a manifestation of the cadenza principle: the ordained sovereignty of the religious text over the music collapses before the sudden and purely musical outpour. The relation of stylistic stricture to cadential freedom is strongly audible in organa and clausulae of the Notre Dame school: after the plainsong has reached its last note, the upper voice continues with a long melisma that, more often than not, breaks away from the rigidity of the preceding rhythmic mode.[1] The same swinging-out beyond the establishment of the finalis—be it a tenor note or chord—is characteristically heard in compositions by Josquin des Prez; one or more voices participate in his cadenzas (cf. the Kyrie from the *Missa Pange lingua* reprinted on p. 14).

It is probably Josquin's overpowering influence on the remainder of the sixteenth century that caused composers like Don Luis Milan and Girolamo Cavazzoni to transplant a similar technique to their lute and keyboard pieces. In such works, the fingers run their course in a cadenza after the final cadence. Cadenza and cadence become reunited by the familiar four-six chord at the end of a concerto movement. Corelli and Vivaldi supply early examples of this type which extends through the classic and romantic eras. The impromptu character of such cadenzas is related to comparable improvisations in Neapolitan arias; the influence is probably reciprocal. In any case, a vocal cadenza on a concluding four-six chord is still often heard in Verdi's operas.

In the first movement of his Violin Concerto, Mendelssohn places the cadenza at the end of the development section. It thus punctuates the end of a section rather than of a whole piece and creates a temporary conflict between the concluding tendency of the cadenza and the necessity of continuation. Mendelssohn's solution has become rightly famous. He had models before him. Beethoven had placed short cadenzas at the same place in his Fifth and Sixth Symphonies (mm. 268, 282–88); and Bach, anticipating sonata form in the D major Prelude from the second volume of the *Well-tempered Keyboard*, did likewise (m. 40, but perhaps reaching as far back as the middle of m. 36).

---

[1]For examples, see Codex Florence, Bibl. Laur. *plut.* 29, I, fols. 86v, 87r; ibid., 88v. Reprinted in Davison and Apel, *Anthology*, nos. 28c and 28e.

The freedom shared by all cadenzas is usually that of meter. Other musical liberties are possible. The harmonies may roam very far between the limits set by the four-six suspension and the eventual resolution (cf. the written-out cadenza in the finale of Mozart's Piano Sonata K. 333; Beethoven's cadenzas for his Piano Concertos, particularly for the first movement of the one in G major in which the key signatures reach from four flats to three sharps;[1] and others). Yet the reference to an element of time remains the most plausible. A composition creates time. In order to end, the "piece" has to be cut off. For this purpose, the dissolution of meter, of the measure of time, as expressed by a cadenza, has proven very effective throughout the ages.

CANON

The literal Greek and Latin meaning of the term is 'rule'. As originally used by musicians, it signified a composition written according to a definite precept, which was usually spelled out at the beginning. In Franco-Flemish works, we find such canons as "Canit more Hebraeorum" ("Sings in the manner of the Hebrews," that is, from right to left); "Cancer eat plenis et redeat medius" ("The crab proceed full and return half," that is, backward in full, and then forward in halved, note values); "Ne recorderis" (a pun to be read "Ne re corderis," "Do not sing *re*"); and many others. Eventually the term *canon* was narrowed to refer only to one particular precept: exact imitation by all participating voices. In this sense, it will be treated here (for other possibilities, cf. *Augmentation-Diminution; *Echo; *Polyphony; *Retrograde).

When strict imitation is understood in the sense of "aping," the connotations are rather comical or unpleasant because bound up with a mechanistic idea contrary to organic and intelligent life. People sensitive to the aspect of aping implied by imitation often profess aversion to canons. Understandable as it may be, such a reaction, supported by instances of purposefully comic canons, is contradicted by the long and distinguished career of canon techniques documented by a rich and purely musical literature.

To clarify the possible misunderstanding created by the word *imitation*, let us observe the genesis of a canon:

[1]*Werke*, 9/2:24 ff.

The pure imitation of the beginning (mm. 1–4) is actually an *echo. Under certain conditions, mainly due to the nature of the text in a vocal canon, the effect of the imitation might be mechanical and comical in a sense that is indeed not entirely missing in any echo; for what amuses us in an echo is precisely the quick automatic response. There are, however, aesthetic virtues to a musical echo. For the lead-off voice, the fascination of echo is rooted in the possibility of eliciting an unexpected response. Something we have sent out comes back to us. We feel the power of having forced the outside world to speak, to confirm our call; and we are elated. For the imitating voice, the fascination lies in behaving as if one were an intelligent automaton. One is receiver and sender at the same time. Ideally, the second and any subsequent voice in a canon should imitate by ear, that is, follow the leader for ever new instructions while simultaneously acting out the already given order. In this as well as the literal sense, any dictation is a "canon."

In our example, the situation changes completely when both voices are heard simultaneously (mm. 6 ff.). A new texture is born. The One has become Two (or Many, as the case may be). The technique, to be sure, is still imitation, but the overall result is a polyphony in which multiplicity is created out of oneness. Our feeling and awareness of imitation recede and give way to our consciousness of a creative process which has produced Many out of One. This textural multiplicity derived from One, and not the mechanical imitation, makes canon meaningful and removes it from depreciatory connotations.

With the number of voices in a polyphonic canon, the difficulty of following it increases. The hearer will tend to become more and more appreciative of the polyphonic web at each moment while remaining mindful of the background presence of the One. Josquin's setting of the Agnus II in his Mass *Hercules Dux Ferrariae* is a strict canon for three voices, at the fifth and octave, in which the richness of the texture, free of metric and harmonic restrictions, becomes the paramount acoustical, aesthetic event. The typical caccia of the *ars nova* places a free bass under two imitative voices. It adds a fresh outside layer which counteracts the otherwise mechanical aspect. Because transformation of this kind helps obliterate the suggestion of "aping," the function of various contrapuntal devices assumes added significance. Whereas an exact canon mimics the flow of both melody and time, a canon in augmentation remains strict in regard to the former but not to the latter; an inversion, to the latter but not to the former; and in retrograde, usually to neither. Thus understood, canonic complications are more than just tricks, for they rather contribute to an independent "geometry of music." The ten canons from Bach's *Musikalisches Opfer* delineate the scope without exhausting it. Much is inevitably lost to the ear. A melody played backward, for example, is impossible to recognize (unless specifically constructed for the purpose) because all rhythms are reversed. The borderline sometimes blurs between meaningful art and hollow *virtuosity. Contrapuntal canonic devices justify their existence by reconciling in a particular way unity and multiplicity.

Having recognized two distinct roots of *polyphony, we must also recognize two kinds of canon. Thus far we have actually dealt only with canon demonstrating a purely melodic, gignetic behavior. There is another type in which canon grows out of a total *Klang*. Our increasing knowledge of medieval Celtic harp music sheds light on some qualities of Western polyphony otherwise inexplicable.[1] Apparently the Celtic system operated by contrasting within a piece two chords built similarly on two adjacent tones of a diatonic scale:

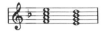

This system is remote from formal harmonic theory. "On the contrary, it developed because Celtic musicians sought some means whereby harmony could be improvised to melody, and whereby harmonic compositions could be improvised in concert."[2] The patterned alternations of two basic chords were known and systematized as the "Twenty-Four Measures." "Any melody based on one of the Measures will harmonize with any other melody based on the same Measure, so long as the harmony changes on the same beat in each melody. And, since a particular note will always be assignable to a particular one of two chords, one needs merely to know the Measure of a melody to be able to improvise an harmonic accompaniment to it, or any number of variations on it; or, again, a group of musicians, by recognizing a common Measure and a common rhythm, can each improvise melodies which will harmonize with those simultaneously improvised by the others in the group."[3]

The system admits a wide variety of formal types.[4] The most revealing for our purpose is the Reading *rota*, "Sumer is icumen in," a six-part double canon written down around A.D. 1240 and often reprinted.[5] All six voices conveniently fit into the following Celtic "Measure":

"The simplicity and ingenuity of the harmonic and compositional system underlying both the Reading Rota and medieval harp music is in truth such that anyone, knowing the system, can improvise a six-part composition such as the Reading Rota almost as rapidly as the notes can be written. Children could easily learn to improvise polyphonously on the basis of the Measures, and thus verify, across the centuries, what Giraldus wrote of the polyphonous singing of the children of Wales."[6]

[1] See Travis, *Celtica*.

[2] Travis, p. 8.

[3] Travis, p. 8.

[4] Travis, pp. 12 ff.

[5] Manfred Bukofzer was so puzzled by the presence of a complex canon at a period when traditional polyphony on the European continent was in its infancy that he tried to push the date forward to at least 1310. Travis, *Celtica*, pp. 48 ff., and others have persuasively refuted Bukofzer by linking the "Sumer" canon to Celtic practices.

[6] Travis, *Celtica*, p. 61. In his travelogue *Descriptio Cambriae*, Giraldus Cambrensis wrote around the year 1200: "In Wales, you will hear as many different parts and voices as there are performers, who all at length unite, with organic melody, in one consonance. . . . What is still more wonderful, the children, even from their infancy, sing in the same manner." Here quoted in translation from *Itinerary through Wales*, pp. 74 f.

In an endless circular canon like "Sumer is icumen in," the constant presence of the One is strongest. The polyphony is in continuous motion, but there is outward immobility. One can compare the effect to that conveyed by a wheel turning on a stationary axis. The old technical term *rota* for a perpetual canon refers to more than simply the "roundness" or "turnover" of the melody: it points, in addition, to the overall structure and morphology. A modern Western ear, attuned to dynamic drives, might consider this kind of canon monotonous in the long run, but an ontically inclined Oriental might understand and approve.

Popular canons of the eighteenth and nineteenth centuries, be they by Haydn and Mozart or of the order of "Row, row, row your boat," are much more closely related to the Celtic than to the Netherlands model. The artful works by the classical masters frequently are bound by an oscillation between two chords and are circular. The twelve measures of Beethoven's famous "metronome" canon can be reduced to four three-measure phrases in which only the first half of each third measure abandons the tonic for the dominant. Mozart's somewhat longer canons—such as "Bona nox" and the "Martin" canon—manage to widen the cadence by inclusion of the subdominant and relative functions; but the underlying technique and morphology are those of the *rota*. To the extreme simplicity of "Frère Jacques," "Row, row," and similar canons, the harmonic restriction to only one simple chord bears witness.

Even in these simplest canons, however, the polyphonic texture alone produces a drastic morphological change affecting the monodic dux. If the structure of the original melody is metrically determined, as in "Frère Jacques" and most classical canons, it is destroyed as soon as the canon begins; for the metrical build also occurs in canon and, unrecognizable in this form, disappears as an aesthetic factor.

In either kind of canon, the time lapse between statement and imitation, if extremely short or extremely long, can weaken the feeling of underlying unity. The long viola line at the beginning of Bach's Sixth Brandenburg Concerto, for example, appears in canon at a time lag of one eighth so that the leading voice has no chance to establish itself and sink in before the answering voice interferes. Moreover, the rhythmic shift within the measure gives each line a totally different individuality:

Many caccias of the Italian *ars nova*, on the other hand, let so much time lapse between the two canonic voices that one often has difficulties relating the answer back to the statement. Memorable spots, particularly after rests, can mislead one into thinking of two strophes.

CANTATA

The term was necessarily introduced at a time when instrumental music broke away from the authority of vocal music and became autonomous. The distinction between cantata and *sonata, first recorded around 1600, is morphologically not very meaningful. Whereas sonata, for whatever reasons, developed some morphological significance, cantata designates any number of possibilities. Early cantatas by Caccini are mostly monodic recitative; late cantatas by Vaughan Williams, mostly choral song. Bach wrote one-movement cantatas, undistinguishable from a da capo aria (no. 53) or a chorale prelude (no. 118), and he also piled together entire cantatas in a complex superstructure of multipartites (Christmas Oratorio).

The only characteristic of permanence in cantata is that it is sung. Hence any formation is conditioned by the relationship of *word and tone. Cantata subsumes all morphological possibilities of *vocal music.

CANTUS FIRMUS

The term denotes a "firm" given melody usually appearing in relatively long metric values. Preexisting as an accepted musical entity, it thus becomes the backbone of a fresh organism, the steel structure around which a new edifice is built.

In whatever form it appears, a cantus firmus provides unity. Strangely enough, the unity is often gained on the strength, not of real experience, but of two assumptions. One assumption is that the given cantus firmus possesses artistic unity of its own which it automatically transmits to the new composition based on it. In many cases, this assumption is backed by facts, particularly when it involves an entire plainchant melody. One may wonder, however, about the actual unity when the cantus firmus is merely a fragment of a larger melody which begins and, even more often, ends rather arbitrarily. Musical unity is even more doubtful when the cantus firmus derives from songs not necessarily of the highest musical quality, or from extramusical considerations such as word games translated into solmization syllables. The other assumption is that the given cantus firmus is actually audible as a unity. Again, this assumption is often justified. When the notes of the cantus firmus, however, are stretched beyond spontaneous and recognizable continuity, or distorted in isorhythmic repetitions, or hidden in a middle voice, one hardly hears them as a unified musical event. Yet the mere presence of a cantus firmus seems to provide unity whether based on assumptions or facts. The reality apparently lies in the idea as much as in the materialization.

A cantus firmus contributes to the morphology of a piece in two distinct manners. It may feed motivic material to the participating voices, or it may appear as a tenor. In the first case, it supplies seeds for growth. In the second case, it provides a ready-made limitation. The two techniques may appear simultaneously in varied degrees of interpenetration. All these possibilities strengthen unity.

Josquin's *Missa Pange lingua* is a good example of the first manner. Every one of the five movements begins with the opening phrase of the Corpus Christi hymn. All four voices always share in it in imitation. The Gregorian melody is never heard in its entirety as a continuous entity, though isolated motives beyond the opening phrase occasionally sound through. Each one of the five movements continues to grow in its own manner, as if the Gregorian phrase stimulated unlimited development. The tenuous unity of the *Mass cycle is sufficiently served by the reaffirmation of the same known theme at crucial and representative moments. Growth is checked by the given structure of the liturgy.

When, on the other hand, the cantus firmus stretches across one voice—usually the tenor in medieval and renaissance music, and any voice in later music—it supplies by itself the *limitatio prius facta*. The formal outline of such a composition is thereby predetermined. A chorale prelude on a hymn tune in barform inevitably assumes the same form whether the entire chorale melody is presented plainly or in elaboration. The musical limitation being given, the play of the purely generative forces can be all the freer. Bach reveals his imagination nowhere more opulently than in his organ chorale preludes. Within the given form, each section may be fancifully lengthened; the epode may introduce fresh counterpoints; each fermata may become a free interlude. But the overall proportions and balances remain the same.

Because the principles involved are still fairly obvious, much can be learned from the use of a cantus firmus in early polyphony. The first clausulas, for instance, employed the Gregorian melody literally; but not later than about the year 1200, the liturgical intactness found itself subordinated to musical needs. In a *Domino* clausula of the Notre Dame school, to mention one example, the cantus firmus is repeated with a shift of the rhythmic pattern in the second *cursus*, thus allowing for both growth and limitation:[1]

One wonders whether the Gregorian melody remains recognizable when each note becomes extended to extremes in the organa by Leoninus and Perotinus. At the end of most of these compositions, the cantus firmus suddenly falls into the tempo and meter of the organa voices and asserts itself sufficiently to be really heard. While the immediate result is obviously a climactic effect, the true accomplishment may well be to render audible the hitherto hidden melodic force of the tenor. In the somewhat later motets of the Codex Bamberg and Codex Montpellier, the cantus firmus limits the total structure not so much by its own length as by the definition of consonance and dissonance by which it binds the upper two voices.

The concept of cantus firmus includes *ostinato basses. Because the upper voices of a chaconne or passacaglia hardly ever partake of the motivic material supplied by the bass, and because the bass itself may suffer endless repetitions, the direct morphological contribution of a basso ostinato is small. It deserves, however, to be considered as a variant of cantus firmus technique.

[1]Reprinted in Davison and Apel, *Anthology*, p. 25.

In an article written at the end of his life, the Dutch composer Matthijs Vermeulen confessed that he had utilized a hidden cantus firmus in his Seventh Symphony. He did not say how, but he expressed his faith in the morphological virtue of the technique.[1] His confession prompts the raising of interesting questions, pointing both forward and backward. Whatever the course of music, in no case can it exclude phenomena and concepts of general validity. Any cadence, be it classic or other, incorporates the idea of a cantus firmus. In this sense, so does the succession of keys or points of reference in a *multipartite work, such as a symphony or oratorio. Studies made in this respect have always been based on functional harmony, and the results have often produced fresh insights. One might try, however, to jot down as a coherent cantus firmus the tonics of the numbers of, let us say, Bach's *Passion According to St. Matthew*. Whatever appears can be profitably approached in terms of melody. The relation of the beginning in E minor to the ending in C minor, for instance, becomes more readily comprehensible. We gain a hint for this approach from the significance of basso continuo. Bach, even when "harmonizing" a chorale, obviously guided his thoughts along basses rather than chords; the latter came naturally out of the former, according to the grammar of the time. In his concerto movements, the main pillars, generally identified by harmonic functions, can be understood as melodic points of a cantus firmus, surrounded by veritable jubilations and sequences.

CHROMATICISM

Chroma is the Greek word for 'color'. Chromaticism, in the most general and literal sense, implies the coloring of a given thing. It thus points toward a nonstructural quality. In music, the "given thing" is the particular tonal system. Each tonal system results from the definite number of tones chosen from among the infinity of available pitches within the octave. Theoretically a system thus established is complete and self-sufficient; in the course of history it indeed remains so for some time. Sooner or later, however, musicians begin to use tones lying in the interstices between the tones of the system. A necessary distinction arises between tones essential and inessential to the system. In Chinese music theory, an essential tone is called *lü*, an inessential one *pien*. English terminology, less concerned with the distinction, yet refers to "accidentals."

Chromaticism as a principle is therefore possible in any system. It pertains to the accidental, nonessential tones. The intervallic relationship of the nonessential to the essential tones varies according to the system. It need not at all be a halftone. Even in our traditional major-minor system, the halftone is not necessarily a chromatic progression. In C major, for instance, the steps E to F and B to C are diatonic because belonging to the system. The step F to F-sharp, on the other hand, is truly chromatic because F-sharp lies outside the tones essential to C major.

[1]"Seventh Symphony: Dithyrambes pour les temps à venir."

101

The halftone has remained the smallest interval in Western traditional systems because of the particular nature of the adopted scales. In the continued generation by fifths, the seven-tone *scale is the first to produce the halftone. Here the halftone appears as lü, essential to the character of the scale; but it may subsequently assume the role of pien, simply because it is the smallest interval available for accidentals.

The diatonic seven-tone systems of Western music (Greek modes, Church modes, major-minor modes) admit of five additional tones. Any one or all of these accidentals may be used diatonically, as in transpositions of a mode:

They may also be used to combine modes:

On the other hand, the additional tones may be considered as produced by *alteration. This process creates two truly chromatic, reciprocal modes:

Bearing in mind that genuine chromaticism resulting from piens is thus inseparable from alteration, we hear the material of dodecaphony not as a chromatic scale but as a natural twelve-tone scale (cf. *Atonality). All twelve tones are in fact lüs; flats and sharps, though kept for the convenience of notation, have no more "accidental" meaning. Piens are absent; the original piens of the seven-tone scale have all become essential.

One can readily speculate on the continuation of this process. If the twelve-tone scale is taken literally, the theoretically existing interstices between these tones can eventually yield new piens, which would obviously be smaller than halftones. Such intervals exist in many tone systems (Arab, Indian). The future will show whether Western tonality will expand its material to include new microtones.[1]

Strictly tied to alteration, chromaticism shares the dangers inherent in alteration. Excessive use of chromaticism may indeed first weaken, then obliterate, the hearer's consciousness of the diatonic pillars. As a result, the experience of alteration also disappears. The process eventually affects the concept of tonality.

CLASSIC-ROMANTIC

The term *classic* connotes two different though basically related meanings. It originally points to that which is of the highest class, of the first rank. When we call a work of art a classic, the attribute expresses a supreme lauda-

---

[1]Yasser, in *Evolving Tonality*, pursues the theoretical possibilities. As the next development he stipulates the "supra-diatonic scale" which, quite logically, consists of twelve essential half-tones plus seven new accidental microtones.

tory judgment independent of any tendency or style. In the other meaning, the term designates some characteristic period in history. By assigning a statue to classic antiquity, or a symphony to the Vienna classics, we do not imply a judgment but merely place the work in a context.

The term *romantic* plays the same double role. It stems from the medieval French word *roman* or *romance*, a fictitious tale characterized by freedom of fancy in conception and treatment, imaginative adventure, and picturesque variety. Thus it points to an aesthetic relevancy of the irrational, for instance, when referring to somebody's romantic attire or behavior. In the other meaning, however, the term, like classic, also designates a particular period—in music, most of the nineteenth century.

The pair "classic-romantic" is sometimes raised to the level of a grand rhythmic principle contributing to the shaping of cultural history. For the purpose of a morphological investigation, we need not pursue the implications of these concepts that result in judgment and opinion. We shall attempt to elucidate the relationship of classic and romantic both in regard to more narrowly defined historic periods and rhythmically wider stylistic cycles.

Looking at the familiar example of Germany in the one hundred years from about 1750 to 1850, we notice at least three stages in literature and music. There is first the most truly romantic period of *Sturm und Drang* represented by such writers as Bürger and Lenz and such composers as C. P. E. Bach and the group in Mannheim. The American and French Revolutions supply the political counterpart. Around the turn of the century, classicism rules, whether we think of Goethe and Schiller, Haydn and Mozart, or the Capitol in Washington. The next generation, however, is again romantic. Literary and musical tendencies become united in the life work of Schumann and Wagner. Are the two romantic periods, before and after the Goethe-Haydn classicism, sufficiently similar to be designated by the same criterion?

The differences are more revealing. Summits in the history of all the arts, unless they terminate abruptly, are always followed by a "decadent" phase in which things literally "fall apart." In the visual arts, such decadence characterizes hellenism, late romanesque sculpture, flamboyant gothic, and many others. In music, the generations after Josquin des Prez provide analogous symptoms. Similarly, the generations after Beethoven, specifically called "romantic," have often been qualified as decadent; but advanced age, while obviously past the summit, has its own kind of productivity, like late autumn. To avoid the negative implications of decadence, we had best characterize such periods as "late styles" (*Spätstyle*).

Sturm und Drang, on the other hand, is an early style in the process of fermentation. No doubt, it shares some symptoms with late style because in some respects beginning and end of an evolution, infancy and old age, resemble each other. Both, for example, show a propensity for the irrational. They do so, however, for quite opposite reasons. What in youth is sensuality, in old age becomes refinement or morbidity. Sentiment may turn into transcendence or sentimentality; vigor, into an empty gesture or pathos. The external similarities do not justify both periods being called by the same name, for they differ fundamentally from each other by their function. While there is little harm in calling "romantic" a single work or a historical phase endowed with a certain character, great confusion arises from connecting distant style periods by the same term unless one clarifies which is to be understood as an antecedent and which as a consequent. If we call the composers after Beethoven "romantic," we cannot apply the same name to the *Sturm und Drang* composers before him.

There are proponents of the theory that *Sturm und Drang* is the real romantic period and that, by extension, romantic periods are always antecedents. In support one indeed admits that, ontogenetically and phylogenetically, the evolutionary state dominated by instinct, feeling, emotion, passion, imagination always precedes cerebration. In this sense, primitive man could be called romantic, and certainly his relationship to nature was typically so. On the day he was prompted to deal with the spirits of nature by conjuring them, he performed a "classic" act of dealing reasonably with the unknown by erecting mental barriers and limits. Viewed thus, romanticism is the deep well from which everything springs. The ensuing classic period is the result of the preceding romantic one—a kind of distillate. It follows the earlier upheaval as old wine follows young fermenting grape juice. According to this theory, the world begins with fertile night, not with clear day.

As we consider the relationship between the period of the Vienna classics and that of the romantics following it, we become inclined to the opposite interpretation. Real romanticism, we submit, is a reaction to classicism. It needs an antecedent classicism with which it shares the foundations in order to develop its own characteristic countertendencies.

In art, literature, and music, there is one hallmark common to all periods called classic: the existence of artistic canons recognized by all and taken for granted. In the period of the Vienna classics, the canons related primarily to the mature concept of triadic tonality with all its implications. Older canons concerning interval quality and counterpoint remained in force. The greatest achievement of the period was the elaboration and reconciliation of all these forces in *sonata form. Recognition and acceptance of the canons defined the expectation of the listeners. Haydn could not have attempted to portray chaos in *Die Schöpfung* and Beethoven would not have produced a shock by the opening secondary-dominant chord of his overture to *Prometheus* unless by a clearly understood referral to the underlying and unquestioned canons concerning the immediate and unambiguous establishment of tonality. An experience reported by Mozart from Paris (in a letter to his father of 3 July 1778) would not be possible in any but a classic period: "Having observed that all last as well as first allegros begin here with all the instruments playing together and generally in unison, I began mine with two violins only, piano for the first eight measures—right afterwards came a forte—hence the listeners (as I expected) said 'hush' at the soft beginning—then came promptly the forte—hearing the forte and applauding was one for them."

The romantic symptoms of the following period appear to a great extent as licenses from established procedures. Romantic freedom is based on inherited classic canons accepted as implicit. Schumann can end the first song of *Dichterliebe,* and Chopin the Prelude in F major, on an unresolved dominant seventh chord; and Mahler, *Das Lied von der Erde* on an unresolved appoggiatura—the underlying concept of tonality clearly projects to the listener the implied resolution and hence the intended lack of fulfillment. Romantic harmony is basically an expansion of classic tonality. Against the implicit background of the latter, the chromaticism of Wagner's *Tristan und Isolde* is as understandable as the earlier Schumann song. Romantic license, like any other, creates fresh dangers along with obvious accomplishments; for when in the nineteenth century the checking factors gradually weakened, the emancipation ended in the tonal nihilism expressed by the negative word "atonality" which had to devise its own new controls and restraints—tone rows, series, parameters, etc.—just to keep functioning.

Form stability, passed down from the classics to the romantics, accounts for the relatively great number of high-ranking composers and compositions in the nineteenth century. This phenomenon applies to all romantic styles— the baroque as much as the nineteenth century. A style evolves through the contribution of many talents, great and small. The style security consequent to a classic highpoint of evolution favors the flowering of many a talent that otherwise would have succumbed under the tasks and problems posed by style difficulties. The multitude and excellence of the romantic production derives from the stable aspect of forms. We have spoken elsewhere of the relative independence of form and content (cf. pp. 181 ff.). Form permanency from early Haydn to late Brahms and even Mahler permitted the change of meaning of a given form by letting romantic composers "fill the old vessel with new wine." Of this conservative strain within romanticism, Schumann and Mendelssohn are typical representatives.

The classic inheritance is felt even in the supposedly original romantic contribution of the "character piece." Whether this kind of short composition bears the title impromptu, nocturne, intermezzo, prelude, or even a poetic name, the form is always very clear—in fact, "classic" and, compared to such "character pieces" as Beethoven's *Bagatellen*, morphologically rather conservative. The recapitulation in Chopin's D-flat major Prelude is greatly abbreviated and suggestive rather than spelled out, but reference to a classic bow form is the one factor letting us recognize it at all as a recapitulation. The dissolution of form in Beethoven's Bagatelle op. 119 no. 7 sounds far more licentious.

As to the symphonic poem, it is morphologically a logical outcome of the evolution of sonata form after Beethoven. The instrumental drama into which sonata and symphony had developed toward the end of the classic period tended toward an ever-increasing unity of the whole. The now readily available symphonic dramatism and popular opera transformed each other. Liszt's one-movement Piano Sonata, a totally romantic work, stands solidly on the tradition of classical sonata form (for a detailed analysis, see Appendix A, pp. 321 f.).

Understood as "late" symptoms, other romantic traits fall into place. The typically romantic spirit with its predilection for the dark, mysterious, even horrible; for the fairy world, the faraway in time and space; for excessive emotion and passion, even the transcendent insofar as it is mirrored in feeling—all this is certainly a reaction to classicism. So is the tendency to blur the lines separating the various arts from one another and art from nature. Mixtures of literature and music appear in different forms. Naturalism takes over. The

sympathy for folk music—actually a minor factor—stems from a related attitude. The essential point is that in all these efforts the classic fundament behind the reaction is never questioned. The flight of fantasy in the romanticism
of a late style occurs in clear consciousness of a secure basis and in total un-
awareness of the possibly dissolving effects of that fantasy on the basis itself.

In this way, Richard Wagner could create the illusion of a beginning, a
"music of the future," which, judged by the consequences in the twentieth
century, actually turned out to be a closing phase, a late style. A romanticism
of which the roots are firmly sunk in the soil of a classic tradition can be a
healthy phenomenon. The particular difficulties of the present *Sturm und
Drang* period are tied to the thorough rejection of, and even contempt for,
canons and to the negation of limitations.

Faced with the conceptual muddle that careless usage of the terms *classic*
and *romantic* has produced, we must ask ourselves in each particular case
whether the romantic period in question is an antecedent or a consequent of
a classic phase. The resulting style distinctions are fundamental and morphologically significant.

CLEARNESS-UNCLEARNESS

In 1915, Heinrich Wölfflin introduced five concept pairs in the theory of
visual arts: linear-painterly, plane-recession, closed-open, multiplicity-unity,
and clearness-unclearness.[1] Although initially abstracted from a comparison
of renaissance and baroque art, they soon proved their validity as general style
distinctions between two basic trends recurrent throughout art history. The
sequence renaissance-baroque is easily paralleled by classicism-romanticism.
A baroque period, Wölfflin stipulated, always follows a classic period, inevitably growing out of it. He saw, for instance, a classic and a baroque stage also
in Gothic architecture.

Wölfflin's concept pairs describe different modes of feeling and seeing the
outer world. Because the subject matter of music remains enclosed in the inner
world, an entirely different orientation ensues to which visual concepts cannot readily be applied. The first two pairs, linear-painterly and plane-
recession, are as clearly out of place in music as *pneumatic-kinematic would
be in painting. The other three pairs, however, possess sufficient universality
to shed light also on musical behavior. Cf. "Multiplicity and Unity" (pp. 39
ff.), *Open-Closed.

Clearness-unclearness are notions identified with, respectively, classicism and romanticism, understood not as periods but rather as poles between
which art oscillates in the course of history. Ars antiqua, Franco-Flemish
renaissance, Haydn, neoclassicism—the music of all these styles is "clear" in
essence. Whatever elements one investigates enhance the clarity of the whole.
Separate movements—be they sections of a motet or Mass, numbers of an opera, or movements of a string quartet—are clearly set off from one another.
Their function is independent within the whole. Within any single movement, phrases, periods, sections, and themes are neatly separated, often be-

[1]*Grundbegriffe.*

106

cause of the organizing power of metrics but also because of other particular techniques. Texture, for example, avoids blends, whether we think of the three individual voices of a thirteenth-century motet or the orchestration of a Mozart symphony. In all respects, the entire piece is carefully proportioned.

In any of the style periods lying at the other pole, structure is deliberately veiled. Clear rhythmic modes yield to the extreme rhythmic complications of the late fourteenth century; separate numbers, to through-composed units; individual instruments, to sound blocks. The artistic result may be equally valid. The recapitulation in the slow movement of the Second Symphony by Brahms (m. 67) exemplifies deliberate unclearness in the hands of a master. The theme, consisting of two scale fragments in contrary motion toward each other, appears when least expected after three previous false recapitulations (mm. 57, 62, and 65). Whereas the earlier attempts were all "clearly" introduced by articulation, dynamics, and orchestration, the real recapitulation slides almost unnoticed into the general movement above an established organ point, without break in the continuous flow, one line in the unobtrusive bassoons, and the other line heterophonically obscured by figuration. Of all tones, moreover, the tonic B is replaced, as it was at the very beginning, by B-sharp. Compare this attitude with the clarity of recapitulation in a Mozart sonata, let alone the additional emphasis at this point in a Beethoven symphony.

Although the separation of elements for the sake of clarity seems to associate clarity with multiplicity, one must beware of all too easy identification of clearness-unclearness with the parallel concept pairs. Clearness may characterize either open or closed forms, polyphony or homophony, unity or multiplicity. Unclearness does not mean lack of order but rather deliberate veiling of otherwise clear artistic intentions.

As a convenient summary, we may suggest a comparison of two extremes such as the respective overtures to Mozart's *Le nozze di Figaro* and Wagner's *Tristan und Isolde*:

	Clear	*Unclear*
Style	Classic	Romantic
Form	Sonata	Energy curve
Role	Independent	Introductory
Tonality	Defined	Suggestive
Scale	Diatonic	Chromatic
Harmony	Triads	Seventh chords
Cadences	Authentic	Deceptive
Melodies	Distinct	"Infinite"
Bass line	Functional	Ambivalent
Rhythm	Metricized	Free-flowing
Meter	Organizing	Fermatas
Tempo	Constant	Fluctuating
Dynamics	Structural levels	Crescendos and descrescendos
Orchestration	Individualized	Mixtures
Fabric	Transparent	Interwoven

107

CLIMAX

Climax is originally the Greek word for ladder; then, metaphorically, it indicates a series of states of increasing intensity; finally, it means the highest rung of the ladder or, metaphorically, the culmination of a development. In this last sense only, the word is used in music.

The relevance of the term is rather recent, because prior to the nineteenth century there had apparently been no need for it. The use of the term is tied to the emergence of musical dramatism in the sense of an inner development somewhat paralleling theatrical drama with its exposition, development, climax, and catastrophe. Thus it is really symptomatic of the general romantic attitude which deliberately blurs the borders separating the various art forms and freely borrows terms applicable to one art for exploration in another. Climax in music is a term borrowed from drama. Opera doubtless acted as a go-between; but the element of excitement bound up with theater soon became a prominent feature of much nineteenth-century music even when direct operatic connotations were missing. The mere notation reflects the new concern. Suddenly dynamic markings, almost totally missing before the *Sturm und Drang* period, appear everywhere in music. The orchestra, which had earlier served the clarification of lines, now begins to minister to the projection of climax. The extent of the orchestral contribution can be easily measured by one's playing the piano reduction of any Berlioz score: it sounds deprived of climax and hence uncharacteristic (whereas a score by an earlier composer need not similarly suffer).

Sonata form is the most complex musical transformation of a dramatic concept. Hence it always contains a climax. To Beethoven, the dramatic event, more often than not, was the return to the abandoned tonic. The moment of recapitulation is usually marked as culmination of a special kind. In the opening movement of the Eighth Symphony, the triple forte, coupled to the shift of the first theme from the top to the bottom range and to the resulting strange inversion of the tonic chord, illustrates well the kind of climax characteristic of the nineteenth century.

One need only compare this moment with a recapitulation in a composition by Bach to appreciate fully the change in attitude. In the B-flat minor Fugue from *The Well-tempered Keyboard I*, for example, the return to the tonic is clearly marked by a quintuple stretto of the theme, but the effect is hardly climactic in a theatrical sense. Even when Bach approaches sonata form, as in the finale of the Fifth Brandenburg Concerto, the recapitulation, though clear, is almost casual—anything but dynamic. Modern orchestrations of Bach fugues usually tend to dramatize such moments. It is true that a fugue by Bach can usually stand the additional dynamic accent, but it does not need one. The suggested spelling out of a climax here distracts. It would be impossible in the kind of significant spot that occurs frequently in Bach—a turning point that has dramatic implications without being climactic. This ontic attitude is well illustrated in the *Actus tragicus* by the appearance of the chorale tune, promising salvation, in the barely audible flute above and against the active ensemble (no. 2, mm. 150 ff.). The drama, if any, is not externalized but rather turned inward. It does not excite—it exists.

To the music before Bach and before opera, the idea of climax is even more foreign. It is totally inapplicable to a Netherlands motet, or a thirteenth-century motet, or Gregorian chant.

Today the sort of excitement provided by theater is still the value criterion of many people in their relation to music. They expect a climax; otherwise they are disappointed. This attitude is typical of the prevalent interpretation of gigneticism as something positive, and of ontism as something deficient. For a short while between the two World Wars, the so-called New Music brought a reaction against anything labeled romantic and subjective, hence also against anything climactic. But since at least the Second World War, this attitude has given way to a renewed onrush of almost brutal continuous stimulation. At this extreme point, climax loses its meaning and, replaced by permanent maximum intensity, disappears as a morphological factor.

CLOSED-OPEN. See **OPEN-CLOSED**

CODA

A coda has several functions. It summarizes. It resolves. It confirms. Sometimes it also prepares.

The coda of the second movement of Beethoven's Eroica Symphony will serve to illustrate these points. The generating force of the movement, as has been shown, is the irritant note A-flat in the opening melody (m. 6; cf. pp. 18 ff.). The events of the movement flow out of it. The coda (mm. 209 ff.) summarizes the role of that note by the immediate tonicizing of A-flat with the help of a deceptive cadence, and by the exposed, expressive oboe solos (mm. 215–17; 232–35). It resolves the initial dissonance by signally incorporating it in a scale leading down to the real tonic (mm. 225–32; 236–38). It confirms, in a final summary and resolution, the function of the critical note within a restatement of the initial melody (mm. 238 ff.). One wonders whether the very last appearance of a_2-natural (m. 246) within the cadential run from dominant to tonic is not a final answer to the immediately preceding step from a_1-flat to g. The coda as a whole reestablishes the precarious structural balance characteristic of the movement. The expected symmetrical ternary arrangement of the traditional march is here distorted by the enormous detour after the false recapitulation (mm. 105–72). One hears the following main sections:

March	Trio	Detour	March	Coda
68	36	68	36	39

The coda corrects, by its mere presence, the intentional lopsidedness of the main movement.

This particular coda does not seem to prepare the following scherzo. For an example of preparation, one may turn to Beethoven's Piano Sonata in D minor, op. 31 no. 2, in which the last melodic progression of the coda of the first movement, f^1–d^1, is promptly answered by the opening melodic phrase of the following adagio, $d^1 - f^1$. In his last Piano Sonata op. 111, the coda of the first movement dissolves the basic motif G-C, which then reappears in the second movement in mirror image, and it transforms the initial rhythm in preparation for that of the next movement. The coda of the last movement reverses the direction: the work closes with G-C. Thus the whole sonata is a symbol of D-T; T-D, D-T.

All the coda functions observed in the Eroica example can be found—to give one more, particularly succinct illustration—in the two coda measures of the theme that opens Mozart's Piano Sonata in A major, K. 331 (see also Appendix A, pp. 309 ff.). The melody had begun on c^1-sharp, the major third of the key. The summarized drives toward the tonic in both directions, up and down, are reconciled by the span of the octave $a^1 - a$ (from mm. 17 to 18). The final three notes, like a coda to the coda, confirm the identity of the main line. They also provide a rhythmic seed for the behavior of the following variation.

To be recognized, a coda often is set apart from the main body by a signally different musical attitude. In the Mozart example just given, the two coda measures are the only ones marked forte. The coda to the whole movement (at the end of the sixth variation) continues beyond the metric frame strictly observed before. In other styles we find, with similar intent, extensions of the last Kyrie exclamation in Gregorian Masses; isorhythmic setting of the "Amen" in Machaut's otherwise syllabic Credo; polyphonically intensified "Amen" fugues at the end of later Credo movements; free *cadenzas contrasting with the preceding strictness; organ points; and other such devices, all of which distinguish the coda by some contrasting behavior.

The question arises whether morphologically a coda lies outside the structure proper or is one of the formative elements. In the first case, it is literally a "tail" hanging outside the essential body. In the second, it must be considered as influencing proportion. In the works of Beethoven, the extreme instances of codas seem to lend weight to the second alternative. The first movement of the Fifth Symphony, for instance, divides the total of 502 measures with almost exact equality among exposition, development, recapitulation, and coda. Yet we submit that the coda is a "tail," even in the instance just quoted. If we think of the underlying basic *sonata form as binary, the double exposition matches development plus recapitulation. If the exposition is not repeated, it balances the recapitulation in the resulting ternary structure, of which the development is the center. In either case, the coda remains outside the main morphological idea.

The reason, then, for having a coda at all—apart from the specific accomplishments listed initially—must be sought in the manner in which we experience time and the devices by which the flow of time created by a piece of music can be stopped. The respective roles of *time and space in music are the reverse of what they are in the physical world. Hence we may allow ourselves the analogy with the roof of a house. It does not function like the main structure but rather indicates the termination. Houses without visible roofs are possible, just as musical compositions without codas. Structurally they may be considered complete and rainproof. Aesthetically, however, they lack something, as anybody knows who has seen a roofed and gabled town. They lack the expression of the artistic intent to terminate. Without roof or coda, the *end appears or sounds more arbitrary than it already is. A coda satisfies by giving shape, that is, a clearly audible sign of an expected limitation, to an otherwise abrupt moment of cutoff.

COLORATURA. See ORNAMENTATION

COMMUNICATION

There exists communication between a maker and his material. We call it "art." There exists communication between man and man. We call it "expression." In this view, expression is a special case of communication and thus a possible, but not a necessary, function of music. Our judgment of a composition is greatly determined by our sympathy for the one or the other kind of communication.

The maker communicates with the work, with the thing he is making. The finished product testifies to the interaction of the maker and his material. It is a monument, enduring as artistic record of a creative achievement. End and goal for the maker are reached as soon as the work has come into existence. From then on, it is there for all to behold or hear. The receiving listener becomes a witness to an action, to a happening long since passed, of which the work is a testimony. He may or may not be moved by it—the work will in any case remain unaffected.

The maker concerned with expression, on the other hand, bears in mind the intended effect on the listener. Communication here takes place primarily between the composer and the public. The work is used for a purpose. It is aimed at the listener, whom the composer has deliberately integrated into the composition.

These two concepts of music are not mutually exclusive. On the contrary: each composition is both testimony and expression, but the emphasis shifts. Traditional Oriental philosophy cares little for individual expression: "Man ought not to work for any why, not for God nor for his glory nor for anything at all that is outside him, but only for that which is his being, his very life within him."[1] In Western music, the deliberate reaching-out from work to public is minimal in chamber music and strong in opera (although one remains witness precisely in the case of the best operatic examples by Mozart and Verdi). The Roman Catholic Mass is a borderline case: on one hand, the music is destined to make "the faithful more easily moved to devotion and better disposed to receive in themselves the fruits of grace"; on the other hand, it clearly rejects participation and remains a testimonial to "the glory of God."[2] Although neither of the great Masses by Bach and Beethoven meets the official standards set by the *Motu Proprio*, the latter's *Missa Solemnis* exhibits greater concern with expression, as indicated by the very motto: "Von Herzen—Möge es zu Herzen gehen" ("From the heart—may it reach the heart").

[1]*Upanishad* iv. 5, 6.
[2]*Motu Proprio*, p. 1.

Some historic facts will help elucidate the two aspects of communication. From about the year 1000, when Western polyphony came into being, to about the year 1600, when opera began its phenomenal rise, we hear very little, if anything, about music as expression. Both functions of music obviously existed then as they do now, but the emphasis was clearly on the interpretation of music as testimony. Music theorists wrote voluminously, but none of them cared about "appreciation." They studied the testimony, not the listener; the work of art, not its effect. The medieval visual representations of musical scenes all confirm this general conviction. The paintings, drawings, and sculptured reliefs show exclusively, before the Renaissance, the music being made, the singers and instrumentalists, but never the audience. This is true even of the characteristic angels' concerts, which convey the idea that paradise was filled with "doers" and not with "consumers." When Dante asks the composer Casella, whom he meets in Purgatory, for some music "to solace the soul," he promptly earns a severe rebuke from Cato, who shouts at him that this kind of standing around and listening to music "non lascia a voi Dio manifesto" ("lets not God be manifest to you").[1] But what Dante still describes as negligent self-indulgence gained force in the following centuries. The crisis of the musical Renaissance culminated in the planned creation of opera by an aesthetic club of intelligent Florentines at the end of the sixteenth century.

The highly critical and articulate essays written by the members of the Camerata all deal with the conflict between the monumental aspects of the older music and the expressive demands of the new. Polyphony was attacked as "unworthy of a free man for lacking the power to move a man's mind."[2] The new music, and the only one worth having, must be based on expression and passion. The immediate result was the condemnation of earlier achievements (such as the superior works of the Netherlands composers) and the introduction of the new art form, "opera." Vincenzo Galilei pinpointed the dichotomy:

> Music exists primarily to express the passions with greater effectiveness and to communicate these passions with equal force to the minds of mortals for their benefit and advantage. Hence the rules thus far observed by composers as inviolable laws are directly opposed to the perfection of the true music. These rules may be excellent and necessary for the mere delight the ear takes in the variety of harmonies, but for the expression of conceptions they are pestilent. Consider the composers until now. They aim at nothing but the delight of the ear, if it can truly be called delight. They have not a book among them for their use and convenience that speaks of how to express the conceptions of the mind and of how to impress them with the greatest possible effectiveness on the minds of the listeners; of this they do not think and never have thought since the invention of music. The last things composers consider is the expression of the words with the passion that these require. I say that it is not enough merely to take pleasure in the various harmonies heard in a musical composition.[3]

[1]*Purgatorio* ii. 106–23.

[2]Giovanni de' Bardi, "Discourse on Ancient Music and Good Singing," in Strunk, *Source Readings*, p. 294.

[3]"Dialogo della musica antica e della moderna," in Strunk, *Source Readings*, pp. 306 ff.

These words were written about fifteen years before Galilei's colleagues in the Camerata translated his theoretical concern into action by writing and producing an opera. Describing the first opera performance, *Dafne* by Peri and Caccini, an eyewitness reports in a letter that the chief aim of the venture "was to improve modern music and to raise it in some degree from the wretched state to which it had been reduced, chiefly by the Goths."[1] The Goths referred to are composers like Ockeghem, des Prez, and Willaert, all of whom had written music which contained a life force that came from within. The new style, on the other hand, insisted on being representative. The *stile rappresentativo*, sponsored by the Camerata, won the battle hands down. The rise of opera in the following three centuries is a clear symptom of the acceptance of music as a means of communication and expression. On the whole, modern man takes this attitude for granted.

Yet three hundred years are a short span within the course of universal history. Although the Renaissance has been generally interpreted as "human progress," an opposite view is equally possible. The gain may have been freedom of individual expression, but the price paid for it has been isolation of the individual from universal forces. In the twentieth century, we are still the heirs of the European Renaissance, whether we like it or not. The general assumption is that we like it. But opera taken as a post-Renaissance phenomenon might well be merely the most audible symptom of an artistic fall from grace. Ananda Coomaraswamy's knowledge of both Western and Oriental philosophies of art enabled him to place his faith in "art as testimony" above the popular notion of "art as expression." He writes:

> It is demanded of the artist to be both contemplative and a good workman. Contemplation is not a passion but an act: and where modern psychology sees in "inspiration" the uprush of an instinctive and *sub*conscious will, the orthodox philosophy sees an elevation of the artist's being to *super*conscious and *supra*individual levels. What is for the psychologist the "libido" is for the metaphysicist the "divine Eros." There is also a sense in which the man as an individual "expresses himself," whether he will or no. This is inevitable, only because nothing can be known or done except in accordance with the mode of the knower. But the artist whom we have in view is not trying to express *himself*, but *that* which was to be expressed. Our conception of art as essentially the expression of a personality, our whole view of genius, all these things are the products of a perverted individualism and prevent our understanding.[2]

The educative role of art has often been discussed. Many misunderstandings can be avoided if we compare the teacher's moral activity with the process of artistic creation. The educator (though needing some artistic qualities) makes no work of art. His activity aims at influencing human beings through expression. The creative artist, on the other hand, does not address himself to the public but to his materials. His work of art is neither moralistic nor educative. Its influence, if it has one, is that of a monument, which will or will not evoke reactions. From a moral point of view, the art work can be an example— neither more nor less. What message one receives from it derives from that

[1]Pietro de' Bardi, "Letter to G. B. Doni," in Strunk, *Source Readings*, p. 364.
[2]*Christian and Oriental Philosophy of Art*, pp. 38 f.

special communion in which one shares an experience and at the same time keeps one's distance. The question, whether there is an intimate transformation as a consequence of the aesthetic event, interests the educator but stays outside the domain of art. When we contemplate living nature or the planetary systems in heaven or in the atom, we may possibly find ourselves affected by the experience. What is certain is that the artist—*artifex maximus*—as well as the opus will remain indifferent to this fact.

The issue of communication is relevant to morphology. A composition does not persuade the listener of its form—it shows it.

COMPOSITION

Although it will stay with us forever, the word *composition* is somewhat unfortunate. Literally it means something 'put together', like a compote. In this sense, the term correctly designates a motet of the thirteenth century, when the art of composition consisted in putting together three otherwise independent melodies. It also properly describes a quodlibet. In all other instances, however, one wishes for more appropriate and correct connotations. Goethe said to Eckermann (20 June 1831):

> It is a mean word. . . . How can one say that Mozart "composed" his *Don Giovanni*! Composition indeed! As if it were a cake or biscuit that one puts together of eggs, flour, and sugar! A spiritual creation it is, the parts and the whole all of *one* spirit and *one* mold, and diffused with the breath of *one* life. And don't let it be supposed that the author went about it by trial and error and in piecemeal fashion— rather the daimon of his genius had him in his power so that he could not help doing as he did.

The statement is a bit partial, for Goethe himself often speaks of struggles, hesitations, arbitrary or seemingly arbitrary decisions, chance occurrences, and hard labor, all of which may participate in the making of a work and determine its growth. The statement, however, is correct in presupposing the existence of an *eidos and in emphasizing the difference between mechanical growth resulting from the "putting together of parts," and organic growth. In the former, the parts are made separately and afterward assembled, "composed." In the latter, the parts are organs growing from a seed by development and transformation. Yet in the cook's mind—to keep Goethe's simile—the idea of the cake (the whole) must be present if the ingredients (the parts) are to fulfill their function. Nothing mechanical is entirely devoid of organic connotations, and a modicum of the mechanical is present in all things organic; but the difference has to be kept in view. A mechanism is fashioned after an extrinsic rule. It cannot heal itself, and any imperfection is fatal. It functions or it does not function. In contrast to it, an organism is fashioned by an intrinsic norm. Hence it possesses self-healing power and retains its value beyond casual injuries. A musical work or a musical performance does not need perfection in order to exist. We can overlook weak passages in a symphony, and we would be foolish to stop a performance because of an accidental wrong note. A Greek temple in ruins is still awesome, but a ruined automobile is a disgust because it is useless.

The problems encountered in composing—gift and technical skill being presupposed—stretch between the poles of substance (matter, contents) and form. A short musical idea, the substance, is of course inseparable from its form but only on a level that might be likened to that of building-stones. Above this level, substance and form have independent lives. The form of a cathedral is not suggested in that of the stones. The cells of a living organism do not prefigure its total shape. The cell form of musical thought is *breathing form, which is also the smallest possible form of a self-sufficient, complete musical piece. Musical "ideas" conceived as in a flash of inspiration are always more or less short. In general, their length varies between that of a motive and that of a self-sufficient breathing form—units that can be created "in one breath." In rare instances, such a unit is acknowledged to be the whole piece. For musical as well as practical reasons, however, such a short piece is generally not left alone but placed in an array of similar pieces. If the succession is haphazard, the result is merely a collection. If, on the other hand, some general morphological idea, some thought of an inner development, presides over the choice and arrangement of the collection, the result is a suite. This simple example should elucidate the concept of relative independence between *matter and form.

If the composer envisages a larger work, new situations and problems arise and multiply rapidly. He decides to write a work of a certain type, a symphony. A type implies definite notions of magnitude, number of performers, and the like. The point of departure here lies on the formal side, and the creation of substance will be guided by the exigencies of the project. Musical ideas unfit for the particular purpose must be eliminated and only those retained that, so to speak, grow by themselves into the preconceived idea of the work. In the process of composition, new ideas might spring up that appear not only usable and important to the work but that might modify to some degree the original formal plan. Such occurrence is possible because substance and form are not absolutely independent of each other. Musical ideas are to an extent self-propelling, that is, they are like a seed that contains its own specific possibilities of growth. Martin Luther overlooked this point when praising Josquin des Prez for being the first composer to make the notes go where he wanted them to go. At the other extreme lies the belief that substance will and should grow automatically, so to speak, into its adequate form. This belief holds true only up to a certain magnitude above which growth becomes wild without the regulating influence of an overall form concept.

The quality of a musical idea being a seed containing its own potentialities for growth admits the possibility of starting a composition with the concrete musical thought and letting it grow for awhile until one can see "where it wants to go." This procedure means starting from the substance instead of the form. But if the method, the path, differs, the outcome must be the same. In the first case, a form idea seeks substance, which might modify it. In the second case, substance seeks a form for itself but will in turn be molded by the suggested though fundamentally independent form concept. Form and substance thus emerge as basically independent factors joined by the concept of mutual adequacy. This adequacy contributes much to the uniqueness of great works by making possible the vision of unity between form and substance which such works generate.

The basic independence of substance and form results in a relative substance indifference toward form and a reciprocal relative form indifference toward substance. The same substance can receive different formal treatment, and the same form can be used in different compositions.

Substance permanence is by itself of high artistic standing, for great imagination and artistry are required to exhaust the possibilities inherent in a given musical substance. The foremost example in Western music is Bach's *Die Kunst der Fuge*. Similar accomplishments are cantus firmus Masses in which every movement utilizes the same given material. The attitude, detectable in plainsong formulas and standardized visual representations of the Madonna or the Crucifixion, apparently fell victim to the Renaissance.[1] In present Western music, substance permanence as a universally valid concept and technique is nearly inexistent. It continues to prevail in music and art of the East, where composing on a given raga is as characteristic as painting or sculpturing Buddha always in the same position.

Form permanence, with the inherent risk of leading toward stereotype, is easily the most common part of a musical grammar. It is identified by any generic term, such as virelai, allemande, courante, sonata form, etc. First-class works in this category generally introduce some subtle form variation without challenging the underlying principle. Around the middle of the eighteenth century, form permanence was used extensively for pedagogic purposes. Appearing as "composing recipes," they are intimately tied to the idea of classic symmetry and therefore not totally devoid of merit.[2] By instructing the student how to develop a long period out of a short one, they also correctly reveal that the student's first and main concern is less with form than with substance. Form permanence, as offered by these recipes, frees the student by stimulating and sustaining his musical imagination.

The inertia of form types is so considerable that a form hardened into a type often outlives style changes. The first movements of Schönberg's Third and Fourth String Quartets adhere to sonata form notwithstanding his explicit denial of tonality. This kind of viability has led to overestimation of, and overemphasis on, set forms. They have become the war horse of music popularization, for they are rather easily verbalized. Yet all forms change although sometimes slowly. The exception is forms so simple and close to principles as to be practically identical with them. As manifestations of the basic underlying breathing form, we can presently distinguish only two such forms: within the binary principle, barform; within the ternary principle, bowform. The innumerable pieces written in these two forms attest to the indifference toward substance in both principal binary and ternary structures.

In times of style change, some forms may grow inadequate because incompatible with the new idiom, the new grammar. The merit of a composer

---

[1]For extensive treatment of this idea, see the writings by Coomaraswamy.
[2]Cf. Ratner, "Eighteenth-Century Theories."

here rests on developing fresh forms out of the exigencies of the substance while not contradicting the perennial form principles. He must divest his mind of preconceived ideas and listen to his musical material in order to discover its immanent form tendencies. Such efforts, if successful, are high spots of spiritual history: Monteverdi's *seconda pratica*, Haydn's string quartets from Opus 33 on, Beethoven's fugues in his late works. On the other hand, the reaction against an established style together with other forces might prompt a revolt against recognized forms. Such was the case around 1600 and again in this century. The problem is to find new forms and new substances adequate to each other, as did early opera.

Whitehead, in his lecture on "Forms of Process," speaks of "the transition from accident towards necessity as we pass from the smaller to the larger units of composition. . . . There is transition within the dominant order; and there is transition to new forms of dominant order. Such transition is a frustration of the prevalent dominance. And yet it is the realization of that vibrant novelty which elicits the excitement of life."[1]

CONCERTO

The only factor of morphological interest derives from the original meaning of the word *concertare*, 'to strive, contend, fight, compete'. The characteristic principle of concerto is competition among the participants for musical ascendancy. This principle has remained constant throughout the almost four centuries of concerto history, appearing in ever-varying forms and guises dictated and supplied by style.

Whereas one associates the term today primarily with instrumental virtuosity, it was actually first introduced in connection with vocal compositions to characterize certain competitive features of the then new style. The *concerti ecclesiastici*, written in the North of Italy around 1600, could involve double chorus or monody. In either case, the vocal entity was for the first time set off against an accompanying thorough bass. Schütz, carrying this usage from Venice across the Alps to Germany, often used the term *Konzert* for pieces in which the voices are not only accompanied by a figured bass but contend against a group of comparably treated instruments. This habit persisted in Germany into the eighteenth century.

The instrumental concerto as well takes its start from the *stile moderno*. In the early seventeenth century, the indebtedness to vocal models remains audible in featured contrasts between two instrumental ensembles or a solo instrument against a group. The gradual emancipation of instrumental music brought new stylistic and technical developments but actually never abandoned the early established basic principle. In all later concertos, we find some physical musical competition between variously grouped forces. In Bach's Brandenburg Concertos (which are representative of the whole period), the strife is both among the soloists and between the united soloists against the tutti. In the Italian Concerto, Bach's transcription of this form for one harpsi-

---

[1] Reprinted in *Modes of Thought*, pp. 86 ff.

117

chord, the competition remains between solo and tutti passages, carefully marked by the composer and phenomenalized by different registrations on the two manuals.

As a result of the romantic appreciation of the individual, the concerto literature of the nineteenth and twentieth centuries characteristically features virtuoso pieces that pitch a solo player against the orchestra (thus actually repeating the early monodic tendency). Against the romantic background, double and triple concertos (as Mozart, Beethoven, and Brahms still wrote them) are not adventures but atavisms. Similarly, modern concertos for orchestra by Hindemith, Stravinsky, and Bartók are experimental departures only in technical respects; the underlying principle is old and unchanged.

To become realized, the concerto principle has evolved three devices:

(1) *Antiphony* is essential when the contending elements are otherwise unified in regard to sonority. Antiphony is the most persuasive manner of projecting contrast within the unity of a given sound, such as that of a chorus or string orchestra. The competition becomes externalized by being carried out of the unified timbre into a separating space.

(2) *Imitation* in a concerto fulfills the opposite function to antiphony. When the given situation already contains and supplies contrast, imitation serves to introduce an element of unity, necessary to the overall artistic purpose. Recorder, oboe, violin, and trumpet—the concertizing instruments in the Second Brandenburg Concerto—seem to come from different worlds; but they are held together by imitating each other in the use of the same thematic material.

(3) *Virtuosity*, compared to antiphony and imitation, seems a secondary means, notwithstanding its supremacy in the nineteenth-century solo concerto. Whereas the other two devices make a direct morphological contribution, virtuosity remains an external trim. Yet it is justifiably welcome in the flourish of a musical contest.

Among the many classical compositions derived from the thorough-bass sonata—symphony, quartet, trio, sonata, etc.—concerto is the only one that has consistently rejected the introduction of a separate dance movement. A few isolated exceptions merely confirm this particular attitude. Bach, who tried everything at least once, placed a minuet movement after the finale of the First Brandenburg Concerto, almost as if to keep it out of the established fast-slow-fast arrangement of all his other concertos. Mozart combined a minuet with the finale of his Violin Concerto in A major, thereby continuing the old practice of "menuet en rondeau." Generally, however, concertos remain restricted to three movements; the dance movement, so readily accepted by analogous classical structures, here remains excluded.

Historic tradition of an accidental and almost paradoxical kind supplies the explanation. The thorough-bass sonata existed in two forms—*da camera* and *da chiesa*. The former, played in secular surroundings, freely admitted dance movements. The latter, intended for the church, did not. Until at least the middle of the eighteenth century, concertos were performed mostly in the church; for the walls of a home were apparently too intimate for virtuoso display, and public concerts with orchestra were few. One associates Northern Italy with the development of concerto writing. Giuseppe Torelli, who is credited with the composition of the first solo concerto for violin and orchestra, emerged, as did Giovanni Vitali, from the luxuriant church orchestra of San Petronio in Bologna. Giuseppe Tartini, who died as late as 1770, made most of his concert appearances in Padua in the sanctuary of Saint Antonio. The concerto, in short, stems from the *sonata da chiesa*. In all its later history, with all its secular leanings and accomplishments, the concerto remained faithful to its origin by resisting the invasion of a dance. Brahms's experiment with four movements assimilates his Second Piano Concerto to the contemporaneous sovereign symphony (in a spirit similar to the derivation of his First Piano Concerto from a symphonic plan).

In turn, the violin concerto made an impressive contribution to the development of sonata form in symphony and chamber music. The establishment of a new key, away from the tonic, is the main event of the exposition. In early sonata forms—by Scarlatti, Haydn, and others—the event could be marked by various devices: the repetition of the first theme in the new key, or a fresh invention, or a different musical behavior. The typical device in the nineteenth century is the establishment, together with the new key, of a new melody characterized as lyrical or singing in comparison to the opening tonic subject. For this feature, sonata form is indebted to the violinist Giovanni Battista Viotti, whose close association with opera prompted him to transcribe the Italian bel canto style, in contrast to the dazzling instrumental virtuosity, at a suitable spot in his opening concerto movements. The second theme of Beethoven's Violin Concerto, for example, shows the composer's clear awareness of the vocal origin.

CONCERT PROGRAMS

The cohesion of a true *multipartite is internal. The purely external occasion of presenting divers pieces as a whole can nevertheless be strongly unifying. Without such assumption, the problem of building a good concert program would not exist. In the absence of material connection among the various numbers of a program, the unifying process is located solely in the mind (cf. Multiplicity and Unity, pp. 39 ff.). The idea behind a good program is the creation of a total event out of a multitude of separate compositions—a "symphony" the length of the program.

The challenge lies in making the whole occasion a work of art in itself. Solutions reflect the creative abilities of the responsible person. Schumann speaks with admiration of Mendelssohn's idea to "compose a whole concert."[1] There is no formula for an ideal concert in the abstract, just as there is none for composing any successful multipartite. The morphological principles of growth and limitation; beginning, middle, and end; and multiplicity and unity all enter.

In general, one can distinguish between mechanical and imaginative solutions. The former kind—evidence of some, albeit helpless, concern—is fre-

---

[1]"Wie Mendelssohn einmal die Idee gehabt haben soll, ein ganzes Konzert zu komponieren mit Ouvertüre, Gesangstücken und anderem Zubehör (man kann die Idee getrost veröffentlichen zur Benutzung)." Schumann, *Gesammelte Schriften*, 1:479 f.

quently encountered in various forms. Adherence to chronology provides the least thoughtful semblance of order. How many voice recitals begin with "old-Italian" or "old-English" songs and, slowly wading through the nineteenth century, end with contemporary numbers! Geographic order often participates; for the chronologically arranged songs may, moreover, fall into the four predictable groups of Italian (very old), German (classical), French (impressionistic), and English (modern). Pianists almost inevitably place Bach at the beginning, Beethoven in the middle, and Bartók at the end, of their recital, whereby the pernicious alliteration of the names seems to add pseudomusical comfort. Equally mechanical are orchestra concerts held together by the same key and even by the same numerical identification of symphonies by different composers: the Second Symphonies by Beethoven and Brahms, both in D major, have become popular roommates. When preceded by one of Bach's orchestra Overtures in D major, the mechanical devices of unification by chronology, nationality, alliteration, key, and partly number join in triumph.

The unity of a program devoted to the works of one composer is partly mechanical, but educational and purely aesthetic considerations may prevail. All-Beethoven programs seem particularly well established, probably because the inherent dramatic juxtapositions convey some notions of morphology. Why are there so few all-Haydn or all-Mozart concerts? Is it because an opus by Haydn or Mozart is so clearly and audibly a finished whole that it cannot easily unite with others of its kind, whereas in general a work by Beethoven is not really rounded off at its conclusion and more readily propels toward another (cf. *Open-Closed)? One suspects the convenience with which Beethoven's sonatas, trios, quartets, and symphonies lend themselves to subscription series. Yet such events may become artistically unified if chronology and other mechanical factors do not predominate. In an ideal sense, there should be a musical structure, not only to a single evening, but to a series of season concerts.

Imaginative, rather than mechanical, solutions can best be elucidated by samples. On the whole, there is good sense to the plan of placing difficult, demanding pieces at the beginning, when attention is fresh, and playful, light pieces at the end. In this regard, the structures of a single symphony and of a whole program often follow the same norm. The first edition of Beethoven's Eroica Symphony carries, in the first-violin part, a comment of general validity: "This Symphony, being purposely written at greater length than usual, should be played nearer the beginning than the end of a concert, and shortly after an Overture, an Air, or a Concerto; lest, if it is heard too late, when the audience are fatigued by the previous pieces, it should lose its proper and intended effect." The word *effect* leaves a door open to program builders concerned primarily with the audience. Thus a modern editor of the many numbers that form Bach's *Musikalisches Opfer* places the six-voice ricercare at the end of the hour-long presentation, doubtless because of the modern finale effect of the impressive polyphonic fabric. Bach's version printed in his lifetime follows musical rather than external logic by rendering this piece right after the opening three-voice fugue, of which it was meant to be an artful improvement, and by ending the entire work with a brief, canonic bourrée in the wake of the "playful" trio sonata.

Any guiding principle can serve the constellation of a program, though in varying degrees. In the absence of a limiting principle, none of the following examples creates a real morphology, though each is held together by an idea. A famous pianist derived both unity and multiplicity from devoting an entire evening to fantasies ("Sonata quasi una fantasia," "Fantasia quasi una sonata," etc.). Different manifestations of the same musical idea can be profitably grouped. They may center on diverse utilizations of the same cantus firmus; or on arrangements of works by other composers (Brahms's settings of duets by Handel, Geminiani's orchestrations of sonatas by Corelli, Bach's adaptations of models by Vivaldi); or on various settings of identical or similar or related texts; etc. Among the subtlest such combinations are those of which the "theme" is purely musical: dissonances considered revolutionary in their day could well be pointed up by following, not preceding, a string quartet by Bartók with that in C major by Mozart.

CONSONANCE-DISSONANCE

Only the morphological implications concern us here, and not the various theories that try to explain a generally accepted and intelligible phenomenon (cf. *Intervals; *Triad). Whatever the reasons behind consonance and dissonance, they have been correctly identified with, respectively, rest and strain, relaxation and tension, blend and friction, simplicity and complexity, and even pleasure and discomfort. From all these and other descriptions, dissonance emerges as an element of growth, and consonance as one of limitation. Dissonance literally drives the "sounds apart" and thus initiates and maintains musical movement. Consonance brings the "sounds together" by reconciling them in the One. Thus understood, the unison is actually the only consonance, compared to which all other musical experiences are dissonances of varying strength. Hence the norm of *beginning and ending a composition with the unison—the former as a reference point of departure, the latter as a signal that all growth has ceased. The octave, by its very nature, partakes of consonance. Plato's assignment of the octave to a "cycle of barrenness" points to the same quality we have called "limiting."[1] Consonance does not produce.

All other tone relations, even the fifth, generate by virtue of the degree of dissonance inherent in them. To Plato, the fifth is the agent in a "cycle of bearing" which theoretically begets all tones of the scale and, in a wider sense, all possible tone combinations. Dissonance is the source of all growth and hence of all music. It is the split of the original cell, which our Discourse has stipulated (cf. pp. 21 ff.). It requires continuation toward the final limit set by the supreme consonance.

By extension of the unison concept, the triad shares the basic quality of consonance. In this role, the triad must be thought of, not as a mixture of three different pitches, but as a harmonic unity in its own right.

Consonance and dissonance each reveal two meanings which must be separated. They refer to the quality of a particular moment or situation but

---

[1] *Republic* viii. 546.

also to the function of this moment or situation in the larger context. The terms *consonance-dissonance* are exact only in the former sense. For the latter, the terms *static-dynamic* have often been suggested. While recognizing the need for the distinction, we do not subscribe to these terms; for no music is ever static, and the association with dynamics has been appropriated by loudness. Our alternative—a necessity in any case—is the concept pair *ontic-gignetic.

Consonance is usually ontic but it may be used gignetically. A major triad, for instance, symbolizes harmonic unity and normative consonance. Occurring as a dominant on a half cadence, however, it plays a gignetic role by demanding continuation and eventual resolution. Similarly, dissonance is usually gignetic. One need only add a seventh to the triad to experience the drive. Dissonance, however, may be used ontically. In the total sound of the beginning of "Les Augures Printaniers. Danses des Adolescentes" from *Le sacre du printemps* by Stravinsky, dissonant ingredients can be easily isolated; but in function, the sound is ontic, defining the limits of a given situation.

CONTEXT

When we single out a particular point as a center of observation, the notion of context arises from the relationship between the things or events observed. Choosing a viewpoint is a morphological act. Relations arrange themselves with respect to a center around which they form a more or less immediate environment according to the area coming under observation. The center—the viewpoint from which an individual or a group observes—and its environment influence each other mutually. Because of sheer weight, the influence of the environment on the individual is normally more evident than that of the individual on the environment—a bias further exaggerated by contemporary thinking.

Environment as just defined does not exhaust the notion of context. Something else enters that is not to be found in the interrelation of things or events, that transcends both center and environment, and that envelops both of them. It is a presiding thought, a unifying mood, or perhaps some other overall notion to the influence of which the interrelation of things and events finds itself subjected. We may call it "atmosphere." It is the most impalpable contextual factor, but its presence and influence can be demonstrated as readily as those of other elements that determine context. Always bearing in mind that context interprets facts, we may differentiate five levels on which, to one degree or another, context permeates morphological considerations.

(1) In *sensorial* perception, the modification of an element through varying contexts is common knowledge. The perception of a color is modified by the presence of neighboring colors; of a taste, by the accompanying food and drink; of a tone, by the surrounding tones. If a tone, say C, is heard first by itself and then together with C-sharp, the resulting natural dissonance is not only a new whole but also modifies the perception of the constituent elements so that both tones stand out more crudely than when sounded separately. The contrary happens when we hear an octave. Here the individuality of both tones is weakened; they tend to blend and "melt together" (Stumpf's *Klang-*

verschmelzung). Because no composition consists of a single event, we do not ever hear music out of any context. In Elliott Carter's Etude VII for Woodwind Quartet, in which the four instruments play nothing but *g*, the context is provided by varying qualities of timbre, dynamics, and rhythm.

(2)   Artistically much more significant than such purely physiological phenomena are those observed on the *psychological* and *spiritual* levels. The harshest dissonance by Bach is smoothed because logically introduced and resolved as the result of voice-leading. Play the same dissonance by itself, isolated from what precedes and follows it, and you will hardly recognize it as the same tone combination. Context explains why forbidden parallel octaves and fifths could creep into the works of masters who believed in avoiding them: they heard with their ears, not with their eyes. The following parallel progressions become inaudible because of, in the first case, figuration and, in the second case, coincidence of a resolution with an appoggiatura:[1]

Bach, *Mass*, "Laudamus te," 56.

Beethoven, Opus 106, I:243.

In the context of a style like Debussy's, on the other hand, which endeavors to utilize the particular quality of parallel fifths, our not noticing such a progression would entail an aesthetic loss.

To musical psychology belongs, among countless other examples, the manner in which in the last scene of *Falstaff* (between rehearsal numbers 28 and 29) we hear the same note F in the twelve different harmonizations given to the midnight bell by Verdi. These measures, moreover, may serve as an illustration of an instance in which the individual influences the environment: the persistence of one tone F, symbolizing the "individual," finally draws the environment back into its orbit. Actually every organ point functions in a similar manner, providing a fixed center above which all other musical events pass muster. In the widest sense, such is the role of the tonic in any long work such as an opera. The first *Figaro* finale, for example, which stands on E-flat, projects a striking complication when heard against the remembered observation point formed by the tonic D major. Context on this level (to give one more example) permits Berlioz in the "Tuba mirum" of his *Requiem* (mm. 7 ff.) to let the tone D-flat, introduced as the seventh of an E-flat major chord, prevail as the root of a D-flat major chord.

Instances of forceful reinterpretation of a given situation seem more frequent in the nineteenth century than at other times in which individual and society lived together in a greater degree of harmony or at least mutual understanding. The prevalence of the nineteenth century in this respect is generally

[1]For an admirable study of this question, see Brahms, *Oktaven und Quinten.*

due—but not always, as the Berlioz example shows—to the increasing independence of chromaticism, which finally dethroned tonality altogether. In
other periods, when the hierarchical (ontic) position of the scale tones is
stronger than the melodic (gignetic) power, conflict between environment
and individual is rare, for the latter submits to the former. Hence the psychological level of context is morphologically relatively unimportant in most
music of the Middle Ages.

(3)   *Topology*, the position of a musical entity within a whole, belongs
directly to the notion of context. Here we need only point to the different
possibilities of understanding a triad. The function of a triad is entirely determined by context: depending on where it stands, a major triad may be heard
as tonic, dominant, or subdominant.

(4)   On another level, we encounter phenomena such as the acquisition
of different *meanings* by the same passage (or by similar passages) in different
works. Beethoven used a simple contredanse theme for the finale of his heroic
symphony, not to mention further employment of the same theme in the
ballet music to *Prometheus* and the Eroica Variations for Piano. A striking
similitude in totally different works can be heard in the respective endings of
the first movement of Beethoven's Piano Sonata op. 111 and Chopin's Etude
op. 10 no. 12. The "Frère Jacques" theme conveys anything but a childish
meaning to the third movement of Mahler's First Symphony, which is built
on it. Meaning is often, though not necessarily, changed in parody Masses and
in Bach's diverse utilizations of the same or sometimes transcribed movement.
Musical quotations may preserve their original meaning, as when Hans Sachs
in the third act of *Die Meistersinger* describes the unhappy fate of old hus-
bands with young wives to the accompaniment of King Marke's music from
Tristan und Isolde. They may, however, change their meaning entirely. When
Alwa, in the backstage scene of Alban Berg's opera *Lulu* (mm. 1095 ff.) says of
the heroine, "Über die liesse sich freilich eine interessante Oper schreiben"
("One could certainly write an interesting opera about her"), the accompanying orchestra quotes the beginning of the same composer's earlier opera
Wozzeck. Unlike the *Tristan* quotation in the preceding example, this one has
no intrinsic significance apart from the "private joke."

A passage can also acquire various meanings according to the wide frame
of its context. The impact of Beethoven's Ode to Joy differs according to
whether it is heard as an isolated melody or a function of symphonic movement. When popular music picks up classical melodies, the context drags
them down into vulgarity even when no parody is intended.

(5)   On the highest level, as already suggested, context merges with the
concept of *atmosphere*. This is a powerful factor of unification, capable of
drawing together extreme contrasts by infusing them with an overall idea.
The fool in a tragedy by Shakespeare is not only, and not even primarily, a
contrast to his environment: we are unable, and not supposed, to delight in his
jests and wits as we would if the rest did not exist. In fact, he makes the tension
more painful and the gloom more tragic because what we know we superim-
pose on what he has to say. In music, any single movement of a tightly unified
multipartite may serve as illustration. In Schubert's essentially tragic song
cycles, there occur pieces that sound pretty innocent when heard out of con-

text, as is often the case in a song recital. When heard within the entire cycle, "Des Baches Wiegenlied" in *Die schöne Müllerin* or "Die Post" in *Winterreise* are heartrending.

Severe or even somber passages or parts may occur in an otherwise gay work; they are prevented from becoming actually tragic by the overall idea of the work. Almost every opera buffa or comic opera of the eighteenth century contained by popular demand a lamento aria. The contribution of the Countess, of Dorabella, and of Pamina to this literature does not turn either *Le nozze di Figaro, Così fan tutte,* or *Die Zauberflöte* into a tragic opera. Nor does the variation in the minor mode change the basic atmosphere of the slow movement of Haydn's "Surprise" Symphony.

Context affects every detail of a work. Morphology being the study of form, and form being the study of context within an individual entity, context plays an essential role in morphology.

COUNTERPOINT

Whereas harmony is a morphological force, and of the highest order, counterpoint is not. Counterpoint is a technique of writing, and it also denotes the product of the technique.

The technique is relevant to our purpose only insofar as the reasons behind the rules of counterpoint have morphological implications. Two considerations are fundamental: contrary motion and consonance. The primacy of these two conditions, overt in first species, is not at all challenged by modifications admitted in more complex situations. Both considerations serve the morphological task of unification and reconciliation amidst the contrapuntal drive for independence. The two melodic possibilities of "up" and "down" assert their simultaneous rights. The opposing motions in space join forces through contrapuntal relationship. Consonance defines this relationship by virtue of the hierarchy it projects. The ban on any dissonance in first species, for instance, issues from the consideration that the relations specified by passing or neighboring positions in subsequent species remain undefined when the two voices move simultaneously. The characteristic figure of the *nota cambiata* illustrates the essence of both fundamental conditions, for the balance of up and down is further illuminated by the alternation of consonance and dissonance.

The product of the technique begins a new life of its own as *melody and creates *polyphony. The only remaining morphological question pertains to the intensity gained by the addition of one or more counterpoints to a given melody. The intensification affects several levels. The most obvious is the mere increase of musical events. Listening to two or more distinct sound sources at the same time is a major accomplishment which man mastered relatively late after thousands of years without it. Subjective perception has a bearing on the musical morphé. One generally perceives a polyphonic web as a whole, that is, as a field produced by a play of forces, of motions. One can also voluntarily focus on one voice, whereby the others lose clarity by being adjusted to the general level of sharpness. The contrapuntal practice of differentiating the parts by rapidity of motion or by rhythm (think of almost any countersubject to a fugue theme by Bach) leads the ear to focus now on one and now on the other voice, sometimes in rapid succession. The question has been raised whether an additional counterpoint divides or doubles the hearer's attention. In the first case, the morphé remains intact. The increased musical movement is absorbed by the corresponding change in the hearer's attitude. In the second case, the tempo suggested by the composition will seem subjectively slowed down. Everybody can make the quick experiment of humming a familiar fugue theme by itself and then humming it again while imagining and pursuing a counterpoint against it. Considering that in a good performance the objective tempo remains constant, we can measure the contrapuntal intensification by our effort not to resist the impact of the double current.

Hearing several coherent conversations at the same time is chaotic if not impossible. What permits hearing several coherent melodies at the same time is their potential of mutual elucidation. A counterpoint to a given melody interprets the ontic and gignetic roles of every single tone as well as of the melodies as a whole. In the opening duet of Kyrie II from Josquin's *Missa Pange lingua* (cf. pp. 14), the positional roles of G and C, for instance, become clear in the course of their contrapuntal relationship; and the symmetry of the soprano line (3/4 3/8 4/8 5/8 || 5/8 4/8 3/8 3/4) is all the while challenged and simultaneously brought in relief by the progressive and supplementary rhythm of the alto (3/4| 3/8 4/8 5/8 6/8| 3/4). This kind of intensification is exclusively the product of counterpoint.

In all contrapuntal settings, the bicinium remains the governing force. Textures for more voices spell out what the inherent polarity of two voices already contains; for neither the character of up and down nor that of consonance and dissonance can be drastically changed. It can only be further clarified and intensified. Double counterpoint demonstrates the most specific case of intensification gained by the realization of a contrapuntal potential. At the octave, two voices invite two different solutions. At the tenth, the two voices yield two additional three-part settings. When the two voices, moreover, also constitute a double counterpoint at the octave, both inversions can be combined to produce a four-part setting. The contraction or inversion of the tenths into, respectively, thirds and sixths opens the possibility for further combinations. Double counterpoint at the twelfth, besides admitting similar possibilities, furthermore involves a change of key.

Counterpoint, properly understood, deals with principles of general and lasting validity rather than with the idiom of a particular style.

CYCLE

The Greek word *kyklos* means 'wheel' or 'circle'. The image evokes the notion of return to a starting point, hence of recurrence. In time—the realm of music—nothing can ever turn back to a beginning. A moving wheel becomes a cycloid. The musical use of the term *cycle* would be possible if precisely related to the inherent notions. In practice, however, improper application has done more harm than good by creating confusion instead of separating principles. Thus there is nothing "cyclic" about any of the examples given under this entry in the *Harvard Dictionary of Music*. A musical form including several movements (sonata, suite, cantata, etc.) is not a cycle but should be called a *multipartite. A composition utilizing the same material in different movements (Masses built on a cantus firmus, Schubert's Wanderer-Fantasie, Berlioz's *Symphonie fantastique*, etc.) shows thereby concern for unity but does not ever retrieve its starting point. Nor should a brief quotation (Beethoven's Ninth Symphony, several of Bruckner's, etc.) be confused with a morphologically meaningful recurrence. A song cycle, like Schubert's *Die schöne Müllerin*, is a series of songs of which neither the music nor the underlying plot admits of a "turning back."

A fundamental and systematic nomenclature embraces not only existing, but also possible, forms. Cyclic quality characterizes all those structures determined by the idea of return or recurrence. The operative technical terms are ritornello and recapitulation. Here belong the various phenomenalizations of *bowform, *sonata form, and symmetrical (that is, centered) *rondos.

DANCE MUSIC

People dance on two legs. Hence the basic morphological orientation of dance music is binary. Duple meter prevails fundamentally in the small unit of a left-right phrase and imposes itself upon the larger unit of a complete dance figure and its answer. The medieval *ductia* and *stantipes* illustrate the point by balancing an even number of beats leading to an open ending by its duplication leading to a closed ending. In stylized form, antecedent and consequent in music of the eighteenth and nineteenth centuries demonstrate the same phenomenon. The participation of both sexes in a dance—be it as a separate couple or as the components of a larger group—intensifies the binary principle. The aesthetic satisfaction gained from an American square dance is closely related to the obvious exclusive rule of this principle: four couples on sixteen legs bring to life the four sides of a square in musical units strictly built on powers, or at least multiples, of 2.

Goethe has said that all music lies between the poles of dance and religion. The polarity can be traced, both historically and theoretically, through many features. Dance music is instrumental, kinetic, metrical. Religious music is vocal, pneumatic, rhythmical. Morphologically relevant is the recognition that the binary organization of dance music stands against the spiritual organization of the *tempus perfectum*. Just as the Trinity symbolizes cosmic perfection, so the one-two of dance befits earthly shuffling. The secularization of all activities brought about by the Renaissance bestowed upon dance music a new legitimacy which soon led to the subjugation of many unrelated musical forms under its somewhat mechanical step. The primacy of triple meter yielded to that of duple meter: unlike medieval man, we take *alla breve* for granted and react to a third beat in a measure as an extra. The dot after a note reflects this attitude in our notation. The double bar in the middle of a composition appeared first in dance movements of which both halves have to be repeated. Every movement in every baroque dance suite up to Bach testifies to this orientation. Soon, however, this double bar dictated the form of early sonatas—Scarlatti's, for instance—and maintained its morphological power long after the sonata form had overcome its indebtedness both to dance and the binary principle (see, as one example of many, the first movement of Mozart's Piano Sonata in A minor in which not only the exposition but also the now much longer development and recapitulation sections together are surrounded by repeat signs).

The musical tendency toward ternary structure, clearly observable in the history of *sonata form, asserts itself in the very territory of dance itself. Just as the secular force of binary meter eventually invades all music, so the spiritual force of triple meter influences dance music early and apparently everywhere. Wilhelm Fischer has established the existence of an *Urpaar*, an archetypal pair, in the morphology of the dances of most European societies.[1] It consists characteristically of a dance in duple time followed by a faster variation of the same dance in triple time. The structure of Fischer's pair is always the same, whether we know it in France as *Branle simple* and *Branle double* or *Allemande* and *Courante*, or in Germany as *Dantz* and *Nachdantz* or *Reigen* and *Hupfauf*, or in Italy as *Pavane* and *Galliarde*. Even in the late stylization of such dances by Bach, allemande and courante always follow each other without interruption—a stately duple meter relieved by a fast triple meter. Morphologically interesting is the appearance of triple meter as a variation of duple, everything else in the music originally remaining constant. For the dancer, this variation necessitates his adjusting two legs to three beats. To do so, he must hop ("Hupfauf"), and the psychological result is increased excitement—a desirable development on the dance floor. This aura of something special attaches to all dances in triple meter—the lascivious Spanish sarabande of the fifteenth and sixteenth centuries, the sophisticated French minuet, the wild polonaise, the Viennese waltz. Minuet and polonaise succeeded in imparting this ternary force to the whole form by inserting a contrasting trio between initial statement and its recapitulation. More significant, however, is the eventual succumbing of dances in triple meter, such as the waltz, to the primeval binary force of left-right. In the present century, the waltz has been danced often with one step to the measure, not three, so that the original duple organization (like the jungle retrieving the formerly cultivated farm) supplies by regular eight-measure phrases the morphological experience. Young people in 1982 report that triple meter has disappeared altogether from the dance floor and that all music there is binary.

In all periods, dance music shows the tendency to form series. The organization is initially loose, motivated by the dancers' desire for continuation rather than by morphological principles. Thus the medieval *ductia* and *stantipes* extend to any number of *puncti*, and later dances in the Renaissance and baroque periods readily string themselves into suites. In the contemporary ballroom or nightclub, the band traditionally plays a group of different dances in a row before allowing a respite. Against this apparently unrestrained and uncontrolled growing process, a limiting morphological force

[1]See his chapter on "Instrumentalmusik von 1450–1600" in Adler, *Handbuch*, particularly pp. 351–53.

often asserts itself to produce the best examples of the species. The gigue need not be the finale of a suite (in Bach's Second Orchestra Suite, for example, it is not) but it assumes that place and is soon understood as indicator of the end. Johann Strauss, writing waltz sequences in the home of sonata form, elevates the loosely organized entertainment by a creditable and delimiting recapitulation.

Dance music, in whatever period, seems to pass through three morphologically distinct phases. First, any dance is simply popular amusement. The music is danced by the people. Second, if it gains favor, it is adopted by society and becomes refined. The main characteristics remain recognizable, but the movements are gentler, the tempo usually slower, and the accents (pumps replacing boots) less bouncing. Third, if the dance endures, it becomes stylized in the hands of serious composers. The music is no longer danced but listened to. The original function of the piece becomes submerged in purely musical demands.

Not every dance survives all three stages, but existing samples are plentiful. The sarabande was a fast, lascivious dance in sixteenth-century Spain. It became respectable and slow in the seventeenth century. A Bach sarabande for unaccompanied violoncello is idealized beyond any recognizable connection with a dance step. The *Ländler* betrays its rustic origin by its name. In mellowed form, it was danced as waltz in the most refined salons of the nineteenth century. Waltzes by Chopin, Brahms, or Ravel are completely removed from the dance floor. Significantly, many New York nightclubs, appealing to a sophisticated clientele, advertise today that they offer "music but no dancing."

The polarity of dance and religion permits a historic speculation. As all life became secularized as a result of the Renaissance, so dance music, in the widest sense, replaced religious music. The rise of instrumental music in the last four hundred years, with the concomitant metrical mechanization, is one very clear symptom of the general decline of religion. When the philosopher Rudolf Pannwitz subtitled a book, published between the two World Wars, "The Rebirth of Vocal Music through the Spirit," he thereby prognosticated man's return to religion.[1] Dance music helps a musician hear these sociological trends.

DEVELOPMENT

The gignetic implications of the term are obvious. In music, they refer to a process associated primarily with the middle section of a sonata form. The dramatic tendency of sonata form is undeniable, but the suggestion that something has to be developed in a certain place is unfortunate, in both the literal and conventional understanding of the word.

Literally, a development section should unwrap, reveal something. Conventionally, it should manifest a process of growth or evolution. The average listener's expectation of a development section in a sonata form is influenced,

---

[1]Pannwitz, *Kosmos Atheos*.

if not formed, by the promised meaning. He is misled, for there are very many such sections that neither unwrap nor evolve. Haydn, Mozart, and Beethoven would not understand the word, for (like the more appropriate German *Durchführung*) it was introduced after they were dead by well-meaning but—in the spirit of their century—gignetically oriented conservatory professors.[1] To the classic masters, the section between exposition and recapitulation was known as the middle section.

This correct name explains both the morphological origin and function. A middle section came into its own right as part of the da capo *aria—the most popular piece of music for most of the seventeenth and eighteenth centuries. The influence of vocal on instrumental musical forms, obvious throughout the Renaissance, continued to assert itself here, even if the path from an easy entertainment number to an abstract instrumental structure seems tortuous. The same influence is more directly audible in many slow movements of sonatas and symphonies, which are fundamentally instrumental aria-transcriptions. The middle section in all these cases at the least separates the main part from its literal repeat, and at its best modulates back to the abandoned tonic. In no case is there any need for developing anything.

In this respect, the German term *Durchführung* (of which development is a miscarried translation) is not incorrect, for all it announces is a "leading through" from one main section to another or from one key to another. But because *Durchführung* had earlier designated any fugue section (except the opening exposition) in which the subject appeared by itself or in imitation, the modern German association is not far removed from the English *development*. The word presupposes that a theme, be it the first or the second, appear in imitation, that it be used, that it be broken up into its elementary fragments. This technique is obviously of polyphonic origin. Transplanted to the homophonic field of a rococo sonata, the old polyphony assumes a fresh behavior. The "new manner" that Haydn attributed to his String Quartets op. 33 is probably the synthesis of the two given eighteenth-century textures. Classical polyphony—on a different level from Bach's—holds its own particularly amidst the dramatism of sonata form. The dramatic development section, by its natural appeal and on the strength of such examples as Mozart's "Jupiter" Symphony or Beethoven's Ninth, was subsequently interpreted to represent all such sections. In this light, the introduction of a new theme in the middle of the first movement of the Eroica Symphony (mm. 284 ff.) is not so much a startling innovation as an atavism. Parallel to the dramatic type, there exist countless classical development sections in which the theme is not developed even in the conventional sense of utilization and fragmentation and which are really only modulatory middle sections.

True to their dramatic tendency, many sonata forms demonstrate the idea of development. In classical compositions, however, the sections that do so are, more likely than not, the recapitulation and coda. Haydn and Beethoven in particular often present the main theme at its first appearance in a manner that makes it sound incomplete and, in the literal sense, underdeveloped. The complete unfolding of the theme is withheld—and continuous dramatic in-

[1]Mainly in Leipzig and München. Cf. the textbooks by Moritz Hauptmann, Adolf Bernhard Marx, etc.

130

terest thus assured—until a statement late in the recapitulation or even coda. The development of the theme toward melodic and harmonic fulfillment becomes the final function of the sonata movement after the tonic has been definitely retrieved. A characteristic example of this common technique is offered by the first movement of Haydn's "Surprise" Symphony. From the beginning, the first theme appears fragmentary and interrupted. Only very late in the recapitulation do we hear it fully developed, and the second theme reveals itself at that moment as the necessary completion of the first theme in the process of melodic growth. Only here "the motive is . . . ready and able to develop into a complete musical thought."[1] The middle section of this movement does not "develop" at all. If anything, it delays the final "unwrapping."

This technique of putting a theme together before our ears—a real development technique—was readily extended by Gustav Mahler. His gradual unfolding of the thematic material usually occurs in the section between exposition and recapitulation, which in his symphonies actually begins to deserve the title "development section."

DIALECTICS

The idea of a conversation or discourse shines through the various meanings agglutinated in the course of time to the basic word *diálectos*. Today we hardly associate dialectics with light conversation, a play of questions and answers, although the origin of the word warrants such a use. Dialectics no longer refers to just any conversation but rather to one undertaken with a serious purpose in mind. It has come to mean disputation, discussion, argument rather than simple discourse. A connotation of dramatism (see *Lyric-Dramatic) is inevitable because the process itself is dramatic, not in the sense of external but of internal action.

The purpose of dialectical process is to reach a higher state of being. The process often takes the form of a syllogism by synthesizing opposites in a higher concept, but it may also achieve that higher state through idiogenetic arguments. The latter, very fertile kind of discussion was on the mind of the man who said, "I can only argue with somebody who is of my own opinion." Like all grand principles, dialectics can assume many different forms that are in turn based on archetypes. In logic, the confrontation of statement and counterstatement is a common example. In music, these forms become persuasive by virtue of the inherent adequacy of the substance.

In the following consideration of some outstanding musical forms of dialectics, the first three are based on heterogenesis, the next two on idiogenesis, and the remainder on the united contribution of both.

(1) The three-step *cadence* subdominant-dominant-tonic is an obvious musical reflection of the type of syllogism associated with Fichte. The postulated "common characteristic" is T, implied in both S and D. For S and D, any chord or group of chords may be substituted so that all tonal music appears to

---

[1]Marco, "Musical Task." The article gives a detailed and very persuasive analysis of the whole movement and thereby elucidates the technique we are describing.

be based on a dialectic process. The largest tonal composition can be understood as an expansion of the underlying cadence.

(2) *Barform* manifests the same principle. Whereas cadence is a rather abstract pattern, barform is an actual shape; for its constituents, smaller or larger units, possess extension by definition. The Pindaric ode, consisting of strophe, antistrophe, and epode, is the classic example. In both cadence and barform, the third term has always the tendency to be understood as conclusion. But whereas in a cadence it is clearly implied in the preceding two terms, in a barform the synthesizing character of the epode must be sought in equivalence. The external balance of the epode against the combined strophes is furthered by its topologic advantage and by new substance.

(3) *Cantus firmus* may initiate heterogenic dialectics under circumstances that are best illustrated by the opening number of Bach's *Passion According to St. Matthew*. The double chorus and orchestra that carry the main movement are self-sufficient. One hears them alone at the beginning and end, and one follows their unfolding throughout. The melodic substance is independent of the superimposed cantus firmus. Yet the joint discourse of the two unlike elements achieves a synthesis much higher than summation.

Cantus firmus is not necessarily a partner in dialectics. As a backbone in a Netherlands motet it serves a delimiting function. In compositions where it supplies melodic substance to the other voices, it becomes part of the general imitative process.

(4) Idiogenetic dialectics characterizes the *fugue with a single theme*. Here there are no antitheses, no antinomies, no syntheses. The subject is One. A state is created. The evolution bears on the state which it causes to change by means of autodialectics.[1] The overall form resulting from the changes is indetermined, individual. The episodes are moments of repose. Counterpoints to the theme are not really opposites or conflicting outside forces; even their melodic substance, in which they differ from the theme, is controlled by it.

(5) *Imitation* is fugal technique in more general situations. In a circular canon, there exists, of course, one state only: it is ontic absolutely. In a continuous, or noncircular, canon, imitation is more a matter of texture than of dialectics where a definite "subject" is called for. Other applications of imitative technique, such as short imitative sections within longer movements, do partake of fugal essence but are commonly removed from its dialectic overall purpose and effect. In their more playful instances, they approach the original "conversational" meaning of the word *dialectics*.

(6) *Fugues with more than one subject* unite both idiogenetic and heterogenetic dialectics. The emergence of dramatism is unmistakable; it arises from the symbolism of personification suggested by the participation of two or more "subjects." The dramatic contraposition is particularly strong in those double fugues where both subjects are introduced simultaneously, whereas in double, triple, and quadruple fugues in which the subjects are developed separately to be united later, the strophic-syllogistic character is more in evidence.

(7) *Antiphonal* structures may be either idiogenetic or heterogenetic,

---

[1]In this sense, Goethe commented on organ music by Bach: "As if eternal harmony were speaking to itself." (Letter to Zelter, 21 June 1827.)

depending on the particular case. In his *Confessions* (ix. 7), St. Augustine describes an early instance in Western music. When St. Ambrose, bishop of Milan in the fourth century, found himself and his community besieged in the basilica by imperial military forces, he kept his flock awake and spirited by a musical game. "After the manner of the Eastern Churches," the people were divided in two groups and sang hymns and psalms antiphonally, that is, alternately on the same melody for each pair of verses. Later Gregorian antiphonal practices eventuated structures of varied complexity, from the framing of a psalm tone by a soloistic short antiphon of different substance to the insertion of a new textual and melodic phrase after each two verses. In all cases, the new form is the result exclusively of dialectics, be it in appearance a simple bowform or an intricate rondo with refrains. Alternation between soloist and chorus intensifies the discourse. A characteristic example is the responsorium "Libera me."[1] The full melody begins and ends the piece, each time initiated by a soloist. The refrain-like responses between the verses successively shorten this melody from the beginning.

(8)   Dialectic procedure underlies all *concertos* and defines the morphological principle, whatever the particular form and style. Both idiogenesis and heterogenesis may be involved. The former seems to prevail in concertos for several instruments, in which the same material is worked out by different timbres; the latter, in the typical nineteenth-century piece, which pitches the extreme capabilities of the soloist against the accompanying orchestra.

(9)   Because *opera* is by definition dramatic, dialectics appears as a necessary ingredient without always supplying the musically formative force. It does so, however, in a noteworthy special case, namely, the duet between two lovers who begin with individually distinct and separate musical statements and end up in unison or at least some parallel motion. The formative principle is really the abandonment of heterogenetic dialectics in favor of idiogenetic; the gain is characterization not achievable by other means. When in the opening number of Mozart's *Le nozze di Figaro* the music associated with Figaro disappears halfway through the composition and he joins Susanna's music in parallel lower tenths, one senses immediately their entire future relationship in which Susanna remains superior. This kind of musical characterization is explainable by dialectics alone and not by reference to the more obvious switch from a strophic to a rondo form. Verdi operas abound in this technique.

(10)   Both idiogenetic and heterogenetic dialectics may also be present in the Beethoven type of symphonic *development*, but actually the former outweighs the latter. More often the "second theme" remains outside the dialectical process. The element governing sonata form is harmony, anyway, rather than melody. The character of idiogenesis is here very different from the one exhibited in fugue. Despite the frequent absence of antithetical melodic material and a consequent lack of the syllogistic factor, development sections in nineteenth-century sonata forms give, not so much a succession of states, but rather an impression of strife and struggle. To understand how dramatism can grow out of idiogenetic dialectics, one has to shift the symbolism of the missing antinomy in this case to the composer himself, and consequently also to

[1]Sung at Exequies, *Liber usualis*, p. 1767.

the listener, as the hidden bearer of the antithesis. One term of the dialectic process remains unexpressed. The strife is not between musical elements but between the composer and the music, which in this case is so to speak only half of the total event. Herein lies the real meaning of the often felt but not always correctly interpreted "subjectivity" of Beethoven as compared to the "objectivity" of Bach. The not entirely explicit statement, the required participation of the listener, is a typically romantic symptom, to which analogies can be found in all the arts. In music, it exemplifies *musica musicata* rather than **musica musicans*.

(11) The lonely phenomenon of *Anton Bruckner* foreshadows a possible new association of dialectics with the strophic principle. The general trend of symphonic music after Beethoven was toward equivalence with the contemporary operatic development. Bruckner's dialectics are not based on syllogisms and conflict but rather, allied to the idea of a succession of states, on dramatism that arises from a series of "terraces." This technique was somewhat anticipated by Schubert, whose musical substance did not bear his attempt to be like Beethoven. His strophic arrangement of sections within a sonata form hardly ever exceeds juxtaposition. Bruckner's strophes within a symphony traverse states of being. The former misappreciation of his symphonies is doubtless due to the misplaced application of Beethoven's symphonic principles as criteria. Bruckner's symphonic dialectics are his own.

DIMINUTION-AUGMENTATION. See AUGMENTATION-DIMINUTION

DISSONANCE-CONSONANCE. See CONSONANCE-DISSONANCE

DOMINANTS

Although in common usage the dominant identifies the chord on the fifth degree of a diatonic major or minor scale, we shall use the term in its double role as either an upper or under dominant. We can continue to call the latter "subdominant" provided the prefix "sub" is understood as a designation not of something inferior but only of something that happens to point in a direction opposite to that of the dominant proper. Because dominant and subdominant are polar forces around the tonic, they can be jointly thought of as dominants, the subdominant being the counterdominant in our tellurian thought system that, earthbound, always seems to favor up over down, or one side of almost any *polarity over the other.

The genesis of dominant and subdominant demonstrates their morphological equivalence and supreme significance. They result from the application to a given pitch of the ratio 3 in symmetrical operations. Whether one thinks in terms of frequency or string length, multiplication and division of a given unit by 3 produce the two dominants a perfect fifth on either side of it.[1]

The operation is a morphological act of paramount consequences for

[1]For more about this fact, see the authors' *Tone*.

music. The one simpler operation of multiplication and division by 2 produces the octave in either direction. The octave sets the musical frame, but the frame remains empty. Musical life has not yet begun, for any further operations with 2 merely repeat the same tone in different octave ranges. The situation changes completely by the operation with 3, for the two dominants provide the minimum conditions for a pronounced musical morphology. By pursuing the generation of ever new dominants in both directions (the basis for our cycle of fifths), one lays the foundation for the creation of tone systems. Brought within the same octave range, upper and lower dominants (the dominant and its counterdominant) define the fixed tones around which a musical life may now develop.

The dominant (and by implication this term always includes the subdominant) occurs in the music of all civilizations and all periods. Greek theory provides a most articulate illustration. Within the octave frame, the two dominants occupy the immovable points, whatever the mode or genus. The other pitches have to arrange themselves. The semitones shift. Variants arise. But all authentic and plagal modes and all their diatonic, chromatic, and enharmonic variants take their shape from relating to the fixed dominant tones. (The Gregorian Lydian mode is only apparently a small exception: the upper dominant is intact, and the position of the lower dominant as an augmented fourth has either kept Lydian removed from practical use or modified Lydian by lowering the fourth to a legitimate subdominant place.)

In modern Western harmony, dominant and subdominant are the two polar forces which act upon the tonic. Said differently, any tension the tonic suffers is either dominant or subdominant. All other chords, practically used and theoretically possible, are functions of one or the other.

The polar genesis of the two dominants explains why the upper dominant is basically major, and the subdominant minor:

These inherent qualities are so strong that the minor mode has customarily borrowed the major dominant ("harmonic" minor); and the major mode, the minor subdominant (A-flat in C major). The diminished seventh chord, in which this last tone characteristically appears, gathers its peculiar ambivalence and strength by equally combining elements of both dominants:

The polar function toward the tonic is intensified by harmonic extension of either dominant:

The resulting cadence is the most forceful, complete expression of the dominants in classical tonality:

T or t   s6   D   7   T or t

The nature of the dominants determines the fundamental law of harmonic behavior: Every major triad has the tendency to act as a dominant. Every minor triad has the tendency to act as a subdominant. From this law spring all rules concerning movement and resolution of chords.

The main functions help define the other triads on the tones of the diatonic major and minor scales. The "relative" chords are substitutes (C-a, F-d, G-e; c-E♭, f-A♭, g-B♭). The diminished triads are fragmented dominants. The second dominant, one notes with interest, has a subdominant function; for it shares with the subdominant the drive toward the dominant and, with one chromatic variant, all constituent tones:

S   (D) D   D

The analogous situation on the other side of the tonic can be symmetrically developed. It may seem less familiar an experience only because of the tellurian ambivalence of the subdominant in the *polarity of dominants. The second subdominant assumes an upper-dominant function in its closeness to the various forms of the augmented sixth chords (German, Italian, and French):

(s) s   D   T or t

This interpretation of second dominants resolves—to give one example—an old argument surrounding the "Tristan" chord. With full recognition of g-sharp as an appoggiatura, Ernst Kurth considers f a melodic lowering of f-sharp and takes d-sharp at its face value.[1] Alfred Lorenz, on the other hand, hears d-sharp as a melodically raised d and accepts f as a basic chord tone.[2] Here are the two possibilities:

---

[1]*Romantische Harmonik*, pp. 42 ff.
[2]*Tristan*, p. 195.

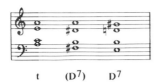

Kurth's emerges as a second dominant with a lowered fifth; Lorenz's, as a complete subdominant (that is, with *sixte ajoutée*) with a raised root. We can reconcile the two interpretations by understanding the inherent subdominant function of either. Leading toward the clearly spelled-out upper dominant of the assumed tonic A minor, the "Tristan" chord represents in both cases the subdominant in a complete tonic-subdominant-dominant statement.

The primary tendencies of the major and minor triads, that is, of the upper and lower dominants, create two currents in opposite directions. Whereas one current strives toward the cadence on a central tone—the dominant from above, and the subdominant from below—the other leads away from it. The two currents thus appear as centripetal and centrifugal. The first includes the expanding series of major dominants and minor subdominants. The latter includes the contracting series of minor dominants and major subdominants. We thus distinguish between (1) primary centripetal functions (major triads of the major zone; minor triads of the minor zone) and (2) secondary centrifugal functions (major triads of the minor zone; minor triads of the major zone). The following table, with C major and minor at the intersection of four roads, illustrates the tendencies:

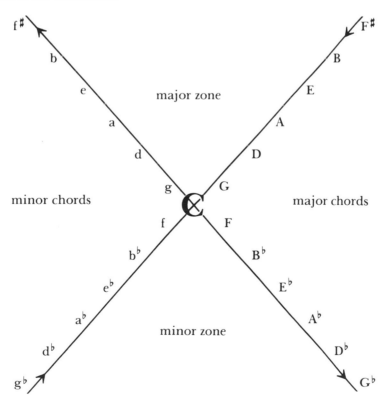

Two roads proceed toward C, the two others lead away from it. The former normally "fall" in a series of cadences; the latter, in contrary motion, give the impression, not of falling, but of expending energy to maintain motion.

DRAMATIC-LYRIC. See **LYRIC-DRAMATIC**

DYNAMICS. See **LOUDNESS**

ECHO

In Greek mythology, which almost always projects a general truth, Echo was the name of a nymph. For having distracted Hera with long stories during one of Zeus's escapades, she was punished by losing her voice except for foolish repetition of somebody else's shout. Later Echo pined away in love for Narcissus until only her voice remained. She had a daughter with Pan, Iynx, who was turned into a wryneck, also as punishment by Hera for assisting Zeus in another love affair.

In music, echo behaves like the unhappy nymph. It has no body of its own; it is "voice only, for the bones are turned to stone." There is no independent structure to musical echo. It "likes to chatter but has no power of speech."[1] The creative power of echo, like the nymph's property as well as progeny, twists backward. Behind all lies the recurrent notion of a shortcoming imposed by outside force. Echo, in fact, may frequently sound a bit unmusical; for the mechanical, lifeless quality prevails. Compared to the model, it is by its very function incomplete and softer. These weaknesses can be turned into virtues by a composer's wit. Orazio Vecchi's "Giustiniana. Dialogo in Echo" for six voices, for example, gains some kind of continuation by echo cadences that change *rumori* into *mori*, *nascosto* into *osto*, *ostaria* into *ria*, *pizzoni* into *zoni*, *impara* into *ara*, and finally *becco* into *echo*.[2] (When Narcissus rejects Echo by crying, "I would die before I give you a chance at me," she answers, "I give you a chance at me.") The necessarily reduced dynamics may help create a feeling of space perspective.

In essence, however, musical echo functions as a *fermata. It stops the movement. The morphological accomplishment is restricted to reiteration of the last sound held in our ears. Nothing advances.

*Repetition, of which echo is a particular form, normally is the basic and strongest manifestation of *idiogenesis. The "punishment" afflicting echo deprives it of original productivity and forces its sole and violently, that is, mechanically, begotten offspring Iynx to look backward. The inherent incompleteness distinguishes echo from all other kinds of musical repetition. *Imitation of one voice by another in a Franco-Flemish motet is significant; truncated reiteration of the last few notes is not. The inevitable brevity of echo furthermore limits the fertility.

[1]Ovid *Metamorphoses* iii. 341–401.
[2]*Convito Musicale*, pp. 199–207.

*Canon may be a borderline case. The echo is continuous and hence, though generally softer, not shorter. On one side of this "threshold" condition, canon may contribute to structure. On the other side, it seldom fails to sound mechanical rather than alive. Anybody who has persisted in pursuing a canon knows the experience, even after initial pleasure, of eventual "boneless" sterility.

Completeness and intensification, rather than fragmentation and weakening, remove most antiphonal and responsorial singing from the category of echo. Polychoral structures by Schütz, for example, usually give equal weight to identical successive statements by opposing groups. The dynamic effect is that of increased intensity. When softer echoes are prescribed, they deliberately serve to enhance the feeling of space necessary for such pieces. Gregorian responses, such as the many "Benedicamus Domino. Deo gratias" formulas, also separate themselves from mere echo—apart from utilizing new words— by being musically complete, sufficiently long, and dynamically increased by the congregation response following the solo intonation.

EIDOS. See **AESTHETIC STANDARDS**

END

The end of a piece sometimes produces the impression of being a bit arbitrary. Although, in a different manner, the *beginning is equally arbitrary, there is a fundamental distinction which parallels the dissimilar attitudes we adopt toward birth and death. The former is usually evaluated positively, the latter negatively. Moreover, the instinctive postulate of the permanence of existing things, myopic as it may be, asserts itself immediately after a birth, a debut, a beginning. A reflex and symbol of eternity, permanence appears to us as a normal thing. The end, however, the thought of turning into nothingness, we keep at a distance by contravening it with countless turns of our mental faculties. Yet one must not forget the absolute interdependence of beginning and end. Without end, no beginning.

The lack of stringent necessity for an end to the musical work is justified by the inherent, never-exhausted potential. Expressions like "piece" (or *pièce* or *Stück*) reflect this condition by suggesting that one work is basically only a fragment, a piece of music. This conception is common to all temporal arts. To Paul Valéry, the flowing life of the work in the course of gestation and elaboration had almost more reality, and certainly more interest, than the product, the object, which he always considered essentially unfinished. Upon completing a work, many a writer or composer has experienced the sentiment that a finished work is an abandoned work. This sentiment slides into the predominant sensation of satisfaction and liberation under the aspect of doubt or regret. This rather curious experience, which has hardly attracted the attention of theorists, is worth considering because it reflects a particular manifestation of the grand principle of polarity. To the concept of definitive fixation of an art work is opposed that of continual production, of variations and changes in process which remain always possible. To the final form symbolized by the image of the crystal—the external expression of a definite internal structure—is opposed the fluidity containing a thousand modes of potential incarnation. Discontinuity is opposed by continuity, the definite by the indefinite.

The study of discontinued, definite phenomena is called morphology, the study of forms. These attributes do not negate their opposites, for we deal with a relation of polarity and not of mutual exclusion. Without continuity, without the indefinite, their counterparts would not exist. Continuity includes all that nourishes the life of forms. The indefinite engenders the definite. Because the indefinite generally appears under a menacing aspect—chaotic and uncontained—art raises barriers against it. The definite can thus be conceived as a piece cut from the indefinite. This thought renders to the term *piece* all its significance. The cut determines beginning and end.

The prevalence of one or the other pole helps determine the style of a work of art, be it that of a single author or an epoch. The acute sensation of the indefinite prompted Valéry to bridle it in his poems by singularly firm restraints on form. In his prose writings, on the other hand, which he considered more a means of communication than a work of art, he yielded readily to the attraction of the other pole. The rigor of his thought notwithstanding, they often give us the impression of the unfinished. The variable proposition of the two factors as an element of style lies behind the notion of *open and closed forms.

In literature and the visual arts, the material employed—there words, here wood or stone, pencil or color—is inert and adapts itself indifferently to both types of form. The situation is not the same in music. The separate elements of meter, rhythm, melody, and harmony each seem to reveal a kind of natural preference for one or the other pole. Meter, rhythm, and above all metricized rhythm tend by themselves toward the formation of well-defined entities. One can predict in most cases when a phrase of eight or sixteen measures, regardless of the particular contents, will end. The reason lies probably in the closeness of *rhythm and meter to our physical nature. This orientation is reversed in the case of melody and harmony. When not subordinate to either meter or harmony, melody tends toward fluidity and continuity. Harmony in any case, is oriented toward the indefinite, for every chord calls for an implied resolution. A major chord has the tendency to function as a dominant and hence to move downward in the cycle of fifths. A minor chord has the tendency to function as a subdominant and hence to move upward in the cycle of fifths. The composer's will exercising itself thus encounters unequal resistance from the diverse musical elements. His decision will lie between following the released musical forces and bending one or the other musical factor to his artistic purpose.

These distinctions, which are not to be taken too literally, help one understand better certain properties of a style. Think of the end of a Beethoven symphony. The whole energy of classic tonality allied to that of meter was necessary to tame the propelling force of harmony. Because this force by definition inheres as a potential in every triad, not even the final chord is entirely at rest. In the terminal cadences of the high period of triadic tonality, the energetic character, the forceful dynamics, and the insistent reiterations that often form a chain are all means aimed at reducing the generative power of the perfect triad, isolating the "piece" from the indefinite, and affirming the end of the movement. Metric regularities contribute. The almost exaggeratedly exact allotment of 124 measures each for exposition, development section, recapitulation, and coda in the first movement of Beethoven's Fifth Symphony makes the end predictable.

In earlier periods, the potential of a piece remains open to continued development. Plainchant is universally recognized as the purest flowering in occidental music of the melodic element. It is free of metric and harmonic drives. Nobody would think of criticizing plainchant melodies for lack of form; and yet they conserve the fluid character, the faculty evocative of the infinite, that comports so well with their source and spiritual aims. The same style characteristic holds for the polyphony issued from Gregorian monody. The end of a Franco-Flemish motet is therefore often predetermined by auxiliary devices, among which the underlying text or an underlying cantus firmus are the most obvious. Subtler but at least as effective is the reliance on what we may call a "geometric" design. The exact measurements and proportions in the polyphonic pieces by Obrecht have been recently uncovered and described.[1] The last tactus appears theoretically and practically fixed in space and time without prior concern for the flowing contents of the preceding movement. Bach's Goldberg Variations, too, terminate only because the preconceived and arbitrary chain design of ten-times-three variations has run its course. As a signal of the interruption, the strict canon expected in the design at the end of each group is relieved by a carefree quodlibet.

Although a good composition will always present a balance between the two poles, all arts in the present century show a general tendency favoring process over form, fluidity over crystallization, the indefinite over the definite. A comparison of old and modern dance music clearly reveals the contrast. The dances of the seventeenth and eighteenth centuries, and still the later waltz, present well-defined crystal forms. Jazz and rock, on the other hand, apart from often beginning in an ill-defined way, never have an end. A modern dance does not finish: it interrupts itself. Instead of employing the formative power of meter, jazz ignores it by turning meter into a metronome by means of incessant repetitions of a beat. Along the same line, though on a more sophisticated level, is Josef Matthias Hauer's conception of pure melos as repetition without end of the series of twelve tempered tones. For this general trend toward the infinite, Wagner's "infinite melody" supplied an earlier model.

Similar symptoms characterize literature and architecture. The technical term *roman-fleuve* (a "flowing novel" to be continued ad libitum, like Galsworthy's *A Forsyte Saga*) reveals more to us now than it pretended to signify when it was coined. The object of the great novel by Proust is precisely the "infinite flow of time." James Joyce pursues fluidity to the limits of the written word. Architects express modernism in either utilitarian apartment and office buildings, which uniformly follow the principle of indefinite repetition, or fanciful structures on fair grounds and airports, which most fre-

---

[1] See the editions by M. Van Crevel of Obrecht, *Opera*, vols. 6 and 7.

quently seem to gain dynamic inspiration from forms intended to produce a sensation of negating gravity. Common to both is the absence of symptoms indicating a vision of the closed form of an ensemble. The simple additive principle (one floor above the other until an arbitrary stop) and the excessive presence of glass (unjustified by practical reasons) both manifest the tendency toward open form. These buildings, in their own way, push toward the outside, toward space, toward the infinite.

A change toward the other pole comes when the tentative behavior of our epoch is replaced by a strong faith in a new orientation. Most artistic production, today as always, mirrors the conditions of society and the minds of men. A small part of the production remains essentially outside the times by being prophetic and traditional in the metaphysical sense of these terms. Whereas the sporadic appearance of superior creative artists transcends the confusion of the contemporary world, a new historic style can affirm itself when the spirit that inspires the solitary has taken possession of the entire society. In a phase of cultural crystallization, musical morphology, like that of all the arts, orients itself again toward the pole of closed, crystallized form.

ENERGY

Contrary to common notion, a composition in its course, like a hurricane, gathers energy before spending it. The initial impulse required for the *beginning of any piece must be created by the composer; but, far from losing strength, this impulse continues to generate energy throughout the movement. The composer may, of course, choose at times to create intentionally the impression of fading energy. In general, however, what we have called "arbitrary" about the *end of a piece may be comparable to the turning-off of a light switch, not the running-out of current. In the Funeral March of the Eroica, for example, the crucial note A-flat is a small but sufficient irritant when first heard. By acting on its surroundings and, in turn, suffering reactions from them, it continues to produce increasing complications each one of which demands, creates, and passes on fresh energy. As a result, modulations reach out in many directions, melody tones develop independent phrases and sections, dynamic fluctuations charge each other, and the movement, as this one, may unfold to great length. We encounter musical energy in its transformation into *matter and form.

EQUIVALENCE

The parts of a morphé, by their position within a whole, acquire a formal significance that remains to some extent independent of substance. We call it their topological significance. Equivalence pertains to *topology, of which it is one particular mode. Topology is concerned with identical elements acquiring different values in different places. Equivalence deals with different elements having the same weight in different places.

In the last analysis the phenomenon of equivalence, because involved in time, is of the nature of rhythm. If we repeat a motive the two occurrences do not have quite the same meaning, for a second measure is by position rhythmically different from a first measure. We may therefore change the second occurrence to without losing the feeling for the topological permanence. The more we increase the change, the more important the substance becomes in relation to topological significance:

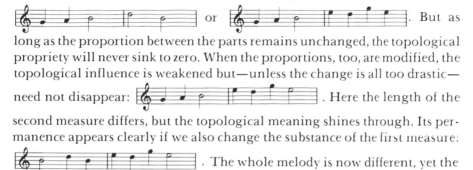

or . But as long as the proportion between the parts remains unchanged, the topological propriety will never sink to zero. When the proportions, too, are modified, the topological influence is weakened but—unless the change is all too drastic—need not disappear: . Here the length of the second measure differs, but the topological meaning shines through. Its permanence appears clearly if we also change the substance of the first measure: . The whole melody is now different, yet the topological permanence can still be felt so that we are able to recognize some relationship between our original model and the last version. The one can be replaced by the other. We say that the two melodies are equivalent.

Equivalence on the basis of rhythmic-metric permanence is not the only possible kind. In fact, permanence may be established on any element of music. The following references are samples of countless other possibilities.

In the finale of his First Symphony, Brahms substitutes at the point of recapitulation the horn theme from the introduction for the main allegro theme. The equivalence is tonal as well as metric. The memorable quality of either theme assists in fixing the topological correspondence. In the B-flat minor Fugue from the first volume of Bach's *Well-tempered Keyboard*, the five entrances of the subject in the exposition (mm. 1–16) are in the recapitulation telescoped to approximately one-fourth of their original length by a quintuple stretto (mm. 67–70). Equivalence of this kind cannot be measured by beats but only by the inherent intensity. The C major Fugue in the same volume answers the strophe of the exposition (mm. 1–6) by a parallel antistrophe (mm. 7–13), except for the substitution in the last entrance of the subject of the relative for the tonic. Harmonic-cadential equivalence of this kind is very common. It may assume complicated realization in the hands of a romantic composer like Richard Wagner. In *Tristan und Isolde*, the equivalence of C major (associated with affirmation) and A-flat minor (associated with negation) has been rightly explained by Alfred Lorenz as a distant but symmetrical polarity around the central tonic E major.[1]

$$C \longleftarrow a \longleftarrow E \longrightarrow B \longrightarrow a^\flat$$
$$sR \qquad s \qquad T \qquad D \qquad Dr$$

[1] *Tristan*, p. 178.

In this sense, the whole art of variation is based on equivalence. The use of identical or highly similar forms for various compositions can only be explained by the relative independence of substance from form. In the multipartite structure of a classical sonata, first and last movements, though very different, are generally felt as equivalent. When equivalence approaches identity of eidos and behavior, as in the finales of Bruckner's symphonies, the result is an aesthetic loss. Perspective of time, in which unequal durations appear equivalent, justifies the convention to omit the minuet repetitions after the trio. It makes the minuet da capo, although reduced to half of the original length, sound perfectly full-fledged. Romantic composers, in line with their general philosophy, carried this possibility to an extreme by merely suggesting, instead of writing out, a symmetrically expected recapitulation. Chopin's D-flat major Prelude matches an exposition of twenty-seven measures by a recapitulation of only fourteen.

ESSENCE. See **REALITY**

EXPOSITION. See **FUGUE; SONATA FORM**

EXPRESSION. See **COMMUNICATION**

FABRIC

Distinguishable from the outer contours of a musical work, its shape in the ordinary sense, is its internal morphology, which we shall call *fabric*. We avoid the term *texture* because it has become too narrowly associated with the distinction homophony-polyphony; and the term *structure*, because common usage has blurred it by too great proximity to form. But both these terms are related to fabric because of their inherent material qualities, and they point toward it together with such terms as *scale, instrumentation*, and others.

To some extent, fabric contributes to outer shape. When the originally vocal canzone, for example, came to be treated instrumentally, it underwent transformations because of the new fabric and for no other particular reason. A classical *sonata, similarly, changes fabric and remains not quite the same when it becomes now a symphony, now a trio or quartet, now a concerto. The differences are due to internal rather than external morphology.

It is in *polyphony, however, that the role of fabric can be most strikingly observed. Here the outer contour loses all essential meaning before the power of internal morphology. The "fugueness" of a fugue, its proper morphology, is not caught by an analysis of its successive parts. The pattern of the succession could be readily realized by conventional means, but not so the internal morphology resulting from fugal technique. A fugue imagined to lack sectionalization altogether still remains a fugue. One misses the point trying to analyze a fugue (or any other product of true polyphony) only or mainly with the tools of external rather than of internal morphology, thus dealing with the shape rather than the fabric.

Unfortunately for our field, conceptual tools of internal morphology have not yet been developed. Whereas a succession of sections can be readily grasped and demonstrated by geometrical analogy—from a simple ABA bow to a complex graph—fabric escapes comparable attempts. Analogies, which are sometimes useful because music is basically inexplicable in nonmusical terms, are of no help in regard to polyphony. The successive entrances of voices in a canon, for example, may be grasped geometrically qua succession as juxtaposition of a sort, but the formal effect of the canon may not. For as soon as all the voices have entered, the graspable factor disappears: the canon is "turning about itself." From this moment on, conventional morphological terms become inapplicable, for there are no more space analogies, no before and after, no sections succeeding each other. The experience holds true in all polyphony, of which canon is an extreme mode. To the extent to which homophonic elements in a polyphonic piece increase, one can resort to description. Nevertheless, what remains of polyphony proper also remains indescribable by a homophonically conditioned morphological vocabulary.

A yet to be developed analytic technique which disregards all nonpolyphonic factors will focus on the predominance of ontics in pure polyphony. Changes occur, not by way of tension and release as in homophony, but by way of increment and decrement. The result is different from, and at best analogous to, the breath of homophony. What happens is a densification and rarefaction of musical matter. Compare a stretto to the normal answer of a fugue subject, or consider the increasing and diminishing participation of voices. Climax is not postulated. When one occurs, it is always due to a superimposed idea or element basically foreign to polyphony.

Polyphony is not only ontic—motion within a fundamental immobility—but also essentially kinematic. A vocal, pneumatic character of a single voice is thereby not excluded; but the polyphonic texture as a whole is necessarily kinematic, for we cannot identify with it (as we can with the "Oneness" of harmony). By the same token, polyphony belongs in the category of *musica musicans* of which it is the foremost example.

Recognition of polyphonic fabrics as pure time-shapes results in a curious situation. Normally time can be represented by some spatial feature; the face of a watch proves the point. In music, however, where the roles of *time and space are inverted and time is of the essence, the possibility of representing time by geometric image vanishes. Purely musical time has no coordinate in space, and its projection in musical notation becomes irrelevant as far as internal morphology is concerned. Purely logically, the inversion might admit the representation of music by some manifestation of space without time coordinate.

FERMATA

The word, in its literal meaning, indicates a halt of motion, an arrest, a stop. (In modern Italian, a bus stop is called a *fermata*.) A musical fermata interrupts the flow of an established rhythm or meter. It may concern a note or a rest. Because all musical elements are interpreted as either *ontic or gignetic (cf. a tonic chord at the end or in the middle of a piece), the fermata, too, has a twofold function which is not indicated by the notation. It may be final, confirming the definitive cessation of movement; or it may be temporary, demanding to "hold one's breath" in the course of an action. The first kind we may call *terminal*; the second, because of the inherent tension it creates, *suspensive*.

A terminal fermata, as we find it in music of many periods, tears a piece of music out of the continuous and measured flow of time. The arrest may happen in a number of ways, for which the modern fermata sign is merely a shorthand notation. Thus in many thirteenth-century motets of the Codex Montpellier, the relentless modal triple meter of the composition is interrupted by the addition of a written-out extra beat in the penultimate measure so that the end becomes metrically indeterminate. For a similar purpose, Dufay utilizes our modern fermata sign. In his well-known setting of "Alma redemptoris mater," the fermata in the middle of the piece, indicating the end of a section, is preceded by a written-out ritardando suggestive of a hemiola; and the very end dissolves the polyphonic flow by eighteen consecutive fermatas over homophonic units, interspersed by general pauses. Throughout the Renaissance and early thorough-bass periods, the terminal fermata is often notated by a value not found in the course of the composition, for instance, a longa or maxima where the semibrevis has normally become the longer note.

We may interpret the closing and opening chords of the Allegretto in Beethoven's Seventh Symphony as intended fermatas and support this interpretation by a revealing analogy to the Sanctus in Haydn's Lord Nelson Mass. In the manuscript of 1798, Haydn notates the rhythm of the two opening exclamations of this movement as follows: ♩. ♩ | 𝅝 | ♩. ♩ | 𝅝 |. The first edition printed by Breitkopf & Härtel in 1803, however, changes this notation to: ♩. ♩ | 𝅝 ♩ ⌐ ♩ 𝄽 | ♩. ♩ | 𝅝 ♩ ⌐ ♩ 𝄽 |.

A suspensive fermata modifies the note or rest over which it appears by an unspecified but always irrational amount of time. Usually the modification prolongs the note. C. P. E. Bach, in his famous mid-eighteenth-century treatise, speaks of fermatas mainly as a device to invite ornamentation, "for they awaken unusual attentiveness" ("sie erwecken eine besondere Aufmercksamkeit").[1] The increasingly pedantic teachers of the following hundred years try to spell out the metric equivalent of a fermata. Daniel Gottlob Türk, in his *Klavierschule* of 1789, for instance, is an early advocate for holding a fermata twice the specified time value in slow tempi, four times in fast, thus misinterpreting the inherent irrationality of a fermata (I. vi. 84). Leopold Mozart must have gained a true insight in the course of his career. In the first edition of his *Versuch einer gründlichen Violinschule* (1756), he explains the fermata traditionally as a suspensive prolongation; but in the third edition, published in the year of his death, 1787, he specifically announces that a fermata may either prolong or shorten, the latter particularly over a pause: "Dergleichen Sachen kommen auf den guten Geschmack und eine richtige Beurtheilungskraft an"

---

[1] *Versuch*, Das zweyte Haupstück, Neunte Abtheilung, par. 2.

("such matters depend on good taste and correct judgment").[1] This interpretation, though not common, touches on the true nature of a fermata. Carried out by a sensitive conductor, a shortening of one or both fermatas at the beginning of the *Tristan* Prelude, for instance, has been heard to be effective. In any case, the modification must in proportion to the context, which means that at the end of the stop the energy curve extrapolated from what has preceded should reach exactly the level required for the continuation. This level may be higher or lower, that is, the energy may accumulate during the fermata or diminish. In rarer instances, the energy level remains equal; but to maintain it after the interruption, an effort is nevertheless required.

A fermata does not occur in nonmetrical music where time production is irrational by definition. In metrical music, a fermata is understood as momentarily suspending the rational time production; its effect is indeed inseparable from the resulting contrast.

In a wider sense, fermata is related to *cadenza. The first movements of both Beethoven's Fifth and Sixth Symphonies provide good evidence for the connection. In each case, the area of the onset of the recapitulation is marked by a little cadenza (mm. 268; 282 ff.); the exact corresponding spot in the exposition, by a fermata (mm. 21; 4).

Fermata is also related to *echo, during which the musical movement does not progress. Even more obviously than cadenza, echo is a written-out fermata.

The use of fermatas in Protestant chorales has no connection with the established meaning. It refers not at all to the music but only to the text of which it marks the ends of lines.

FIGURATION. See **ORNAMENTATION**

FINALE

The concept originated in opera. Like other operatic features (*rondo, *aria), it was subsequently adopted by particular instrumental forms—a continuation of the very old instrumental tradition of transcribing primary vocal models. In either situation, finale is the end piece in a multipartite of which the unity is highly developed.

In the number operas of the seventeenth and eighteenth centuries, finale had the main function of indicating the approaching end. It thus served the principle of limitation. In the most general way, a number was marked as finale merely by being different. In early opera buffa, for example, the two standard protagonists, after alternating in arias throughout, joined in a duet only at the end of an act. The external explanation that neither would concede the final curtain and applause to the other, though correct, is incomplete and a bit frivolous. The *end of a composition always being somewhat arbitrary, morphological considerations demand signal musical behavior for terminat-

[1]I. iii. 19.

ing any piece. Such is the case in the otherwise strophically unlimited variation sets, and such is the need in a number opera. Characteristically enough, finale as a concept disappears from through-composed opera: the need of limiting a series has disappeared, and the end, if successful, appears as a consequence of the preceding structure. But even here, the termination is often indicated by musical behavior differing from the rest: witness Isolde's *Liebestod* or the ensembles at the end of Richard Strauss's *Der Rosenkavalier*.

Among the many possibilities of being "different," opera finales seem to favor, on the whole, denser fabric and increased length. Early Neapolitan composers, like Nicola Logroscino, accomplished this kind of intensification by continuing the action of the play, normally restricted to the recitatives between numbers, into the finale. Baldassare Galuppi extended this technique by organizing a "chain finale" of which the continuum is broken up into short separate pieces. Nicola Piccinni gave form to his long and intricate finales by holding together the links of the chain with the help of a ritornello. The French vaudeville finale, based on a recurrent refrain, shows a similar tendency. In the hands of Mozart, finale becomes ultimately a purely musical structure of high complexity ("an operetta all by itself," as Da Ponte saw it). The first *Figaro* finale, for instance, is 939 measures long—more than twice the sum total of all the preceding numbers in the act; and the overall organization surpasses in subtlety and scope any other music written even by Mozart.[1]

This kind of finale invites, and perhaps is partly inspired by, symphonic thinking. In any case, the notion of finale in an instrumental multipartite arises exactly at the moment in history when dramatism, popular in opera, begins to affect *sonata in all its manifestations (symphony, concerto, etc.). Our initial qualification that only compositions meeting particular conditions admit of a finale becomes understandable against the operatic background. Hence characterizing as finale the Agnus Dei movement of a Mass would be absurd. Nor is a similar quality inherent in the gigue at the end of a *suite; for the conventional set of baroque dances lacks both drama and any higher degree of unification. Haydn could still place at the end of his sonatas carefree rondos successful by themselves. Under the ever stronger spell of opera, however, the notion of finale focuses less on the piece so designated than on the relationship of this end piece to whatever comes before. This dramatic attitude, a matter of course in opera, is implied in the concept of the late classic and romantic sonata.

As the instrumental version becomes increasingly emancipated from its operatic origin, the changing role of finale may be interpreted as an indication of search for larger unity. In the total perspective of sonata, entertainment yields to climactic experience. The finale of Mozart's "Jupiter" Symphony, unlike earlier finales, becomes musically the most demanding of the four movements. From Beethoven onward, dramatic orientation predominates. Key areas are dramatically identified and contraposed. Middle sections turn into dramatic "developments." The developmental idea spreads over the whole of the sonata so that the middle movements have to adapt themselves to the dramatic influence of the strong outside movements. A symptom of this evolution is the transformation of the original dance movement from a styl-

---

[1]For a detailed analysis, see Levarie, *Figaro*, pp. 107–23.

ized minuet into a scherzo and subsequently (mostly under the influence of Brahms) into a new kind of movement occurring in two variants—one fierce and turbulent, the other subdued and tender. The main task of the finale is now no longer merely to terminate a multipartite but to balance in the overall structure the dramatic force of the opening movement. To this end, finales by Beethoven embody the most diverse experiments. With each work, he had to find a new solution of the finale problem because the spiritual data and hence the formal consequences were different in each case. The Eroica finale is unprecedented in its particular variation technique. The Fifth and Sixth Symphonies gain intensity for their respective finales, here by the unexpected repeat of the scherzo, there by the interpolation of storm music. The addition of human voices in the Ninth, with all the concomitant complications, was his extreme experiment. Nowhere did Beethoven fall into the error (consistently committed afterwards by Bruckner) of letting the finale compete with the opening sonata movement. His closing fugues are not atavisms, like those in Haydn's Opus 20, but breakthroughs. Variation sets close the Piano Sonatas op. 109 and 111, neither of which contains the four traditionally expected sonata movements. The finale of Opus 109 synthesizes the dialectically opposed elements of the preceding two movements. Opus 111 has only two movements. The dramaticism is twofold: each of the movements is dramatic by itself, but superimposed on them is an implicit polarity between the outward struggle of the opening movement and the inward ascension of the finale.

Experimentation continued after Beethoven. The finale of Brahms's First Symphony shows the effort; that of the Fourth, original and mature mastery. Tchaikovsky placed the Adagio lamentoso of his *Pathétique* Symphony after a movement sounding like a traditional finale; by the number of people breaking into applause or leaving their seats after the penultimate third movement, one can measure the extent to which the original function of finale has succumbed to dramatic effect. In a historically important experiment, Liszt in his B-minor Piano Sonata changed the multipartite into a through-composed structure. The sonata here becomes a drama played without interruption, in which the finale is made to be identical with the recapitulation (cf. Appendix A, pp. 321 f.). As in through-composed opera, the concept of finale henceforth becomes superfluous. Multipartites of the future are likely to find new difficulties and new solutions.

FORM. See **MATTER AND FORM**

FUGUE

A fugue is not a form but rather a manner of using techniques of *poly-phony. It is, in the words of Luigi Cherubini, "the complement of counterpoint."[1] The first volume of Bach's *Wohltemperiertes Klavier*, a representative witness, contains a wide variety of forms.[2] Almost exactly one-half of the

[1]*Contrepoint.*
[2]See Levarie, *Fugue and Form.*

twenty-four are in binary form, the rest ternary. There is considerable variation of form within the binary and ternary categories. One hears barforms
with recapitulation (6, 9, 13, etc.) and without (1, 5, 6, etc.). Bowforms are
arranged parallel around the center (3, 23) and mirrored (7, 16, 17). One fugue
has no episodes at all (1), another loses the theme in the second half (5). There
is blossoming sonata form (3, 21), concerto behavior (20), and rondo (12). The
diversity of these musical facts precludes the possibility of a unified underlying formal principle.

Yet on another level, fugue follows a morphological law of its own. The
minimum definition of fugue as a "polyphonic, imitative piece of music"
evokes, if nothing else, a *fabric. The concept of *theme may serve us—as it
does every fugue—as a starting point. The literal translation of *theme* is 'proposition', the 'task laid before one'. The task of a fugue is to utilize the proposition to its fullest potential, to let the theme do all it can. Different themes
contain different possibilities. Hence we find fugues in all degrees of technical
complexities—from simple statement-answer arrangements through aug-
mentations, diminutions, strettos, and canons to mirror, duple, triple, and
quadruple fugues. The morphological interest remains concentrated on the
contrapuntal fabric and the resulting energy curve. What matters is not one
more statement of the theme but the new surroundings in which it finds itself.
(A good performer will bring the counterpoints into focus.) Between different
kinds of situation, episodes may provide breathing points. The piece is finished when the propositions have been developed and demonstrated according to the eidos, which really determines the morphology of a particular
fugue.

The ancestry of fugue in the baroque ricercar permits one to think of
fugue as basically strophic. In the early seventeenth century, two types of
ricercar prevailed, both instrumental adaptations of the earlier Netherlands
motet. The principal difficulty of the instrumental version lay in the maintenance of unity among sections no longer held together by either a text or a
cantus firmus. Sweelinck in the North unified the various sections of the ricercar by retaining one main subject throughout the composition while changing the counterpoints to that subject with every new section. Frescobaldi in
the South tied the sections together by using them for variations of the theme
itself. Whatever the particular affiliations with other formative forces, the appearance of a constant factor in ever-changing situations suggests a strophic
principle.

The historic association of fugue with motet has further consequences.
Equality among the voices remains relevant as does the insistence on an advance definition of the number of voices. Thus the fabric of a fugue—to which
we have initially assigned a prime morphological significance—sets up the
framework within which the formative contrapuntal forces have a free play.
The vocal origin intensifies the strophic orientation. Both vocal and strophic
behavior are demonstrated in Bach's E major Fugue from the second volume
of the *Well-tempered Keyboard*. On the whole, we must remember, *polyphony demands a morphological approach *sui generis*, that is, not borrowed
from homophonic forms and yet to be developed.

Fugues are ontic in principle but may be used for gignetic ends. Such is the case when they are made to serve a plan that lifts them into a different context. In the finale of Bach's Fifth Brandenburg Concerto, fugue helps build the concerto movement; in that of Mozart's "Jupiter" Symphony, the dramatic tensions of sonata form. When Beethoven, for whatever purposes, employs fugue, it may remain *musica musicans but ceases to be ontic. In his Piano Sonata op. 106, fugue is used for sonata development; in op. 110, for the crowning of the entire work. His Grosse Fuge op. 133 is a string quartet in three movements. The overall orientation is not unlike that of Bach's big organ fugue in E-flat major; Beethoven's own subtitle describing the fugue as "tantôt libre tantôt recherchée" points back to the idea of ricercar.

Beethoven's fugues are the strongest explorations of a possible synthesis of "old" and "new" values. The role in the eighteenth century of fugue was assumed in the nineteenth century by sonata form. Indicative is the transfer from fugue to sonata of terms like *exposition* and *development (Durchführung)*. Both fugue and sonata form, each at its time, were the most comprehensive type of instrumental music, accommodating any kind of musical structuring from the simplest archetype to the most complex and involved organisms. Each could give purely musical shape to any kind of contents, that is, to acoustic-musical as well as to aesthetical and psychological motives. In the confrontation of fugue and sonata, Beethoven accomplished a maximum of order and unity for a maximum of complexity and multiplicity.

GRAMMAR

Musical grammar has two roots. One is natural and immediately and instinctively understood. It brings to life all elementary musical phenomena such as tonal relations, triadic functions, meter, rhythm, tempo, dynamics, etc. The other root of musical grammar is conventional in varying degrees and must be learned. It comprises all that is peculiar to a particular style, including modifications of the elementary. Here belong, first of all, the diverse utilizations of consonance and dissonance. A sounding together of third and fifth above a bass has different meaning in a Perotinus conductus, an Ockeghem motet, a Haydn quartet, and a Stravinsky symphony. Convention can also explain changes in rhythmic organization and orientation. A new grammar represents a major accomplishment of a good composer as it becomes, at best, "instinctively understood" by the next generation. In this respect, Monteverdi, Haydn, Wagner all did their share. The required harmony between our reaction and a particular grammar can be brought about by study whenever it is not supplied by musical instinct and special inclination.

Grammar is a system. In the most general sense, system is a creation of the mind to protect instinct and intellect alike against unexpected events (literally, to 'place together' what otherwise seems chaotic). The quest for order, an axiom of both science and art, is humanly basic and irrepressible. In the face of an unexpected event, our total organism directly tries to fit it into a known pattern or to produce a new accommodating pattern. The creation of a system against the eruption of disorder signifies the regulation of expectation.

In all epochs the importance has been recognized of delineating the system in use right at the beginning of a composition. The most condensed form of identifying a system is the old counterpoint rule of starting a melody on the tonic note or on a closely related substitute like the fifth or third. Mozart still wrote an initial sixth as an appoggiatura to give it, if not the sound, the appearance of correctness (see Piano Sonata K. 333). The complete cadence forming the opening measures of almost any Bach prelude extends the same concept. In principle, the incipient statement of a twelve-tone row expresses similar concern. Whenever the system is both new and unclearly stated at the outset, it evokes confusion which lasts until the individually conceived convention becomes accepted as universal norm. As is well known, the harmonic and rhythmic uncertainties at the beginning of Beethoven's First, Fifth, and Ninth Symphonies, or of Wagner's *Tristan und Isolde*, were at first upsetting. The reaction of contemporaries hearing these works for the first time is indicative of the universal validity of canons in the nineteenth century and the sensitivity of classic consciousness to every slight deviation from these canons. The attenuation of the exceptional effect of these and similar passages in the minds of later listeners is due to the subsequent widening of the tonality concept. The rooting of grammar partly in convention contributes to the difficulties of understanding styles of the past. The "natural" and unchanging roots of musical grammar facilitate the adjustment, which may be often automatic for people with affinity for a style. Usually, however, a rectification of our "hear point," particularly when works of a remote past or culture are concerned, must be brought about by study and experience. A listener conditioned by the traditional classical cadence must change system to appreciate fully the impact of a Landini cadence or a double-leading-tone cadence.

In music, where grammar and contents are identical, the grammar of a particular piece must be known for expectation to function. Because a work exists as a whole, expectation is not—as some people have suggested—a question contingent on repeated hearing but rather a built-in permanent feature of the work. The handling of expectation, identical with the handling of grammar, becomes an artistic tool at the disposal of the composer.

Grammar thus regulates expectation; but the regulation, producing the feeling of the familiar, far from excluding adventure, precisely grants a play among possible and unforeseen relationships. Thus system contains the potential of surprise. Within the set limits, a certain arbitrariness can freely develop without turning chaotic. The surprising interruptions of the first subject in the opening movement of Haydn's "Surprise" Symphony No. 94 always keep their effect because they grow out of the given grammar, not out of our familiarity or lack of it.[1]

Heaping of surprises might cancel the feeling for the system. Many experimental compositions produce this result. In Anton Webern's instrumentation of Bach's Ricercare from the *Musikalisches Opfer*, the sonorities are unexpected throughout. In such a case, either boredom ensues or the events have to be accommodated by a new pattern. Such a change of system occurs when,

---

[1]For a most perceptive explanation of the musical behavior of this movement, see Marco, "Musical Task."

for instance, an atonal passage is introduced in an otherwise tonal piece. Change of grammar is always symptomatic of the eternal human need for adventure.

GRAVITY. See **TIME AND SPACE**

GROWTH. See pp. 11 ff.

HARMONY

Harmony is a natural force inherent in tone. It governs the behavior of tonal relationships. Harmony—originally a carpentry term indicating a joint, and later identified with concordance of parts and right proportion—is that which holds together the musical phenomenon in all its elements. Specifically, harmony is the generating principle of both melody, that is, tone relations in time, and of harmony in the narrower technical sense, that is, tone relations in musical space. At the crossing of the two lies *scale. This interpretation elucidates the role of harmony at one stage as directly dependent upon melody by virtue of being a realization of a more or less deep perspective of the structure of tone. All parallel chord motions exemplify the kinship—from organum, the point at which melody-bound harmony and nascent polyphony part ways, to faux bourdon and the many parallel progressions in the music of Debussy. In such styles, harmonic function is absent from both melody and harmony. The melody tones have positional value within a scale considered as an entity, and harmonization follows this signification. In free organum (see the Compostela example in the Discourse), the scale tones acquire an additional meaning from the interval value in respect to the chant tone below, which acts as if it were a temporary tonic.

Thus seen, harmony is first of all a spatial projection of the tone perspective. Before 1600, the concept of *tonality is not missing but one detects no independent, let alone determinant, role of harmony. A radical change occurs with the discovery of the *triad as a basic harmonic unity, that is, with the rise of classic tonality. Two aspects coincide. The older concept of taking the entity of the scale as tonic supplies the positional hierarchic view of tonic-subdominant-dominant as the harmonic projection of the scale material. The decisive new concept, however, arises from the discovery of the gigneticism implied in the major and minor chords, namely, the tendency of a major triad toward its minor subdominant and, inversely, that of a minor triad toward its major dominant. From here proceeds the development of tonality based solely on functional harmony. All subsequent theories of harmony stem from these concepts.

The harmonic morphé in organum was strictly determined by, and identical with, the melody of which it was a dimension. Functional harmony reverses this relationship. It develops an autonomous harmonic morphé which sets a rigid framework for melody. It does so together with metricised rhythm, which is predestined by its rational character to serve the purposes of a morphé based on cadence.

There is a tendency to reject chord formations that cannot be explained harmonically as belonging to the field of "melodic modification." Unquestionably chords often undergo such modification. Yet a chord at one time understood as a melodic modification of another chord will under other circumstances have to be conceived as a real chord, as a harmonic entity. Actually a harmonic theory should be ready to explain, without calling melody for help, any tone combination occurring as a chord. We do not suggest that any tone agglomerate or tone cluster is *eo ipso* a harmony, but it may become one by a mental act of organization on the part of the hearer. This organization must follow certain lines suggested by the nature of harmonical tone development. It is carried out by the isolation, within the agglomerate, of several generators and the tones dependent upon them. Any chord, then, is a tone agglomeration organized by one or more generators according to harmonical principles. The various trends of resolution in the most complex chords should be subject to purely harmonic reasoning.

Initiated mainly by Bartók and Stravinsky, harmonic practice in many contemporary styles once again proceeds from the tone perspective. By employing chords for coloring and accentuating melody and rhythm, composers have in a way returned to prefunctional concepts of harmony though with considerably deepened interpretation. Harmony thus taken at its face value is now not inherent in either melody or tonality. The chances of further evolution rest with the possibility of renewed concepts of tonality with which the modern use of chords may be coupled. The point of departure is implied in the very concept of tone perspective. The cadential form of a tone fanning out in its rising and falling harmonic series and then returning to its original simplicity can thus create a new kind of tonality. The "fan" principle, though basically nonfunctional in the traditional sense, may also be coupled with the idea of functional harmony by the conferring of functional signification upon the fanned-out chordal agglomerates. The scope and power of harmony admit ever wider and different interpretations of the concept of tonality.

HETEROGENESIS. See **IDIOGENESIS-HETEROGENESIS**

HETEROPHONY

The term ('otherness of tones') was used by Plato[1] from whom musicologists have taken it over. Of the original meaning we cannot be sure. The modern sense given to the word generally implies the simultaneous rendition by several performers of slightly modified versions of the same melody. Heterophony is often referred to as a primitive type of polyphony. A melody and its varied version, or versions, are heard at the same time. On the face of it, the

---

[1]*Laws* 812d.

statement describes correctly a number of cases. But considering heterophony as a whole, we soon come to recognize that its nature differs completely from the premises on which Western music is built and that the cases covered by the usual definition form only a branch of a system that cannot be satisfactorily explained by means of our traditional conceptual tools.

The very nature of heterophonic melody differs from our usual notion of melody. The tones in a heterophonic melody are not points in an energetic curve but belong to an essentially ontic whole formed by a complex of sounds, a *Klang*.[1] This is a "symphony" in the original sense of "sounding together." Out of the total sound, which lacks functional connotations, melodies or melodic fragments arise but remain embedded in it. Church bells ringing together give us an approximate idea of heterophony: a sound complex, changing yet always the same, with melody fragments emerging here and there. For a precise impression and knowledge, one must turn to music of the Far East, especially to the Javanese gamelan.

The texture arising from this situation is fundamentally alien to what we are wont to designate as polyphony. In no case is heterophony a "primitive" imperfect stage of Western polyphony, which is based on energetic melodies that cohere according to laws of functional harmony. The difference in concept is illustrated by the proper or improper use of carillons, as traditionally found in European and American provinces that border the Atlantic. Western melodies are ill suited to rendition by bells of which the sound is complex and prolonged. The effect is comparable to, but much worse than, that of a melody played on a piano with all dampers lifted. For such sound source, heterophony would be the right style.

Yet heterophony and heterophonic effects are not missing in the history of Western music. A persuasive case has been made for the participation of the *Klang* concept in the origin of *polyphony. But even plainchant may invite heterophony, particularly those melodies of faint gignetic drive. The likelihood of an approximate performance by a group of monks—heterophony in fact if not by intent—is merely an additional, but almost inevitable, factor. In this sense, organum is all heterophony. The voices sing no longer at the unison or octave but at the fifth, and eventually they do not move at the same time. But even in the apparent freedom of a St. Martial organum, the reference to a single outline is unmistakable. Theory supports practice: the demand for perfect intervals at the main points of the melody shows the uniform backbone behind the apparently diversified voices. The principle is still recognizable in motets of the thirteenth century, although other forces begin to predominate. In any case, no heterophony is left in the music of the *ars nova* so that one may wonder whether the now solitary authority of gignetic melodies is not perhaps the real "new" element of this style.

Heterophony seems antipodal to the polyphony of the Netherlands composers and of Bach. The enormous accomplishment of Western polyphony makes one all too readily overlook the concomitant role played by heterophony. As if entering by a back door, it characterizes all realizations of a figured bass. The harpsichord cannot help but be heterophonic against the

[1]Cf. *Polyphony, in particular our indebtedness to Rudolf Ficker.

155

solo lines. By itself, of course, an early keyboard does not favor heterophony, but the modern piano does because of the right pedal. Already Haydn experimented with the manner (Piano Sonata in C major, Hoboken XVI:50, first movement, mm. 73 f., 120 ff., "open Pedal"). Beethoven repeatedly prescribed a similar use of continuous pedal for several bars in his piano sonatas (op. 31 no. 2, first movement; op. 53, finale; op. 110, Adagio ma non troppo) and also in the middle movement of his Third Piano Concerto. When the classical orchestra took over from the harpsichord the function of harmonization in addition to carrying the melody lines, it necessarily absorbed heterophony in the process. The symphonies by Beethoven show all kinds of possibilities. The opening eight-measure melody of the Eroica Funeral March moves above a heterophonic bass that duplicates the same line though not at the same time. The slow movement of the Pastorale and the finale of the Ninth abound in examples—often diminutions—without monopolizing them. There is also heterophony when in the first movement of the Second Symphony the string

motive  is simultaneously doubled by horns and trumpets as

 . This use of heterophony

for an outline is the opposite of that for diminution; but they are related inasmuch as both comment on foreground material.

Heterophony against the background is clearly audible in impressionistic music. The amorphous whole-tone scale here contributes, just as any twelve-tone row produces heterophony by definition in Schönberg's kind of *atonality.

Not every tone material lends itself to heterophonic treatment. Because in a heterophonic piece the total *Klang* is necessarily ontic, the scale derived from it must not by itself form a gignetic melody. The pentatonic scale, unlike the diatonic major or minor, fulfills the condition. Other scales are entirely possible if intervals smaller than the wholetone are deprived of their directional energy, for instance, through octave transposition.

In conclusion, we notice that the term *heterophony* is not such a happy one after all for the phenomena discussed. Must we draw the deduction that Plato's heterophony was something different from what we assume? Or was Greek heterophony simply less developed than Javanese?

HEXACHORD. See SCALE

HOMOPHONY

Homophony is a texture distinct from monophony on one hand, and from polyphony on the other. We speak of homophony when chords characterize the *fabric. Chords are simultaneous combinations of three or more tones heard as a unit. Whatever their particular constellation, they can assume one of three roles: (1) reinforce a melody, (2) progress according to inherent harmonic laws, or (3) accompany a melody.

(1)   The earliest and most characteristic examples are triple and quadruple *organum and faux bourdon. Debussy's parallel chord progressions a millennium later demonstrate a similar technique; sounding advanced in their own time, they actually renew an old practice. The resulting homophonic movement, at any style period, is completely subordinate to the behavior of the given melody. The result rightly sounds like a first level of homophony. It illuminates the relationship of monophony to homophony: the stronger the melodic force, the less autonomous the chordal life. If one remembers that harmony as an idea is fundamental, one wonders at its weakness at a moment in history when the long autonomous rule of monody was at last challenged and superseded by the development of two and more simultaneous sounds. The apparent paradox is explained by the flow of history: because monody is chronologically the earliest phenomenon, harmony entered first by a back door, so to speak, as reinforcement of melody. Several centuries passed before the real and independent force of harmony could assert itself.

(2)   This happened in the sixteenth century, articulated by Zarlino's fundamental and revolutionary theories as clearly as by the new Protestant and Roman Catholic experiments with homophony. There had been earlier but isolated breakthroughs of "pure" homophony, that is, of chord progressions not at all or barely determined by melody. Expressive reasons must have encouraged Machaut to interpolate strongly noticeable, free-floating homophonic sections on the two occurrences of the words "Jesu Christe" in the otherwise melodically and rhythmically conditioned Gloria of his Mass. Homophonic passages in the works of Dufay and Josquin serve similar purposes, although some indebtedness to the guidance of melody can usually be observed. The apparent homophony in the following section from Josquin's "Ave Maria" is really determined by the canon between soprano and tenor:[1]

The less the danger of being subjugated by melody, the clearer the autonomous role of homophony.

(3)   The thorough-bass period (which term Hugo Riemann appropriately substituted for musical baroque) and also the subsequent centuries show homophony at its fullest. Here the earlier two stages are actually combined: the realization of a figured bass phenomenalizes progression according to harmonic laws, while the harmonization of a melody unfolds and explains the inherent tendencies of the otherwise monodic line. In this kind of homophony, each melody tone, quite apart from its gignetic value, plays a role by

[1]*Werken*, 1:3.

force of its position. Each melody tone has its harmonic counterpart. The situation differs drastically from a comparable one in a polyphonic texture in which—though the whole may be heard as ontic—each individual melody tone serves a gignetic tendency.

Homophony and polyphony are, of course, difficult to separate within a piece of music. Many Palestrina motets sound homophonic while actually determined by polyphonic behavior, and even the most intensely polyphonic fugue by Bach is likely to respect homophonic tendencies. Yet a theoretic distinction is necessary, for it touches on essentials. The concept pair homophony-polyphony designates two extremes. For practical differentiation, a shift in emphasis suffices. We call homophony a texture in which the homophonic factor prevails. We call polyphony a texture in which the polyphonic factor prevails. In principle, homophonic chordal texture determines voice leading; in polyphony the constellation of voices produces harmony. Attempts at isolating "pure" homophony or polyphony have in general failed and proven unfeasible. In a four-part chorale harmonization by Bach one can always recognize the primacy of the bass as a fresh counterpoint to the given melody and the subsequent addition of one after the other middle voice in accordance with the demands of both good voice leading and intended harmonic frame.

One symptom of polyphony is a fixed number of well-defined participating voices. Polyphony pushes toward homophony as soon as the melodic tensions inherent in each voice begin to yield to chordal unification. The process can, of course, be reversed. Style, only, determines the extent to which harmonic laws are observed or disregarded in a total polyphonic texture, or contrapuntal laws in a homophonic texture. Music history has often been explained in terms of such styles—as an interaction of, and oscillation between, the two extremes of homophony and polyphony.[1] From an overall view of morphological tendencies, one may call the first five hundred years of post-monophonic Western music "polyphonic," because in principle and time closer to melody, and the last five hundred years "homophonic." Thus far, there seem to be only these two large waves, whatever the ripples of shorter style periods.

HUMOR

In a sense, every work of art is serious. Therefore, however one might define humor in music, no music is humorous by itself. It can become so only through comparison with something else already known. The humorous in music, in short, is always parody, caricature. If one dispenses with the model, the caricature disappears together with the humorous effect.

There is an occasional difficulty in the definition of *model*. One might contend that the conscious reference to a created model (for example, to an existing melody) is dispensable because the caricature could be brought to bear on an innate model, that is, on an archetype. A badly drawn circle needs

---

[1]For a stimulating development of this idea, see Lorenz, *Rhythmus der Generationen.*

no particular model to be found distorted. In music, however, the objection, though well taken, has little practical importance. Musical archetypes are known through compositions so that the parody of an archetype must needs become a caricature of the composition embodying that archetype.

The special humor arising from incongruousness is not of a different kind, for it, too, depends on reference. Bach's *Bauernkantate* illustrates the point. The parody is not of one particular model but, so to speak, of all models of the day. The incompatibility of style and purpose distorts whatever model one has in mind and produces caricature.

A brief consideration of the following instances confirms the parodistic nature of musical humor:

Hans Newsiedler, Der Juden Tantz.[1] The rhythm and structure of the most common German dance of the early sixteenth century—Tantz in duple meter followed by Hupfauf in triple meter—were as obvious to the composer's contemporaries as his antisemitic intentions. The tuning of the melody one halftone lower than the accompaniment may sound to us polytonal. To Newsiedler it was merely caricature.

Mozart, Ein musikalischer Spass, K. 522. A classical piece arouses the clearest possible expectation. Hence any deviation from it was readily understood. If the variant was an improvement, the audience might break into spontaneous applause (see Mozart's letter to his father from Paris, 3 July 1778). If the variant fell below the norm, people would boo if they felt short-changed, or laugh if they realized the composer's purpose of parody. The model behind Mozart's joke is so strong that the composition can well be used to teach classical norms by showing the violations. Noticeable are the inability to modulate, establish an arrival point, build a good melody, distinguish melody from accompaniment, maintain rhythmic fluency, achieve continuity in place of "stop and go," and many others.

Beethoven, Violin Sonata, F major, scherzo. The model is spelled out in the composition. The coordination of the two players is parodied in the repetition of the eight-measure theme. Notice that even in this repetition, the first measure is still played properly so that there may be no misunderstanding about the intended model.

Beethoven, Eighth Symphony, second movement. The whimsical melody becomes funny when related to the rigid metronome interpretation of the accompaniment. The final cadence (mm. 79 ff.) may strike even the uneducated listener as inappropriate because of the suddenness and brevity of its behavior. The expert who knows the Italian opera model will enjoy the parody all the more.

Berlioz, Symphonie fantastique, finale. The composer himself refers in both versions of his program notes to the "parodie burlesque du *Dies irae.*" The introduction of the Gregorian melody and, even more so, the simultaneous rendering of the *Dies irae* and the deliberately vulgar rondo theme are not humorous to man, who should only react with terror. There is immense humor in the situation, however, from Satan's viewpoint. The listener is invited to identify with the devil, who is a caricature—God's—himself.

---

[1]Facsimile and discussion in Apel, *Notation*, pp. 78 ff.

Liszt, Faust Symphony, third movement, "Mephistopheles." The themes are all parodies of the Faust themes heard in the first movement; for the devil, the spirit of negation, is incapable of original creation. He can only distort. In the contrasting middle section, the Gretchen theme from the second movement makes a brief appearance—untouched by the devil, in line with Gretchen's character.

Debussy, "Golliwogg's Cakewalk," Children's Corner no. 6. The middle section of this deliberately naïve entertainment piece repeatedly quotes the beginning of *Tristan* (*Cédez, avec une grande émotion*) in alternation with a Negro dance rhythm (*a tempo*). The incongruousness might be lost on any listener not acquainted with Wagner's music and Debussy's attitude toward it.

Medieval music, to the extent to which we know it, seems strangely devoid of humor. The reason lies probably in the strength of a hierarchic sense that pervaded all activities. The models were clear and occupied a well-defined position which it would have been blasphemy to parody. We may safely assume that they were occasionally caricatured, but spontaneously and impromptu so that no records are left.

Neither the use of a secular cantus firmus in a sacred Mass nor the practice of writing parody Masses can be interpreted as humorous. The first is a symptom, characteristic of all medieval life, of the total interpenetration of the religious and secular spheres.[1] The other is not a caricature but rather an homage. When Willaert writes a parody Mass on a Josquin motet, he thereby shows his respect for the older master. The later production is not a reduction of the model to another level but, on the contrary, the elevation to greater complexity.

Humor in music of the twentieth century, first intended as a reaction against nineteenth-century romanticism, suffers from the absence of a generally accepted and intelligible stylistic model. When everything seems possible and is freely admitted, caricature often remains indistinguishable from serious intent. Characteristically the models for humorous attempts in music of recent generations had to be borrowed from remote but stylistically clearly defined periods: Prokofiev's parody of a classical symphony; Stravinsky's use of themes from a Rossini opera or a Lanner waltz; Weil's imitation of a Handel finale.

In the visual arts, the human face behind a drawn caricature can always be recognized. In music, the model that makes humor possible has to be consistently redefined.

IDIOGENESIS-HETEROGENESIS

Musical growth can be accomplished only by either idiogenesis or heterogenesis (cf. p. 27 and *Matter and Form). To continue a given musical

---

[1]Cf. Huizinga, pp. 156 f.: "All life was saturated with religion to such an extent that the people were in constant danger of losing sight of the distinction between things spiritual and things temporal. . . . It occasionally happened that indulgences figured among the prizes of a lottery. . . . Nothing is more characteristic in this respect than the fact of there being hardly any difference between the musical character of profane and sacred melodies. Till late in the sixteenth century profane melodies might be used indiscriminately for sacred use, and sacred for profane."

unit, one can repeat it exactly or varied, or one can juxtapose a contrasting musical unit. There are not other possibilities of growth.

Any multipartite, such as a sonata or song cycle, exemplifies the most stylized mode of juxtaposition. The pieces form a series merely by lying next to each other. Topological considerations strongly influence cohesion. Apart from submitting to the unifying force of one key, the eighteenth-century dance suite, for instance, builds a structure by a convincing juxtaposition of heterogenous meters, rhythms, and tempi.

IMITATION

(1)   As distinguishing art from nature; (2) as distinguishing music from the other arts; (3) as a technique of music.

(1)   The question has been extensively treated ever since Aristotle, at the beginning of the *Poetics*, defined all poetry (which in Greece included all vocal music) and most instrumental music as modes of imitation. Although the *Poetics* does not concern itself with painting and sculpture, one can safely extend Aristotle's view of imitation as characteristic of all the arts. It distinguishes them as a whole from nature. This general point, well known, need not be further developed by a book that deals specifically with music. We may accept Aristotle's statement that "man is the most imitative creature in the world" and that we all "delight in works of imitation" (1448b). Art is an outgrowth of these two human characteristics. Aristotle distinguishes the arts from one another "in three ways, either by a difference of kind in their means, or by differences in the objects, or in the manner, of their imitations" (1447a). The first five chapters of the *Poetics* explain and support these generalizations by extensive examples from the poetic arts.

(2)   To distinguish music from the other arts, one can profitably proceed from identifying means, manner, and object of imitation in music. The first two pose no special difficulties. The means used by music are rhythm, melody and harmony—either singly or in combinations. This definition is already stated by Aristotle. The manner in which music projects whatever it projects can be inferred by us in analogy to Aristotle's examples from the poetic arts. We suggest that the distinction between vocal and instrumental music suffices.

The object of imitation in music has escaped all those thinkers who looked for it in the outside world, where the objects for other arts lie—action with agents in drama, forms with colors in painting. The most obvious acoustical phenomena in the outside world—bird calls, wind, thunder, breaking waves—have nothing to do with music, although desperate attempts at establishing a connection have been made (not to mention more removed phenomena such as sounds produced by machines, cities, and transcribed graphs). None of these outside objects has the slightest bearing on music, on a Haydn quartet, a Mozart concerto. Music differs precisely from all other arts by having an object of imitation that lies not in the outer world. It lies in our soul and in no other place. It is the form of the operations of the soul. If mechanistically inclined thinkers will reject this definition as being too vague and lacking concrete shape, Platonists, musicians, lovers, and the like can assure them that the form of the soul, the *eidos*, is *reality and that everything else in the outer world is shadow and reflection. Our experiences in this life are based on *mimesis*, imitation. Creative artists imitate the supreme Creator— painters and poets by imitating objects of the outer world, musicians by imitating objects of the inner world. We understand music because of this direct correspondence between the processes of our soul and those of music. Plato says outright that melodic movement imitates the passions of the soul.[1] The morphology of music reflects necessarily that of our soul. The two illuminate each other.

Safeguarded by this basic distinction between music and other arts, one can now raise the question to what extent all arts, including music, reflect the general condition, both physical and psychological, of the society from which they spring. Today one is certainly struck by the coincidence of fragmentation and disintegration of established forms in both art and society. We insist that such a coincidence is rare and happens only at high points or low points of an evolution. Art in general—music particularly so—is a mirror, not of an outer reality, but of an inner reality that need show little congruence with the state of outer affairs. Hence art, if we consider it at all a mirror, reflects aspirations as well as conditions of society. In this sense it is basically prophetic. It shows, not an image of the present, but a vision of the future. The convergence of both functions—reflection and aspiration—at high points or low points of an evolution indicates a turning point, literally a "catastrophe." By thus interpreting contemporary music, one may gain confidence in the imminence of a new beginning.

(3) As a specific technique in music, imitation falls within the more general concept of *repetition. We say that a visual motive is repeated, not imitated. Repetition, however, is felt as imitation when it occurs in time, as when a musical motive is heard in immediate succession and in a different layer or voice of a composition. Imitation presupposes a before and after. It is a concept proper to time.

The morphological gain produced by imitation lies in the area of growth. Imitation is a means of extension by idiogenesis. Hence it also serves the cause of unity. Exact imitation can easily run into conflict with tonality, particularly when the "sensitive" semitones of the scale are involved. Tonal imitation resolves the conflict in favor of tonality; real imitation, in favor of exactness. An extreme case of real imitation is canon at the unison or octave. The mechanical repetition and artificial unity here bestow on imitation a slightly ludicrous aspect, which has been consciously exploited in deliberately funny instances of canon.

What actually protects imitation in music from becoming a grimace is the receding, while we are listening to musical imitation, of our consciousness

---

[1]*Laws* vii. 812c.

of motivic repetition as the main event in favor of an increased feeling of a new texture. In an imitative piece or section, our concern for the imitated motive soon weakens before the total impression made by the general *fabric. The interest in the development sections (or points of imitation, as some people call them) in a fugue derives primarily from this subordination of a single motive to the overall texture. Within the process, imitation in the narrowest sense has yielded to the projection of inner morphology.

IMPRESSIONISM

The term is borrowed from the nineteenth-century French school of painters who called themselves impressionists. In music, it has been used to characterize the style of Debussy and of composers influenced by his work. Whereas the visual term is precise, in music—like all borrowed terms—it is ill defined. Yet it possesses a significance that the following technical critique might elucidate.

An impressionist painter paints things as they appear to him rather than as he knows them to be. This statement can be expanded but will serve our purpose as it stands. A nonimpressionist painter—to support our thought by a concrete example—represents hair in as detailed a manner as possible. Dürer tended to show every single hair on his famous rabbit. He would approach a lawn in a similar manner by identifying each blade of grass. An impressionist painter, on the contrary, strives to represent a mass of hair, or grass, in the way it appears to him as a whole from a distance. The contrast lies between objective and subjective representation, or between imitating what one knows to be there and what one actually sees. Each mode possesses its own and valid truth.

When attempting to transfer this contrast to music, we must, of course, exclude the outer world. In its place we put sound. To the different ways of the painter's feeling and seeing nature correspond the different ways of the composer's feeling and utilizing sound. The composer's written score becomes the thing to be interpreted. It is susceptible of different translations into actual sound; for just as painters can see the world in different ways, so musical interpreters (composers as well as performers and readers) can hear notation in different ways.

What is an impressionistic musical interpretation? We continue to use the word *interpretation* in the widest sense to include the composer as interpreter of his own notation, which he has chosen. Suppose that in a succession of notes the single note is intended to correspond to the single sound it symbolizes. We may call this translation into sound nonimpressionistic or objective. Suppose that, on the contrary, in a succession of notes the single note is not intended to be heard as such but rather as an ingredient of a sound compound. We may call this translation into sound impressionistic or subjective, because the subjective sound impression does not correspond to the objective notation picture. To illustrate the distinction, think of a scale passage written the same way in piano concertos by Mozart and Grieg. The identical notation admits of different interpretations—in this case, demands them. At the root of the difference lies the possibility of impressionism.

163

The restriction of our example to a succession of notes, that is, a melody or scale, delimits the phenomenon from harmony. According to our definition, harmony qua harmony is always impressionistic, because the simultaneous sound of three or more tones is heard as a total impression. Even when we isolate the ingredients of a chord, the unified harmony provides a different experience. Therefore in regard to harmony, notation and impression never coincide. If thus all harmonic perception is impressionistic, the term, deprived of its distinctive meaning, here loses all further significance. To preserve the concept of musical impressionism, we must restrict its application to cases in which the relation of notation to sound might or might not be made impressionistic through interpretation. This choice, which is relevant in the interpretation of successive sounds, does not exist in regard to a single chord.

For the same reason, dynamics, rhythm, meter, and tempo are not susceptible to impressionism. Orchestration, on the other hand, provides a perfect example of the difference between the timbre of separate instruments and the impression conveyed by their combined sounds. Mozart's orchestra is clear: one recognizes each instrument as it plays a melody, and the various sections of the orchestra are kept distinct. By contrast, Debussy's mixtures, identifiable in the score, defy analysis at the moment of hearing. The blend is deliberately creating an impression based on more than just the aggregate timbres. No wonder that the orchestra sound is a particular characteristic of impressionist style. A piano reduction of *La mer* loses a main style criterion, whereas a Mozart symphony would not comparably suffer.

The first part of the same work by Debussy also provides a strong argument for the possible value of form as an impressionistic device. The notation suggests little connection between the episodes that compose this piece. There is barely anything to abstract from the written document toward a total form. Yet, magically, these rather detached episodes create in the mind a convincingly total form. The many seemingly unconnected or barely connected details give the impression of something unified.

These guidelines help us recognize impressionist elements in a number of familiar musical utterances such as trill, tremolo, Murky and Alberti basses, arpeggio, glissando, and others.

Among them, Alberti basses deserve special attention. They are designed to produce the impression of a chord moving within itself. They prolong the chord and at the same time maintain motion. Disparaging them is easy. Yet they allow melody to soar freely without distraction by harmonic or polyphonic complications. They represent a mode of homophony very near to monody: monody with a revolving harmonic background. (Hint to pianists: never play Alberti basses drily, for they are not melodies, but always with pedal or with a pedal effect.) This aspect makes Alberti bass an ancestor of related modern impressionist figures. One need only eliminate the unessential restrictive word "bass" while keeping intact the core notion "revolving harmony" to discover that Debussy's revolving chords are a modern version of "Albertis." The difference in the chords actually used is less remarkable than the difference in the role these chords play. From background status, the revolving chords have risen to become the main substance. The total sound, moving and changing within itself, has now become the main character of the piece, its actual theme. No longer is melody harmonized, but harmony has become "melodified." After two hundred and more years, Domenico Alberti has experienced a comeback he would not have been able to imagine.

On the basis of the technical musical meaning of impressionism, which determines a style of writing, a few remarks about Debussy are in order. He was led to his style by a conscious reaction against what he felt to be Germanic in nineteenth-century music. He reacted against symptoms such as strictness of form and development, emotive exhibitionism, and the trend toward the colossal. Against these he emphasized the chatoyant play of sonorities, the delicate melodic and thematic hint, and a more capricious employment of ideas. In historical perspective, as a reaction against Germanism, his music appears as the end of romanticism rather than as the new beginning he thought it was. This role of Debussy is true, if only for the musical earthquake that followed his death, but it should not blind us to the possibility of a different sequel. Seeds germinate sometimes unexpectedly after the storms of revolution have died down. The plainsong-inspired recitative in *Pelléas et Mélisande*, anticipated by Mussorgsky's *Boris Godunov*, might be one such seed; the development by terraced episodes, another. Heterophonic use of chords and melodies is already gaining a better foothold in contemporary music than sterile nonfunctional harmony.

Impressionism in its special sense is a historically limited phenomenon. As a general style criterion, however, it is perennial. It characterizes a quadruplum by Perotinus as much as a baroque trio sonata with figured bass; for in both cases and in many others before and after the nineteenth century—the total impression transcends the sober notation. Elements present in Debussy's impressionism may yet reappear in the future in new, unexpected guises.

IMPROVISATION

Improvisation is instant composition. The improvising performer acts as composer. He reproduces immediately his simultaneous mental processes. Hence the essential precondition for improvisation is the existence of an established *style. The connection of improvisation with style is so primordial that one might use the presence or absence of the art of improvisation as a telling criterion for the style power of a period.

In times of a generally accepted style, improvisation flourishes. Organum, faux bourdon, musica ficta, figured bass—these practices were favored by the strength of the prevailing style. Similarly, the great improvisers of the past—Frescobaldi, Bach, Beethoven—all functioned in periods defined by a clear and powerful style.

In stylistically uncertain or weak periods, on the other hand, improvisation withers away. In our own day, for instance, improvisation is practiced regularly only in jazz, the one stylistically secure if limited domain. Otherwise modern composers rarely devote themselves to improvisation. Organists, who are improvisers by necessity and therefore trained for it, generally have to fall back on styles of the past. They use work types such as fugue, theme and variations, and other models which supply, not an actual musical reality, but rather a morphological schema.

Some music cultures are based on improvisation. They include most non-Western music but also extend into plainchant. In the high cultures of traditional music of the Orient, the performer improvises on well-defined melodic models (raga, maqam, patet, etc.), in which style appears sublimated. An analogy in Western music is supplied by standard bass figures that serve the idea of improvisation: Romanesca, Folia, and other *ostinato lines; descending scale passages (the first prelude from Bach's *Well-tempered Keyboard*, the slow introduction to Mozart's "Dissonance" Quartet); predetermined chord progressions in jazz.

In both such non-Western and Western cases, the variation concept is all-pervading. Thus the difference between an improvised and a written-out composition is not one of principle. Apart from stylistic considerations, the enormous importance acquired by notation increases the difficulties of producing an improvised work able to stand comparison with a written one. It is mainly notation as an integral part of musical creation that has caused improvisation to lose the importance it possessed at times. The future of improvisation is tied to that of notation.

INTERPRETATION. See REALITY

INTERVALS

The relationship between any two tones is precise, for it embodies a particular quality that we experience aurally, and it also corresponds to a particular ratio that we express mathematically. Nevertheless we hear intervals in a variety of ways; for the initial precision does not preclude subsequent interpretations, as one might expect, but rather favors them.

The two tones forming an interval may be heard in succession or simultaneously. We call the former occurrence *melodic*, the latter *harmonic*. The distinction has both theoretic and practical implications. Melodic succession of two tones involves both time and distance. Harmonic projection of an interval, on the other hand, ignores time and basically abstracts from space (although distance has some influence on interval quality). Harmonically a twelfth is the same as a fifth; melodically these two intervals lie far separate from each other. The average range of the human *voice no doubt sets the limit; according to our traditional nomenclature, one never speaks of resolving a fourteenth, nor does one call the double octave a fifteenth. Contrapuntal technique treats the ninth differently from the second.

The two harmonic series, ascending and descending, contain all intervals. In the following diagram, both series, which can be continued into infinity, are conveniently stopped at 16, where the smallest interval in our system, the halftone, appears:

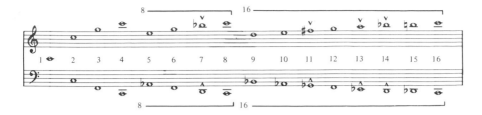

The series are the result of, respectively, string division and multiplication. The intervals produced are identical in both directions; but the tones, except for the octaves, are not. An interval produced in opposite direction from a reference tone is called reciprocal. Dominant and subdominant (G up and F down in relation to C) are reciprocal. They create the same interval but different tones. When, however, not the size of the interval but the pitch of a tone is reproduced on the other side of the reference tone, we speak of inversion. The interval of the fifth G above C becomes inverted when G is reproduced a fourth below C.

The hierarchical order supplied by the framework of the harmonic series is of two distinct kinds. Each tone in the series produces, first of all, an interval in relation to the generating reference tone; but it also produces intervals in relation to the other generated tones. We thus distinguish between primary and secondary intervals. The distinction serves our interpretation of intervals.

The primary intervals appear in order of diminishing degree of consonance (or, if you wish, increasing degree of dissonance).[1] From this order we except octaves because of their inherent quality of identity. The important intervals of the fourth (F in the ascending series, G in the descending series) and of the minor third (E-flat in the ascending series, A in the descending series) are absent. We can find them as secondary intervals between tones excluding the generator (3:4, 5:6). Johann Joseph Fux considered the question of the fourth "infamous and difficult."[2] Whereas he "decided" to classify the fourth among the dissonances because it is not a primary interval, Zarlino and Padre Martini admitted the fourth as a perfect consonance. We are led to resolving the ambivalence by the following explanations.

Except for the octave, all intervals are subject to interpretation according to context. The primary and most powerful factor determining context is the tonal system in use. To establish a tonal system, it is necessary to limit the indefinite unfolding of the generator in the two reciprocal series. The limitation may be external or internal. In our diagram above, the external limit is 16. This external index is not an essential structural principle but rather a practical convenience. The internal index, on the other hand, defines the means with which a system can be built. The internal index of the Pythagorean system is 4 (quaternarius), because all intervals derive from progressive fifths (a procedure still followed when we tune an instrument). The internal index of our present system is 6 (*senarius), for our model, since the admission of the natural third, has been the triad. Like the fifth, the triad is considered a perfect

[1]Cf. the authors' *Tone*, pp. 198–211.
[2]Fux, trans. Mann, *Parnassus*, pp. 20 f.

consonance. Now if a whole is consonant, then any two constituent tones heard as part of the whole are also consonant. Hence both the fourth (complement of the fifth in the octave) and the minor third (complement of the major third in the fifth) are consonant on any degree of the scale, provided they are interpreted as part of a "defective series" which we mentally complete. If we do not, the alternative is to interpret one of the two tones as a hypothetical generator, in which case the interval heard conflicts with the overall model, demands to be resolved into it, and is dissonant. If we listen to the fourth C to F as part of a series generated by a lower F, we assume a defective series and interpret the fourth as consonant. If, in the case of the same interval, the context makes us accept C as the generator, the model triad on C becomes operative against which we hear the fourth as dissonant. The consonant character of the fourth was probably more evident to the ears of a man in the Middle Ages than to our own, for he had not yet experienced our pervasive tendency toward, and our subsequent difficulty of abstracting from, the triadic model.

Similarly the minor third C to E-flat, which does not exist as a primary interval, becomes consonant when interpreted as complement of either the triad descending from G (C minor) or the triad ascending from A-flat.

The notion of complementary intervals can be carried further. The major second appears first as 8:9, that is, as the relation of the generator to the second dominant (and, reciprocally, second subdominant). We also find it between subdominant and dominant transposed to the same octave (F to G, or 2/3 : 3/4), that is, as the complement of one dominant in the other. The case provides good evidence for the influence of spacing. In the original position on either side of C, the interval F to G outlines the stable boundary of the basic minor and major triads. Transposed to lie within a fifth, the interval F to G assumes dissonant character because we interpret it in reference to the strongly suggested model of a triad.

The recognition of the wholetone, in our system, as a kind of intervallic module seems to be justified by the natural limits of the human ear. This interval actually exists in two sizes, 8/9 and 9/10. Whereas almost anybody can absolutely distinguish the two sizes of the next larger interval—the major third 4/5 and the minor third 5/6—even the best musician will have difficulties telling a major wholetone from a minor wholetone in absolute terms, that is, when hearing one or the other by itself out of context. (The distinction is obviously possible relatively, that is, when the two wholetones are heard in immediate succession.)

The harmonic series contain tones not used in our system. They correspond to the numbers 7, 11, and 13, all of which are unrelated to the senarius. Yet the number 7, producing the so-called natural seventh, is probably responsible for the particular function of the dominant seventh by pulling it down. We interpret the interval of the dominant seventh by hearing the smaller natural seventh through the diatonic or tempered seventh. Possibly the number 13, producing a flat major sixth, has an analogous effect by suggesting the lowering and downward resolution of the sixth in certain contexts ("una nota supra la sempre est canendum fa"). The tone produced by the number 11, lying slightly below F-sharp, is well known from hunting melodies appropriate to the natural horn. This interval suggests the tritone which, within the senarius, appears far-out at the ratio 45 (the major third of the second dominant, $5 \times 3 \times 3$, both as F-sharp above, and G-flat below, the reference tone C).

Within the framework of a scale, each interval lies at the crosspoint of the harmonic relation and the actual distance to the generator. The nature of each interval is determined by the interplay of these two morphological forces which, on the whole, stand in no proportion to each other. Thus the octave, the nearest harmonic relative, lies farthest away in the scale; and the fifth, the next relative, occupies a noncommittal approximate middle. The melodic steps of the scale define the intervals as they become coordinated with the harmonic framework.

The characteristic behavior of several intervals can be observed in the first fugue theme of Bach's *Well-tempered Keyboard:*

The main points within the initial scale (until *e,* before the first skip) are the three tones of the tonic triad. They are the points at which the scale changes direction. Between the triad tones, second and fourth are treated as passing dissonances. The fourth, however, shows all the ambivalence typical of this interval. Although a melodic passing note and in this sense a dissonance, it claims a strong place within the phrase (emphasized by the prolongation dot, which is missing in some eighteenth-century sources). The hearer is likely to be misled into interpreting *f* as the tonic, and the preceding second and third degrees of the scale as, respectively, the sixth and seventh degrees. This ambiguity deprives the first sound of *e,* the actual major third, of its triadic responsibility. Only the force of the fifth *g* and of the following *e,* which does not at all act like a leading tone, eventually clarifies the situation. The fourth becomes a motive interfering with the scale progression and thereby putting in relief the melodic contour. The skips are harmonically all consonant. The sixth degree *a* is free to go in either direction, being neutral in the pull between consonance and dissonance. The second degree *d,* however, necessarily retains its function as a passing dissonance. By thus hearing it between *e* (at the end of m. 1) and *c* (the final tonic consonance in m. 2), we understand that the skips split the scale in two. The upper line resolves at its own pace down from the sixth to the unison. Again the tones of the triad appear as markers. All intervallic dissonances are properly resolved except the last vexatious fourth *f;* but turning away from the third *e,* it becomes a passing dissonance pointing toward *g*—the precise pitch offered at this juncture by the entry of the *comes.*

Compared to the relatively restful tones of the triad, to the dissonant passing tones between them, and to the sensitive obligation of the leading tone, the major sixth alone of all intervals remains neutral and free. By expanding the fixed triadic outline, the sixth gives individual profile to a melody:

Haydn, *Die Schöpfung*, no. 30

Schubert, "Des Müllers Blumen"

Verdi, *Requiem*, m. 17

The treatment of the noncommittal sixth may become a style trademark. Schubert, for example, dwells on the neighboring quality of the sixth. In "Der Lindenbaum," the hovering of the never ascending sixth above the fifth forms the musical contents of the entire song.[1] Mozart, on the other hand, usually resolves the sixth as a passing note pushing up toward the octave. The fugue subject from the finale of his G major Quartet K. 387 spans a major sixth; one waits until the final cadences in the coda to hear the interval rounded off by the seventh and eighth degrees of the scale. In his overture to *Le nozze di Figaro*, the sixth of the opening theme gives life and continuity to the whole piece before being resolved in the coda.[2]

INTRODUCTION

The criterion for being an introduction is dependence on what follows. An introduction is insignificant without reference to the piece it introduces. A sonata movement deprived of its slow introduction can survive, but the reverse situation is morphologically impossible. The preludes in Bach's *Well-tempered Keyboard* are not introductions, though they serve a preparatory function. They are potentially independent pieces. The slow section preceding the fugue in a French overture always remains an introduction regardless of how long it may last. The orchestra music before the first curtain in Verdi's *Rigoletto* is in the nature of an introduction and hence never heard in concert performance; that in *La Traviata* is in the nature of an overture.

Noticeable is the slow tempo of most introductions in comparison to the following faster main movement, notwithstanding some exceptions particularly since Beethoven (finales of the Third and Ninth Symphonies, Bagatelle op. 126 no. 6). An introduction serves the same function as an upbeat and thus may be understood in terms of *rhythm. It is always an inhalation. In preparation for an extensive main event, one "takes a deep breath" rather than a quick one. The slow tempo of most introductions seems to be related to this physiological and psychological condition. When the "upbeat" of an introduction is missing, as in an Italian overture, the rhythm of the piece as a whole becomes inverted.

An introduction may serve as a kind of "table of contents"—an indication of what is to follow. Certain opera preludes, particularly of the potpourri

[1]For a detailed analysis, see Jonas, pp. 212–14.
[2]For a detailed analysis, see Levarie, *Figaro*, pp. 3–11.

type, fulfill this function (for example, *Carmen*). The introduction to Beethoven's Seventh Symphony, to give another example, dwells on the relationship of the fifth to sixth degrees of the scale in both the major and minor versions. The step and cadence E to F, or E to F-sharp, remains highly characteristic of all four movements.

Some introductions present the music *in statu nascendi*. The hearer witnesses the slow emergence and coalescence of musical motives. He is present at the birth of an idea which develops—a true *musica musicans*—according to its own necessity. Such is the situation at the beginning of Beethoven's last Piano Sonata; in the introduction to the finale of Brahms's First Symphony; or in the opening of Mahler's First Symphony (which contains the composer's comment: "Wie ein Naturlaut," "Like a sound of Nature").

The preliminary nature of an introduction may place it, as it were, "before creation." The case is obvious in the Introduction to *Die Schöpfung* by Haydn; clarification of the tonal and rhythmic intents occurs literally by hindsight from the appearance of "light" on the famous C major chord. When the guiding laws are less inherent in the piece than in the consciousness of the composer, the resulting "formlessness" manifests an extreme case of *musica musicata*. Ferruccio Busoni, commenting on Beethoven's revolutionary and liberating spirit, refers to the introduction to the fugue in the Hammerklavier Sonata as the highest accomplishment of this kind.[1] He continues: "In general, composers came closest to the true nature of music in preparatory and connecting movements (introductions and transitions), in which they permitted themselves to ignore symmetric relationships and, without knowing it, to breathe freely. Even the much smaller Schumann is gripped in such spots by the boundlessness of this Panic art—think of the introductory passage to the last movement of the D minor Symphony."[2] Such introductions neglect motives and structure in favor of personal instantaneous statements. There is movement rather than gestalt, for the role of memory is minimized.

INVERSION-RECIPROCATION. See INTERVALS

ISORHYTHM

Isorhythm is a principle belonging to the *variation complex. The possibility of varying depends on the permanence of a gestalt. Theoretically, a musical gestalt can be produced by any musical factor. In this respect, however, the roles of dynamics, timbre, and even harmony are limited (cf. *Variation). The elements determining a musical gestalt are mainly rhythm and melody. They are autonomous, notwithstanding their different complexity. They are the means for supplying a well-defined whole, a fixed gestalt, from which any kind of variation can proceed.

---

[1] Busoni, *Ästhetik*, p. 11.

[2] "Breathe freely" may convey the notion that the true nature of music is formlessness, but it certainly does not conform with Busoni's general philosophy (the esteemed Mozart and Bach above all). Nor would the authors have written this book if they agreed.

The variable elements in melody are raga, rhythm, and period. *Raga is the abstraction of pitches from melody. Rhythm is proportion in time. Period is a unit of discourse. Period is an integral factor of metric melody because it plays a role as a variant, and also of rhythm as a morphological entity because it supplies a form-generating force without which rhythm would act exclusively as a substance builder.

In the interplay of raga, rhythm, and period, isorhythm is the morphological result of permanent rhythm and period. In the following example from a motet by Machaut, the period of the tenor "Quia amore langueo" is ten measures long:[1]

It contains at least three different rhythms (♩♩, ♩., ♩♩♩♩), possibly five if one differentiates between the two forms of the iamb (♩♩ and ♩ ♩ ♩) and the two forms of the spondee (♩. and ♩ ♪). In medieval terminology, the period is called *talea*; the raga, *color*. If talea and color have the same number of notes, the resulting melody becomes an indefinitely repeated ostinato. In most isorhythmic motets of the fourteenth century, as also in our example, different melodies are formed by each talea. Said the other way around, the raga appears each time with a different rhythm. Eventually all combinations are used up after the last notes of both talea and color fall in the same place. In our example, the talea has fifteen notes, the color ten. Hence the series repeats after thirty notes, that is, after two repetitions of the talea and three of the color. In the case of a more complicated ratio of talea to color, an isorhythmic motet or Mass movement of the fourteenth century need not exhaust all possibilities.

If color is made a variant while the talea remains constant, melodic variety results at the price of rhythmic monotony. The shorter the talea, the greater the risk of monotony. The obsessive pursuit of this possibility is characteristic of Robert Schumann. In his *Humoreske* op. 20, the rhythm ♩ ♩ |♩ ♩· ♪ :|| repeats twenty-nine times in succession. In the finale of his Third String Quartet, the rhythm ♩ ♩ |♩♩ :|| repeats twenty-two times in succession.

If in addition to rhythm and period, raga (color) is also eliminated as a variant, the phenomenon ceases to be part of the variation complex. No variable element being left, the one remaining quality is *ostinato. When raga is eliminated altogether, isorhythm proper remains, that is, a *ritmo ostinato*. Characteristically, most obstinate basses in literature show isorhythm within the melody, as William Byrd's "Tregian's Ground" from the *Fitzwilliam Virginal Book* (♩ ♪ sixteen times),[2] Schütz's *Symphonia sacra* "Es steh Gott auf" based on a Ciaccona by Monteverdi (♩ o four times),[3] Bach's Passacaglia for Organ (♩ | ♩ eight times), and many others.

[1] *Werke*, 3:52 ff.
[2] No. 60, 1:226–33.
[3] *Werke*, 7:87–97; 191–98.

JUXTAPOSITION. See **IDIOGENESIS-HETEROGENESIS**

KEY. See **PHENOMENALIZATION**

KINEMATIC. See **PNEUMATIC-KINEMATIC**

KLANG. See **POLYPHONY**

LEADING TONE. See **ALTERATION**

LIMITATION. See pp. 11 ff.

LOCUS. See **REALITY**

LOUDNESS

Loudness in music is a means toward an end. Its morphological value depends on the way it is used. The immediate sensory appeal of loudness makes it an efficient tool for clarification of main events. Loudness becomes debased when employed to replace primary musical forces.

The paramount contribution is to rhythm. Dynamic *accent is here a basic ingredient that directly affects articulation and phrasing. Throughout the greatest part of music history, this function of loudness has been regulated by performers rather than composers; and to a considerable extent it will always remain a property of performance practices. The growing concern of composers with loudness (paralleled by that with timbre) is evidenced by a comparison of the almost total absence of dynamic markings in music before 1600 with the ever-increasing number of dynamic signs, symbols, indications, and instructions in compositions of the last four centuries. Two stylistic reasons account for the sudden and steep ascendancy of loudness as a morphological factor: particular emphasis on expression as illustrated by the development of opera, and secularization of *rhythm by meter as a concomitant of the new harmonic language. Both phenomena—expression and meter—are symptoms of a trend from *musica musicans* to *musica musicata*. The former can dispense with the idea of loudness, the latter thrives on it. We can think of a Gregorian Mass or Netherlands motet without reference to a dynamic frame, but we miss structural essentials by ignoring loudness in a symphony by Beethoven let alone by Mahler. The multitude of dynamic markings in the works of the most recent generations of composers is symptomatic of the rapid ascendancy of *musica musicata*—music "to which something is being done."

Giovanni Gabrieli's *Sonata pian'e forte*, of 1597, stands at the beginning of a development toward the end of which we find the entire music between two climactic scenes of Berg's opera *Wozzeck* consisting of a crescendo on one tone.[1] The stages of this development are not always necessarily distinct, but there are significant milestones. While *piano* and *forte* remain relatively rare indications in scores of the figured-bass period, the impression of dynamics could be conveyed by extra voices within a given texture, or the addition of ornamentation, or the juxtaposition of tutti and soli. The contrast of varying masses can shape not only phrases, sections, and movements but also entire multipartites. The three standard movements of an Italian sinfonia or concerto gain overall form by loudness as well as by tempo, texture, and other qualities. The high energy level of the two outside movements implies a general impression of loudness, whatever some internal fluctuations, in distinct dynamic contrast to the slow middle movement. The role of loudness in the formation of finale character is so obvious that Mozart could play a deliberate trick on a Paris audience by beginning the finale of his D major Symphony K. 297 *pianissimo* in order to evoke surprise and delight.[2]

From the middle of the eighteenth century on, loudness contributes ever more significantly toward the morphology of a piece. The popularity of the "Mannheim crescendo" as a new sensual musical device must not overshadow its meaningful occurrence at structurally important moments. The Mannheim composers often used crescendo to confirm an established, or to reach a new, key area.

Beethoven far exceeds his predecessors in specifying degrees of loudness. His dynamic markings always serve the structure by clarifying his plans. They may be simple accents—like the first sforzato, amply discussed by us, in the *Marcia funebre* of the Eroica Symphony—or extensive areas of tension and contrast. Loudness, in one way or another, inevitably participates as a distinct factor in the formation of his sonata recapitulations. Among the first movements of his symphonies, for instance, the recapitulation of nos. 1, 4, 5, 7, 8, and 9 occurs on a dynamic climax (*fff* in no. 8). In nos. 2 and 3, the moment of recapitulation is marked by a "negative" accent—a sudden *piano* after compact dynamic agitation. The Pastorale is special in every way: the recapitulation grows out of a subdominant, not out of the usual dominant, cadence; the first theme sneaks in, as it were, in the second violins; and the continued subdued dynamic level conforms to the overall intended effect.

As in all other matter and by definition, the classical period seems to strike the right balance between the sensuous and structural powers of loudness. After Beethoven, dynamics for their own sake increasingly predominate at the expense of primary morphological considerations. The literature from Berlioz to Boulez is full of examples, among which Ravel's *Bolero* and Honegger's *Pacific 231* are special studies in loudness.

LYRIC-DRAMATIC

Lyricism and dramatism stand in opposition. The former has to do with

---

[1]Act III, between scenes 2 and 3.
[2]See Mozart's letter to his father, dated 3 July 1778.

music (*lyra*, 'lyre'), the latter with action (*dran*, 'to act'). The French designation of opera houses as *théâtres lyriques* emphasizes the visible action by the noun, and the musical component by the adjective.

Lyricism is nonaction. The word points to compositions showing preponderance of a temperamental state or mood (the German *Stimmung*) over change generated by dialectics or struggle. To maintain a mood, lyrical pieces are generally short. Here belong the enormous number of character pieces from the nineteenth century but also from earlier times, whatever their names. Longer pieces exhibiting contrasts may still be lyrical provided the contrasts result from juxtaposition and not from generation. A scherzo-trio-scherzo, for example, is a lyrical piece as we hear the contrasting sections set side by side, whereas the contrast of a second to a first theme in a standard sonata form creates a potentially dramatic situation. Lyricism is basically ontic, and hence the contrasts within a lyrical piece are also ontic, like black and white, each element accepted for what it is.

Dramatism is action. In music, which lacks reference to the outer world, the term can be explained by its history and interpreted by analogy. Dramatism entered music through opera. Except for some forerunners of opera, such as certain madrigals and motets, the dramatic concept was peripheral to music before 1600. Under the influence of the enormously successful music drama, the symphony came eventually to be regarded as a counterpart in absolute music of contemporaneous opera, particularly of Wagner's. The excitements, tensions, and releases associated with such terms as "development" or "climax" have grown synonymous with dramatism in music. These terms had no meaning earlier; even Beethoven spoke only of a middle, and not of a development, section. Operatic dramatism in absolute music is in principle one of effect. It draws the hearer into the event, into the "action." Compared to ontic lyricism, which has always been inherent in music, gignetically oriented music seems to have been introduced from other arts. To this extent, dramatism in music is a romantic feature.

There is, however, another kind of dramatism, not of effect but of structure. Being therefore more specifically musical, it needs no theatrical analogy. It is the dramatism indigenous to contrapuntal techniques, of which fugue is the most prominent representative. Characteristically, predecessors of the fugue before the spread of opera were so undramatic that Frescobaldi, for instance, advised organists to end the ricercari in his *Fiori musicali*, of 1635, wherever convenient to them without waiting for a denouement. Our different inner responses to the two kinds of dramatism are significant. A musical drama like Beethoven's Fifth or Ninth Symphony or any of Mahler's symphonies makes us come out older; the experience is chronal. In an organ fugue by Bach, on the other hand, time stands still; we come out of the event aggrandized. These observations are overstated but help sensitize us to two fundamentally different kinds of experience.

Lyricism and dramatism meet when lyrical means produce a dramatic impression. Pieces lyrical by themselves may form a dramatic progression resulting in what may be fitly called "terrace dramatics." The five movements of the Ordinary of the *Mass or the numbers of a song cycle belong in this category. The concept is applicable to all multipartite works such as suites, sonatas, and the like—aside from works purposefully so composed—whenever the principle of contrast is not the sole determinant factor of succession. Terrace dramatics thus becomes a useful tool for the macro-analysis of multipartite works.

The epic mode is absent from the tone world; for music, being pure presence, can tell no story. Epic works of music are therefore always vocal, the literature alone contributing the epic character. To infer from the music of, say, Chopin's Ballades that they ought to be understood as stories told, is impossible. They are actual musical happenings. Real *program music is not epic but rather dramatic with the help of directed associations.

MAGNITUDE

In the context of discussing *beginning, middle, and end, Aristotle stipulates that "to be beautiful, a living creature, and every whole made up of parts, must not only present a certain order in its arrangement of parts, but also be of a certain definite magnitude."[1] The argument at first proceeds from the spectator's and listener's position. If something is very small, our perception becomes indistinct. If it is vast, the unity and wholeness of it are lost to us because memory refuses to take it all in. Aristotle quickly dismisses this argument relative to the beholder as not falling within the theory of art under discussion. He turns categorically to "the limit set by the actual nature of the thing."

When is a piece of music too short or too long? Is there a morphological defect of magnitude in a quartet movement of twenty seconds by Anton Webern and, at the other extreme, in the four evenings of Richard Wagner's *Ring* cycle, each considered as one complete event? The general respect shown by our investigation of musical morphology for the kind of limit demanded by Aristotle must be understood with our initial qualifications.[2] Music happens within us. Hence whatever morphology we uncover in a composition must correspond to a morphology of our soul. The objectification of a piece of music for which we have declared ourselves is methodically useful and, for a study of this kind, even necessary, but it is in essence imaginary. Thus the two critical approaches to magnitude really merge into one. The Webern movement probably is "too" short to permit our perception to become fully activated; and the entire *Ring* cycle probably is "too" long to be carried on one single wave of our memory; but both works can claim an inherent order and shape of their own.

In all art, magnitude quickly transcends its primary quantitative meaning and points to the relationship between outer size and inner content. Why does the model of a cathedral not affect us like the full-sized building? Schopenhauer gives the correct explanation that the idea of a work, rather than external characteristics, is its theme and gives it real significance.[3] The magnitude of the model is wrong; outer size and inner content, phenomenalization and eidos, do not correspond. The disparity between ideal value and physical dimension finds expression in the story of David and Goliath and similar myths, and in common critical phrases like "a giant with clay feet" or "a paper dragon." We call a work "overblown" when the contents are inadequate to produce the superimposed

[1] *Poetics* vii. 1450b–1451a.
[2] Cf. "Fundamentals and Methods," pp. 3 f.
[3] *Die Welt als Wille und Vorstellung*. Ergänzungen zum dritten Buch, Kap. 35.

size. Wrong magnitude is often comical but also disagreeable. Michelangelo's *Moses* reduced to the size of a paperweight offends. Small works, on the other hand, may gain particular intensity by "bursting at the seams" with content. Good examples are some of Beethoven's last Bagatelles and some of Chopin's Mazurkas.

There is doubtless something impressive about sheer bigness. When we behold a giant at a country fair, we do not ask whether he is intelligent. Some artists are obsessed with large size. Berlioz repeatedly confessed his preference for large means. This attitude links magnitude in music not only to duration but also to the body of performers. The two factors are interconnected, if only because the mobilization of a hundred performers for five minutes of music would be highly impractical. A large performing body is justified by musical thoughts requiring considerable time for unfolding and exegesis. In his *Requiem*, Berlioz succeeded in filling a preconceived magnitude with inspiration sustained by workmanship; but in his *Te Deum*, the substance is hardly a match for the nine hundred performers (among them over one hundred string players and three choruses) employed in the first performance.

In determining magnitude, understood as a relationship, by the scope of the eidos, the masters have generally favored content over sheer extension. The concomitant economy corresponds to our feeling that an unfulfilled potential, though a shortcoming, is preferable to inflated oversize. In any case, real grandeur is never the result of bigness alone. Adequacy of magnitude has been well known to scientists as the "Principle of Similitude." In his famous essay "On Magnitude," D'Arcy Thompson credits Galileo with the earliest formulation. "He said that if we tried building ships, palaces or temples of enormous size, yards, beams and bolts would cease to hold together; nor can Nature grow a tree nor construct an animal beyond a certain size, while retaining the proportions and employing the materials which suffice in the case of a smaller structure. The thing will fall to pieces."[1]

MAJOR-MINOR. See HARMONY

MANIFOLD

A manifold is a piece of music complex in itself but not divided into separate movements. Long movements are always manifolds. In homophony, the complexity derives from the succession of sections; in polyphony, from the superposition of parts. Hence polyphonic manifolds depend less on length than homophonic: a thirteenth-century motet is relatively short but yet a manifold by virtue of the several autonomous melodies. A movement from a sonata by Beethoven is always a manifold; a folksong, almost never.

A manifold is to be distinguished from a *multipartite. Both relate directly to the morphological implications of multiplicity and unity (cf. Discourse, pp. 39 ff.).

[1] *On Growth and Form*, pp. 15–48.

MASS

The formal structure of a Roman Catholic Mass is determined by the liturgy rather than the music. A Mass contains eighteen sections of which eleven are sung, and the rest spoken. An inquiry into its musical morphology would be irrelevant were it not for the arrangement of five selected sections into an artistic whole, as first attempted in the fourteenth century and subsequently adopted as a model. The five sections are liturgically connected by all belonging to the *Ordinarium Missae*—that part of the rite that remains unchanged throughout the year. But in an actual service, they are heard as scattered items within a complex totality. The following table visualizes the arrangement (italics marking the sung numbers, and capital letters the *Ordinarium*):

> *Introitus*
> *KYRIE*
> *GLORIA*
> Oratio (prayers, collect)
> Lectio (Epistle)
> *Graduale*
> *Alleluia* or *Tractus* (with *Sequence*)
> Evangelium (Gospel)
> *CREDO*
> *Offertorium*
> Secreta
> Praefatio
> *SANCTUS*
> CANON
> *AGNUS DEI*
> *Communio*
> Post-communio
> *ITE MISSA EST* or *BENEDICAMUS DOMINO*

Kyrie and Gloria, preceded by the sung Introitus, follow each other without interruption. But there are five items, three spoken and two with impressive music, between Gloria and Credo; three items, one of them sung, between Credo and Sanctus; the recitation of the fixed rule according to which the sacrifice of the Mass is to be offered, between Sanctus and Agnus Dei; and there are three sections after the Agnus, one spoken, and one of the two sung sections, Ite Missa Est, belonging to the Ordinarium. In short, within the service, the five movements in question cannot possibly be heard as a unified structure. On the other hand, the artistic unification of just these movements has become a reality in the hands of composers. The explanation that composers have favored the *Ordinarium Missae* over the *Proprium Missae* because the former can be performed frequently and the latter only once a year is doubtless true though a bit cynical. Nor does this explanation account either for the omission from the usual setting of the Ite, which belongs to the Ordinary, or for the neglect of most composers to set only one or the other movement from the Ordinary instead of bothering with an entity of five.

The morphological reason for the musical structuring of the Mass is symmetry. The unity of the five movements makes no sense within the context of the liturgy, but it has emerged through the centuries as a realization of the potential of symmetry. The articles of faith as pronounced in the Credo form the appropriate center around which the other sections revolve. The inner symmetrical frame is shaped by the jubilant character of, respectively, Gloria and Sanctus; the outer, by the triple plea for mercy in both Kyrie and Agnus Dei.

This particular symmetry projects an energy curve: from the humble beginning, the intensity increases up to the central Credo and then flows back to the final prayer for peace. Throughout all changes of style, this principle of symmetry remains the primary morphological force for the Mass as a whole, although other elements may contribute. In the Renaissance, the presence of a *cantus firmus provided unity. In later periods, key relationships, much more than motivic correspondences, reinforce the architecture.

The individual movements are structured to the extent permitted by the text. Musical principles seem to be favored by the three-times-three exclamations of Kyrie-Christe-Kyrie, the refrain "eleison," and the syllabic paucity inviting melismas. The implied bowform is more often created by the different behavior of the Christe section than by an actual recapitulation. Thus in the Third Gregorian Mass (of which Kyrie I has served our inquiry all along), the rise and fall of the Kyrie melody becomes inverted by the fall and rise of the subsequent Christe.[1] The closing Kyrie section then reestablishes the original kind of curve without offering a melodic recapitulation. In later Masses, the contrast of the middle section is accomplished by the devices of the particular style. Among them, a change of texture is most common, as from chorus to soloists in the Bach and Beethoven Masses. Key relationships participate. Exact recapitulations are rarer than one may assume. Of the eighteen Gregorian Masses in the *Liber usualis*, only five utilize a literal da capo (nos. 5, 11, 12, 16, and 18) although a few others contain some melodic correspondences. The bowform is blurred, if anything, by the practice of setting the word "eleison" as a melodic refrain. Such is the case in the Third Mass where the gain is the articulation of a different kind of unity. The principle of bowform asserts itself by invading each of the three sections rather than spanning the whole movement.

The expansion or other modification of the very last Kyrie exclamation, a frequent occurrence, is a limiting signal pointing to the imminent end. In all styles, the magnitude of the Kyrie movement is open to fluctuations, depending on the manner in which the sparse text is musically expanded. The melismas common in plainchant easily evolve toward freely invented themes that produce fugal structures in polyphonic Masses. In Bach's grand Mass, for instance, both outside sections of the first movement are fugues, though on different themes, framing a more relaxed Christe section in which parallel thirds and sixths between the two solo voices predominate.

The Agnus Dei has a comparable ternary organization. Instead of a refrain, however, the incipits of the three sections are identical; and the text

---

[1]*Liber usualis*, pp. 22 f.

variation lies not in the middle of the whole movement but at the end. Both these characteristics often point toward strophic structure. The two text variants ("miserere nobis" and "dona nobis pacem") have exactly the same number of syllables and the same rhythm so that one setting satisfies all three strophes. When composers, as often happens, write new music for the closing Agnus statement, the potential barform may become realized, thus superimposing a binary orientation on a ternary basis. In Josquin's *Missa Pange lingua*, for example, the third sentence with the prayer for peace forms an epode against the preceding two identical strophes by virtue of new material and more than double length. In Bach's Mass, the epode quality is clearly marked by the weight of the chorus after a solo aria. Archetypal ternary form proves stronger than the text when the composer specifies that the third sentence be sung to the music of the first. In Josquin's *Missa La Sol Fa Re Mi* for four voices, an "Agnus tertium super primum" creates a musical, though not textual, bowform around a central duo.

The Benedictus-Sanctus unit hardly admits anything but a binary structure because of the "Osanna" refrain which terminates each half. Tradition, more than anything else, has preserved in most Masses of all periods the musical identity of both Osanna sections. This almost mechanical repeat is compensated for by the distinctly contrasting quality of the two preceding strophes. The exuberance of the "Three Times Holy" yields to the welcome greeting of the gentle blessing. The expansive Osanna refrain notwithstanding, a decrescendo of intensity is the main morphological contribution.

Gloria and Credo supply the musically least pliable texts. Both abound in words, most of them not at all lyrical, so that the composer, in his effort to maintain overall proportions, is often driven toward syllabic recitation. To salvage an independent musical life, composers have frequently sacrificed the liturgical supremacy of the text. Bach made eight separate numbers out of each of these movements, against the spirit and letter of the Roman Catholic service and for the gain of musical structure. His placement of the Crucifixion at the exact center of the whole work (in the subdominant, in the minor mode the strongest functional tension) reconciles the musical with the religious current. Among the separate numbers, alternation of texture, key, and tempo assures a musical form where none was given. Haydn repeatedly sacrificed the sacred text in favor of musical proportions by letting the chorus recite different sentences at the same time (cf. the early *Missa brevis* in F major, of 1749–50; the *Missa Sancti Nicolai*, of 1772; the *Missa Sancti Joannis de Deo*, also known as the *Little Organ Mass*, of about 1775; and to a certain extent, but less so, the late *Missa In tempore belli*, of 1796). Haydn, as the story goes, may thereby have accommodated the priest waiting at the altar, but he was not the man to yield to pressure without a musical gain in return. In his *Missa Sancta Cecilia*, of 1769, to mention another device, he shapes the Credo into a rondo by repeating the profession of faith as a refrain. Five years later, Mozart proceeds similarly in his short F major Mass K. 192. (As if the musical violation of the sacred untouchable text were not enough, Mozart takes the exceptional trouble of marking *piano* several appearances of the word "Credo" and ending the whole movement with the refrain in a soft imperfect cadence.)

The main legitimate musical outlet of both Gloria and Credo is the closing "Amen" exclamation. Against the preceding length of each movement, a cadence on two tones or chords, one for each syllable, would be a most abrupt and unsatisfactory termination. Even in the generally syllabic Gregorian Gloria and Credo settings, the respective Amen formulas admit of melismas. In polyphonic Masses, these "free" spots soon became a musical playground unhampered by liturgical text and restrictions. The traditional "Amen Fugue" of later centuries is clearly anticipated by corresponding extensive contrapuntal subtleties in Netherlands compositions.

Mass composition, particularly the Ordinary, presents the unique case of the same text inspiring music of distant and different styles. The history is continuous, and the effort unaffected by changes of taste. Whereas a lyrical poem, by contrast, remains bound to a specific situation, the Mass text is universal. Not only does the Roman Catholic Church consciously claim this universality, but the admission of monody, homophony, and polyphony; of soloists and choruses; of small ensembles and huge apparatuses; of all known styles and techniques; and of all countries and centuries—this unique adaptability of the text gives musical support to the religious claim. The influences of style produce variants, but the principle remains intact. We recall how the Kyrie may change appearance or how the Agnus may approach barform. The lines may blur and the limitations be shifted: the original ternary force of both these movements survives. So does the morphological potential of the whole Mass cycle.

MATTER AND FORM

*Phenomenalization means limitation, which is the most general principle of order. The process of becoming, of individuation, involves unlimiting and limiting. They are the basic and universal polar forces of creation. The terms "unlimited" and "limited" are Pythagorean. Goethe observed and described the effect of these forces in plant growth as, respectively, alternate expansion and contraction. Modern scientists have suggested identifying this concept pair with energy and organization.[1]

The process of becoming points in the general direction of differentiation. It builds a morphology. In the inorganic world, magma leads to elements; in the organic, plasma to organs. The morphé of becoming is characterized by successive expansions and contractions (inhaling-exhaling, diastole-systole, life-death). That the general trend toward differentiation might itself be subject to the law of expansion-contraction is assumed in the hypothesis of a pulsating universe. According to an old Hindu myth, one exhalation of the "unknown God" creates the world, one inhalation makes it again disappear.

Differentiation arising from the interaction of unlimiting and limiting eventuates in a certain mutual independence of matter and form. In nature, the variety of vegetal and animal shapes exemplifies the presence of similar matter in different forms; the identity of crystal shapes produced by different

---

[1]Needham, *Biochemistry and Morphogenesis*, p. xxxiv. Organization here has to be taken literally as a process of growing organs.

elements, the presence of different matter in identical forms. In art, the examples are legion—portraits of the same person in different media, rondo forms in different compositions, the same composition in different instrumentations, etc. In the phenomenalized world, the two forces of unlimiting and limiting become polarized in the concepts of matter and form.

Here unlimiting is manifest in endless repetitions of the structural units, of matter. The growth would result in "cancerization" of the world unless checked by the polar limiting force of form. This limiting first affects the internal structure of matter. Thus it appears early as a necessary condition in atoms and molecules. Although in "free energy" the distinction between matter and form is hardly possible, limiting asserts itself already in the quantum concept. External form clearly appears in "directed energy," as in a magnetic field. As soon as matter becomes polarized with form, it becomes identical with content. This new opposition of content to form carries into the open the original dyad of the unlimited and the limited.

Although music is a psychic phenomenon possessing no external *reality and using no outside models, analogies with outer processes must be expected to exist. *Tone may be viewed as a sort of musical atom; of deceptively simple outer aspect, it possesses a far from simple internal structure. Analysis of tone ultimately leads back to the concept of energy in both a physical and musical sense. Chords, melodic motives, rhythmic motives are primary building particles like molecules: they possess a form that cannot be abstracted from their matter or content. These "atoms" and "molecules" initiate a process of proliferation, of musical extension. Music at the magical stage of culture is characterized by endless repetition of a small unit. It is music formed internally but not externally (cf. the remarks on jazz in *End).

The limiting that has caused the internal formation of matter can subsequently serve the external formation of matter. This presupposes an abstraction of the concept of form that is actually an enormous morphological step. Henceforth matter can be distinguished from form, form from content. The composer is well aware of these forces which he experiences directly and with which he has to cope in the process of composing. Let us assume that he has phenomenalized a first idea in the shape of a melodic theme or harmonic succession: how will he continue? This question concerns not the fashioning of the musical matter but the very creation of this matter. The two processes should be distinguished. Cell division does not explain the form of the plant or animal. The form of a brick does not foretell that of the finished house. The equilibrium attained at the end of the labor of individuation is the result of two polar forces acting in opposite directions. One force is unlimiting, extensive, generating: it creates matter. The other force is limiting: it creates form.

The principles of extension generating musical matter are actually only two: repetition or variation of the same material, or juxtaposition of different entities. The first kind we call *idiogenesis* (Greek *idios*, 'the same'); the second, *heterogenesis* (Greek *heteros*, 'other', 'different'). The principles limiting musical matter are less easily defined, as the *end of a piece always contains an element of the arbitrary. The solution worked out in a particular composition can usually be isolated (cf. the six cases treated in detail in the systematic Discourse of this book), but further generalizations remain elusive. The

182

principle of proportion in the widest sense seems related to all limiting processes.

The interaction in music of the two polar forces of unlimiting and limiting underlies explicitly or implicitly all thoughts directed, as in this book, toward a musical morphology. The following table need not be taken too literally, but it serves as a means to clarify and order ideas underlying the process of musical phenomenalization:

AESTHETIC PRINCIPLES

Growth-Limitation
Matter-Form
Multiplicity-Unity
Open-Closed
Abundance-Economy
(Etc.)

EXTENSION FACTORS	SHAPING FACTORS
a. *Idiogenesis*	1. Breathing
Repetition	
Variation	2. Metrics (incl. Symmetries)
(incl. Metamorphosis)	
	3. Contrast
b. *Heterogenesis*	
Juxtaposition	4. Dialectics

SHAPES

Gestalt	Extension Factors	Shaping Factors
Breathing Form	Indeterminate	1
Bowform	b	2, 3
Barform	a	4
Sonata Form	a, b	4

Above everything stands, and into everything enters, the grand general aesthetic principle of growth and limitation. Below it, extension is distinguished from shaping. The final results are shapes or gestalts. A few traditional, crystallized forms listed in the left column are explained by corresponding extension and shaping factors in the parallel columns to the right. Not all participating extension and shaping factors have been marked, but only those necessary for the form concerned and characteristic of it. Breathing form has indeterminate extension factors because, being the basic form, it is present in almost any combination.

MELISMA. See **ORNAMENTATION**

MELODRAMA. See **WORD AND TONE**

MELODY

Technically, a melody is the togetherness of single tones in time. It is a time gestalt. It exists as a whole in time; and any part of it, large or small, exists as a function of the whole.

One can treat melody gignetically. In this approach, one distinguishes between up and down, and step and skip, both subordinate to the general forward motion from a *beginning to an *end. One is left with few morphological norms which might permit one to judge a melody "good" or "bad," in the way in which harmonic norms permit one to judge a cadence. Hence the teaching of melody has remained incomparably more difficult than that of harmony. The latter can be rationalized, whereas the former remains dependent on either intuition or imitation of samples. Intuition, which cannot be taught, can to some extent be formed by such limiting devices as arbitrary restriction to the number of tones that may be employed ("write a melody on only two different pitches," "three different pitches," etc.). Imitation of samples can be taught at the risk of sterility. In short, while our perception of a melody as we hear it is gignetic, this process by itself does not elucidate the melody as a whole.

By treating melody ontically, one has a better chance of arriving at meaningful morphological norms. Melody understood as a gestalt rather than as a process is essentially ontic. It is probably the purest time shape. Its "prime mover" must be sought in something lying behind the tones. The tones themselves, not unlike points in a graph, are guide marks of a continuous line. This line arises from the morphé produced by an energetic process. In addition to this function as the phenomenalized points in an energy curve, tones form relationships with each other according to harmonic principles. We are thus faced with three layers: tone relations at the surface, tone points behind them, and an energetic process at the source. While merging into one total quality in the actuality of melody, the separate phenomena possess properties specific to each which contribute to the character of the final product.

In the foreground of tone relations, different interval steps clearly exhibit expressive powers of their own not present in, nor deducible from, the deeper layers. If a melody changes from the major to the minor mode, the new character is due to the changed interval relations and not primarily to the somewhat modified energy curve. At the next layer, the tone points are a rhythmic phenomenalization of the energetic morphé. One must imagine them to be initially not completely determined as to exact pitch. A somewhat deformed melody can still be recognized. The contribution of the tone points lies precisely in rhythm. The morphé of the energy process finds itself affected by the application of different rhythms. This morphé itself is not a sensory, but rather an inner, phenomenon. It needs tone to reach us through the ear. Anyone following the composer can only conclude back to its existence through apperception of the actual melody. Yet it must not be supposed to exist in the mind as a mere hypothesis. It is a real though incompletely determined morphé.

Melodic forces are more or less regularized by harmonic forces. Defined as widely as possible, "harmonics" act also on a plainchant melody, although the workings are best shown by way of a typical case. Mozart's Piano Sonata in

A major, K. 331, begins with a closed melody that subsequently serves a chain of variations. The morphé of the energy process is related to the tonal orientation of the given key, that is, the scale and triad of A major. We sense that the harmonic force is spread out in time in a particular way indicated by the tone points. The third and the fifth heard in the first measure each start a line down toward the reconciling unison. The entire first half of the melody can be plotted by points showing the way, but neither line reaches the expected goal. The metrics of the style admit two more or less parallel drives (mm. 1–4 and 5–8). In the second half, the octave span is completed or, if you wish, the goal first attained in the wrong range before the restated drives unite and finally succeed. All along, the particular relations of the points on these lines create surface tensions and resolutions which contribute to, and clarify, the total behavior of the melody.[1] Considered as a whole, the morphé—to the extent to which it can be at all described—appears harmonically energized and ontic.

The relative brevity of this entry exemplifies the difficulty of reasoning about melody. The immediacy of all musical elements is, of course, everywhere inexplicable; but at least we understand certain fundamental laws of harmonic or rhythmic systematization. If, as has been said, harmony finds resonance in the rational part of our being, and rhythm in our muscular nature, melody needs intuition as the mode of apprehension.

MEMORY. See **TIME AND SPACE**

METER. See **RHYTHM AND METER**

MODALE

In the traditional system of Western music—explicitly since the sixteenth century but de facto much earlier—the triad is the model for harmonic norms. We are used to defining relationships in terms of the triad and its constituents, fifth and third. In antiquity, the prevalent generating interval was the fifth; for whereas the octave, resulting from division of the monochord string by 2, continued to repeat the same tone in different ranges, the fifth, arising from division by 3, produced ever-new tones and eventually the entire tone system. Pythagoras still sacrificed the major third, the result of division by 5, to the particular *temperament of his tuning. This attitude has carried over into modern times so that we traditionally relate all tonal functions to either the upper or lower *dominants.

The sovereignty of the triad justifies the consideration of the third as a normative determinant in its own right. Because the third is the interval that defines the mode of the triad, we shall call it, for harmonic purposes, *modale*. The reciprocal (lower) third can analogously be called *submodale*. The recognition of the modale as a direct function within tonality stems from the

---

[1]For a detailed analysis of this melody, see Appendix A, pp. 309 f.

musical practice of at least the last four hundred years. There is a precedent: our admitting the direct relationship of the minor third in the concept of relative chords; and what applies to a derived interval such as the minor third should be all the more convincing in the case of a primary interval such as the major third.

The nearest examples in C major of the modale are the major triads on E and A-flat. They might, of course, be understood in dominant terms—the former as a secondary dominant of the tonic relative and hence a dominant substitute; the latter as the minor-subdominant relative and hence as a subdominant substitute. All depends on the context. Classical harmony is likely to relate the keys in question to the main functions of dominant and subdominant; romantic widening of the harmonic concept, to the modale and submodale. Beethoven's experiments are noteworthy. The middle movement of his C minor Piano Concerto (1800) is in E major. So is the second key area in the opening movement of his C major Waldstein Sonata (1805). The *Leonore* Overture No. 3 (1806), also in C major, balances the E major key of the second subject by heavy emphasis on A-flat major. In the *Missa Solemnis* and also in his Ninth Symphony, both in D (and both first performed in 1824), the frequent occurrences of B-flat major are significant. When Brahms places the four movements of his First Symphony in the key sequence C-E-A^b-C, the harmonic function of the two middle movements is readily interpreted as a symmetric play of the modales around the tonic center.

MODE. See PHENOMENALIZATION

MODULATION

Over the centuries, the term *modulation* in music has come to mean passing from one key to another. We define key as the realization of a mode at a certain pitch, that is, at a certain tone. Mode, in turn, is the functional organization of tones expressible by a cadence. This organization crystallizes melodically in a scale, and harmonically in a cadence in the narrow sense of the word.

The question does not interest us here whether in a given case we deal with a real modulation or an enlarged cadence. The evaluation involved is essentially a function of duration and of elevation of viewpoint. It is correct to say, for instance, that a chorale by Bach never modulates. If a European travels to America for one month, that is a cadence. If he stays there a quarter of a century, that is a modulation. But if he then returns to live in Europe and looks at his whole life, it will have been a cadence after all. If, on the other hand, he had died while in America, it would have been a definitive modulation. But if one considers the earth as a unity and each person as a citizen of the planet, the change appears insignificant and one can no longer distinguish either cadence or modulation.

The classic definition of modulation, sufficient and valuable when applied to certain styles, is nevertheless not universally valid. Assume that we move from G major to A major, or from G minor to A major. The operation meets the conditions set by our definition. Does it still when we move from G major to G minor? One could say yes but with some hesitation. We have changed the mode and not the tonic; but within the spirit of the classic definition, the change of tonic seems to be more important than that of mode.

When a phenomenon or a group of phenomena refuses to fit a given concept, one can either enlarge the old concept or create a new one. In the present case, a conveniently enlarged definition provides a sufficiently elevated viewpoint for discerning that what is called modulation today is only one aspect of a grand principle that admits varied applications.

The term offers no opposition to manifold interpretation. *Modulation* comes from the Latin *modulus*, which signifies 'measure' in a most general sense. *Modulus* is the diminutive of *modus*, which originally meant the same. Subsequently the two words developed so as to form a multitude of meanings. Mode in music signifies different particulars in melody, harmony, and rhythm. In French (and German) the word changed from masculine to feminine when *le mode* (manner) became *la mode* (fashion). The module of architects most closely approaches the original meaning of the term. Related to it is St. Augustine's definition—of which the fame matches its ambiguity—that "musica est ars bene modulandi" ("music is the art of modulating well"). The evident capacity of the word allows us to ask: which is the most general possible definition of modulation that will still remain musically meaningful, that is, useful?

Let us regard plainchant attentively and, so to say, naïvely without being prejudiced by any modal theory. We notice that frequently within the same piece the centers of gravitation are mobile; that within the same piece B-flat can alternate with B-natural. The "modules" (tones and semitones) shift according to the centers of gravitation. Whereas modulation in the classical period consists of transposition, here it is made by change of mode. This fluctuation of modes within a composition doubtless played a role in plainchant and polyphony until the middle of the sixteenth century comparable to that of modulation in classical tonality. From this viewpoint, the labyrinth of opinions by theoreticians of the Middle Ages and until Glareanus is suddenly illuminated, and their efforts at a theoretic comprehension of the given musical matter appear as what they were: efforts with conceptually inadequate tools.

The incertitude of Gregorian modality indicates to us the path toward an enlarged concept of tonality. Tonality is always tied to the notion of function; but the way toward a unique tonic, well defined and represented by a definite pitch, was long and slow. The end, historically speaking, lasted only one moment. One can imagine periods in which melodies were rather badly defined. If we may speak of a system—simply for the convenience of the expression—we can say that it received its support from one or several tones (doubtless the privileged tones of prime, fifth, and fourth) but that it was very mobile concerning the pitches of the other tones which were changing and often ill defined. Plainchant has preserved many examples of this early state.

According to this concept, the ensemble of utilized tones possesses actually an importance superior to that of its elements. This means that one must attribute the quality of tonic to the entire ensemble. Consequently, the interior modifications, that is, changes of mode, acquire the quality of modulations. We must imagine a deformable, plastic system as the primary entity and consider the tones as functions of that system. One might call this interpretation a simple change of viewpoint, but the change is important. By our affirming the primacy of the system over the tones, the reduction of the ecclesiastical modes to the sole major and minor modes during the Renaissance appears in a new light. The importance of mode diminishes because there are now only two. That of key, on the other hand, increases because henceforth a great many can be employed. The tonic acquires a hitherto unknown preeminence. Modulation no longer occurs by virtue of the plasticity of the system, which has become rigid, but by a displacement of the system on the scale of available tones. Modulation through change of mode on the same tonic continues, of course, but plays only an insignificant role compared to transposition.

How does contemporary music fit into this perspective? To answer this question, we must first eliminate all those extremist tendencies characterized by the negation of any order, of any system, and by the essential utilization of noise or almost-noise. Nor shall we have anything to say about that segment of contemporary music which is deliberately written in a style of the past. Dodecaphony is a special case.[1] The remainder is characterized by the employment of new modes or by the new utilization of established modes. Here the internal changes of a sounding system become again more important than the external changes by transposition. Modulation by an interplay of modes is once again honored. The possibilities of a plastic system combined with those of transposition open wide perspectives.

In summary we say that any modification of a tonal system constitutes a modulation. Giving to the term *system* the strictest meaning, we see that both internal modifications of a scale (for example, C major—C minor) and external modifications by transpositions of a fixed system (for example, C minor —D minor) fall under this concept. Thus defined, modulation is the passing from one tonal system to another.

MONOPHONY. See **MELODY**

MONOTONE. See **VOCAL MUSIC**

MOTIVE

A musical motive is the shortest unit that maintains independent identity. A motive, in its literal sense, indicates a moving power. While the characteristic identity makes a motive recognizable in recurrences, the potential of the motive makes these recurrences altogether desirable.

Any musical element may serve the identification, and usually several elements participate. For a better understanding of their morphological contribution, one must try to think of examples in which each element functions

[1]See Levy, "Essay sur la dodécaphonie."

in relative isolation. Melody and rhythm are the most common formative powers. Purely melodic motives can be found in Netherlands compositions. The Phrygian halftone (E-F-E) at the beginning of the Gregorian hymn *Pange lingua* is probably the most characteristic motive unifying the various movements of Josquin's Mass of the same name, notwithstanding the presence of considerably longer phrases throughout the work. One recognizes the Phrygian motive regardless of rhythm, texture, or timbre. In Bach's Third Brandenburg Concerto, on the other hand, a similar halftone progression at the head of the opening theme (descending in this case) is so much tied to rhythm that the motive subsequently maintains its force even when a whole-tone replaces the halftone, provided the anacrustic shape is preserved. In the hands of Beethoven, the preponderance of rhythm becomes ever more audible. Thus the opening motive of his Fifth Symphony exercises its force even when totally deprived of pitch connotations. In a less extreme case, as in the opening Allegro of his First Symphony, the melodic part of the motive

, except perhaps for the halftone progression, soon loses

out before the rhythm; and in the first movement of the Seventh Symphony, one barely thinks of the otherwise attractive first melody in comparison to the motivic drive of the dotted dactylic rhythm.

In addition to melody and rhythm, harmony contributes significantly to motivic formation in Wagner's operas. The sound of the "Tristan chord" alone suffices to create a particular experience. But even when melody and rhythm contribute, in many of Wagner's leitmotives, harmony provides the more striking identity, so in the *Ring* the augmented triad of the Nothung motive and the descending inverted triads of the Sleep motive. Part of Wagner's leitmotive technique is modification for expressive purposes. When a motive is changed, one can pinpoint the morphological elements that are intrinsic and those that are variable. The shift of the Youth motive from major to minor when Freia is abducted in *Rheingold* keeps intact the characteristic rhythm and melodic line. In the many appearances of the Contract motive, only the idea of a descending scale remains constant.

Under circumstances, even timbre alone may serve as a motive. The single horn tone in Verdi's *Ernani* is an example, not of a common technique, yet of a persuasive one. The dramatic meaning of the particular sound is clear enough to push the action to the final tragic point.

MOVEMENT. See **MULTIPARTITE**

MULTIPARTITE

We call *multipartite* a musical work forming a whole but composed of separate pieces. In suites, symphonies, and similar works, the separate pieces are usually referred to as movements; in operas, as numbers and acts. The idea of a whole is essential though it varies in force. One can measure this force by the relative dependency of the parts on the whole.

Here a historic distinction proves useful, for multipartites eventuate from one of two diametrically opposed tendencies. A musical continuum may grow so complex and long that it eventually falls apart, or various short pieces may group themselves along some line to form a more comprehensive entity. The final products may seem similar, but the role of the underlying cohesion varies.

Instrumental canzoni and ricercari of the early baroque illustrate the first case. In the hands of Andrea and Giovanni Gabrieli, they were relatively long continuous pieces consisting of many short sections. A generation later, these sections asserted their inherent motivic independence by separating from one another. The newly gained freedom let each individual section grow in size and complexity so that by the middle of the seventeenth century, within the extension of the original "sonata," the reduction of the number of sections to four had been fairly regularly established. Even when these movements of the multipartite seemed to lose any obvious interrelationship, as in most later baroque sonatas, the idea of an original whole remained a strong morphological factor. In the eighteenth and nineteenth centuries, when concert programs often featured single movements from larger works, we find complaints about "interrupted" and "partial" performances. Whatever unifies the movements of a classical sonata or symphony, the cohesion is paramount. The result is a true multipartite.

Dance suites, on the other hand, are looser structures. The idea of a unit remained strong only in regard to the two opening movements which developed from the archetype of a dance in duple meter followed by a faster variation of the same dance in triple meter.[1] Known as pavane and galliarde, pasamezzo and romanesca, dantz and hupfauf, reigen and nachtanz, these two dances supplied the seed for the later baroque dance suite under the names of allemande and courante. Any number of other dances were added, each suitable for a satisfactory independent performance. Under the influence of the four-movement sonata, the sequence of allemande-courante-sarabande-gigue eventually crystallized as the French norm. But although the insertion of other movements remained free, none ever interrupted and broke apart the original entity of allemande-courante.

Between the true multipartite structure of a classical sonata and the looser stringing of a baroque suite, some hybrids make it difficult to judge how independent the parts really are. How does one approach the question of inevitable unity in the case of Bach's borrowing a movement from one of his own concertos for inclusion in a multipartite cantata?

The reasons for multipartition vary in significance. The most obvious and pragmatic reason is the threat of fatigue. Works of considerable duration, such as operas and symphonies conceived to be played without interruption, make great demands on attention span. The required mental breath transcends the capacity of most listeners, who at some point will disengage themselves from the music through sheer fatigue. The performer, who simply cannot allow himself to become disengaged, has a better trained mental breath, and the stimulation of performing militates against mental as well as physical

---

[1]The *Urpaar*, in Wilhelm Fischer's terminology. Cf. Adler, *Handbuch*, pp. 351–53.

fatigue. Yet the considerable exigencies of concentration produce both mental and physical fatigue so that, in fine, performers and listeners alike welcome the opportunity of a break to draw a restorative "deep breath." String players use interruptions also for tuning up. One might say that "going out of tune" is the result of "fatigue" of the instrumental material.

Fatigue is most effectively remedied by a change of motion—a new "movement." This term points to *tempo, which is indeed a weighty cause of multipartition. The inertia of any given tempo is great. Long stretches can be characterized by a common density of time production. Contrasting tempi are therefore readily associated with breaks in musical continuity—much more so than keys and melodic substances. The alternation of slow and fast—slow-fast-slow-fast in the traditional eighteenth-century sonata and suite—provides a welcome relief from musical weariness.

Multipartition is an element also of style. It offers discontinuity against the apparent continuity of life. The mere stylization, always an attribute of an artifact, is in itself a morphological factor. Moving pictures are not stylized to the extent to which they dispense with distinct "acts." With increased continuity, a movie runs the risk of drifting from artifact to documentary. For similar reasons, a "number" opera is always more "artistic" than a through-composed attempt at realism, although the mere presence of other elements, such as singing, safeguards the inherent stylization.

In works combining text and music, extramusical factors contribute to multipartition. The musical organization of a song cycle seems to stem from the morphology of the poetry; of a *Mass, from that of the liturgical ritual. In its higher types, however, such morphology is always consonant with the principles of musical morphology. The strong inspirational power of the Mass text on composers is due not only to its contents but also to its eminently musical organization. Symmetry and proportion similarly determine the poetic and musical flow of the twenty songs that form *Die schöne Müllerin* (see Appendix A, pp. 309 ff.).

With growing size an organism grows also in complexity. It develops increasingly distinct organs while becoming more unified in the sense of centralization. In a musical work with a strong central unifying idea, the actual separation into parts articulates the continuum less than the breaks would indicate. In such a case, the style factor remains the most prominent feature of multipartition.

MULTIPLICITY AND UNITY. See pp. 39 ff.

MUSICA MUSICANS-MUSICA MUSICATA

The two terms are, respectively, the active and passive participles of the Latin verb for 'making music'. *Musik in Geschichte und Gegenwart* defines *musica musicans* as music determined by immanent laws of musical structure and by the grammar of musical language, *musica musicata* as music serving the unfolding of passions.[1]

The distinction is helpful, for it touches on a basic polarity. It is related to that between music as testimony and music as expression (cf. *Communication). In one case, music "actively" unfolds from its core by following inner necessities. In the other case, music "passively" is employed to convey a message for an outside purpose. The polarity relates to many opposite musical experiences encountered under divers names. We find it at the two extremes of the aesthetic scale which the *Motu proprio* sets up and identifies with Gregorian chant (*musicans*) and Italian nineteenth-century opera (*musicata*). We recognize it in the pendulum between fugue and toccata, classicism and romanticism. Practically, compositions and styles do not demonstrate one or the other quality in pure isolation. Yet the usefulness to morphology lies in making possible the diagnosis of a tendency.

NORMS. See **ARCHETYPES**

NOTATION

The fixing of music has passed from memorization to writing and now to recording on disc and tape. None of the later stages has made its predecessors obsolete so that today all stages coexist. The art of dance finds itself at present in the position of music long ago, for attempts at fixing the dance work in written symbols are in an early experimental stage. Possibly in the future dance will appear to have skipped the middle step in the process of passing directly from memorization to recording of the physical manifestation in a motion picture.

Each mode of transmission has its peculiarities both in regard to what is being transmitted and what is left to interpretation. The peculiarities in turn affect the composer's task, that is, his mode of phenomenalizing the spiritual essence of the work. In other words, the mode of notation becomes an element of style. This influence ought not to be underrated, nor should the concomitant limitations be considered as annoying fetters to be shed in due time. All individuation owes its existence to limitation. What we call style in particular is always the result of a definite set of limitations. The very selection of discrete tones for the establishment of distinct scales is an effect of limitation that forms recognizable style characteristics.

Notation reflects style. The assumption is erroneous that early notations were necessarily more primitive than ours. To the extent to which they served a different style from ours, they were entirely adequate. Our own notation of the last few centuries has proven as practical as the composers using it needed it to be, but it harbors its own deficiencies. It contains, for example, no special symbols for triple meter, which has to be written down as a makeshift variant—and often a misleading one—of duple meter. By comparison, Re-

---

[1] In the article "Levy, Ernst."

192

naissance mensural notation was far superior in this respect. The style demanded it.

Closest to memorization is notation which is content with suggesting and reminding. Neumes give a perfect illustration. Long before Gregory the Great, the Greeks had devised various systems of exact pitch definition. The early Church could have utilized any one of them had style and tradition demanded it. Instead, emphasis on living transmission (and perhaps a bit of esoteric secretiveness) professed the conviction that performances are meant to be but passing suggestions of immortal ideas. Memory is a living recording apparatus; successive performances are witnesses to the ever-changing aspect of the work in the mind of the transmitter. The role of the performer as a collaborator of the composer here becomes evident. Plainchant neumes kept this cooperation unqualified for a long style period. The active participation of the performer can be equally observed in the transformation processes undergone by many folk tunes. The immortality of great melodic essence shining through superimposed accidental interpretations is amply documented by the survival of chants and songs through approximate notations and inappropriate renditions.

Most systems of notation, old and new, employ visual symbols; and for an understanding of the principles it hardly matters whether these symbols are letters of the alphabet, original designs, or dots and dashes. Systems that indicate mechanical fingering rather than musical processes we take to employ signs rather than symbols. Already the Greeks distinguished between a symbolic notation for vocal music, and a fingering notation for instrumental music. Later, lute and organ tablatures fall in this category. Society today, in a general distrust of symbols and with a strong inclination toward mechanization, has revived fingering notation in sheet music and all those instruction books for beginners on the recorder, electric organ, and whatnot that promise quick mastery of music by nonmusical means.

One basic style change among all other notations, occurring around the year 1000, signifies a drastic revision of man's view of the symbolism of music. The modern staff, credited in its incipient form to Guido d'Arezzo, represents properly the morphology of the tone field as formed by *time and space. The horizontal direction of the lines reflects chronology; the vertical arrangement, pitch. Among the many variants evolved in the last one thousand years, the modern score, compared to individual parts common until the sixteenth century, represents an increase of spatial orientation.

Discs and tapes provide a particular form of notation; for, like a written score, they serve the transmission and storage of sound. The typical and common experiencing of music through radio and recordings rather than in live situations has brought about a confusion of values that touches the morphology of music. Mechanical recording transmits just one state of utterance of the work—a state depending on a particular place, a particular time, and a particular performer at a particular point of his life. It freezes the appearance of the work on one single occasion. The performer's responsibility approaches that of the composer. His utterance, which cannot be thought of except as happening at an incidental moment, gains permanence and is made to endure. Yet there is no listener witnessing the interpretation except an electro-mechanical device. The spiritual artistic collaboration with the audience is split into elements of performance and listening. The complete event, involving together composer, performer, and listener, is left to a chance happening in the future. If the recording is made at a concert performance, its main value is still only suggestive; for at best it will have the power to conjure up the performance in the minds of those who actually attended it. Imagination here, too, proves stronger than the physical *reality.

Considering the growing popularity and success of electromagnetic notation, one has encountered the question whether concerts, by and large, might not eventually grow obsolete altogether. Let us assume the possibility of recordings so perfect as to be absolutely identical with the performance. Has notation abandoned its role as symbol and usurped that of the work itself? A distinction remains. The ultimate goal of the musical experience does not dwell in the sound of a work but in the idea it phenomenalizes. The essence of a work cannot be obscured by the substitution of the symbol for the thing symbolized. The sheer technical excellence of discs and tapes entails the danger of falsifying the locus and essence of musical reality.

ONTIC-GIGNETIC

Every phenomenon can be considered in two different manners:

(1)   Outside time, or absolutely. The phenomenon appears under its eternal aspect, unaffected, immobile. We shall call this character *ontic* (from the Greek word for 'being').

(2)   In time, or relatively. The phenomenon appears under its natural aspect, changing, charged with multiple forces. We shall call this character *gignetic* (from the Greek word for 'becoming').

The words *static* and *dynamic* have been used to convey a similar distinction, but in music they only produce confusion. Music, first of all, is never static, regardless of the viewpoint from which it is considered; and dynamics has become so closely associated with, and appropriated by, sheer loudness that it has ceased to serve any other function.

According to our initial distinction, any tone or agglomeration of tones can be thought of in two different manners. Ontically, it is isolated from the notion of time and heard as a definitive entity (*sub specie aeternitatis*). Gignetically, it is considered an experience in time and heard as an evolutionary entity (*sub specie momenti*). To listen to a musical phenomenon in the ontic sense is to listen to it for itself. To listen to a musical phenomenon in the gignetic sense means to charge it with currents. In reality, all music presents at the same time both aspects. By analogy, we can experience the sea ontically when we see it or think of it as a whole, but also gignetically when we follow or are hit by the separate waves.

The usefulness of the distinction may be illustrated by our applying it to a specific example, for the sake of convenience to the opening eight measures of the Funeral March of the Eroica Symphony.

Ontic Aspect	*Gignetic Aspect*
The melody exists as an idea that I can evoke instantaneously. I know it without having to imagine the detailed sequence of musical events.	The melody moves from the fifth degree of the scale up a ninth. It builds up energy as it goes, and creates dissonances that call for resolution.
The G major triad at the end of the first four-measure phrase is a perfect consonance.	The G major triad confirms a half-cadence within the key and thereby carries a dissonant tendency.
The first tone g_1 is an isolated sound.	The first tone g_1 induces a current that flows somewhere.
The dotted rhythm of the first three notes is a definitive event.	The dotted rhythm pushes forward toward an expected evolution.
The tempo as set determines the flow of time.	The tempo is slow in relation to my normal pulse.
The volume is consistently soft.	The restrained dynamics will eventually lead to an outburst.
The sound of the instruments is defined in advance by my concept of the "Beethoven orchestra."	The various instruments and sections of the orchestra are bound to concertize against each other.

Music history could profitably be studied from the aspect of hidden forces—the forces that are "backstage," polarized in ontic and gignetic principles but constantly interlacing and combining. The ontic, hierarchic principle clarifies particularly certain typical, but for us unusual, features of Oriental music. As for Western music, a quick glance at the sequence of the main historic periods seen in the light of our antinomic pair might validate the usefulness of the case in point.

For almost a thousand years following St. Gregory's revision of chant, the hierarchic principle rules. The music which it determines, at first monodic, then polyphonic, reveals a tonal space rigidly structured, which the gignetic-melodic influence is slow to penetrate and modify. We deal here—and the statement is only an apparent paradox—with an art essentially harmonic. The art lacks harmony in the modern sense, of course, entirely so and by definition during the monodic period, and in principle and to a large extent during the polyphonic period. "Harmony," in this music, means first of all the totality of the employed scale, which is the melodic projection of mode but of which the treatment depends on the value of the position of the notes more than on their tendencies and tensions. The sounds of a quadruplum by Perotinus cannot be explained and understood in any other way.

Later, in the thirteenth century, we encounter a play of consonances and dissonances of the intervals of the mode. The relationships, however, are still not triad-directed. The interplay bears upon the value of intervals, on the "more or less consonant," on the "more or less important," rather than on the disturbance of a consonance that would demand and engender a "resolution" of the gignetic kind.

When in the Renaissance the musical consciousness of the perfect triad becomes specific, the triad continues to be used in a hierarchic sense. It serves most frequently as a rather "viscous" base, hardly mobile, yielding under stress rather than generating it. Any pseudo-harmonic piece by Josquin illustrates this attitude, for example, the famous section "Ave vera virginitas" from his four-part *Ave Maria* which hides the motivating canon behind apparently simple triads. Let it be said in passing that every true polyphony evolves on a harmonic basis, manifest or hidden, which it is difficult to deform.

Alteration, in a style based on a space so well defined and of a structure so firm, is slow to appear and assert its role. There had been attempts to introduce chromatic alterations in Gregorian chant, reaching as far as E-flat and C-sharp, but they were repressed or hidden through transposition as a result of the opposition of the Church to any kind of chromaticism.[1] In a polemic pamphlet of 1487 against musical novelties, Nicolaus Burtius explicitly states that among the diatonic, chromatic, and enharmonic genera, "mater ecclesia ex his tribus dyatonicum delegit" ("Mother Church chose from these three the diatonic").[2] The ambivalence and extreme care accompanying *musica ficta* for centuries reflect the justified fear that a gradual defiguration of the system would bring about an eruption of dynamism. One could say that in its long fight against alteration, the Roman Catholic Church showed apprehension—more or less consciously—of the danger of chromatic gigneticism in its role as a destroyer of hierarchy.

During the century of the Protestant Reformation, chromatic dynamism made lightning progress. For a few generations, extremist tendencies in the hands of the young eclipsed the hierarchic structure of tonal space. The revolutionary drive of Gesualdo's music pushed so far as to suppress and delete any points of density that might resist the deformations. At the same time, popular microtonic experiments were undermining the habitual positions for orientation.

Paradoxically, these forceful innovations failed to join the main current of the development. The event important for the future was the recognition of the triad as a functional unit. Zarlino's formulation of this insight, almost exactly contemporaneous with Nicola Vicentino's most effective chromatic and enharmonic experiments, set the course for the music of the next three to four centuries. In fact, the drastic change of style around 1600 disregarded the immediately preceding accomplishments. Opera, the big new venture, emerged as a product of the conservative Counter-Reformation.[3] One can say that this *stile moderno*, this *nuova musica*, was in many respects a renewal of ties with a remote past.

[1] See Jacobsthal, *Chromatische Alteration.*
[2] As quoted in Lowinsky, *Secret Chromatic Art*, pp. 111 f.
[3] Cf. Levarie, "Early Opera."

The new reign of functional harmony did not hesitate to utilize for its purpose melody, rhythm, and meter all at once. The new system, which lasted into the beginning of the twentieth century, is no longer based on intervals but on the perfect triad, of which the latent gigneticism is brought into full value and thoroughly explored. The tonal space is organized by a hierarchic system of harmony, but now openly energized. From this concept stem all the rules governing the treatment of dissonances in the music of the last three hundred years. Chords and tones are understood as carriers of tendencies. Subdominant and dominant triads point in a direction, suspensions have to be resolved, sevenths brought down, augmented intervals stretched. This reinterpretation of musical space makes intelligible the tonal language of the classical masters.

The crisis challenging the primacy of functional harmony has been identified with Wagner's *Tristan und Isolde*[1] Isolated thrusts had been experienced earlier. When Berlioz, in the "Tuba mirum" of his Requiem Mass (1837) placed the note D-flat below a well-established E-flat major chord and then simply moved to D-flat major, treating the apparent third inversion of a dominant seventh chord like an independent sonority, he asserted the ontic aspect of dissonance—an acoustical gain to be weighed against the insinuation of a different structure. Gignetic forces have been attacking ever since, and the hierarchic style has found itself dissolved. Most modern composers, Schönberg first of all, have exploited the inherent anti-hierarchic (if not anarchic) possibilities. In the cyclic alternation of attitudes, one can observe the reappearance of the ontic principle today in such trends as pandiatonicism,[2] neoclassicism, and various individualistic expressions of faith in new concepts of tonality.

This brief historic sketch has interpreted variations of musical grammar, that is, style variations, as foreground manifestations of changes bearing on the structure of tonal space and arising from the interplay of ontic and gignetic forces. The study of the background of music presents, apart from any theoretic interest, an immediate practical advantage. When indeed a musical grammar appears to us uncomfortable to approach, the reason lies in our not having penetrated, in our inability to hear, the particular structure of the tonal space which is the hidden source of style.

OPEN-CLOSED

The concept pair *open-closed* stems from visual art theory into which it was introduced by Heinrich Wölfflin.[3] He abstracted this concept pair, together with four others, from a comparison of renaissance and baroque art, which he saw as recurrent tendencies throughout art history rather than as specifically limited eras. Concepts valid in the visual arts cannot generally be

---

[1]Consider the mere title, aptly chosen, of Ernst Kurth's book, *Romantische Harmonik und ihre Krise in Wagners "Tristan"* ("Romantic Harmony and its Crisis in Wagner's *Tristan*").

[2]Well described by Nicolas Slonimsky in the article "Pandiatonicism" in the *Harvard Dictionary of Music.*

[3]*Kunstgeschichtliche Grundbegriffe.*

applied to music, but the pair open-closed possesses sufficient universality to warrant consideration.

The notion is certainly not foreign to music. We speak of open and closed cadences. Expectation, a basic concept in music, includes the possibility of not being satisfied and thus experiencing the effect of openness. These examples pertain to details. The morphological question is: are the concepts applicable to musical form as a whole? Are they as meaningful in music as they have proven to be in the visual arts?

Visual arts favor closedness. Paintings are tied to a definite format, of which the borders may moreover be accentuated by a frame. Architecture—which, of the nature of crystals, is whole by definition—may take over the role of a frame for both painting and sculpture. When freestanding, sculptures are usually confined by a pedestal; but already their very nature, tending toward the architectural, favors closed forms. The norm in the visual arts, in brief, is definiteness; and elements pointing toward the open, the unbounded, occupy an antithetical position.

The reverse is true in music. By nature, musical flow is continuous, indefinite. The *end of a piece is never quite free of a certain arbitrariness. Whereas the painter or sculptor, let alone the architect, is from the beginning preoccupied with form, that is, with limitation, the composer's very first concern is with creation of musical substance, that is, with growth. The artist finds space a given entity to be limited and shaped. The composer must create time, for clock time is nothing to him. His techniques of composition—repetition, imitation, variation—serve primarily the building of substance.

The natural tendencies of the visual arts and music thus show themselves to be contrary to each other. The former go in the direction of the bounded within space (the given medium of the visual arts), whereas the latter go in the direction of the continuous in time (the substance music has to create). In consequence, the prime reactions by painters and composers against these conditions or states are also contrary to each other. In the visual arts, the creative artist reacts against limiting form; in music, against formlessness. The painter tries to "break out" of the form, to "overcome" it. Think of Fra Filippo Lippi's *Madonna and Child with Angels* in the Uffici or Veronese's frescoes in the Villa Maser. The composer, on the other hand, always tries to limit and shape the primevally boundless. Every "rule" of composition in every style, even the mere fact of putting notes down on paper, attests to this concern. Involvement with form belongs to both the visual arts and music, but the approach is from opposite directions.

The primeval trend of music to remain open is illustrated in basic situations. A small child will repeat without end a motive or short phrase that pleases him. Tribal dance music builds substance by being continuous, and so does jazz, its offspring in many respects. The trend is unmistakable in oriental music, which favors endless production by repetition and variation. The active principle underlying all these examples is continuation, not shaping.

Music thus begins by being open and evolves toward becoming closed. It is originally nonarchitectural and exhibits Oneness of substance. Overall shaping architectural principles are concerns of a later stage. Continuity, first achieved by undiversified repetition, develops by means of diversifying variation toward multiplicity. Multiplicity, in turn, produces a trend toward unity, a new Oneness in diversity. The history of the dance *suite illustrates the development. The reversibility causes a dialectic process where either trend may be expected to appear as a major style characteristic of historic magnitude.

In the most general terms, one can associate open forms with monophonic and polyphonic periods; closed, with homophonic. In Western music, Gregorian chant is an admirable example of the former. The amazingly long period of nearly a millennium during which it prevailed can, of course, be explained by the political attitude of the Church and moreover by the absence of notation; but the inherent reason may be the great inertia of a monophonic music representing Oneness, that is, unity as yet little touched by multiplicity. Polyphony issuing from plainchant understandably shows a similar trend toward openness. The organa by Leoninus and Perotinus flow freely and uninhibited by architectural principles, which are gradually imposed from the outside by the behavior of the tenor. Netherlands polyphony sounds similarly open-ended and hence eventually calls for singularly forceful restraints, such as the structural proportions worked out by Obrecht. The mere fact that fugue, for instance, is not a form points to its basic openness. True polyphony is open by its very nature. Homophony, on the other hand, favors closedness because melody here grows powerfully cadential under the influence of metrics and harmony. The long historic development toward functional harmony is in itself an illustration of the evolutionary musical direction from openness to closedness.

The suggested stylistic distinction must be understood as a tendency only, for a masterpiece is always closed in some sense. The arbitrariness of the *end of a piece is a permanent reminder of the original condition of music. The manner of closing can serve as a convenient style criterion. Compare the almost casual swinging-out of a Josquin motet with the forceful tearing-off of a Beethoven finale. In isolating such a style criterion, one need consider only the actually present tendencies and not the original trends, with which they might or might not coincide. The power of a Beethoven cadence reverses or at least minimizes the basic inner drive of functional harmony toward the indefinite (as witnessed by the reciprocal urge toward each other of a major triad and the minor triad a fifth below). The motive or phrase sung by the small child may be naturally closed when considered by itself, but it becomes open through indefinite repetition. The same holds true for rhythm, without which there would be no melody.

The oscillations of the concept pair open-closed (originally paralleled by polyphony-homophony) are not of the nature of dialectics. The terms are antinomical and incapable of being dialectically developed toward unification by a third term. Thus far the evolution of the concept pair in music seems on the whole to have been unidirectional—from the openness of primeval monophony, past various style fluctuations between homophonic and polyphonic periods, to the extreme degree of integral closedness reached toward the end of the nineteenth century.

The contemporary efforts to reverse the trend are all symptomatic of a desire to return to a primeval state of openness. The question presents itself whether a grand historic cycle has been closed, perhaps reaching again the undifferentiated open One. Symptoms are not wanting. Foremost is an openness of both microforms and macroforms—a fragmentation, even a shattering of form incomparable with any former state. As never before, audiences can no longer tell the end of a piece from the music alone; they get the signal when the performer stops. The openness of jazz (to which we have alluded earlier) appears conservative in comparison with a work like Stravinsky's *Canticum sacrum*. Dodecaphony and serial writing are by definition not only open but also undifferentiated. So is the appeal to sonorities that approach or attain noise. This return to a One is fraught with the mass of acquired multiplicity become liquescent. Experiments in all directions have filled nearly three quarters of our century without producing a generally accepted and valid style—a symptom unparalleled in all music history and itself reaching toward openness. Whether we consider the grand historic cycle as closed or still open, the inevitable oscillation will push music in the direction of crystallization. The "rules" made by many modern composers to govern their own behavior, though often extramusical and hence not generally and naturally persuasive (rows, parameters, etc.), all point up the need for an eventual closing of musical forms.

OPERA

An opera is a vocal work sung by characters who also use words and act their parts. Both ear and eye are involved, and the appeal to the ear by *word and tone moves, moreover, on two different channels. The law governing the development of the passions and the symphonic law are not identical. Schopenhauer drew the merciless conclusion: "Strictly speaking, one might define opera as an unmusical invention for the pleasure of unmusical minds."[1] At all times, opera has caused difficulties because of a profound incompatibility between the laws of the various participating arts. The relationship of text and plot to music varies and accordingly produces different results.

Ideally, one likes to think of a complete amalgamation of the different arts so that their inherent morphological forces will cooperate rather than compete. This ideal may have existed in the *musikè* of the ancient Greeks, of which already Plato speaks with the regretful melancholy attached to a lost accomplishment.[2] The recovery of the ideal has guided the ambitions of every opera reformer, among which Wagner's *Gesamtkunstwerk* may be the most articulate formulation. The continuous struggle for a union of the arts takes on the meaning of a longing to restore an aboriginal state of affairs. From the viewpoint of an opera composer, what is artificial is the separation of the arts, not their reunion. Since the era of *musikè*, however, the conditions of the partners have radically changed. Poetry and music have developed away from each other. In the process, both have suffered a loss of their inherent magical essence and now find themselves relegated to a place apart from what modern man deems to be reality.

[1] *Parerga und Paralipomena*, vol. II, ch. 19, par. 224.
[2] *Republic* ii–iv. Also *Laws* ii.

In the light of these thoughts, we can examine the problem of opera by proceeding downward from postulates, from ideals. For man on the magical level, art is reality—a higher kind of reality than ordinary life. On this level, the distinction between creator, performer, and public is minimal and irrelevant. The member of the audience at one moment may be the creator and performer at the next. The unity of experience is perfect. Furthermore, all modes of expression—word, tone, gesture—are intimately tied to each other. To think of such a state in other than theoretic terms is difficult, because we have no experience of it. The nearest approximations available today might be dances of so-called primitive tribes, some song-plays of children, and religious ritual. The common quality of such manifestations is the creation of a community experience. There is no distinction between performers and audience. Words, music, and gestures all contribute jointly. "Opera" on this ideal level has two characteristics. First, the "work" is known to everybody. As a practical outcome, there is no problem of text that must be clearly understood. Second, realism in the vulgar sense does not exist. Nor does any of its consequences, above all "dramatic speed." Whenever this ideal primary state is abandoned, operatic difficulties arise, which become increasingly insoluble as the various elements draw farther apart.

Opera has been criticized for being unnatural. People do not sing arias when they are about to die. Such criticism misinterprets the meaning of art. Realism is the doom of art. If anything, life ought to be viewed in terms of art, and not inversely. A source of profound misunderstandings has been the use by poetry of words and phrases shared with ordinary speech. They do not mean the same thing in poetry and in daily life. The portion of realism in a Shakespeare drama is artistically the least important part of it. Modern movies have compounded the misunderstanding. The concert hall is somewhat protected, because the setting and the music itself are removed from any realistic interpretation. Opera, however, contains all the prerequisites for nourishing the misconception. The development of opera has done everything to feed it.

Granting that the operatic work should not be judged on the level of ordinary reality, we still encounter dilemmas built into the situation. The separation of the original community into a performing and a receiving portion is complete. The public is not inside the performance but outside. Hence dramatic speed is measured in terms not of inner time production but of clock time; the public brings to the performance a reaction speed taken from ordinary life. The "theme" is unknown to the public. Therefore the text ought to be clearly heard and understood; but poetry and music have developed away from each other, with divergent form tendencies.

Constrained by these facts, the composer has to do his work. The separation of the community into a performing and a receiving sector entails the necessity of a sort of "rape" of the audience: it has to be forced into participation. The immediate result is a striving toward effect, toward excessive tensions and climaxes. Opera has to become dramatic in the more vulgar sense of a "thriller." Drama being conveyed mainly through dialogue, the words ought to be clearly perceived by the public. But musical forms, being essentially architectural, use musical means—repetition, recapitulation, polyphony, etc.—which are in opposition to dramatic speech, still more to ordinary speech. Hence they are fundamentally incompatible with the postulates of both realistic dramatism and intelligibility of the text.

All these dilemmas can essentially be reduced to the difficulty of reconciling dramatic speed and literary clarity with a musical unfolding of forms. Because these two sets of postulates are incompatible, all operatic solutions have to be based on some sort of compromise. The history of opera reveals three compromise solutions. Either the music is subservient to the text, or the text is subservient to the music, or the two divide the field.

The first two categories contain least of a compromise and have therefore remained the most problematic. Text rules in the operas of the Florentine Camerata. Recitative from beginning to end generates little musical interest. Later examples of similar literary concern are some works by Gluck and Wagner, at least according to their own writings on the subject. Here also belong such operas of the twentieth century as Debussy's *Pelléas et Mélisande* and probably Berg's *Wozzeck*, although the latter shows a trend to revert to closed musical forms, not arias but purely instrumental structures like passacaglia, variation, et al. The other extreme which sacrifices text and dramatism to the exigencies of music is heard in those operas of which the librettos have been maligned, be it *Euryanthe* or *Il Trovatore*. Carried through consistently, this extreme would be the end of music drama in any current sense; it could exist only on a magical level. Nearest to this type comes the madrigal comedy. Exactly contemporaneous with the antipodal effort of the Camerata composers, Orazio Vecchi's *L'Amfiparnaso* spells out the attitude in the prologue: "This spectacle appeals to the imagination through the ear, not the eye."[1]

In a much-quoted letter (13 October 1781) Mozart wrote to his father: "In an opera the poetry must be altogether the obedient handmaiden of the music." Yet the solution Mozart followed in all his operas, and which he inherited partly from the Neapolitans and partly from popular comedy, can be best described as a "division of labor." The text leads in the recitatives or dialogues between the musical numbers; during the numbers, in turn, it becomes ancillary. Repetitions of words and phrases in arias make no literary sense but supply material for the musical form. The alternation of musical pieces and literary stretches is obvious in all eighteenth-century operas and modern Broadway shows. It may be less distinct in the *through-composed operas characteristic of most of the nineteenth century; but Wagner's attestations to the contrary, it exists as much in his works as in Meyerbeer's and Verdi's. The "literary" stretches are all those of which the music is not developed and structured according to purely musical laws. On the other hand, purely musical units recur, either in the form of arias and ensembles (Gralserzählung, *Meistersinger* Quintet, etc.), or tonally unified "periods" (Tristan's Awakening and Yearning),[2] or pseudo-symphonic pieces in which the voices are part of an instrumental web (Wotan's Farewell). The technique is recog-

---

[1] "Spettacolo, si mira con la mente,
   Dov'entra per l'orecchie, e non per gl'occhi."
[2] In Alfred Lorenz's terminology.

nizable in most post-Wagner operas, be they by Richard Strauss, Alban Berg, Britten, or Menotti, The result can be viewed as a "number opera" on the symphonic level.

Do these operatic numbers—the result of a compromise that has lasted three centuries—make a particular contribution of their own to musical morphology? The da capo *aria has done so; for beside serving the purely musical needs of an operatic situation, it has doubtless contributed to all instrumental compositions that contain a recapitulation. C. P. E. Bach's concept of a "veränderte Reprise" ("recapitulation with changes") stems in some way from the opera aria.

Otherwise the forms of numbers in operas seem to have followed general musical, rather than specific operatic, principles. One need not consider the overture, which, lying outside the opera itself, has always reflected the instrumental conviction of the day. The pieces within the opera are as conventional or as free as the composer cares to shape them. There are open and closed forms, strophes and rondos, variations and fugues. The employment of a form for characterization is an ingenious practice of Mozart's. In the opening duet of *Le nozze di Figaro*, for example, the expectation of strophes generated by the initial recurrent alternation of two distinct melodies associated, respectively, with Figaro and Susanna soon yields to the recognition that the disappearance of the Figaro theme halfway through the piece is producing a rondo based on the musical (and personal) superiority of Susanna—a superiority which the remainder of the opera amply demonstrates. For a morphological inquiry, however, only the opposite practice would be important; but the employment of dramatic characterization to create a musical form does not, to our knowledge, exist.

Closest to it come key relationships. The tonal organization of the whole of *Le nozze di Figaro* hinges upon subtle interplays of sharp and flat keys.[1] Tonal interactions also govern the structures of finales. The first *Figaro* finale parallels the increasing imbroglio of Figaro by a steady drop across five keys through the circle of fifths. In the first *Don Giovanni* finale, the huge C major structure gains cadential articulation from the most noticeable recurrence of the minuet, first in F major and then in G major.

Although questioned and attacked more than any other type of art, opera has proved its vitality again and again, in one guise or another, surviving onslaughts of aesthetic theory and practical sarcasm alike. Often declared dead and gone, it has kept alive on all levels from sheer entertainment to religious contemplation. This phoenix-like nature of opera has repeatedly puzzled observers, but one need not look far for an explanation. Human endeavors firmly anchored in the world of ideas are not jeopardized by the imperfections and vices of temporal realization. Though opera as a magical communion does not and cannot exist in the present state of society, the original quality of magic has not left opera altogether. The fascination with opera, we submit, is like a faint remembrance of its magical essence and of the pristine togetherness of language, gesture, and tone.

[1]For detailed analyses, see Hermann Abert's foreword to the miniature score (New York: E. Eulenburg, 195_), and Levarie's *Figaro*.

ORATORIO

As a musical structure, oratorio is best understood by comparison with *opera. Both were created at about the same time. Both grew out of the spirit of the Counter-Reformation—oratorio overtly so.[1] The musical development of both is at first almost identical. The emphasis on the chorus in oratorio reflects external conditions rather than morphological differences. To the epical character of oratorio, opera adds a further dramatic dimension; but when the epic quality becomes dramatically intensified, or the dramatic quality lyrically weakened, the difference between oratorio and opera begins to blur. Such is the case with some operas and oratorios by Handel.

At this point in history, the morphological development of oratorio stopped. The form froze while opera continued with new experiments. Apparently the eighteenth-century organization by separate numbers serves the purpose of oratorio better than any other structure. Haydn's *Die Schöpfung*, for instance, is morphologically no more advanced than Handel's *The Messiah* from which it is separated by more than half a century. The reason lies in the absence from oratorio of the basic conflict of eighteenth-century opera between separation by numbers and desirable continuity of action. Through-composed opera of the nineteenth century tried to resolve this conflict while oratorio, spared by virtue of its epical nature, retained a structural orientation which it is not likely to abandon.

ORGANUM

Singing in parallel fifths differs from singing in parallel octaves or unisons in degree rather than in kind. Any single melodic line contains morphologically parallel lines at many intervals. These parallel lines are clearly and inevitably audible at the initial relations of the intervallic hierarchy (1/1 unison, 1/2 octave, 2/3 fifth, etc.). They gradually decrease in loudness and eventually become only a theoretic potential. A mixture stop in a pipe organ is essentially the artificial reinforcement of one or the other or several parallel lines to the main melody. Labeled 6 2/5, for instance, it sounds parallel major thirds.

Organum originally functions in the same way. The new second voice phenomenalizes a line parallel to, and contained in, the given chant. The need of both low and high voices, basses and tenors, to sing the chant at a comfortable and appropriate range may have contributed to the creation of two simultaneous pitch levels. The interval chosen varies, as Marius Schneider has shown, with different spheres of culture.[2] The Franco-Italian sphere favors the fourth; the Northern French and thus also early English sphere, the fifth and third; the far-Northern sphere, the third and sixth. The peculiarities of different spheres crossed at places that thereby emerged as geographic and musical centers of a new style, notably so Limoges and St. Gallen. Morphologically only one basic distinction need be made: between the fundamental

---

[1]For the relation of the Counter-Reformation to opera, see Levarie, "Early Opera."
[2]*Mehrstimmigkeit*, vol. 2.

orientation toward the fifth in the south of Europe and toward the third in the north. Fourth and sixth are secondary intervals which necessarily come into being if an organum at either fifth or third, respectively, is doubled at the octave—a situation that naturally arises when boys or women join men. Parallel seconds (and, by inversion, sevenths) seem to be indigenous to the Balkan countries. Banned from the main development of Central European .polyphony because of their obvious dissonant character, they were consciously cultivated by Béla Bartók. This rather recent introduction into the main stream of art music has doubtless been preceded by centuries of similar practice in the folk music of Hungary, Bulgaria, and neighboring countries. If we think of the inherent hierarchy of intervals, we must recognize in this Balkan practice a wider exploration of possible tonal relationships, hence a higher level of artistic accomplishment, than in traditional organum.

English faux bourdon, as correctly explained by Leonel Power, offers an ingenious reconciliation of the generally prescribed, theoretical superiority of octave and fifth with the locally demanded, practical preference for thirds and sixths. The upper two derivative voices read the given chant a third lower than written ("false bass") and thus imagine singing parallel octaves and fifths while actually sounding parallel sixths and thirds. The new morphological accomplishment, almost as a by-product, is the materialization without octave doubling of three real voices.

At the early stage of organum, when parallelism is, on the whole, exact, the result seems an expansion of monophony rather than a fresh polyphonic morphé. The threshold between the two is crossed as soon as the organum voice takes liberties that eventually lead to independence. As part of this process, the notes of the given chant gain in length. Each serves an ontic function that permits the upper voice to unfold ever more freely. The morphological gain of organum lies in this gradual emancipation of the inherent force of a melody.

ORNAMENTATION

The concept of ornamentation belongs in the *variation complex, with which it shares definitions and descriptions. Ornamentation in music is melodic variation. Delimitation between the two is difficult. Variation is the basic morphological principle. The shapes it produces possess their own intrinsic values that are not exclusively the result of their descent from shapes standing behind the variation. The very term *ornamentation*, on the other hand, connotes subordination of the ornament to that which is being ornamented. The degree of indebtedness differentiates ornament from the more general concept of variation.

When does a configuration cease to be an ornament and become an independent shape? The question can best be investigated by means of a single ornamented tone. The usefulness of this approach arises from our interpreting tone as a center of attraction. Tone appears to us as an entelechy. It is invested with the qualities attributed to entelechies, above all with mass and inertia, and consequently with power of attraction. If we think of the musical field as generated by a play of forces manifested in tones, the attributes induced in tones may change from instant to instant. A tone heard at one moment as center might suddenly become attracted by another tone and become, as we say, a "function" of this new tone. As long as a tone exerts a strong attraction, it is felt as "structural," that is, as of primary, nonreplaceable importance. In such a case, variation may be deemed truly ornamental.

One's judgment concerning a particular case is guided by the ambitus and duration of the variation. Both bear on the power of attraction emanating from a tone. The greater the ambitus of the ornament, the less chance for the main tone to retain supremacy. The shorter the duration of the ornament, the stronger the impression of inertia in the main tone and hence the less chance for the variation to escape its sovereignty. Much can be learned from the behavior of melisma. Although embellishments are indigenous to both vocal and instrumental styles, the primacy of the human *voice suggests norms here as elsewhere. If one sings one syllable on more than one note, the resulting shape will be subject to the physiological tendency of the voice to move by step. The basic forms of melisma are all those that extend in time one particular tone, the carrier of one syllable. In their simplest manifestation they are:

Significantly these are the forms that, by virtue of their fundamental pervasiveness, are reduced to shorthand symbols in our notation:

All such and similar symbols have to do with a single tone and its neighboring notes as the prime carriers of ornaments. The tugging at the tone itself is present in vibrato and trill, which are premelodic pitch fluctuations. (Tremolo, by definition, is loudness fluctuation of one tone and hence, strictly speaking, not an ornament.) The rapid movement counteracts melodic tendencies. By defining an inverted mordent (pralltriller) as a "half trill," C. P. E. Bach introduces a quantitative restriction concerning duration and thus frees the inverted mordent for a possible task.[1]

The following few examples illustrate the gradual weakening of a single tone as embellished center and the concomitant increasing power of attraction of other tones leading to relative independence. In the borderline cases, the distinction between true ornament (that is, embellishing adjunct) and autonomous variation (that is, liberated melody) remains necessarily ill defined.

[1]*Versuch*, Das zweyte Hauptstück, Dritte Abtheilung, par. 30.

Example 1(a) is a mordent. When performed "fast enough," it is doubtless a true ornament. The interpretation of "fast enough" varies with context, general tempo, and dynamic and agogic accents and nuances. Played as in 1(b), it sounds purely ornamental (that is, not essential), whereas in version 1(c) the neighboring note becomes an integral part of a melody. No doubt is left if we think of this emancipated melody as harmonized by tonic-dominant-tonic. The same observations apply to the schneller of example 2. By omitting the faster middle stage in the realization of the inverted turn of example 3, we have made 3(b) unmistakably melodic. The parallel case 4(b) is the beginning of "Dove sono" from Mozart's *Le nozze di Figaro*—a turn become entirely melodic. Example 5 deals with a wider ambitus ornamented with an appoggiatura. If in 5(a) the latter is performed at the speed of about an eighth note, it is felt as a true ornament. The realization at 5(b) belongs to the ambivalent stage encountered at 1(c), but the skip brings it close to melodic independence. Within the same ambitus of example 6, the former appoggiatura note b now appears as an autonomous tone. The space between d^1 and b is filled with a schleifer. The tone b occurs twice—as the end of the schleifer and the beginning of an appoggiatura. Depending on the performance, and particularly on the speed, these figures might still be felt as ornaments in 6(a), hardly so in 6(b), and not at all so in 6(c).

The history of ornamentation is in the main one of increasing integration of embellishment into melody. When the ambitus widens and the tempo slows down, melisma becomes the main line. The opening notes of the Kyrie accompanying this book (cf. p. 11) constitute an amplified turn. So do those of the Eroica Funeral March after the preliminary fourth (which disappears, anyway, in the course of the movement). The widening, though a morphological event in its own right, also increases the melodic obligations of the initial melisma. What was at first a playful modification of one central tone now assumes also an independent role that contributes toward shaping a line. The ornamental neighboring notes become contrapuntal dissonances demanding a resolution of their own. The melisma thus breaks away from the centripetal force of one single tone and becomes a link between two or more main points of a fresh melodic phrase. Because melisma imparts life to an otherwise inert tone, it often serves as the initial melodic impulse at the *beginning of a piece.

In the following random examples, the incipient melismatic dissonance has been marked by *x*, the resolution by *R*.

Bach, *Well-tempered Keyboard I*, Fuga XV

Mozart, Piano Sonata K. 331

Mozart, *Le nozze di Figaro*, "Dove sono"

Beethoven, Piano Sonata op. 22, second movement

Beethoven, Piano Sonata op. 27 no. 2

Schumann, "Warum?" op. 12 no. 3

Schumann, Studien für den Pedal-Flügel op. 56 no. 2

Chopin, Nocturne op. 15 no. 2

Chopin, Nocturne op. 32 no. 1

These examples, which can be readily multiplied from the literature of all periods, suggest the hypothesis that melismas of yesterday become melodies of today. The melodies of any period—said the other way around—contain the residue of earlier ornamentations, which can thus be traced. Ornaments are not—as some people believe—shriveled melodies, just as good decorations on a piece of architecture are not leftover visual devices. On the contrary, melisma lies at the source of all further melodic unfolding, just as a Gothic rose may give the clue to the idea permeating an entire cathedral. Throughout his famous essay, Carl Philipp Emanuel Bach emphasizes the singing, melodic character of all keyboard ornaments and warns against treating them falsely as curlicues and noises. "They help explain the contents" of a melodic line, he states at the very beginning of the *Zweytes Hauptstück*, for they give cohesion and life to the notes.[1]

OSTINATO

Ostinato is a constant, obstinate repetition of a pattern. Theoretically any musical element may serve. Practically, however, there is little to be gained from an ostinato of, let us say, timbre or dynamics. The most common repetitive patterns are rhythmic-metric, melodic, harmonic, or combinations of these elements. A question of magnitude enters. To remain recognizable, the ostinato figure cannot be overly long. Beyond a certain length, repetition loses its obstinate character and produces strophes. On the other hand, the pattern must be repeated often enough to become really obstinate.

A rhythmic-metric ostinato is called *isorhythm. It is a main characteristic of non-European music: a percussion instrument incessantly repeats a rhythmic unit, above which a melody pursues its independent course. Erich von Hornbostel saw in this arrangement a seed of polyphony.[2] The situation may grow complex through the simultaneous participation of several different obstinate rhythms and meters. The example on page 210 transcribes music of the North-American Pawnee Indians.[3]

In Europe, isorhythm appears most clearly isolated from melodic and harmonic forces in music of the fourteenth century. Whether the repetition of a rhythm, the *talea*, could always be heard becomes a moot question vis-à-vis the realization that it served the principles of both unity and growth. In a few cases where melodic and rhythmic repetitions (*colores* and *taleae*), though of different lengths, were so coordinated that their respective ends would eventually coincide, the isorhythm participates also in the morphological limitation of the composition. Machaut's isorhythmic structures are not progressive experiments but rather last explorations of a technique inevitably suggested by the rigid rhythmic modes of the preceding *ars antiqua*. Significantly, the sixteenth century is almost devoid of ostinato compositions. The new flood from the seventeenth century to our time, arising from the ascendancy of dance and instrumental improvisation, shares with the medieval ostinatos one characteristic rhythmic feature: in at least three out of four compositions, the

[1] *Versuch*, Erste Abtheilung, par. 1.
[2] "Ueber Mehrstimmigkeit."
[3] Buttree, *Rhythm of the Redman*.

entire ostinato phrase contains an additional internal rhythmic ostinato. Bach's Passacaglia is no exception: the theme by itself is built on eight repetitions of the rhythmic motive ♩|♩ .

Melodic ostinato occurs most commonly in the bass. A basso ostinato affords the other layers melodic freedom, whereas an obstinate higher voice congeals the melody so that the repetitions quickly grow tiresome and irritating. The indebtedness to dance is particularly audible in the generally regular organization by groups of four or eight measures.

Harmonic ostinato is closely related to basso ostinato because of the double function of the lowest voice in Western music of the last four hundred years as both melody and defining carrier of the realized or implied harmony. Thus Beethoven's Diabelli Variations, although arising from some kind of melody, are much more readily understood as differentiated repetitions of an underlying harmonic-metric scheme. The first known musical examples of passacaglie, in a tablature by Girolamo Montesardo, of 1606, consist of simple I-IV-V-I patterns for all keys.[1] Interestingly enough, here, too, the four-measure phrases are rhythmically obstinate within the harmonic ostinato. The same

[1]C.f. Walker, "Ciaccona and Passacaglia."

210

four harmonies continue to serve Frescobaldi in his thirty organ *Partite sopra passacagli*, of 1627.

In ostinato compositions of all types, unity (provided by the repeated element) and multiplicity (provided by the other voices) are not interwoven but assigned to separate and parallel layers. The only other instance of similar separation is heard in those compositions in which a cantus firmus provides the backbone but not the melodic material to the other parts. But whereas an ostinato remains always an intrinsic part of the substance of a composition, the unity provided by a cantus firmus may remain extraneous to the behavior and organization of the piece as a whole.

The multiplicity contraposed to the unity of an ostinato composition stems from the principle of variation. Both ostinato and variation are substance-producing principles, because neither repetition nor variation implies limits. The shaping of the whole in a piece containing an ostinato is therefore determined by the same morphological principles that govern *variation.

Ostinato offers a great technical advantage, particularly to improvisation. "In song or poetry of improvisors, simple and cultured, repetition of sounds, syllables, words, phrases, whole sections, etc. provides the opportunity and means to fill a gap and to gain time when thought 'loses the thread', 'does not know how to go on', until a new idea is found for proper continuation."[1] In this sense, *cum grano salis*, one may consider the obstinate metrics of an epic narrator, such as Homer's, as providing a pertinacious basis for the free recitation line. A similar technique of obstinate repetition can often be heard in folk tales following a primitive tone, for example, many stories reported by the brothers Grimm. The freedom gained through the limitation set by an ostinato is considerable—not only for the organist playing a passacaglia who can soon forget pedaling and concentrate on the manuals, but for all improvisors and creators. "On tolére bien des choses à cause de cette contrainte, qui ne seroient pas régulièrement permises dans une composition plus libre," we read in a French text of the early eighteenth century.[2] One tolerates many things because of the ostinato constraint which would normally not be permitted in a freer composition. The hearer, too, finds relief in not having to focus on both soprano and bass voices all the time, taking the latter for granted.

Throughout the centuries, ostinatos have noticeably served concluding movements as if to confirm and intensify a desired impression by incessant repetition. In Franco-Flemish Masses, it is preferably the Agnus that harbors an obstinate bass: witness Josquin's *La Sol Fa Re Mi*, Obrecht's *Malheur me bat*, or Agricola's *Le serviteur*. Suites, sonatas, and cantatas of the thoroughbass period assign passacaglia and chaconne almost exclusively to the finale, so Biber in most of his violin sonatas, Buxtehude, Handel, and Bach. The use of ostinato in an opera finale stretches from Monteverdi's *L'incoronazione di Poppaea* (1642) across Lully's *Persée* (1682) to Hindemith's *Cardillac* (1926). The great symphonic writers of the nineteenth century, within a different

---

[1]Lach, *Wiederholung*, p. 36.
[2]Brossard, *Dictionnaire*.

tradition, employ ostinato, if at all, as coda ingredient. Beethoven (who liked to do things twice if he did them once) places an ostinato in the coda of both outside movements of his Seventh Symphony, and also in the first movement of his Ninth. Bruckner's ostinatos in the codas of the opening movements of Third, Fifth, Eighth, and Ninth Symphonies all emphasize the originally rhythmic momentum. Brahms, in the Haydn Variations and his last symphony, and Reger, in his First Organ Sonata, renew the tradition of the old variation set.

The same qualities for which an ostinato is placed at the end of a piece also led composers, around 1700, to the idea of beginning a multipartite work with an ostinato. Purcell utilizes chaconnes to open opera acts (*Dioclesian* and *King Arthur*); Buxtehude, sonatas; and Bach, occasionally cantatas. Kuhnau, with good insight and success, structured his entire Suonata Sesta by a da capo of the opening Ciaccona at the end of the composition.[1]

PAUSE. See **FERMATA**

PHENOMENALIZATION

The becoming of music may be separated into two processes. Morphology starts with the musical phenomenon as such. It is concerned with the making of a work—with a "composition"—and aims at enunciating principles of extension and formation. The extension principles are only two: *idiogenesis, which is either *repetition or *variation; and heterogenesis, which works by juxtaposition. The shaping principles are breathing, proportion (including metrics), and dialectics (including contrast). Together they supply the material and contents for this entire book. The study of phenomenalization on this level is identical with morphology.

There is another process preceding musical composition that is essential for the becoming of music. It is a process of continuous selection leading from the infinity of possible sounds to musically meaningful tone relations. First, noise is eliminated so that tone remains as the basic building material. Then discrete tones are distilled out of the pitch continuum (the siren) according to proportion. Practically, all musical proportions can be heard on the monochord string divided by integers.[2] The resulting individuation of tones thus follows a principle that is harmonic rather than melodic. Operations with the number 2 create infinite octave repetitions. Operations with the number 3 produce new and distinct musical entities:

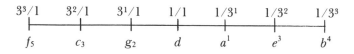

$$3^3/1 \quad 3^2/1 \quad 3^1/1 \quad 1/1 \quad 1/3^1 \quad 1/3^2 \quad 1/3^3$$

$$f_5 \qquad c_3 \qquad g_2 \qquad d \qquad a^1 \qquad e^3 \qquad b^4$$

If we project these pitches within the microcosm of one octave and ar-

[1]*Klavierwerke*, pp. 99–106.
[2]For more details, see the authors' *Tone*, particularly pp. 1–40.

range them according to pitch, we recognize (a) at the first power, the two fixed tones of the Greek tetrachord system or the two dominants in ours; (b) at the second power, the tones of the pentatonic system; and (c) at the third power, the seven tones of the diatonic scale:

A new, melodic kind of interval has appeared, representing the logarithmic projection of harmonic ratios. The diatonic scale thus established is still an abstractum; for all we have are five wholetones and two semitones a fifth apart (we started from the note D as a convenience; the procedure is possible anywhere). If we fix the place of the semitones within the scale, thereby determining a definite succession of wholetones and halftones, we create a mode. By symmetrically surrounding the halftones—as one possibility—by wholetones within each tetrachord, we identify Dorian. The principle of phenomenalization applied is variation of the scale; but mode, too, remains an abstraction. Only through the realization of mode on a definite pitch do we at last obtain a concretum—a key. A mode realized on a definite pitch supplies the first concrete gestalt for the becoming of music. The example quoted (c) is Dorian on D. On this first gestalt—the mode phenomenalized by key—the shaping artistic imagination proper goes to work. Here begins extension of musical substance by idiogenesis and heterogenesis.

PHRASING-ARTICULATING

These concepts are morphologically of secondary importance but help interpret the laws of musical language. Just as the sounds of spoken language unite in syllables, words, and phrases, so musical discourse is formed by tones grouped in ever larger organic units. The deciphering of a literary text is made easy by the separation of words from one another and by punctuation. Musical notation, however, offers no visual correspondence to the meaning of the discourse. It contains, moreover, elements like barlines, connecting beams, and others that are liable to lead the reader astray.

Phrasing is the art of bringing out proper values of musical discourse. It is primarily a manifestation of rhythm and hence related to breathing without necessarily always coinciding with it. Phrasing is generally independent of meter and suffers when subjugated by it. A result of musical studies at every level, phrasing does not constitute a special branch of music theory. If properly understood and executed, it confirms, corrects, and enlarges the impulses of instinct which lie at the base of all musical comprehension.

Musical articulation is the material separation and connection of sounds by the devices of staccato and legato. It must not be confused with phrasing. Whereas the sense of musical discourse and consequently of phrasing is beyond personal opinion, the manner of articulating is subject to interpretation. A given musical thought admits of only one phrasing but of several manners of articulation. To play a phrase all staccato or all legato is neutral.

Different mixtures of staccato and legato accentuate more or less the meaning of the thought. Articulation may become false when it goes against the course of the thought.

The phrasing of the C minor fugue theme from Bach's *Well-tempered Keyboard I*, for example, is as follows:

Any other phrasing would distort the meaning. Notice how the meter set by the barlines and by the connecting beams contradicts the phrasing and must not be taken as a guide. The note d^1 in the second measure brings into the open an ambivalence: melodically it belongs to the preceding rather than to the following note while rhythmically driving only toward the latter. The articulation could conceivably (though not advantageously) be all legato or staccato, or (better) gain life by combinations of the two:

The following excerpt from the first Intermezzo op. 119 by Brahms shows how the careful composer had to employ any number of indications (ties, slurs, dynamic signs) to overcome the obstruction of the barline:

Legato slurs in scores rarely coincide with phrasing, which must be understood and derived from the music itself. In principle, all slurs refer to articulation. A small distinction must be made between legato slurs and bowing slurs. They look alike but are not quite the same. Bowing slurs give the string player the mechanical instruction of changing the direction of the bow. Prac-

214

tical problems of bowing technique adjust to the superior concept of articulation. Hence bowing instructions to a string player need not have any bearing on breathing. The conflict between two comparable kinds of markings (mechanical, technical *versus* breathing, interpretative) seems to have been present in all periods, witness the use of ligatures in mensural notation or the distinction between ♩♩ and ♪ ♪ in more recent vocal writing.

PNEUMATIC-KINEMATIC

There are two kinds of melody of profoundly different morphological implications. Compare, as an example, the theme of the last movement of Beethoven's Piano Sonata op. 109 with the runs and passages opening Bach's Clavier Toccata in F-sharp minor. Our inner reaction to these two examples is not the same. The Beethoven theme "takes hold of us." We live it, breathe it, sing it. We participate. The runs and passages of the toccata, on the other hand, are observed by us. What we observe as if it were an event in the outside world is the unrolling of an energetic process that manifests itself in the displacement of an acoustical point. From all evidence, we deal in both cases with melodic production. From all evidence, we also deal with melodies of different essence which call forth characteristic interior attitudes.

Of the two kinds of melody, that illustrated by the Beethoven theme approaches the vocal genre whereas the toccata displays instrumental bearing. To stop at this statement would be insufficient, for the reduction of the distinction between the two species to one between vocal and instrumental styles pinpoints merely a technical difference. The wide discrepancy between our internal attitudes toward the two kinds of melody leads to a profounder distinction. The terms *pneumatic melody* and *kinematic melody* will facilitate the discourse (from Greek *pneuma*, 'air', 'breath'; and *kinema*, 'motion').

The relationship of the two melody types invites an analogy with that of the vital centers in the thorax of our body to the limbs. Whereas we "form a block" with breathing and the heartbeat, we become "multiples" the farther we get away from the center. This fact manifests itself in a certain independence of the extreme limbs—particularly of the hands which, unlike the feet, do not have a function exclusively dictated by terrestrial gravity. We can assume a relatively objective attitude toward our hands and their movements, whereas we inevitably identify with our heart and lungs, the seats of our life. The relation of the kinematic to the pneumatic is like a relation of periphery to center, like the relation of the branches of a tree to its trunk and roots. By keeping this image before us, we can risk the remark that the pneumatic is more "important" than the kinematic, and further that every renewal of music is made by a return to vocal music. Extreme kinematism could effectively end up by uprooting music. By placing pneumatic melody in the center, and kinematic melody in the periphery, of the human body, we speak in analogies and do not wish to suggest a relation of cause and effect. Pneumatism and kinematism are thus totally independent—theoretically in any case, and some times also technically—of the means of execution. The popular statement that Bach's treatment of the voice is often instrumental sounds like a reproach. The

truth is that countless composers (Bach among them) have employed kinematism and pneumatism almost indifferently in vocal and in instrumental
music.

Awareness of the existence of these two melodic poles can prove useful to
the interpreter. Gallant style, above all its culmination with Haydn and Mozart, exhibits a rapid and almost continual oscillation between the pneumatic
and the kinematic. The latter manifests itself not only in runs and passages
but in everything that falls under the notion of *ornamentation. Such style
demands of the interpreter the frequent and instantaneous passing from expressive to detached elegance, often several times in a single measure. The
following, basically pneumatic opening of the second movement of Mozart's
Piano Sonata K. 309 abounds in kinematic details:

There are, moreover, nuances within kinematism. A phrase may well be
kinematic and depend on the hand rather than on breathing: yet it can be
charged with sensitivity and demand to be executed like a rapid caress. The
nuances and transitions resulting from combinations of the kinematic and
pneumatic are infinite. In certain variations in the last works by Beethoven—
think of the slow movement of the Ninth Symphony or of that of the Piano
Sonata op. 106—the dissolving of the theme remains essentially pneumatic in
spite of the rapidity of the melodic motion. One deals here with a pneumatism
that belongs to a more refined organism than the human; one has expressed
this sentiment by saying that the melody has become "spiritualized." A kinematic interpretation would here be out of place.

In the music of Chopin one finds side by side with a kinematism frankly
opposed to the given pneumatic background (think of the singable yet pure
ornaments in the middle of a slow lyrical line) another kinematic element
which is the particular property of Chopin (think of his physical pleasure in
fast runs). There exists in the slow movement of Beethoven's Piano Sonata op.
106 a phrase which, heard out of context, could be taken for one by Chopin
(mm. 113 ff., particularly mm. 118–19). One observes here the same extraordinary equilibrium between the pneumatic and the kinematic characteristic of
Chopin. Yet one senses that Beethoven achieves this equilibrium by a push of
the pneumatic toward the kinematic, whereas Chopin arrives there by the
opposite path. The comparison sheds a light on the two melody types.

In vocal music, one might be tempted to equate pneumatism and kinematism with, respectively, lyricism and dramatism. Balance between the latter
two creates one of the real difficulties in the singing of Schubert *Lieder*. Actually there is no special connection. Lyricism may be both pneumatic or kine-

matic, and so may dramatism. All one can isolate are the dosages. Against the correct assumption that vocal music, carried by breath, is basically pneumatic, one must not forget that it also contains a legitimate kinematic element. A singer's need for kinematic melody is spontaneous. The following passage from Schubert's "Wohin?" is not a vocal transcription of an instrumental thought:

The largely kinematic character of the Alpine yodel is unmistakable. The falsetto execution of yodel emphasizes this character by making the chant less "natural," that is, more impersonal, more instrumental. A similar artifice can be observed in the strange nasal execution of oriental slow coloraturas, where the effect is also antipneumatic.

If anybody complains today that many new pieces lack melody (a criticism that did not spare Bach in his time), he thereby professes his pneumatic conception of melody. Much modern music, born of an antiromantic attitude, is deliberately kinematic in the main varieties of its style.

POLARITY

Polarity, a principle pervading the universe, denotes the condition of two complementary forces acting in opposition to each other. They are complementary because together they form a conceptual whole. The opposition is genetically centrifugal. It is symbolized in the *Pythagorean Table by the splitting of One. The result is genesis. The centrifugal quality produces growth. Polarity is also centripetal to the extent that the two opposite forces tend to reunite and to cancel each other at a point of ideally perfect equilibrium. In this respect, polarity is limiting. Morphologically, growth and limitation are a paramount expression of polarity. The implications for all fields have been extensively treated by philosophers from Plato to Whitehead. The importance for music has guided the thinking underlying this book.

Two elements occupy a position of polarity if they lie in the path of two polar forces in symmetrical relation to the point of origin. Polarity and symmetry are related but not identical. They belong to different categories (in the Aristotelian sense). Polarity is viewed in perspective from a center, symmetry from an external point of observation. Polarity has to be imagined as limitless in principle; symmetry appears as a concomitant of limitation. Polarity and symmetry are each a conceptual morphé which we tend to impose upon processes and phenomena. Both principles, in varied degrees of embodiment, are also found in nature. Day and night, male and female, positive and negative electricity are each members of a polarity. The magnet unites both polarity and symmetry; it is gignetic and ontic at the same time.

The following list of specifically musical manifestations deserves critical investigation:

Major	—	Minor
Up	—	Down
Consonance	—	Dissonance
Loud	—	Soft
Fast	—	Slow

Concept pairs like binary-ternary, vocal-instrumental, open-closed, etc. do not belong in the list; for, whatever the contrast between the members, they do not complement each other.

Major-minor phenomenalizes the supreme musical polarity. The two modes are reciprocal phenomena, and a reciprocal mathematical operation presides over their physical production—division of the string for major, multiplication of the string for minor. They are created by the splitting of One in opposite directions and hence exert attraction on each other which, if successfully accomplished, results in neutralization of both:

A major triad is heard as a dominant of, that is, to be resolved to, a minor triad. A minor triad is heard as a subdominant of, that is, to be resolved to, a major triad. The polarity up-down, in its harmonic implications, parallels the experience of the two *dominants, which act on the central tonic from opposite sides. In its melodic implications, the concepts up and down determine factually the only directions in which a line can extend.

Consonance-dissonance is a concept pair to which we can assign polarity if, recognizing the same genesis as for major-minor, we identify the triad (in both its ascending and descending versions) with consonance, and everything else with dissonance. The distinction seems natural. The triad is the musical equivalent of the *senarius, and consonance and dissonance complement each other. The very polarity of the two triads is a source of dissonance, for it gives birth to wholetone (F-G in relation to the generator C) and halftone (E-F and G-A♭). The transition from consonance to dissonance, thus explained, is neither quantitative nor indefinite. One may rightly wonder, however, whether consonance and dissonance do not represent a borderline case of polarity, for they are susceptible to other explanations imposed upon them by other forms of our mind.

The other two cases on our list fall in a different category altogether; for though they may be polar, they are so only if we voluntarily group them around an arbitrary neutral middle. In fact, they show primarily quantitative differences in degree. Loud-soft can be measured in decibels down to zero audibility; fast-slow, by a metronome along a sliding time scale. Yet the sense for polarity imbedded in our psychic constitution imposes even upon these quantitative gradations a mental model so that they appear arranged in polar perspective. Because loud-soft, fast-slow, and other pairs, though measurable, are also qualities, we group them around an assumed human middle value. A "normal" pitch region, "normal" loudness, and "normal" pace establish a generally accepted center, in relation to which the two members of each pair, by our volition, appear polarized. A telling extramusical example out of many is the Celsius temperature scale. A point is arbitrarily chosen as a center, in this case the neutrality point between the fluid and solid states of water. From this assumed zero point, two series develop in opposite plus-minus directions.

In true polarity, both members are ideally of equal value. Yet our bondage to gravity, our tellurian orientation, makes us instinctively favor one pole over the other. Depending on one's disposition, one prefers either day or night, North or South, up or down. In our list above of musical pairs, one is likely to associate all members in the left column with each other, and all members in the right column, although there is no obvious inherent connection among most of them. The Renaissance gentleman considered soft sounds "positive," unlike his twentieth-century counterpart. The nineteenth century proclaimed the supremacy of major over minor (and of male over female). The physical existence of overtones in contrast to the ideally equivalent, but spontaneously nonexistent, phenomenon of undertones is a strong symptom of our general tellurian one-sidedness.

Music demonstrates well the possible simultaneity of opposites. A composition is fixed as a gestalt but also fluid in time. We can hear it ontically and gignetically. The major and minor modes can be apprehended as opposites or as nuances of each other. One single held tone contains within itself the potential of many polarities.

POLYPHONY

The generally accepted definition of polyphony refers to the simultaneous movement of two or more voices, each of which preserves its individuality. The underlying element is melody. Both historically and theoretically, the concurrence of several melodies creates polyphony, be it the addition of parallel fifths to a given chant and the eventual emancipation of the new line, or the construction of a *counterpoint according to tested principles. The melodic foundation of polyphony is not in the least challenged by the relation of melody to harmony. We can understand the former as an unfolding of the latter, or projection into time of the potential force of a chord or cadence. Either way, the polyphony depends on defined consonances and dissonances, on tensions and resolutions. It is based on relationships.

This common view of polyphony is inadequate and one-sided. It ignores another main source of polyphony and thereby makes our understanding not merely incomplete but erroneous. We submit that all polyphony, as we know it, is the resultant of two very different musical atittudes acting upon each other. One stems from the Near and Middle East. The other is European, probably Northern. They first became entangled in Greek music of antiquity. The supreme accomplishment of Western polyphony is their reconciliation.

The first meaningful reference to the double origin of our polyphony comes from Rudolf Ficker, to whose insight ours is indebted.[1] To our knowledge, he did not pursue the morphological implications, nor does he seem to have influenced the thinking of other musicologists. He proceeds from the plausible assumption that any Greek player of the lyra or kithara cannot possibly have refrained from plucking more than one string at a time, and he backs his speculations by persuasive examples of non-European practices preserved to this day.

The Eastern source of polyphony is melody. With this concept we associate movement, currents, drives toward formation, cohesive connection. In traditional Arabic music, one can still hear the main characteristics. Within the set frame of the octave (which no music and no attitude can deny), the tones lie close to each other, at many intervals smaller than our halftone. The leading quality of such tones and intervals is strengthened by the characteristic vibrato production of each individual tone and the equally characteristic portamento between the tones of each interval. Melismas and other ornamental devices all contribute toward giving direction to the melodic motion of the line. The melody is in a state of "becoming" before our very ears. This Eastern type of melody is basically gignetic.

The Northern European source of polyphony (usually overlooked or subjugated to the Eastern) is a total *Klang*. This German term may seem a regrettable introduction, but it has the advantage of being free of other associations (apart from being the term used by Ficker). "Sound" includes noise and would be incorrect. A *Klang* is a given complex of tones within which voices may move polyphonically without mutual ties of consonance and dissonance and without forward drives. Ficker focuses on pentatonic complexes because they exclude by definition any leading tone and directive current. His caution is understandable, but the principle holds for other manifestations of *Klang* as well. The main condition of such a complex is that it is not going anywhere. It exists. Melodic lines arising from it unfold the momentary sound in a temporal process, but they are no farther at the end than they were at the beginning. This Northern type of melody is basically ontic.

An example of *Klang*, still audible today though not polyphonic, is change-ringing as practiced in England. The total contributing pitches are predetermined by the number of available bells. The listener down in the village sooner or later hears them all as a unit. The order in which the pitches reach him, though determining the game for the ringers, is musically irrelevant. Whatever motion there is does not alter the situation. Whereas melody as a current depends on a definitive lapse of time, the melody arising from ringing changes is tied to no time at all. It merely lasts, but beginning and end are morphologically of no importance. Ordinary church bells produce a similar effect on a simpler level.

This attitude is probably a leftover of very old Celtic practices which, hazy

[1] "Klangformen."

220

as they are to us today, yet illuminate one aspect of early polyphony. The *Klang* was probably predetermined by instruments, such as a pair of lurs with their overtones, or harps with a fixed number of open strings, or perhaps bagpipes. In most of the compositions, which defy analysis by standard concepts of later counterpoint, two contrasting chords alternate into which any number of voices improvise apparently independent melodic lines. The chords are regarded as either *cyweirdant* or *tinniad*—quite analogous to repose and tension, or, if you wish, to tonic and nontonic in the widest sense. The Sumer Canon, a puzzle if investigated in the usual contrapuntal tradition, may well have sprung from this source. The risk of endless repetition was controlled by "the Twenty-Four Measures of instrumental music, all conformable to the laws of metre, as they were settled in a congress, by many professors skilful in that science, Welsh and Irish, in the reign of Gruffyold ap Cynan," around the year 1100.[1]

Not much later, the Northern *Klang* ideal, wedded to a Gregorian basis, produced works like the *quadrupla* by Perotinus. No reference to counterpoint can explain the behavior of the three upper voices. They move as if most of the time the concepts of consonance and dissonance did not exist. The plainchant in enormously long values defines the *Klang*. The three organa voices unfold it, fluctuate within it, but they do not present directional, independent counterpoints. They are linear events which lack melodic tension and drive.

Ficker suggests that Alpine yodels and their inevitable echoes also are not primarily melodic but rather *Klang* phenomena. The characteristic alternation of deep chest tones and high falsetto tones reveals a typical desire for the widening of the *Klang* space. The canon-producing echo renders the yodel polyphonic, particularly when a real second voice replaces the natural duplication.

The rich gamelan literature of Java and Siam belongs to this kind of polyphony. So does consequently any kind of heterophony. What matters to us is the recognition that our accepted polyphony has two sources and that the unique accomplishment of Western polyphony has sprung from the meeting of the two types. Like so many great achievements, polyphony appears as a synthesis of two originally different forces. The gignetic, melodic type seems to have prevailed; and there is no denying that in this sense our musical heritage, like all other, is basically Mediterranean. Yet the *Klang* concept asserts itself and might gain new usefulness in the hands of modern composers.

Two examples given by Ficker deserve to be quoted.[2] In Wagner's *Tristan und Isolde*—the composition of the nineteenth century with gignetic energies carried to ecstatic extremes—the hunting sounds at the beginning of the second act awaken primary *Klang* effects by the tensionless fluctuation of F major and C minor sounds which extinguish any harmonic drive. In the midst of stirring excitement, there is suddenly a hovering above an ontic *Klang* event, like a message from a distant world. Debussy's music signals a decisive return to primary *Klang* experience with dampening and even exclusion of

[1]Travis, *Celtica*, p. 25.
[2]"Klangformen," pp. 31 f.

221

harmonic functional tensions. In the excerpt above from *La mer*, all apparent movement is a tensionless play of the pentachord D^b-E^b-F-A^b-B^b. The melody in the French horns is part of the same *Klang*, the notes C^b and G to be understood as appoggiaturas.

Quite possibly, Western polyphony—which has been rightly hailed as one of the major achievements of Western man—could materialize only because these two sources of polyphony combined; for singly their inherent qualities needed complementation. The Eastern source, gignetic by nature, permits a melody to grow but it lacks built-in limitation. The muezzin can

spin out his long melodies, because the leading tones give it direction; he can move freely at any moment and thus does not readily admit of a related counterpoint. The Northern source, ontic by nature, lacks melodic currents but it provides a fixed limit set by *Klang*. The Celts could sing many-voiced canons, rotas, which were going nowhere—turning back on themselves like wheels. By joining, tentatively in antiquity and decisively in the Middle Ages, these two attitudes produced a new art, polyphony; for together they met ideally the morphological conditions of both growth and limitation, of both melodic independence and relationship.

PROGRAM MUSIC

Program music is not to be considered a union of literature and music. Each art follows its own rules (cf. *Word and Tone; *Opera). Verbal thought unfolds in a manner quite different from musical thought. A composer cannot transpose the sequence of one into that of the other. His work must stand on its own merit, which he cannot borrow from literature. In the best examples of program music, the connection between the two arts is therefore the loosest imaginable. If it is not, the result is invariably and necessarily bad.

Bach's *Capriccio on the Departure of his Most Beloved Brother* can be heard as a suite without necessary reference to the subtitles. The Adagissimo lament by the friends, for instance, is built on the same chromatically descending bass that baroque composers employed as a standard expression of grief, and the posthorn signal is quickly turned into the subject of the concluding fugue. The first Biblical Sonata by Kuhnau, Bach's predecessor at St. Thomas in Leipzig, depicts the "tremor of the Israelites at the sight of the Giant" by a similar descending chromatic bass above which the intonation of "Aus tiefer Not" produces a musically excellent chorale prelude. One can even argue that the sudden runs in a later movement, meant to illustrate the "stone slung into Goliath's forehead," are a musical cadenza on the dominant chord. Here, however, the music comes so close to being descriptive that the result sounds like a literal, nonanalogical translation from one tongue into another. The inappropriateness felt when a musical microform derives from a literary description is intensified in the case of a macroform (such as Strauss's *Don Quixote*) where the sequence of events is largely literary and not musical. The situation is related to opera, but in program music the two main participating arts are not synchronized.

The literary contribution to program music varies from a simple title to an elaborate story. When the literary piece is in itself a work of art, the inherent poetic value might justify a recitation preceding the music. One can imagine hearing the Scotch ballad "Edward" before the piano ballad by Brahms (op. 10 no. 1). Ludwig Spohr wanted a poem by Carl Pfeiffer, *Die Weihe der Töne*, printed and distributed or recited aloud before the performance of his Fourth Symphony. In such cases, word and tone become united, not in the work of art, but in the hearer's mind, and the term *tone poem* properly defined becomes applicable (cf. *Word and Tone). There have been performances (in Basel, Paris, and perhaps elsewhere) of Liszt's *Harmonies poétiques et religieuses* in which the playing of each of the ten piano pieces (which fill an evening) was preceded by a recitation of the poetic text belonging to it. The listener's experience is at least wholly acoustical and artistically more elevated than if divided between the visual reading of words and the aural perception of tones. The successive artistic impacts are romantically understood as convergent, and the total effect is expected to assume a peculiar tint and depth without undue injury to the specificity of each mode.

In all other cases when the literary piece is not in itself a work of art (such as the words accompanying Smetana's *Moldau*), the printed program is interesting mainly as a glimpse into the composer's mind or as a point of convergence for the listener's extramusical imagination. In no manner does it add value to the music or increase one's understanding. Wisely and characteristically, Debussy placed the titles at the end instead of at the head of his piano pieces, as if he wished the imagination of the listener to solidify only after absorbing the music. The musical touchstone is the feasibility of omitting the story without impairing the structure. Strauss's *Till Eulenspiegel* can be heard as a rondo; *Also sprach Zarathustra* falls apart without extramusical propping.

Program music which tries to tell a story should theoretically be kept apart from a kind of music which purports to duplicate impressions received from the outside world. We may call this kind "extrinsically imitative" to distinguish it from "intrinsically imitative" music which finds the legitimate object of *imitation in its own substance (a fugue, for example, or any other polyphonic imitative texture). Extrinsically imitative music (sometimes loosely identified as descriptive or as word-painting) is always part of program music, whereas the latter can do without it and only occasionally slides into it. The value of extrinsically imitative music, doubtful in principle, stands in inverse relation to the degree of realism attained. It becomes nil when the imitation succeeds completely to the point of illusion. This danger exists in fact only in the case of acoustical imitation. Wind machines and thunder machines are indeed not musical instruments but theater props. So are Respighi's Roman nightingales, and one minds the possibility of electronic sound reproduction of the moving sea. Imitation of lightning—a nonacoustical outside event—must needs remain analogical; yet the mere intent is somewhat embarrassing, and the imitation requires insertion into a highly musical context to be bearable. The storm in Beethoven's Pastoral Symphony is (in the composer's own words) "more an expression of feeling than painting." The bird quotations in the same work are evocative and amusing only because they fulfill the function of a structural cadenza. The imitation, moreover, is played by real woodwind instruments. Schumann's Florestan nevertheless "loved the Pastoral and Heroic Symphonies less because Beethoven himself gave them these names and thereby set limitations to one's phantasy."[1]

Word-painting, eventuating in the eighteenth century in a veritable dictionary and recipe book of expression, and abundantly employed by Bach, is essentially analogical. Like Wagner's leitmotivs, it operates by fixing definite associations. Here, too, the preponderance of a purely musical discourse or the lack thereof marks the difference between good and bad result.

PROPORTION

The phrase *portio pro portione* implies a relation of parts. The essential perception of proportion consists in comparison, the *tertium comparationis* in the widest meaning being called "module." Proportion is a universal principle. It permeates everything and is found everywhere. In music it affects the single tone with its harmonic series, harmony, melody, form, rhythm, meter,

[1]*Aus Meister Raros, Florestans und Eusebius' Denk- und Dichtbüchlein.*

construction of instruments—in short, every conceivable aspect. Most profitably understood by way of examples, it underlies almost all inquiries of this book. The idea of proportion is implied as soon as one speaks of "parts of a work." Whether the parts be compared in relation to technical features (correspondence of durations, keys, chords, motives, etc.) or to moods, proportion rules both. Morphologically it is a limiting force endowing growing elements with shape.

Proportion can be interpreted literally or metaphorically. In the literal sense, it concerns a comparison of sizes. Vitruvius's classical work *On Architecture* proceeds from this concept. St. Augustine's *De musica* employs it to demonstrate cosmic principles by way of metrics. Throughout medieval and renaissance music theory, *proportio* remains a measuring device of time units. The precision of proportion in mensural notation relaxes in later stylizations: the ten-times-three groups of Bach's Goldberg Variations, though phenomenalizing the governing formative principle, are hardly audible as literal correspondences. The comparison of sizes in music is not restricted to time units. Intervals, scales, chords all become comparable by way of rational modules. The mathematical concepts of arithmetic and harmonic proportions identify the two musically polarized legs of the *Pythagorean Table. Geometric proportion defines progression by identical intervals, such as octave relationships.

In a metaphorical sense, proportion relates to "irrational modules" such as "importance" or "weight" of parts. In all arts, this interpretation of proportion has as much reality as the literal one. The listener remembers moods or levels of musical experience and relates them to each other. He rationalizes the irrational time proportions of plainchant or of irregular beats. He replaces the exact module of the geometrician by his sense for *equivalence and the significance of *context.

Module in music has meaning both literally and metaphorically. In *modulation it refers technically to the general tonality as point of orientation. In other areas which artistically escape precision, module is the intangible medial level of a whole. We can criticize the "imbalance" of one movement of a symphony, for instance, only by assuming as a module the general level or curve set by all the movements, or rather resulting from them, and then hearing the questionable movement stray inordinately from this level.

Symmetry is subsumed by proportion in both senses of the term. In music, the metaphorical interpretation is far more significant than the literal, which fundamentally deals with space. Popularly symmetry is defined as bilateral, such as left and right in respect to a dividing axis. In time forms like music, this purely visual notion does not apply without the most stringent qualifications and restrictions. There are extreme cases like the mirror fugues in Bach's *Kunst der Fuge* or *retrograde pieces appearing in the music of Guillaume de Machaut as well as in that of Alban Berg; but the value of such "trick" compositions depends on factors other than the literal symmetry. In these as in all musical works, our notation transforms the durations, which are given, into spatial distances. Aural apperception differs qualitatively from the visually convenient representation and is moreover subject to modifications brought about by time perspective. Space can be filled as by the repetition of an ornamental strip, whereas in music time is not filled but produced. Because of the opposition of *time and space, neither a consequent following an antecedent nor an exact recapitulation of an earlier exposition sounds symmetrical in the perspective of time. What we hear last is nearer to us and hence seems bigger, longer. Thus the omission of the traditional two repetitions in the da capo section of a minuet, far from destroying symmetry, adjusts the real musical experience to the memory of this experience. Exact visual symmetry, that is, repetitions also in the da capo, would give the acoustical impression of excessive length.

Classically but also more loosely defined, symmetry points to some standard of measure (Greek *syn* + *metron*, 'same measure') on which all parts of a work depend. The result is proportion. We can let Vitruvius speak for the artists of all branches who know how to engage symmetry: "It is a proper agreement between the members of the work itself, and relation between the different parts and the whole general scheme." The principles of symmetry "are due to proportion, in Greek *analogia*. Proportion is a correspondence among the members of an entire work, and of the whole to a certain part selected as standard. . . . Without symmetry and proportion there can be no principles in the design" of a work of art.[1] Symmetry in this wide definition connotes not only limitation but the resulting balance of form. Hence it has always been bound up with beauty. Vitruvius called the outcome of good proportions *eurhythmy* (Greek 'harmonious rhythm'). Aristotle concluded that the perfection of a sphere was most suitable to the shape of the heaven and of the stars.[2] Looking at the symmetry of a Greek statue, Hermann Weyl asks

> whether the aesthetic value of symmetry depends on its vital value: Did the artist discover the symmetry with which nature according to some inherent law has endowed its creatures, and then copied and perfected what nature presented but in imperfect realizations; or has the aesthetic value of symmetry an independent source? I am inclined to think with Plato that the mathematical idea is the common origin of both: the mathematical laws governing nature are the origin of symmetry in nature, the intuitive realization of the idea in the creative artist's mind its origin in art.[3]

Symmetry in the wider classic sense is most evident in metrically determined styles. The measure assumes the role of module and forms ever larger corresponding groups. Organization into $1 + 1 + 2 + 4 + 8$, etc., underlies explicitly and implicitly most music of the eighteenth and nineteenth centuries. Among our six cases in the Discourse, the Bach chorale follows this arrangement literally, the Beethoven movement freely, and even the Schönberg piece recognizes the bondage. The feeling of symmetry arises from our hearing the relation of groups as an obvious rhythmic event. In metric music, the given module, assumed to be constant in the mind, continues to act as a determinant so that any modification is recognized as a deviation from the symmetric norm.

[1]*Architecture*, pp. 14 and 72.
[2]*On the Heavens*, ii. 4, 8.
[3]*Symmetry*, pp. 6 f.

The most common devices of modification are shortening or lengthening of the group rhythm. The effect of shortening is metric accelerato. The first sung statement in Schubert's song "Pause," for example, consists of two three-measure phrases which against the analogous four-measure phrases of the keyboard introduction sound distinctly rushed. The intent is clear in conjunction with the mood "ziemlich geschwind" ("rather quick") and the statement following the accelerato: "Ich kann nicht mehr singen, mein Herz ist zu voll" ("I cannot sing anymore, my heart is too full"). This statement, by the way, lasts two measures and thus restores the eight-measure norm though not symmetrically. Similar accelerato passages occur throughout the song. The opposite effect of lengthening a group is metric ritenuto. One hears it as a standard device in cadences of most any eighteenth-century courante. The symmetry of four-measure phrases in 3/4 time is affected by a hemiola in 3/2 time which slows down the group rhythm.

A singularly interesting example pushing in both directions is the slow introduction to Beethoven's First Symphony. It is twelve measures long, unambiguously divided in three sections of 3 + 4 + 5 measures. The module, as to be expected in the style, is the four-measure phrase; the central materialization (mm. 4–7) is explicit in its symmetrical arrangement. The following five-measure unit is heard as ritardando; for the final cadence, by means of a composed "fermata," stretches the D $^{6-5}_{4-3}$ progression from one measure (9) to two (11–12). The opening three-measure unit intensifies the famous harmonic shock by rhythmically accelerated asymmetry. The real first measure is missing; one can imagine a tonic unison, similar to that opening the Second Symphony, preceding the first actually heard measure. It would serve, not only to "introduce" the dissonant seventh of the first chord, but to explain the norm of the rhythmic group. The special feature of this experience, highly characteristic of Beethoven, is asymmetry preceding the establishment of a module.[1]

Many other modifications exist of symmetry in its widest meaning. The group rhythm itself may change, as in the *ritmo di tre battute* section of the scherzo in Beethoven's Ninth Symphony. In the coda of the same movement, the length of the measure itself is altered from 3/4 to alla breve as part of a steep accelerando. In general, variation in the length of a measure introduces new proportions. If the alternation is regular, it will be understood as a module in its own right. From the notation of Brahms's Variations on a Hungarian Theme in a succession of 3/4 and 4/4 measures, a seven-beat norm reaches the ear. His Variations on an Original Theme regularly mix four-measure and five-measure phrases. If, on the contrary, the alternation is irregular, the resulting group rhythm is likely to be appreciated on the basis of the metric impulse of the smaller module, and the hearer may be pulled between the impressions of alternating ritenutos and acceleratos.

But the pulse itself may vary. In metric music, the module will be carried back to the smallest common denominator—as a silent background rather than an actual experience. The finale of Stravinsky's *Le sacre du printemps* exemplifies the case in its irregular changes among 2/16, 3/16, 4/16, 5/16, 1/8, 2/8, 3/8, 2/4, 3/4, 4/4, and 5/4. The Franco-Flemish style, as represent-

---

[1] See Levarie, "Beethoven's First Symphony."

ed in our Discourse by Josquin's Kyrie, requires a different interpretation of an apparently similar situation. The pulse seems to change repeatedly (cf. pp. 14 ff.) but only if one holds to the immediate surface experience. Actually the overall slow pulsation is very regular, an integral value which admits of numerous different subdivisions. Such music must not be approached with the more recent attitude of hearing group rhythms primarily as multiples. The Netherlands composers divided a module to produce their own version of symmetry. The opening soprano melody, as shown earlier (cf. p. 14), is mirrored exactly around a center.

Beyond a certain point, the rhythmic flow tends to approach irrational time proportions. Our notation is based on rational time relations. With all its metric complications, even Stravinsky's *Sacre* remains rational. Our notation touches on irrationality only in special, relatively exceptional instances such as fermatas, "senza misura" sections, and the like. Yet irrational time relationships play a great role in music. Plainsong is an obvious case. One cannot speak of symmetry because there is no module. Proportion, however, is not absent although the term must now be given a very wide meaning. The existence of motivic groups creates time equivalences that need not be measured to be perceived. The Kyrie recapitulation after the Christe is a particular, nontypical case in which the large group of one complete exclamation becomes the module itself. But behind all other forms of plainsong stands some regulative time principle that, being a norm, need not be embodied exactly. As in *agogics everywhere, deviations from rigid symmetry are life-giving. "Symmetry," in the words of Dagobert Frey, "signifies rest and binding, asymmetry motion and loosening, the one order and law, the other arbitrariness and accident, the one formal rigidity and constraint, the other life, play and freedom."[1]

Proportion in art subsumes all these different interpretations. It reconciles opposites by relating them to the idea of beauty and perfection.

PYTHAGOREAN TABLE

The Pythagorean Table is an arrangement of proportions demonstrable on the monochord. Pythagoras has become associated with the correspondence of mathematical numbers and musical intervals, although he doubtless acquired his fundamental knowledge in Egypt. After experimentally determining the string lengths for various tones, he or his followers recorded the results, first along a line representing the string, and eventually in a *diagramma* (literally a 'crossing of lines') in which the relations of numbers and tones were demonstrated by a system of coordinates.[2] Iamblichus, writing a mathematical commentary in the fourth century A.D., gives a precise description of the Table. Placing One at the apex of a right angle, one then aligns the results of consecutive string divisions along one leg, and the results of consecutive string multiplications (in conformity with Plato's prime axiom of po-

---

[1]Here quoted from Weyl, *Symmetry*, p. 16.

[2]For a detailed history of the Pythagorean Table and its immense influence on scientific and philosophic thought, see Thimus, *Symbolik*; and most writings by Kayser, notably his *Lehrbuch*.

larity) along the other leg. Interaction of the two series produces the planimetric Table:

The Table, though an offspring of the human mind, corresponds to some natural order. The case is the same as in Mendeléeff's Table demonstrating the Periodic Law of the Chemical Elements. His particular arrangement of the atomic weight numbers of the elements uncovered a meaningful order, pregnant with consequences, that was not otherwise accessible by observation of the natural facts. Nowhere in nature are the chemical elements neatly arranged according to the Periodic Table and yet their properties follow the periodicity shown in the Table.

The Pythagorean Table can theoretically be extended into infinity. The first six numbers spell out the major triad in one direction, the minor triad in the other. Higher numbers develop ever smaller intervals, each prime number producing a new tone. The interpenetration of the two series creates increasingly complex major and minor constellations, which eventually comprise the total musical cosmos. A line drawn through any identical pitches meets all other such lines at a point outside the system, logically corresponding to 0/0.

The Pythagorean Table helps visualize many abstract concepts. All of the following Greek theorems, and many more, can be directly read off the diagram.[1] Diogenes Laërtius: "Out of the Oneness sprang the indefinite Twoness. The first is cause and motivation, the latter effect or matter." Sextus Empiricus: "To the Oneness belongs the predicate of active motivation, to the Twoness that of passive matter." Archytas: "Necessarily the principles of Being are Two." Philolaos: "Of the Limited and of the Unlimited the world and everything in it is composed." Aristotle: "Harmony is a mixture and union of opposites." Philolaos: "The Similar and the Like would not need harmony; the Dissimilar and Unlike, however, had necessarily to be united by harmony, if it were to endure in the Cosmos." Iamblichus: "But above the Limited and the Unlimited, as prime cause of these two prime causes of the things that have come into being, stands as cause not come into being, God. He has set the Limited and the Unlimited. Before God, the Limited and the Unlimited, the One and the Many, the Monad and the indefinite Diad appear as the Same. But through this, that the things have been limited and shaped by the One, they have become apprehensible by the soul, in virtue of the immanent number, and have become an object of intellectual comprehension. For the Same is known by the Same, and the soul is itself number as to its form, or at least is made according to the law of number."

Restricting ourselves to musical morphology, we can do no better than let Plotinus speak for us. The specific meaning of the following excerpt emerges from the Pythagorean Table:

It is suggested that multiplicity is a falling away from The Unity, infinity (limitlessness) being the complete departure, an innumerable multiplicity, and that this is why unlimit is an evil and we evil at the stage of multiplicity.

A thing, in fact, becomes a manifold when, unable to remain self-centred, it flows outward and by that dissipation takes extension: utterly losing unity it becomes a manifold since there is nothing to bind part to part; when, with all this outflowing, it becomes something definite, there is a magnitude.

But what is there so grievous in magnitude?

Given consciousness, there will be, since the thing must feel its exile, its sundrance from its essence. Everything seeks not the alien but itself; in that outward moving there is frustration or compulsion; a thing most exists not when it takes multiplicity or extension, but when it holds to its own being, that is when its movement is inward. Desire towards extension is ignorance of the authentically great, a movement not on the appropriate path but toward the strange; to the possession of the self the way is inward.

Consider the thing that has taken extension; broken into so many independent items, it is now those several parts and not the thing it was; if that original is to persist, the members must stand collected to their total; in other words, a thing is itself not by being extended but by remaining, in its degree, a unity: through expansion and in the measure of the expansion, it is less itself; retaining unity, it retains its essential being.

Yet the universe has at once extension and beauty?

Yes; because it has not been allowed to slip away into the limitless but is held fast by unity; and it has beauty in virtue of Beauty, not of Magnitude; it needed Beauty to parry that magnitude; in the degree of its extension it was void of beauty and to that degree ugly. Thus extension serves as Matter to Beauty since what calls

---

[1] The following quotations are all taken from the article on "Pythagoras" by Kayser, in *Abhandlungen*. See also Guthrie, *Pythagoras*.

for its ordering is a multiplicity. The greater the expansion, the greater the disorder and ugliness.[1]

RAGA

Isolating in an actual melody the quality of tone relations by abstracting the pitches from rhythm, we are left with what we call *raga*. It is a grouping of intervals producing melodic outline but not melody because it lacks rhythm. Raga is a premelodic gestalt out of which melodies may be formed through rhythmization. The morphé of raga is an abstract of all possible energetic processes outlined by the form of particular tone relations.

Theoretically, raga has a distinct place in the process of musical *phenomenalization:

- (a)   Total tone material available (for example, chromatic material of twelve tones).
- (b)   Mode (for example, Dorian, major, etc.).
- (c)   Key, that is, definite pitch (for example, Dorian on G).
- (d)   Raga, that is, melodic outline, pitch succession.
- (e)   Melody, that is, pitch + rhythm.

In dodecaphony, (a) and (b) are identical; but the concept of (c)—key in a widely stretched sense—is present in the assumption of definite pitches at the original realization of the row. Moreover, twelve-tone composers recognize transpositions of a row to different pitches. Technically, raga (d) underlies the system. Both twelve-tone and traditional Western composers reach melody (e), but the latter bypass raga (d) by inventing their melodies directly on the basis of key (c).

Yet raga, though officially ignored, plays a considerable role in Western *variation technique. Because metrical music ties rhythm to melody, raga composition can be more easily found in nonmetrical styles. The corpus of plainchant supplies the clearest examples. It abounds in melodic formulas that recur in different chants, in different versions, with rhythmically different texts, but always recognizable as an identity, in short, as ragas. The mature technique of the Netherlands composers employs raga for divers kinds of variation. A *cantus firmus, for instance, serving a movement by supplying all voices with melodic material, actually supplies them with a raga. The extended behavior of individual lines is thereby often influenced, as in the following soprano fragment from Josquin's Mass *La Sol Fa Re Mi* (Agnus Dei, mm. 3 ff.):

[1]*Enneads*, pp. 541 f.

The variable elements of a raga are direction and succession of morphemes. Change of direction admits of inversion and retrogression. The original succession of pitches may undergo permutations in which only recognizable groups of two or more tones need be preserved. Transposition plays a role. A constant ambitus facilitates the perception. This technique, bearing on *topology, reaches the borderline of aleatory permutations.

REALITY

We think of a musical work as a reality existing all at once. Without this condition, there would be no musical morphology. Yet the process by which it is built in our mind is inevitably temporal—a succession of events related to each other through memory. The events coexist in the score. We perceive them through reading. The complex of musical reality admits separate investigations concerning (1) locus, (2) essence, (3) relevance, and (4) interpretation.

(1) Locus. Where exactly does a composition exist? The question could be readily answered in the visual arts: Leonardo's *Mona Lisa* is in Paris, Michelangelo's *Moses* in Rome. One may wonder whether such statements are completely correct, but at least they deal with the objective existence of a particular canvas or marble. The musical analogy of referring to a score remains unsatisfactory. Which score? The autograph? A particular edition? A particular copy from this edition? Does the composition exist in thousands of copies? The locus cannot be found in *notation. Music had reality before the invention of notation, when it was either improvised or transmitted from memory. But a performance or recording of music, too, retains a subjective character that lies outside the work itself. Listening to it, we do not say, "This *is* the work," but rather, "This is a performance *of* the work." This distinction remains true even in the extreme case, favored by recent developments, in which the composer fixes his composition directly on magnetic tape. A second copy of the tape does not double the reality.

At one time or other, the work must have lived as a whole in the composer's mind. By an inverse process of that which led from the composer's conception of the work as a whole to its temporal expression in notation and performance, the listener in turn rebuilds it (or is supposed to rebuild it) in his own mind. In either case, it is in the mind that the composition may be said to live.

We can locate the composition farther back. Inspiration, according to observation by those who have experienced it, is an occurrence in the mind of the subject, characterized by flashlike suddenness and a distinct impression of discovery rather than invention, plus the conviction of a meaning transcending the particular content. The experience of inspiration, added to that of his vision and elaboration of the work, leads the composer to believe himself as much a tool as a maker. These circumstances indicate that the ultimate reality, or the ultimate meaning, of music is of spiritual essence.

Die Fledermaus by Johann Strauss is aesthetically a masterpiece, yet we feel that somehow it is not so significant as Beethoven's Ninth Symphony or Bach's B minor Mass. The ultimate criterion lies outside technical perfection and sensuous beauty. We differentiate and judge not on musical grounds alone but according to the degree of spiritual meaning prevailing in a work.

What is the locus of a composition? Music inheres in the spirit and lives in the mind, in the imagination. On this supposition, the symbolic character of the work as a phenomenon becomes clear, whereby it may be fairly evaluated in all its aspects.

(2) Essence. Music has meaning. It is about something. Precisely what that "something" is cannot be translated into words. If we could define or describe it, music would be superfluous and futile. Music is not—as a modern book on acoustics puts it—"something that happens in the air." Music happens inside us. Yet it is not essentially a personal expression but rather a symbol for something common to all humanity. Only in this sense can we call it a message. If it were nothing but self-expression, music could be safely stored away as a psychological curiosity. Music, in any case, is a whole, of which individual works are quite literally "pieces." We see this truth best by considering a distant but stylistically unified body of music. Plainsong, for instance, was composed and compiled during a period of at least one thousand years, yet at once the vision of a whole appears of which the individual chants are felt to be fragments.

Whatever the meaning of music, the spiritual essence of music needs sound as a physical vehicle. The changing role of sound in the history of music leads us to a basic distinction. The essentials of a composition reside in musical *time and space, that is, in rhythm and pitch. They are phenomenalized in relationships: time proportions and pitch proportions. The rest—dynamics, timbre, and in a way even tempo—is of secondary importance. The material, terrestrial contribution of these secondary elements is great but not essential. Until the eighteenth century, scores usually did not bother to specify them. Many pieces could be indifferently sung or played or performed by a combination of both voices and instruments. Bach's *Die Kunst der Fuge* was recognized as one of the great achievements of the human spirit solely from the written-down proportions of time and pitch, long before the work began to be heard in various material embodiments. People of all times, of course, have enjoyed sound. The fourteenth-century composer Guillaume de Machaut, reporting on several festivities, lists for each occasion over thirty different instruments, most of them used in multiples and making "such noise that it was a marvel."[1] Monteverdi's orchestra sounded magnificent in line with Venetian splendor. Yet sound in those days was thought of as the body of music, not its soul. The soul lay within the structure, independent of the physical manifestation.

In the last two hundred years, the secondary, nonessential qualities of music have come into their own as relevant aesthetic factors. Materialism, which for some time has been on the way out in philosophy and art in general, seems to be enjoying a curious comeback in music. Since Berlioz published his *Traité d'instrumentation* in 1844, emphasizing timbre, there has been an increasing tendency toward worship of sound. Actually many people experience music precisely from that "terrestrial" end and thus miss most of what music is essentially made of. There is music, and there is its embodiment in actual sound. Nobody will wish to underestimate the latter, but it is not identical

[1]Machaut, *La Prise d'Alexandrie*. See also Levarie, *Machaut*, pp. 26 ff.

234

with the essence of music. Timbre, dynamics, and tempo deserve every possible care, but they should never overshadow our awareness that a musical work is, to a considerable extent, independent of its acoustical sensorial manifestation. The current overemphasis on externals has produced a regrettable reversal of the scale of values. Excessive concentration on materialistic qualities is likely to distract attention from the essence of the work. The interest in appearances ought not to overshadow that in essentials. Musical imagination ought not to be fired from the outside by experiments with sounds and sound patterns. The tendency to lay undue value upon the physical vehicle in music reflects the materialistic notion that fullness of life and happiness rest in mastery over the physical world. Technical accomplishments, however, are means and not ends in themselves.

A work of music being a spiritual entity, the composition of the work, its notation, its sound, its performance assume the character of approximation to an idea. The embodiment of beauty on the physical level has great value, but it must not overshadow the distinction between essentials and incidentals.

(3) Relevance. If it be true that art should mirror its time, it must by no means mirror only the external and existent. The mirror's field of vision should be widened to reflect also human aspirations and their wellsprings. The art of great epochs has fulfilled this function above all others. Greek art reflects not so much the actual Greek of the time as a certain elevated aspect of the Greek soul. The romantic postulate, that the artist's works are identical with his life, is clearly at variance with fact. A saintly deed, for instance, does not have to wait for an actual saint.

Therefore, one need not boast about "expressing one's time." The secular corporeal person is but half the man; and of this half, biography renders account. Art is much more the record of that other, invisible part of him. It provides those energies which shape the most precious parts of ourselves. For above all, the task of art is to show a way. In medieval terms, it is anagogic. Where art is concerned, one may safely ignore all concern for being "timely." The stylistic traits of an age or an individual will automatically be present.

(4) Interpretation. All phenomenalization owes its existence to limitation. Interpretation is always a form of limitation, hence an element of style. Interpretation means explanation or translation. In a wider sense, the composer himself might be called an interpreter inasmuch as he is personally and symbolically phenomenalizing something essentially permanent and universal; for works of art are indeed symbols of permanent and universal meanings or contents. The listener or beholder is also an interpreter inasmuch as the phenomenalized work is being interpreted through his individuality.

In the visual arts, no middleman is interposed between the work and the beholder. The latter alone, after the creative artist, interprets. Recent techniques in musical composition permit the elimination of the middleman if the composer transmits his ideas directly to a magnetic tape, which thus becomes "score" and performance all in one. Out of a similar concern to restrict interpretation to the composer and listener alone, Stravinsky, arranging some of his works for player piano, is said to have once punched the paper rolls himself. If the story be true, what he actually did was to freeze, not his intentions (which he had phenomenalized in the act of composing), but his view of the work some time after having composed it. Similarly, the modern composer creating directly for the tape obliterates the distinction between idea and manipulation.

The artistic event, that is, the recreation of the work in the mind, must be viewed as the result of a hierarchy or cascade of interpretation. It is the outcome of a necessary cooperation between artist and spectator in the visual arts, and between composer, performer, and listener in music. Some styles, like figured bass and jazz, expressly call for cooperation of the interpreter with the composer. In such cases, interpretation assumes material connotations transcending our usual acceptance of the term.

Our point that the work as an event cannot be fixed is borne out by history. The beauty of Gothic cathedrals lay hidden for centuries; the very word *Gothic* was coined to indicate contempt. The buildings stood there for everyone to behold. Yet the work as a spiritual entity—the essential message of the stones—was not seen, and the symbol was not understood. The event simply did not happen. Likewise Stravinsky's experiment, even if it did achieve the purpose of identifying composition and interpretation, would in no way guarantee the happening of the artistic event. The event, in any case, needs the resonance of the listener who, ironically enough, may or may not respond precisely to the composer's interpretation. The claim is exaggerated that the best tradition can be built upon a composer's interpretation of his own work. The recording of such a performance is interesting mainly as a document of the composer's state of mind at a certain point in his life.

The process whereby a performer penetrates a work is one of progressive identification with the work. He reproduces, that is, he produces anew, the work within himself. Because the composition thus lives within the interpreter, partaking of his own life and the changes entailed by it, fluctuations occur in the rendering of even the most spiritualized conception. Considerable divergences can be heard in different performances of the same work by the same artist. They are symptoms of imperfection, a condition inseparable from life and thus from interpretation. Imperfection inheres in all phenomenalization; and art, being at the same time pure thought and embodiment, concept and life, partakes of it. Actually imperfection is built not only by definition into every interpretation (even the "perfect" performance) but into the very structure of the tone material. Nature forces us to a compromise between the just intonation of the octave and that of any other interval. The compromise, known as *temperament, is an inescapable and limiting imperfection of any conceivable tone system. A remarkable lesson to be learned from temperament is that we are perfectly capable of hearing just intonation through its imperfect realization. This ability, without which music-making would be impossible, is by no means to be explained by habit or conditioning. On the contrary, without a given inner attunement to natural intervals in their original perfection, we should obviously be utterly incapable, lacking any yardstick, of judging intonation as being true or false.

The work of music, subjective embodiment itself, needs a second incarnation. It needs to pass through the interpreter who, being a live person, is imperfect. This very imperfection, a humanizing agent, helps the event to happen. It "makes the work come to life," as one says. This phrase describes not only a kind of awakening of the work but also, and rather, a coming *down* to life from the spiritual realm. The idea of the work experiences a "subjective interpretation." The recognition of imperfection is no excuse for lessening the drive toward perfection. Preoccupation with the outer appearance of the work, however, all too easily overshadows its essence, which "ears to hear" can recognize through almost any decent performance. As long as the distinction between essentials and incidentals is kept clear, technical enthusiasm remains entirely legitimate. When interpretation usurps first place, music is degraded to the level of idol worship or treated like the arena of an athletic competition. Do we not say in highest praise of a performer that he makes one forget him and his instrument?

Interpretation is an act of incarnation. Beauty in any form of incarnation gives us an experience of deep significance. The attitude that predisposes us for such an experience is readiness. It begins with an inner earthquake. The precondition of understanding, which is not at all the same as acknowledging, is awe.

RECAPITULATION. See REPETITION

RECITATIVE. See VOCAL MUSIC

REFRAIN. See RONDO

RELEVANCE. See REALITY

REPETITION

Repetition is the basic mode of *idiogenesis. In music it can never be quite so mechanical as in visual decoration, because the passing of time always modifies the repetition in its relation to the original (cf. "Growth and Limitation," pp. 11 ff.). Of two apparently identical musical statements, the second contains irreversibly the memory of the first.

The recognition that even a literal repetition is heard as variation must have encouraged performers and composers alike to introduce deliberate changes. The habit of singers in the eighteenth century of ornamenting every da capo is a matter of record. Often criticized as a self-indulgence, it deserves some praise for being a vital musical activity.

C. P. E. Bach's concern with "veränderte Reprise" ("varied repetition") shows the fertility of the concept. His *Kurze und leichte Klavierstücke mit veränderten Reprisen* ("Short and easy Piano Pieces with Varied Repetitions") have been compared to his father's *Inventionen* as an "instructional work of the highest order."[1] The emphasis in the title on varied repetition (which in

[1] See the edition by Jonas which contains a very good preface.

these pieces has nothing to do with recapitulation in sonata form) reflects the composer's high evaluation of the technique in the art of composition. Although intended for beginners, these pieces convey anything but a simple notion of how an antecedent phrase—usually 4, 6, or 8 measures long—may be varied in the immediately following repetition by a consequent. Here is an example (*Erste Sammlung* no. 9, Andante e sostenuto):

repeated as

Two decades later, the technique has become very subtle in the hands of Mozart; the first two measures in the following excerpt from his Piano Sonata, C major, K. 545, recur immediately as a "veränderte Reprise":

C. P. E. Bach's *Klavierstücke* were written in the same decade as his more famous *Sechs Sonaten für Clavier mit veränderten Reprisen*. He tried out the concept on small and large forms alike. The subtitle refers here primarily to the written-out repetition, replacing the mechanical repeat sign, of each half of the sonata movement and not to the relation of recapitulation to exposition. The modulatory variant, however, may well have been in the composer's mind; for the principle, on a harmonic rather than melodic level, is similar.

In the case of immediate repetition, the contribution to growth is obvious. A chain of such repetitions produces, as the case may be, strophes and variation sets. The absence of a limiting principle keeps these occurrences short of creating definitive forms. Intermittent repetitions, as of a refrain or ritornello, also favor the continuation of growth. Folksongs and rondos thrive on them. The morphological gain seems greater; for paired with *proportion, symmetry, or number, periodic recurrence can be made to serve limitation as well. The main structure of the rondo in Beethoven's Violin Concerto, for example, is determined by five appearances of the ritornello symmetrically arranged around a distinct center.

Recapitulation is a special case of repetition. The single restatement by a recapitulation or da capo is apparently endowed with special obligations and forces. It is usually longer than refrain or ritornello and hence may accommodate a complex morphé of its own. Length and complexity probably influence the expectation of not more than one repetition. In this regard, recapitulation, while still an element of growth, also limits the form by closing it (cf. *Open-Closed). The canceling of the modulation in a sonata-form recapitulation reinforces the finality. This function of repetition is not lessened by apparent deviations from proportion. The abbreviation of a minuet da capo is justified by time perspective; that of a condensed rather than explicit sonata recapitulation, moreover, by romantic suggestiveness.

Repetition underlies the essential quality of *imitation and *echo effect. Whereas in the first case the activity of a voice, spread across the fabric, is distributed among various participants, in the second case one voice may suffice.

RESOLUTION. See CONSONANCE-DISSONANCE

REST

Rest is potential music, not absence of music. Hence it always denotes a state of creativity, not of nothingness. Once the continuum has begun, all silences, however notated, are elocutionary devices. Silence can be significant in many ways. One can make errors of silence as easily as errors of sound.

Suspense is one of the obvious gains. A rest may be preparatory or an actual interruption. When Mahler in his Eighth Symphony (at number 38) places a seemingly illogical caesura in the middle of the word *Ac'cende*, he thereby intensifies the strong religious request of the hymn text for sudden illumination. The conductor of Haydn's *Schöpfung*, rather than the composer, might act similarly before the C major appearance of "Light." A prescribed interruption, as before the coda in Weber's *Freischütz* Overture, adds structural meaning to the suspense and the subsequent explosion. Even in a polyphonic texture, the silence of only one among several voices creates suspense for the reentry of that one voice. Sounds create suspense by devices of their own, but the musical effect produced by silence need not be smaller.

Repose, at the other extreme, may also proceed from rest. Familiar are quarter rests on weak beats following chords on strong beats. The effect is a suggested prolongation of the sound and a letup between impacts. At the end of a piece, the repose becomes part of the general meter. The empty measure at the end of the first movement of Beethoven's First Symphony, for example, helps clarify the missing measure implied at the very beginning—whatever the intervening events.

Syncopation produced by rests is often difficult to understand, for any corrective counterbeat is missing. A telling spot is the coda of the second movement of Beethoven's Piano Sonata op. 110 where for eleven measures the cadential chords fall exclusively on weak beats and the strong measures remain empty. Such a passage can only be understood by foresight, that is, the right kind of expectation, or by hindsight, that is, the eventual resolution. In our example, the memory of the preceding metric organization may carry the listener across. The final correction is offered by the sustained right-hand chord, the new bass arpeggio, and the unexpected turn to the major mode.

Staccato denotes a rest following a sound, but the detached presentation of a line is really a device of articulation. The reasons are usually expressive. The procedure is related to breathing; for the duration of the interruption one actually holds one's breath.

Rests between the movements of a multipartite work are part of the total musical event and thus influence it like sounds. The caesura may sometimes be composed, as between the movements of Mendelssohn's Violin Concerto, or specified in words, as after the first movement of Mahler's Third Symphony. Usually there is no indication, and the performer will have to decide for how long to interrupt the flow of the music. Occasionally the performer might deny the implied rest altogether. Felix Weingartner argues for attaching the finale of Beethoven's Ninth Symphony directly to the preceding Adagio in order to increase the eminently dramatic effect of the "terror fanfare."[1] In concert performances of Masses, the first two movements might be sung *attacca*, because in the service Kyrie and Gloria follow each other without any interruption from the part of the liturgy. In this respect, a long song cycle, like Schubert's *Die schöne Müllerin*, calls for particular care and understanding; the implied flow of the story and the parallel overall musical structure may be either highlighted or ruined by the placement of pauses. The situation is still more critical in opera houses. A long intermission between the first two scenes of Verdi's *Rigoletto*, for instance, as frequently practiced by major companies, adds undue weight to the preparatory Introduction, so designated by the composer, and weakens the direction and continuity of the drama. Lengthy pauses to shift scenery in the middle of the first *Don Giovanni* finale or the second *Zauberflöte* finale tear the unity of the musical structure wide apart.

RETROGRADE

Scientists differ in their interpretations of space, but they agree on the irreversibility of time. In space, retrograde motion is a common experience. We can move forward and backward, up and down, left and right. In time, retrogression is an unfamiliar experience. Time is unidirectional, and we can only go forward in it. The attempt to reverse the direction of a temporal pro-

---

[1] *Ratschläge*, p. 185.

cess artificially is legitimate, if at all, only in music in which retrogression at least does not destroy the substance. The result, in any case, remains an illusion, for it cannot cancel our memory of the original forward event. Even if the substance is turned back, the event moves forward. In other temporal arts, retrogression is therefore generally ludicrous, as when in a film played backward a bullet leaves the target and returns into the muzzle of the pistol from which it was shot. In literature, the attempt can become wistful in the hands of a skillful writer. In a short story, Vladimir Nabokov describes an old man "who had managed on two occasions already to recount . . . the story of his life, first in one direction, from the present toward the past, and then in the other, against the grain, resulting in two different lives, one successful, the other not."[1] The narrator in another short story by the same author is "listening to the sparrows outside: Who knows, if recorded and run backward, those bird sounds might not become human speech, voiced words, just as the latter become a twitter when reversed?"[2] The last example neatly and wittily makes the obvious point that language used backward ceases to be language.

Music, however, remains music also in retrogression, whatever the result. Particular qualities, of course, are affected. Rhythmically, arsis and thesis change places: every accented beat becomes unaccented, and unaccented beats receive an accent. The more distinct the rhythmic organization, the more distinct also the qualitative change. A spondee, for instance, remains intact (𝅗𝅥 𝅗𝅥 𝅗𝅥), but a trochee (𝅗𝅥 ♩) becomes an iamb (♩ 𝅗𝅥), and a dactylus (𝅗𝅥. ♩♩) played backward sounds so unnatural that it existed in the Middle Ages as the fourth rhythmic mode only in theory but not in practice. Machaut's musical rendering of the text "Ma fin est mon commencement," an early example of extensive and complex retrograde motion, utilizes for good reasons the syncopated and hence neutral rhythm | ♪ ♩ ♩ ♩ ♪ |.[3]

Melodically, every up becomes a down. A smaller interval following a larger turns into a larger interval following a smaller. Together with the qualitative rhythmic shift, these melodic characteristics invert the roles of consonance and dissonance. Hence contrapuntal complications arise when forward and backward versions are played simultaneously, as is the case not only in most of such Renaissance compositions but also, for example, in Bach's Canon 4 from the *Musikalisches Opfer*. In the following juxtaposition of two corresponding measures (6 and 13) from this Canon, not only consonances and dissonances are reversed (DCDCCDDC becomes CDDCCDCD) but the very nature of the dissonances changes identity among passing tones, neighboring notes, appoggiaturas, and suspensions:

[1]*Lik* (1939).
[2]*The Vane Sisters* (1959).
[3]*Werke*, 1:64.

What remains constant are tonality and ambitus. Tempo, on a different level because it is not structural, also usually remains constant although there are notable exceptions. In the fugue in Beethoven's Hammerklavier Sonata, the retrograde theme occurs in augmentation, that is, in a different tempo. It is true that in regard to tonality every going away becomes a returning, every abandoning of the key a retrieving; but the central position of the established tonic remains intact. In an atonal piece (like the third movement of Alban Berg's *Lyrische Suite* which runs forward toward, and then backward from, a middle axis), retrograde motion reinforces, if anything, the static quality of the underlying series. The constancy of ambitus and usually of tempo in all styles is morphologically essential for the maintenance of some balance and identity against the otherwise drastic reversals.

Music played backward challenges our hearing to recognize the retrogression. By comparison, music played upside down is easy to recognize because the inversion is in space rather than in time, as the mere name "mirror fugue" indicates. Hence mirror technique is more common than retrogression, witness the many examples in the works of Bach (*Kunst der Fuge*; *Wohltemperiertes Klavier* I, nos. 8, 15, 20, 23; et al.). Recognition of musical retrogression may be easy in simple melodies with noncommittal rhythms and impossible in complex structures. The hearing difficulties can be gradually alleviated by study and previous knowledge.

Retrograde motion is commonly understood as the inversion in time of a melody, that is, of pitch progression together with rhythm. One is free to apply the term to any one element of music, hence also to raga alone. The technique is basic to dodecaphonic writing. In other styles, it has proven efficient and audible particularly when concerning small cells like motives.

Of these four examples, all from the first movement of Anton Bruckner's Fourth Symphony, (1) is the simplest. One may argue that a rhythmically undifferentiated arpeggio is likely to "go back and forth" the same way; but there are other arpeggios in the immediate vicinity of this one which do not, and the retrogression is obvious. The other examples all show retrograde motion of the raga component. In (2), the rhythm retains the appearance of the forward motion. Because the nature of a scale blurs the distinction between retrogression and inversion, this and the next example remain ambiguous. Yet in (3), the retrogression of the rhythm at beginning and end influences our interpretation of the behavior of the raga. Example (4) comes closest to true melodic retrogression; the characteristic skip eliminates ambiguity with inversion.

Retrograde motion serves both growth and limitation. It contributes to growth by producing a kind of repetition or variation; and to limitation, by suggesting symmetry and perhaps dialectics.

RHYTHM AND METER

(1) General Considerations. (2) Distinction between Rhythm and Meter. (3) Mutual Influence. (4) Pneumaticism and Kinematicism. (5) Relation to Prosody. (6) Illustrations.

(1) General Considerations. Rhythm is the mode of phenomenalization of time by means of proportion. The qualification imposed by proportion is necessary to distinguish rhythm from mere duration. In pure duration—a tone held without any dynamic change—time is phenomenalized solely by the innate time feeling produced by our heartbeat. Even here an underlying rhythm—that of the heartbeat—defines the experience. Perhaps one can never feel pure duration free of rhythm. If we indeed imagine a state in which time feeling is canceled altogether, such a state can be explained by the tendency of pure duration toward chronal lethargy. Time feeling comes to life through rhythm. Space feeling discloses analogous conditions. Space becomes phenomenalized through the presence of objects, which correspond to the "rhythmic points" in time. A theoretically imaginable continuously filled space would be self-canceling. Rhythm is a universal principle.

When our innate time feeling comes under the influence of an imposed rhythm, two layers form. Our time feeling remains undivided as we listen to a clock ticking in unison with our heartbeat, and stopping the clock simply causes the heartbeat to disappear from consciousness. As soon as some external rhythm differs from our heartbeat, however, it creates a new time feeling. Our normal heartbeat, regardless of whether it is actually modified by the new time feeling, remains in any case the standard against which all rhythm is judged. This standard either remains subconscious or immediately becomes so as soon as we hear the new imposed rhythm, which alone henceforth commands awareness. A split has occurred between the standard and the actual rhythm, the former remaining subconscious but setting the norm, the latter becoming the only aesthetically relevant feature. On both layers, time is created through rhythm: the normal human time arising from the heartbeat is modified by the rhythm of the conscious experience.

When we listen to several different outside rhythms at the same time, we still take the conscious layer to be one and not many; for we can breathe only one rhythm at a time. In polyrhythmic complexes, there is *one* vital overall rhythm, below which the various subrhythms are experienced, not pneumatically, but kinematically. We can perform different rhythms simultaneously with different limbs, but our breathing always remains undivided. We can observe a simultaneity of various rhythms, but we cannot breathe them simultaneously. If an overall rhythm is lacking, so will be human resonance.

(2) Distinction between Rhythm and Meter. Meter could be defined as equally proportioned rhythm, but this statement remains a surface description. In fact, what can be reduced by the mathematically classifying mind by means of variables to a special case may actually appear to an aesthetically perceptive mind as a thoroughly new phenomenon. Both rhythm and meter are rooted in proportion; but regularity is not essential to rhythm, whereas it is to meter. Meter is a much more haptical phenomenon than rhythm. It is of a more mechanical nature, being measure and springing from an urge for order, for regularity. Rhythm is rather on the side of the organic, of life. It is an energetic process, a gesture. Rhythm is will, meter is system.

The number inherently associated with meter is 2. It bears on systole and diastole of the heart. Our hearing the ticking of a clock as tick-tock is an irrepressible phenomenon. By mentally interchanging the two phases, one can easily persuade oneself that this binary organization is not prompted by the clock mechanism but by our subjective sense of order. In walking we accentuate one out of two steps. One might think that for the sake of balance alternating accents on left and right would be preferable, but walking in triple time, which would produce the alternation, simply "goes against the grain." The number 2 is also the guiding principle of larger metric units; the progression 2-4-8 etc. is standard. Even ternary groups use multiplication by 2 (3-6-12 etc.) and almost never by 3 (3-9-27 etc.).

The number inherently associated with rhythm is 3. Regularity not being essential to rhythm, the number pertains only to the distinction among parts or phases of a process and not to equality of duration. The basic rhythmic process is breathing. It begins with inhalation. We first gather breath before we can employ it. The first act of a newborn child is inhaling. In normal breathing, exhaling lasts approximately twice as long as inhaling. The breath is let out rather swiftly at the beginning, then more slowly, and finally peters out or comes to a stop. Accordingly we distinguish theoretically three rhythmic breathing phases, which may be notated as follows:

Inhaling creates tension, exhaling brings relief. Hence the exhalation, always long by nature, also assumes an accent by nature. We speak here of the basic form of rhythm and not of possible or incidental occurrences of length and stress. In modern notation, which sets the barline before the strong beat, the normal breathing rhythm looks as follows:

We call this basic form *anacrustic* because it is characterized by an upbeat. The rhythm appears tellurian. Lifting a limb (arsis) works against gravity; like inhaling, it produces tension. Setting down a foot or arm (thesis) works with gravity; like exhaling, it accentuates. Accumulation of energy creates a potential followed by a release of energy which is kinematic. This basic anacrustic rhythm is the normal form of rhythm because exhalation, length, and accent all coincide. It is embodied in the conductor's traditional upbeat leading to a downbeat.

When the inhalation draws the accent, a new rhythm arises that stands in a relation of polarity to the anacrustic form:

Inhalation   Exhalation

We call this form *crustic* because it begins with a beat (*krusis*). It is inscribed between barlines whereas the anacrustic rhythm straddles the barline. Crustic rhythm is characterized by forceful inhaling, which thus falls on the strong beat. The subsequent exhaling is then not felt as a downstroke but as a sinking down, a release from an unprepared effort, from a sudden burst of energy. Corresponding gestures are the throwing-upward and subsequent sinking-down of the arms, or an exploding leap. This form is antitellurian in intent; it works not with, but against, gravity. Both physiologically and psychologically it is "abnormal" when compared to the anacrustic form. One puts an unprepared accent on the inhalation when out of breath or sobbing. Nor is leaping normal when compared to walking. If convention would allow the crustic form to be embodied by the conductor's gesture, the beginning of Beethoven's Fifth Piano Concerto should be expressed by a sudden upward thrust of the arm, not by a downbeat.

The essence of both rhythms remains untouched by a change in proportion, although the character of the individual rhythm will thereby be affected. When the original proportion ruled by 3 is made to approach 2, for instance, the change will always be felt as a quickening of the rhythm, but the distinction between the anacrustic and crustic forms remains intact. Similarly, 3 may be extended to 4 or more. The basic ternary principle, however, is thereby not touched, because the extension merely prolongs the particular phase. The polarity of the two basic rhythmic forms is solely determined by the stress either coinciding with the exhalation or occupying the inhalation. Except in the case of pure proportion, rhythms are either anacrustic or crustic.

Their individual forms arise through proportion variation. The original forms may be changed, for example ♩|♩ to ♩|♩ , and |♩♩| to |♩ ♩| They may be shortened to, respectively, ♩|♩ and |♩ ♩|. Time values may be split in two or more parts and interpreted as fractional breathing (corresponding to *fractio modi*). Fractional breathing always carries an intensification:

(a) I I │ E   (b) │ I E E
     ♩ ♩ │ ♩   │ ♩ ♩ ♩

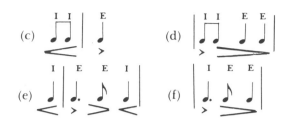

These examples show the most natural, instinctive mode of fractioning a given rhythm. There are, however, other modes. Among them we note the special vitality of those that exhibit anticipated breathing, which comes about when a breathing fraction normally belonging to the preceding time assumes the breathing characteristic of the following phase. Thus, for example, (a) above may be modified to *I E E*, or (d) to *I E E I*. In this last case, the inhalation on the third beat does not constitute an upbeat, superficial appearance to the contrary. It is a true anticipation: the crustic meaning is not changed. The choice of interpreting a spot in one way or another depends, as always, on the musical context. A certain arbitrariness is sometimes unavoidable, and ambiguity can be found to be an integral part of the aesthetic effect. Ambiguity in melody and harmony is frequently encountered, and rhythm makes no exception.

(3) Mutual Influence. Rhythm may become metricized; meter, rhythmicized. When permitted by circumstances, the amalgamation is spontaneous. To separate in actual experience the rhythmic, crustic ingredient from the basically metrical ticktock of a clock, for instance, is a practical impossibility.

Rhythm is metricized when the metric layer, by acquiring a rhythmic meaning, draws the free rhythm, that is, the whole rhythmic layer, into its pattern. There are consequences. The originally irrational proportions become rational. Such is the case when a Gregorian melody is turned into a Protestant chorale (compare the Gregorian Easter sequence *Victimae Paschali laudes* with the Lutheran *Christ ist erstanden*). The originally ternary rhythm may become binary. Examples are supplied by various popular adaptations of classical melodies (compare "Tonight we love" with the opening theme of Tchaikovsky's First Piano Concerto).

Conversely, meter may be rhythmicized beyond the elementary spontaneous amalgamation, with consequences of its own. The originally binary meter may become ternary (cf. Variations 9 and 10 of Bach's Organ Partita on "Sei gegrüsset, Jesu gütig"). The beats themselves may grow irregular while, of course, remaining metrical, that is, in rational proportions to each other (cf. the behavior of the medieval rhythmic modes, particularly as liberated by *extensio modi* and *fractio modi*).

When rhythm and meter are simultaneously operative, they normally coincide, thereby creating the possibility of an abnormal situation. It can be produced by the dissociation of the rhythmic and the underlying metric layers. The result is *syncopation, a temporary tearing off of the rhythmic layer from the metric layer (Greek *syncope*, 'cutting off', 'cutting into pieces').

(4) Pneumaticism and Kinematicism. Rhythm being a modification of

the equal flow of time by varying proportions, each rhythmic form expresses a specific chrono-energetic character determined centrally by breath, peripherally by gesture. Although the original connection with breathing, the basis of all rhythm, is never quite lost, kinematicism begins with gesture and eventually leads to an objectively detached perception of proportion indicative of energy curves with which neither breathing nor gesture can any longer empathize bodily. Because of the physiological limits to actual imitation of rhythms by breathing, the range of kinematic perception is much wider than that of pneumatic perception. Because of the mechanical limits to actual imitation of rhythms by gestures, the range of "higher" kinematic perception of sheer proportion is wider than that of "lower" kinematic empathy with body motions. The immensely greater part of music appeals indeed to mental perception rather than to muscular imitation.

The supposition is wrong—tempting though it may be—that vocal music is pneumatic by definition. Singing is done by exhaling, not by both inhaling and exhaling. In this sense, the singer also "plays an instrument." The identification of voice production with only exhalation disengages the sung rhythm from actual breathing. The sung rhythm becomes objectified, kinematized.

(5) Relation to Prosody. Rhythm and meter belong to both music and language. Questions of prosody could therefore be profitably treated jointly, and findings in one art applied to the other. Over the centuries, rhythmic and metric terminology has unfortunately become so confused as to be of little help to the musician. The reason for the confusion lies in the distinction, often blurred, among the various kinds of *accent. Dynamic accent makes a tone louder; tonic accent, higher; and agogic accent, longer. Latin meter depended on quantitative distinctions, whereas poetry in most modern languages favors qualitative delineation. Stress by length has yielded to stress by loudness. (In versification, tonic accent, always present, plays a small theoretic role.) As a result, the prosodic symbol ◡– does not make clear whether the second syllable is meant to be long, or loud, or both. Webster defines iamb as "a foot consisting of a short syllable followed by a long one, as in *ămāns*, or of an unaccented syllable followed by an accented one, as in *invent*." The offered alternative frustrates one's inclination to identify crustic with iambic rhythm (and by inversion and analogy, anacrustic with trochaic). Whereas *invent* clearly contains an upbeat, *amans* does not. In the first case, the accent is dynamic; in the second, agogic; and neither example considers breathing. The concepts of arsis and thesis each receive in Webster's *Dictionary* two contradictory meanings: either term can refer to the accented or unaccented part of a measure. Nothing is gained for music by the introduction of ambivalent terminology.

Whatever the rules in different centuries and languages, musical rhythmics maintain the independence of quantity and stress. The underlying principle is breathing. The two polar rhythmic modes we have isolated differ by the placement of the stress, the dynamic accent, on either the exhalation (anacrustic) or the inhalation (crustic). In the normal form, exhalation carries the length, but adjustments of time proportions are possible without changing the basic principles.

247

(6) Illustrations. In nonmetrical music, such as the Gregorian Kyrie from the Third Mass (cf. p. 11), the constancy of energy flow is conspicuous (*cantus planus*). This quality, coupled with the absence of metrics, makes this kind of music the antithesis of music for working, marching, or dancing. There is nothing muscular about it. Rhythm is subservient to melody, riding the melodic breath, never crystallizing into self-sustained shapes. Accent as a constituent rhythmic factor is absent. Looking for anacrustic or crustic rhythms would be senseless. All these characteristics—absence of meter, only small deviations from a steady flow, no rhythmic accents—in addition to a neutral tempo make plainchant destined for kinematic perception of high spirituality. Pneumaticism comes into its own, not within each phrase, but in the succession of phrases. The varying lengths of phrases produce an overall pneumatic rhythm. We can experience this rhythm of form directly because the length of any one unit never becomes disconnected from actual human breathing conditions.

For examples of metrical music, see the rhythmic and metric analyses of Schubert's *Moment musical* op. 94 no. 5 and Johann Strauss's *Frühlings-stimmen-Walzer* in Appendix A (pp. 319 ff.).

RICERCAR. See **FUGUE**

RITORNELLO. See **RONDO**

ROMANTIC. See **CLASSIC-ROMANTIC**

RONDO

The word implies that something is "coming around"—the image of a wheel shared with such related terms as rota and round. In all such pieces, something returns. In the case of rondo, we distinguish between two types: in one, the recurring element is a refrain; in the other, a ritornello.

A refrain is a recurring closing phrase. In the early occurrences of the device and of the word in medieval France, the connection with *refringere*, "breaking" the flow of the song, was obvious. The practice is very old and probably the product of a musical social situation in which a soloist alternates with a group. The soloist chants the continuous story; his description of changing lyrical or dramatic events demands variety and skill. His contribution is the main event. The group or chorus responds at certain cadential points with an unchanging and artistically far simpler formula, the refrain. The punctuation gives form by setting a limit to each section—call it verse, strophe, or whatever you will. The form of the whole, however, is controlled by the soloist, who is the center of attention.

A great deal of unrecorded and recorded folk music of all places and periods belongs in this category. The entire Kyrie movement of Missa III (cf. p.

11) is held together by the musical as well as textual "eleison" refrain. Trouvères, troubadours, and *ars nova* composers in France and Italy, all of whom composed with regard to a social group situation, strongly favored refrain forms under varying names such as virelai, ballade, and rondeau itself.[1] In Italian compositions of this period, the refrain is often called *ripresa*.

Ritornello, unlike refrain, is not an appendix but the main section of the piece in which it occurs. Hence it always stands at the beginning as well as at the end. It is the first thing one hears. It demands most of the interest. By returning, a ritornello gives form to the whole. The sections between the ritornelli are heard as interruptions; they remain episodes.

Ritornello is thus morphologically a higher accomplishment than refrain. Characteristic of the relationship is the medieval French rondeau which originally employs refrain but in its more complex and later form resorts to ritornello. A clear example of a piece anticipating the modern rondo is Adam de la Halle's "Diex soit" which symmetrically interposes two longer episodes between three recurrences of a catchy ritornello.[2]

Whereas in subsequent centuries, refrain seems to have remained the property of popular music, such as folksongs, folk dances, and gospel hymns, and therefore barely participates in the development of complex structures, ritornello proved its efficacy particularly in the transformation of various given structures from the seventeenth century on. With the help of ritornello, almost any stylized dance movements of the baroque can be put "en rondeau." The works of Couperin and Rameau abound in examples. At the same time, Italian instrumentalists utilized ritornello to organize their fresh outpouring of concerto movements, whereby the alternation ritornello-episode could easily be equated with that of tutti-soli. From Vivaldi, Bach learned to transfer this form to his own concertos and indirectly to many of his fugues. Concertizing, and eventually other, fugues in which sections developing the subject return after interruptions by subject-free episodes are all indebted to the idea of ritornello (cf. *Well-tempered Keyboard I*, nos. 7, 12, 20, etc.).

The operatic rondo of the day (a stand-by in opera buffa not disdained by either Gluck or Mozart) may have been influenced by dance music "en rondeau" or merely have come into being as a more easily digestible alternative to a da capo aria. In any case, its purposeful transfer to *sonata (in which term we include trio, quartet, symphony, concerto, etc.) in the 1770s and 1780s produced results of unexpected vitality and durability. Haydn had included rondos in sonatas before that time, but they were almost exclusively stylized dances. In compliance with the operatic taste of the period, Mozart replaced the sonata-form finale of his Piano Concerto K. 175 nine years later with a rondo, K. 382, from which he gained much pleasure and success.[3] In the finale of a much earlier String Quartet, K. 157 of 1772 or 1773, he reconciled—probably for the first time in history—sonata form with rondo by equating the first subject in the tonic with the ritornello, the second subject in the contrasting key with the first episode, and by limiting the number of appearances of the

[1]For a detailed study and many examples, see Orenstein, *Refrainformen*.
[2]*Oeuvres*, pp. 232–35.
[3]Cf. his letters of 23 March 1782, 12 March 1783, and 12 April 1783.

ritornello by the exigencies of the recapitulation. The sudden combination in one movement of entertainment, dance, opera, instrumental stylization, sonata form, and easy memorability by virtue of a catchy ritornello catapulted this new type of rondo to the position of sonata finale, which it maintained for several generations.

A refrain rondo has no particular morphology, for the repetitions may continue indefinitely. A ritornello rondo, on the other hand, immediately suggests some kind of symmetry by its placement at beginning and end of a piece. In this simplest appearance, ritornello-episode-ritornello, the form seems identical with the basic ternary bowform. One may argue that more returns are necessary to define a rondo. In this respect, the scherzo from Beethoven's Seventh Symphony may present a borderline case. The traditional A-B-A scherzo structure is here expanded to A-B-A-B-A (not to mention the coda threat of one more cycle): is the result a rondo? In any case, symmetry around a central axis (R-a-R-b-R-a-R, as in the combination of rondo and sonata form) contributes by clarifying in advance the intended shape.

RUBATO. See AGOGICS

SCALE

The first formative work of the musical spirit in the refinement of sound material is the detachment of discrete tones from the continuous and unlimited sonorous flux. The result, for any society, is the total tone material that supplies the basis for further creative activity. The French call it *échelle*; there is no appropriate English or German term. In Western music of the last two thousand years, to give an example, this total available tone material consists of the twelve chromatic tones within the octave. The Arabs happen to have seventeen; the Hindus, twenty-two. Application of the principle of tonality to the tone material yields modes. They are formations of individualized *échelles*, taken from the general tone material. The major mode, for instance, selects an organic and indivisible ensemble of seven tones, in particular and precise relations to each other which are not those of any other of the many possible modes. In the process of gradual musical *phenomenalization, scale is the melodic realization of a mode. Scale is a melodic archetype.

All available tones of a society have to be brought into a system. The chosen underlying organizing principles are indicative of the spirit of a society, and the consequences of the system are very serious. Plato used musical scales as metaphors and symbols to explain both the creation of the world and the ideal state.[1] When in the course of time a new system evolves, it retains the old principle in a new function, as our octaves retain the earlier hexachords. The contemporary attempt to break away from scale is a symptom of the general revolt against spiritual principles.

[1] Cf. *Timaeus* and *Republic*, of which Ernest McClain has made a brilliant and persuasive exegesis in *The Pythagorean Plato*.

The arrangement of the given tones by pitch is a consequence of harmonic operations and not the organizing principle itself. The resulting steps (halftones, wholetones, etc.) are produced secondarily and must not be interpreted as basic originators. The consequences are manifold, admitting of divers solutions and creating in turn new involvements.

The harmonic operations are fundamental, all proceeding from basic proportions applied to tone. They can be materialized by string divisions on the monochord. The harmonic proportions here serve the morphological principle of growth. Theoretically they can be continued into infinity. The problem faced alike by Plato's creator of the world or of the state and by the creator of a musical composition is the realization of a particular limitation without which there would be chaos.

The musical limits are set by the ear which can discriminate only up to a point. The point is not rigidly fixed. It can shift within certain degrees of tolerance, for individuals as much as for entire societies. The influence of supramusical forces has been recognized.[1] The Chinese selection of the pentatonic scale, for instance, corresponds to a general pentadic orientation of Chinese thought, as demonstrated by five elements, five directions of the sky, five colors of the rainbow, etc. Prime numbers and otherwise "sacred" numbers seem to permeate all known systems: 5, 7, 12, 17, 22. Further complications and subtle distinctions are theoretically possible, but practically they lie, if anywhere, in the future.

According to the law of polarity, which Plato takes for granted in all his demonstrations, each proportion is valid in both directions—up and down. Division and multiplication by 2 produces what sounds to us like repetitions of the same tone in different octave ranges:

This result precedes any system. The octave identities set a strong frame which is accessible to any kind of scale. All civilizations of all periods have been bound by this frame. The individual solutions within the octave differ according to both number of tones subsequently selected and relationships of these tones toward each other. Plato refers to these octave repetitions as "cycles of barrenness" (*Republic* 546).

Division and multiplication by 3 generate new tones continuing into infinity ("cycles of bearing"). The limits, defined by the number of consecutive operations, shape the results. One extension in each direction, projected into the octave, yields the tetrachordal system:

The primacy of the tetrachordal system has assigned to it a universal role. One finds it in many non-European societies and, absorbed but not denied, as

---

[1]Cf. Robert Lach, "Die Musik der Natur- und orientalischen Kulturvölker," in Adler, *Handbuch*, pp. 1–26.

part of all later Western organizations of the scale. To us, this scale outlines the cadential points of subdominant and dominant. To the Greeks, it determined the fixed tones of the system between which further movable tones could be placed. These are also the fixed tones that all Gregorian modes share (the Lydian in a somewhat modified form). The wholetone appears as a by-product.

A second extension by 3, that is, by fifths, in each direction produces the pentatonic scale. The given identity of the octave demands here as everywhere reduction to the range of one octave:

This scale must not be understood as an "incomplete" seven-tone Western scale from which the semitones are missing. Rather, it is a complete scale, derived from a harmonic operation in its own right. Notice that it contains the antecedent tetrachordal organization though necessarily reinterpreted.

A third extension by 3 produces our diatonic scale. The particular appearance is Dorian:

This is the first scale that creates, as a by-product, the particular commitment of halftone progressions. The number 7 for the totality of different tones becomes intelligible as the sum of the originator plus the three extensions in each direction: $1 + (2 \times 3)$.

Plato set up the philosophic axiom that any generative operation should extend three times but no more.[1] Music, which he ranked with philosophy, audibly demonstrates the increasing risks of continuing systematic extensions beyond three fifths in each direction:

The fourth extension sets up a conflict between the established and the newly gained thirds and sixths. The fifth extension adds further confusion to

---

[1]*Laws* 893e–894. "But the condition under which coming-to-be universally takes place— what is it? Manifestly 'tis effected whenever its starting point has received increment and so come to its second stage, and from this to the next and so by three steps acquired perceptibility to percipients." Ernest McClain, in *The Pythagorean Plato*, comments that Plato always structures processes through three increases, analogous to the progression from a point through a line and a plane into a solid (pp. 20f.) Plato's method keeps the mathematization of psychic and physical experiences on parallel levels.

seconds and sevenths. The Greek system did not employ the next, sixth extension which creates a head-on collision between F-sharp and G-flat. To Plato, this place in the system was reserved for the "tyrant." Later music theorists associated it with the "devil." It threatens order by the inherent tension of the clashing double identity of the pitch and by the supreme tritone dissonance against the generator. This point sets the limit to our own twelve-tone system. It completes the modern chromatic scale.

The theoretic possibility of generation by operation with numbers above 3 has proven to be practically unfeasible. Within the *senarius, 4 and 6 are octave repetitions of, respectively, 2 and 3. The number 5 introduces a new quality, the *modale; but already the second extension produces split identities (G-sharp to A-flat, and E to F-flat), and further extensions cannot break out of the sterile and yet dangerous cycle:

One system not explained by the genesis of scales is the hexachordal, which dominated medieval thought. The hexachord occupies a melodic middle ground between the Greek tetrachord and the modern octave systems. It gains its main virtue as a system by containing within its unity all three possible tetrachords—the ascending, the neutral, and the descending:

This integration of the basic tetrachords into one system must be interpreted as an attempt at unification. The admitted modal scales were based on D, E, F, or G. Hexachords could be built on C, F, or G. Hence the subfinalis, needed for the cadence in any mode, was always available within one of the existing hexachords. The Hymn to St. John, "Ut queant laxis," which exemplifies the hexachord system, has its finalis on D *re* and not C *ut*.[1] Because the range of the Hymn stays within a sixth, the whole melody can be sung within the "natural" hexachord on C. When a melody exceeded a sixth, the process of "mutation" permitted the smooth passing from one to another hexachord. The interlocking of the hexachords thus allowed for a wider melodic flexibility at the expense, to be sure, of a preferred and fixed tonal center. The beginning of the Dorian Antiphon "Ave Regina coelorum," for example, was sung with the following syllables:[2]

re   fa   re   ut   fa   sol-re   mi   fa   mi   re   ut   re-sol   fa   mi   re

[1]*Liber usualis*, p. 1504.
[2]*Liber usualis*, p. 1864.

253

A later phrase for the same Antiphon finds the following accommodation by hexachordal mutation:

la sol-ut   re   mi   fa   re-la   re   fa   fa   mi   re   ut

The tones B-flat and B-natural, movable in Dorian, are thus incorporated by being taken literally rather than in relation to a given finalis.

Hexachordal thinking reached its end when the melodic framework set by the hexachord was replaced by the new harmonic framework set by the triad. At the same time, musical needs shifted the tonal center from D (*modus primus*) to C and demanded the addition of a leading tone *si*. Because of the supremacy of the triad as a unifying force, the sixth became a signal melodic event—an artistic breakthrough, so to speak, across the natural boundary of the fifth. Hence a multitude of melodies from the seventeenth through nineteenth centuries is based precisely on the archetype of the hexachord, of which the former melodic stability is now contested by the octave-oriented harmonic impulse. The following examples are typical:

Bach, *Well-tempered Keyboard I/1*

Haydn, String Quartet op. 20 no. 5

Mozart, Piano Sonata K. 333

Beethoven, *Leonore* Overture No. 3

Brahms, Symphony no. 2

Wagner, *Die Walküre*, Fire Music

254

The future holds the possibility of many yet untried scales. Their vitality will be directly related to their anchorage in harmonic principles and morphological norms.

SENARIUS

Originating in antique metrics, the word *senarius* identifies the first six numbers taken as a unit. The senarius is a morphological force in all fields including music. The hexagonal system gives shape to the division of the circle (6 × 60) with all astronomic implications (minutes, hours, months, zodiac signs). It has determined the geometric orientation and hence the architecture of Babylonians, Egyptians, Greeks, and all premechanical Western societies. The senarius underlies the hexagonal shape of snowflakes and the orientation of crystals. In poetry, it produced the classic hexameter. In music, it generates pure major and minor triads (through division of the string by 1 to 6 and, reciprocally, by 1 to 1/6).

The prototypic quality of the senarius has provoked a variety of explanations. The identity of radius with the hexagon side inscribed in the circle is as undeniable as the purely practical reconciliation of even and odd, 2 and 3. We suggest that the senarius, apart from its number character, is a basic morphological value. Causal connections between the first six numbers and the triad explain little in either direction. More fruitful is the recognition of the senarius as one more archetypal example of the correspondence, stipulated throughout our investigation, of psychic forms and physical realizations.

Besides generating the major and minor triads and influencing our selection of 12 tones to the octave, the senarius is musically active in all questions of *rhythm and meter. It provides reconciliation between the two possible forms of tempus, perfect (3) and imperfect (2). On the largest musical time scale, the senarius permits the basic distinction between *binary and ternary forms. It is an elemental power which in all fields puts opposites in *harmony.

SEQUENCE

We deal here only with the current meaning of the term, which designates the immediate repetition of a musical unit at another pitch level, and not at all with the liturgical alleluia trope. A sequence is primarily a melodic event. Because change of pitch, by definition, is an inherent condition of sequence, purely rhythmic sequences do not exist; we can speak only of rhythmic repetition. Purely harmonic sequences, however, are conceivable. Theoretically a particular chord progression can be repeated on another pitch without regard to melodic projection. The possibility is approached in Wagner's *Siegfried* by Erda's first sentences above the sequentially repeated "Sleep" motive. Whatever the morphological implications, they are all contained in the concept of melodic sequence.

As a particular manifestation of the principle of repetition, sequence serves idiogenesis. It produces growth and continuation. Unlike other repetitive devices, however, it also possesses a built-in element of limitation, namely, the background design which determines the behavior of the repetition. The sequence material is actually the less significant though more noticeable foreground. What matters in the following measures from a Bach fugue (*Well-tempered Keyboard II*, 15) is not so much the four-times repeated sixteenth-note figure as the underlying progression of the scale from g¹ down to *b*:

While the melodic repetition pushes forward, it is this scale that sets the limitation. Sequence permits a morphological unfolding in time of an otherwise simple cell.

In the Bach example, the cell is the descending tonic scale. As a result, the sequence is not exact—the position of the semitone shifts—but rather tonal. In the case of a real repetition (the terms *tonal* and *real* here have the same meaning as in a fugal answer) the growing power of the sequence increases by virtue of the necessary modulation. The following real sequence from Hugo Wolf's *Italienisches Liederbuch* (no. 13) intensifies the expression by both the raised pitch (marked, moreover, by a slight rhythmic change) and the temporary modulation without obscuring the underlying simple progression from the tonic note to the one above it:

The sequence need not progress by scale at all. Romantic composers in particular favored sequences governed by a chordal background. The main condition for the existence of a sequence is an underlying regular pattern. Whereas the first layer of the chordal background may thus dictate the more obvious behavior, in the widest sense even apparently harmonic sequences obey the basic formative power of the scale.

Characteristic in this respect is the manner in which Anton Bruckner opens the development section of the first movement of his Third Symphony (mm. 266–96). We give the harmonic outline of the long passage which is built exclusively by an interplay of sequences:

The melodic motive above each bass tone consists of only root, fifth, and octave, thereby emphasizing the primary harmonic orientation. The entire passage is divided by a *Generalpause* in two halves, almost identical except for the shift of pitch. Within each half, there are two sets of sequences, distinguished by orchestration and mode, each moving up a perfect fourth. Taken together, they change pitch by descending thirds and thus jointly spell out a major seventh chord (F-D♭-B♭-G♭; and G-E♭-C-A♭). In each half, the last pitch reached is enharmonically changed into the leading tone of a dominant seventh chord, which resolves properly. Beyond the double sequence in, respectively, fourths and thirds, the two halves relate to each other as a large sequence proceeding first from F and then from G. The final resolution toward A discloses that the whole long passage has merely unfolded the incipient scale of F major, the key in which the development section has opened. Moreover, the arrival points of the sequence (E-A) hold out the promise that further pursuit in the direction of the harmonic push will eventually retrieve the tonic D, as it does with the recapitulation some forty measures later.

The morphological limitation behind every sequence can occasionally stifle the growing power, notwithstanding surface motion. A sequence moving across the tones of a diminished seventh chord ends up where it has begun. The gignetic foreground activity is absorbed by an ontic background situation. Literature of the late nineteenth century yields many such instances. Facile utilization of the growing power, on the other hand, may reduce sequence to the routine level of the rightly criticized *rosalia* or *Schusterfleck:*

The inherent double force of both growth and limitation accounts for the presence of sequence in all periods. Gregorian chant knew it as did the polyphonic composers of the *ars nova* and the Netherlands schools. Modern writers have tested the usefulness of sequence in atonal, serial, and other experimental pieces; for the strength of the basic idea transcends stylistic considerations.

SILENCE. See REST

SONATA

In its original, literal meaning as an independent instrumental, rather than a transcribed vocal, piece, sonata is so wide a concept that it lacks specific morphological significance. The tempting parallelism between instrumental and kinematic, on one hand, and vocal and pneumatic, on the other, is not quite correct and hence fruitless. A sonata, like a cantata, can be either kinematic or pneumatic and usually is both. We shall deal here with the term to the extent to which it covers certain instrumental multipartites developed ever since the eighteenth century, that is, sonatas for one or more instruments, trios, quartets, symphonies, concertos, and the like.

The history of sonata exemplifies the fertile relationship of unity and multiplicity. An example had been set by the baroque dance *suite which had strung together otherwise more or less independent separate movements. The path led from multiplicity to unity. The sonata arrived at a similar appearance from the opposite direction. The multiform ricercar fell apart and showed the possibility of developments from unity to multiplicity. The crossing of these two types, mostly in the eighteenth century, resulted in new formal experiments which extend into our own time. Common to both early suite and sonata is a slow-fast-slow-fast archetype. But whereas the movements of a suite were held together at best by a common key and occasional variation, those of a sonata, safeguarded by a unified origin, pushed toward extreme independence and interdependence under the influence of dramatism.

A thorough investigation of the contribution of opera to sonata has yet to be made.[1] Many symptoms, however, are obvious at sight. Dramatic contrast produces key variety—absent from the baroque suite—among the different movements as well as within each movement. Modulation, particularly in larger sonata forms, becomes the essential event and creates such dramatic situations as departure, adventurous development, and return. The pull between different keys is materially intensified by the concomitant contrast between two characteristic themes or subjects. The whole idea that the last movement of a sonata has to be a *finale derives from the operatic stage. This concept is still missing in early works by Haydn but no longer in Beethoven symphonies. The conversion of the original first slow movement into an introduction is probably also related to the practice of a preparatory overture. The slow middle movement of a sonata betrays often its indebtedness to a typical opera aria, of which it is an instrumental transcription. The overpowering popularity of the Neapolitan da capo aria doubtless shaped the idea of recapitulation wherever it occurs in sonata.

The symphony after Beethoven becomes the instrumental counterpart of opera. Titles, stories, and dramatic techniques characterize the musical behavior of the symphonic output by Mendelssohn, Berlioz, Liszt, and Richard Strauss. Less explicitly they also affect the symphonies of Tchaikovsky (*Pathétique*) and Gustav Mahler. Brahms and Bruckner are the notable nonoperatic exceptions.

Haydn's introduction of a contemporary dance, the minuet, into sonata has often been described as a modernism. Yet one may wonder whether sonata thereby did not pay an old debt to the suite which it superseded as the leading multipartite of the day.

The early history of sonata, as we have tried to show, leads from manifold to multipartite, from external unity to external multiplicity. One-movement sonatas, as initiated by Liszt (Piano Sonata in B minor) and pursued into the twentieth century (Fourth Symphony by Franz Schmidt) thus return on a higher level to the early sonata concept by synthesizing different levels of unity and multiplicity.

SONATA FORM

Sonata form is a paramount example of the tendency, observable in all

---

[1]As one of several isolated thrusts in this direction, see Cole, "Instrumental Rondo," which persuasively demonstrates that sonatas by Haydn, Mozart, and others particularly between the years 1773 and 1786 were directly invaded by the popular rondo found in contemporary Italian opera buffa.

centuries and styles, of *binary forms to become ternary. At its origin in the eighteenth century, sonata form is clearly binary. The double bar in the middle, as in the sonatas by Scarlatti, discloses the indebtedness to the binary organization of baroque *dance music. The primary accomplishment of sonata form is the widening of the scope and process within a single movement with the help of modulation.[1] The harmonic scheme is therefore always ternary: home key—foreign key—home key. This scheme is at first in crucial conflict with the binary metric plan. The whole history of sonata form can be fruitfully viewed as the gradual subjugation of the binary by the ternary principle. In this history, the themes function as carriers of the process. They signalize critical moments. They help the listener's memory, but they are morphologically of secondary importance.

The sonatas by Scarlatti alone supply a wealth of material and insight. The first half of a sonata establishes a tonic (seldom with the most attractive material of the piece) and then abandons it. The moment of arrival at the new key is so crucial a morphological event that it must be signally marked. There is no thought here of an independent "second theme" in the sense of later textbooks. Ralph Kirkpatrick, in his definitive study of these works, has rightly coined the name *crux* for this event to escape any preconceived notions.[2] The crux of the matter, that is, the establishment of a new key, can be marked by a repeat of the opening melody in the new key, or by a singularly memorable new melody, or by a change of texture or dynamics, or by any combination of these and other techniques. The first half is thus binary in itself. The second half has as its sole task the recovery of the tonic. It usually succeeds at the halfway point. The event is again marked by the crux and only seldom by the opening theme. The recapitulation is thus purely harmonic. It may be melodic besides if the opening theme happens to be used for the crux. The recapitulation is in any case only about half as long as the total exposition. The external morphology therefore remains tied to the binary power of meter:

Going away—Crux :||: Coming back—Crux.

The internal morphology, however, is steered by the ternary power of rhythm:

Tonic—Foreign key—Tonic.

The situation is basically not much different in many sonatas by Haydn and Mozart. The new key, particularly in Haydn's sonatas, is often not associated with a new theme. In some movements, as the finale of Beethoven's short Piano Sonata in F major, opus 54, there is not even a recognizable first theme. But all these sonata forms adhere to two characteristics: the double bar somewhere in the middle, and the ternary harmonic organization. The latter now expands the harmonic recapitulation to a full-length repetition of the exposition so that the section after the double bar, gaining considerably in weight and length, loses its metric symmetry with the exposition. Containing both the return modulation and the full-fledged recapitulation, it quickly

---

[1]Leonard Ratner has consistently emphasized the harmonic nature of sonata form. See his early article, "Harmonic Aspects of Classic Form."

[2]*Scarlatti.*

abandons its repeat sign at the end and thus restores an appropriate balance to the double exposition. The many sonata movements, particularly by Mozart, where the final repeat sign persists, seem to have retained it as a habit. It disappears definitely with the eighteenth century.

One is left with a sonata form which, always suffering the attraction of the underlying ternary norm, has reached the compromise of recapitulation *barform. The exposition and its obligatory repetition function, respectively, as strophe and antistrophe. They are matched in length by the development and recapitulation which together comprise the epode. Notwithstanding the strength of the recapitulation—now fully armed with a characteristically attractive first theme on top of the satisfactory harmonic return—the morphological orientation remains binary. This overall shape becomes particularly clear in any first movement of a classical concerto where the exposition by the orchestra is answered by that of the soloist without any option of tampering with the repeat sign.

The final step is taken by composers of the nineteenth century. They at last reconcile the original binary dance form with the ternary harmonic norm by omitting the first repeat, that is, the antistrophe, altogether. The ternary power of rhythm takes final possession of the binary power of meter. Brahms shows how conscious he was of this accomplishment. The development section of a sonata form had necessarily always begun in the foreign key. Such is still the case in the first three symphonies by Brahms, where the exposition is traditionally repeated. In the first movement of his last symphony, however, (and equally so of his Violin Sonata in G major) he finally omits the double bar and promptly continues the development section with the first theme in the tonic, as if at least to give the initial illusion of a repeated exposition. He leads the listener gently into the newly conquered territory where all binary sonata-form elements have at last fulfilled their morphological tendency to become ternary.

SPACE AND TIME. See **TIME AND SPACE**

STATIC-DYNAMIC. See **ONTIC-GIGNETIC**

STROPHE

A strophe is a unit of a certain magnitude that invites repetition. Hence the term pertains to two different though related concepts—the basic unit, or strophe, and the ultimate result emerging from the totality of repetitions, the strophic structure.

The strophe proper adheres to no particular form. Anything can theoretically lend itself to countless repetitions. We have stipulated a certain magnitude to insure the primacy of a musical gestalt over mere technique of repetition, but actually a strophe (as is the case with many children's songs and folksongs) can be very short. In practice, strophes are generally *open rather than closed, barforms rather than bowforms. The open end facilitates repetition, or at least continuation, which inheres in the nature of strophe. A closed end, on the other hand, not only counteracts this tendency but moreover might blur the overall strophic structure when the end of one strophe, being a recapitulation of the beginning, is heard immediately preceding the identical beginning of the next strophe (aba‿aba‿aba etc.). The little Swiss Song on which the twenty-year-old Beethoven wrote Six Easy Variations for pianoforte (Sechs leichte Variationen über ein Schweizer Lied) demonstrates this periodic bump. Because a musical strophe generally serves the repetition of differently worded stanzas, it is also bound to a certain simplicity which precludes unwanted and distracting complications.

Strophic structure (a a a a . . .) is the purest example of growth by idiogenesis. One can hardly speak of form, for no principle of limitation interferes. This somewhat primitive feature has made strophic form an obvious harbor for such pieces as children's songs, folk ballads, church hymns, anthems, and the like. Countless strophes can be strung together without any concern for the eventual end. Yet even in this simplest appearance, strophic form contains an element of variation, if only because the repetition, by *topology alone, is conditioned and thus changed by its relation to the earlier statement. The new words for each musical repetition add another element of variation.

The extreme case is reached by strophic variations (a a' a" a"' . . .). They differ from pure strophic repetitions only in degree, not in kind. They serve growth only. One strophe or variation leads to the next without regard for the ultimate outcome and without necessary memory of the preceding events. The absence of any morphological obligation was clearly recognized by Frescobaldi who, in a preface "Al Lettore," advises the users of his *Fiori musicali* (1635) to conclude earlier by a cadence any canzonas and ricercars that appear too long.

This kind of loose strophic structure can assume any kind of formal complexity depending, apart from the specific variation technique, on the principle of limitation applied. The simplest device is the termination of the otherwise shapeless chain by a signal finale that breaks the continuity. Barform accomplishes this end after two strophes by the dialectic device of an epode. Frequently the entire barform is then reinterpreted and used as a fresh strophe for further repetitions. This procedure is typical of most Lutheran hymns. Variation sets by Haydn and Mozart (for example, the latter's "Ah, vous dirai-je, Maman") create finale character by expansion of the given metrical pattern and indulgence in brilliant virtuoso passages that invite final flurry and applause. A similar function is served by the special fabric of the fugue that terminates Brahms's Variations on a Theme by Handel. Actually variation sets by master composers gain morphological significance by subtler and more complex principles of limitation. The strophic form comes to life under the influence of proportion, symmetry, number, or any such other force applied from the outside. The otherwise apparently countless variations in Bach's Chaconne, for example, group themselves, even at first hearing, according to the three stark appearances of the theme in the beginning, the middle, and the end. The same composer's Goldberg Variations are organized into ten-times-three strophes; the parallelism of the ten groups is made obvious by the arrangement of the fabric; and the quodlibet finale, moreover, breaks the chain decisively. Detailed analysis of relationships among the strophes of masterful variation sets will always yield individual morphological results. For some examples, see Appendix A, Variation, pp. 322 ff.

Strophic songs illuminate in a particular way the relationship of *word and tone. Poetic texts change from strophe to strophe, whereas the music remains the same. Often even entirely different poems utilize the identical music, as was the case when the melody of "God save the King," already doing double duty for the American "My country, 'tis of thee," served at the same time the German and Swiss national anthems. The reason lies in the greater generality of music when compared to poetry. The same music can accommodate undefined official solemnity against which specific nationalistic peculiarities become irrelevant. It naturally accommodates parallel patterns of rhythm, meter, rhyme, and assonance—all musical and nonlinguistic qualities of poetry—provided the literary concepts changing from strophe to strophe do not impose themselves too strongly. Refrain-like recurrences reinforce the musical superiority, as, for instance, the phrase "Dein ist mein Herz" throughout the four stanzas of Schubert's "Ungeduld." The musicality of strophic songs decreases as conceptual abstraction increases. (Although highly intellectual poetry can be set to music, the value of the music can reach a point harmful to the poem. Schubert's settings of most Goethe poems—not the simple Goethe songs—whatever their musical attraction, do not help the poetry.) Over-reflective poetry is in fact music-repellent. Hence strophic songs at their best preclude complication by employing rather short stanzas of unified mood. The first stanza, more often than not, inspires the total musical behavior. In Schubert's "Des Baches Wiegenlied," the direct address "Wandrer, du müder" (m. 9) determines the omission of the anacrusis; and the following four stanzas have to adjust in one way or another. On the other hand, Bach's interpretation of a chorale in his organ preludes often derives from a later stanza, which usually can be identified. Strong fluctuations of one or the other stanza can be handled by strophic variants affecting small melodic and rhythmic phrases, dynamics, tempo, mode, or any comparable qualities. The temporary turn from minor to major in the fourth stanza of Schubert's "Gute Nacht" parallels that from reality to phantasy. Further structural modifications necessitated by the text lead song away from strophic form.

In the widest sense, a succession of units may be called strophic even if the connection is not based on obvious variation. In such terms, Bruckner's large structures are best understood. In his sonata forms, the classical disposition is still present but has become morphologically irrelevant. What we hear are diverse sections frequently ending with a full stop and separated from each other by a *Generalpause*. Almost every first movement of his symphonies consists of a succession of such sections. In contrast to Beethoven's technique, the mere manner in which they follow each other now produces an impression of "development." The underlying principle of building is strophic rather than dialectic. The effect is comparable to that of a series of terraces or an arrangement of blocks. Bruckner's sonata forms must not be measured against those of Beethoven. The earlier model is dramatic. Bruckner's inspiration is essentially lyrical, like the strophic form he creates. Neither type excludes the effects of the other, but emphasis and means differ. Bruckner's ancestry is not Beethoven but Schubert. Both Schubert's song cycles and Bruckner's sonata forms achieve a "symphonic whole" through the terracing of separate entities. Both procedures are essentially lyrical and strophic, for the inherent dramatism depends not so much on conflict as on a traversal of states of being.

STYLE

Against the recognition that the essence of *phenomenalization is perennial and permanent, style may be defined as the sum of the temporal characteristics of a work. This definition applies to any kind of manifestation—fashions and motor cars, social forms and paintings, modes of behavior and musical compositions. The word harks back to *stilus*, the pointed instrument with which the Romans wrote on their wax tablets. Today we would say "pen" to denote a personal way of writing. In an enlarged sense, the word came to mean a particular and characteristic way of doing and appearing.

Style is distinguished from fashion (French *la mode*) by having deeper roots and hence being less transitory and fleeting. A time span characterized by a given style may include several fashion episodes. When style is weak or absent, fashion alone can rule. Fashion may thus be the nuance of a style as well as the quest for a new style. Rococo was a fashion of baroque. The present fashions in clothing, frantically changing in rapid succession, are symptoms of a lack of style.

Three roots of style may be distinguished: (1) material, (2) historic-geographic, and (3) individual. They all pertain to a particular mode of limitation.

(1) The most universal influence on style derives from the material out of which a work is fashioned. Wood cannot be treated in the same way as marble, aquarelles demand a different technique from oil colors. In music, material style is determined by the contribution of such factors as *scales, *rhythm and meter, instrumentation. texture, *fabric, etc.

(2) Less universal but still supra-individual is the moment in time and the place in space at which a work is created. Historic-geographic style is the sum of qualities by which we know to what civilization a work belongs. Against the unchanging contents of the *ordinarium missae*, settings by Machaut and Palestrina differ, not by virtue of material style, but in regard to historic style. Similarly, here lies the difference between a fugue by Bach and one by Beethoven. The recent Westernization of the East has imposed one geographic style on another. When Debussy was affected by the exotic music he heard at the Paris World's Fair in 1889, the new style elements he adopted were both historic and geographic; for in relation to Debussy's society, they were older as well as foreign.

(3) Lastly it is individual style that characterizes, and distinguishes between, compositions employing the same materials (for instance, string orchestra, major mode, etc.) and belonging to the same period (for instance, Bach and Handel).

Like all classifying concepts, the one just applied to the main roots of style is by itself also a stylization, a petrification of things that are alive and in constant flux. Material style is affected by changing techniques: the polyphony of Perotinus is not that of Josquin, the pigments of the Italian Renaissance are not those of modern chemistry. A historic style does not suddenly spring into being or end abruptly: the apparently revolutionary musical behavior around 1600 can easily be traced backward through at least two generations. Individual style evolves in the course of the composer's life, and can moreover be affected by changes in historic-geographic style occurring at the same time: an example near us is the case of Stravinsky.

Style, we have suggested, concerns the manner of a work, not the essence. If two persons in identical relation to an event such as the birth of a child each write a congratulation, their letters will be of divergent styles. Funeral marches by various composers differ although responding to the same occasion. Against the variability of styles we may postulate a certain permanence of the musical contents, simply because man has remained essentially the same. The modes of expression obviously have an effect on contents, but they do not influence the core. They illuminate the given essence from a certain direction and put it in a certain light. Style brings out varied facets of our being. The universality of an artist can be appraised by the multitude of facets he brings to light.

Without the ordinary, nothing extraordinary can exist. The condition of the artist's freedom lies in a strong style, that is, in strong, well defined limitations and in a strong, recognized grammar. Rightly the historically great periods of art are those exhibiting a firmly established, strong historical style. Such is the case of classical Greek architecture, Renaissance painting, or harmonically functional music. The contemporary scene lacks historical style altogether. There are many groups, schools, and individuals, but there is no common style. Typically Schönberg himself did not teach his own style but rather conventional harmony of another historical style.

SUBDOMINANT. See DOMINANTS

SUITE

The history of the suite demonstrates the irresistible trend of isolated elements toward subordination under an overall shape. This trend from *open to closed is characteristic of all musical forms and manifests itself on every level of magnitude. The evolution of the suite from a mere array of pieces toward unification in a true *multipartite differs from that of the sonata. The early thorough-bass sonata evolved, not from the grouping of independent small units into a whole, but rather from the breaking apart of a rich *manifold into separately developing movements. Both cases together, however, illustrate the principle of mutual morphological influence of manifolds and multipartites.

We shall reserve the term *suite* for those arrays of movements that have become, or at least exhibit a tendency toward, multipartite structure. For all other arrays of pieces, the French term *ordre* is adequate. It correctly designates most such works by Chambonnières and Couperin, which are to be understood as mere reservoirs of pieces and not as wholes. Whether a unifying key alone suffices to warrant the designation *suite* is a moot question symptomatic of the borderline character of such cases.

Numbers taken from incidental music to plays and then grouped together for concert performance are basically *ordres*. Grieg's music to *Peer Gynt* or Bizet's music to *L'Arlésienne* was not composed to form a unified whole. Such groupings, however, may reveal morphological tendencies, particularly when the composer himself concerns himself with the selection and arrangement. Stravinsky's *Petroushka* Suite, drawn from his ballet music, is a true multipartite. The concept of suite is applicable to such works as the two Serenades by Brahms which gather both symphonic and dance movements into a whole. A similar attitude is displayed by many twentieth-century multipartites entitled *Suite* which, while abandoning the concept of a loose array, yet remain less tightly structured than a symphony.

The earliest formative force uniting separate dances is *variation. The arrangement of a slow dance in duple meter followed by a variation of the same dance in faster triple meter has been recognized as fundamental to the *dance music of most civilizations. It is well documented in the history of medieval Europe, as by *branle simple* and *branle double* in France, *dantz* and *hupfauf* in Germany, *pavana* and *gagliarda* in Italy, and others. English composers in particular used the variation principle in order to expand the original two dances so that entire variation sets came into being. Such multipartites are real suites though initially they often lack a formative principle of limitation and thus of intrinsic organization. Growing power increased the number of pieces from the original two to six and more before contraction to four movements established something like an "ordinary" of the suite. It consists of allemande, courante, sarabande, and gigue. Tempo alternation slow-fast-slow-fast prevails. The opening duple meter of the allemande is released by first a fast, and then a slow, triple meter before the closing gigue combines both metric orientations in a characteristic 6/8 or 12/8 movement. The new cohesion is so strong that the organizing principles together with a unifying key remain valid long after the primary variation idea has disappeared. Nor is it disturbed by the eventual inclusion of extra movements which supply the suite with a kind of "proper."

Bach's suites complete and summarize the development. The three Partitas for Unaccompanied Violin illustrate the potential of this type of multipartite. The first, in B minor, doubles each of the four movements by a variation, thus acknowledging English origin. The second, in D minor, consists of the four "ordinary" dances, the closing chaconne confirming the French orientation by a display of contrapuntal mastery. The third, in E major, is indebted to the concertizing style of the Italians. In his keyboard suites, Bach openly discloses the national variants by the respective titles. The underlying principle in all, however, is multipartite formation.

SYMBOL

The musician is concerned with three kinds of symbols: (1) artificial symbols, such as the notation of music; (2) natural symbols, such as the relationship of number and tone; and (3) psychogenous symbols, such as the meaning of music. Of these three kinds, artificial symbols are conventions. Both natural and psychogenous symbols are more deeply rooted. Number and tone, like meaning and music, do not act one on the other as cause and effect, nor are they a poetic representation of one by the other: they literally and precisely coincide. The suggested distinctions among three kinds of symbols are convenient and possess significance in spite of their being a stylization of given situations. Finally, all symbols are produced by our mind.

(1) Notational signs are wholly arbitrary and thus devoid of any deeper significance. Lute tablatures, for example, use letters and numbers practically at the discretion of a particular tuning in a particular country. Yet the power of symbolization asserts itself in the mutual influence of notation and style. The latter must reach a high degree of stability before admitting the need and possibility of notation. A more or less long development of the kind of music to be fixed by written signs always precedes the invention of a notation. The nature of a notation will express as closely as possible the peculiarities of the music, that is, its style; but no notation is ever complete. Ours, for instance, has no independent and unambiguous symbols for triple meter. Fixing one particularity means neglecting another so that there always remains what could be called a "notational deficit." The mere practical necessity of keeping notation down to what are considered essentials carries with it a fatality, for the very judgment concerning essentials implies a decision that determines the further evolution of style.

To give an example, the transition from neumes to square notes on a staff stressed definiteness of pitch to the detriment of the delicate melodic shadings characteristic of earlier music. The microtonic liquescences gradually lost their power as active ingredients of a style, and the positive forces inherent in the fixed elements began to blossom forth. Without the invention of the particular notation initiated in the ninth century, often since modified but never essentially changed, the later harmonic and polyphonic developments are hard to imagine.

The specific case of Franconian notation provides another example. When the *Ars cantus mensurabilis* was written in the second half of the thirteenth century, rhythmic differentiations in polyphony had been practiced for several generations. On the other hand, the principles evolved by Franco's system, particularly as refined by Petrus de Cruce around 1280, first invited the somewhat wild rhythmic experimentation of the French *ars nova* one century later—which sounds as if the composers were testing the new rhythmic notation to its limits—and eventually helped in some respects determine the style of all Renaissance music. The written sign possesses a power of suggestion and inertia that may transform the tool, as which it had been created, into a master. Thus even a conventional symbol partakes of the life of an objectivated psychic reality.

(2) The number-tone relationship is symbolic in the original meaning of

the term. Both factors are literally "thrown together." They have to be considered with equal seriousness. Division of a string by 2 yields the octave; by 3, the fifth; by 4, the double octave; by 5, the major third; and so forth. This correspondence means that merely by ear one can exactly divide a string by 2, 3, 4, 5, and so forth. Every violin player does so correctly and musically without conscious mathematical division. Number and pitch coincide. String length is directly related to wave length, so that the numbers point to both musical tone and mathematical frequency, depending on the interpretation one chooses. Number allows an exact intellectual, scientific operation. Tone carries a meaning. The quantity of the former and the quality of the latter can be symbolically transformed one into the other. No other sense but the ear possesses this faculty of perceiving proportion in a spontaneous and precise manner. The rainbow colors are also scientific facts and aesthetic experiences, but nobody is visually able to define the exact interval formed by any two shades.

The symbolic relationship of number and tone obviously permits not only a mathematization of music but equally so a musicalization of mathematics. It has often been pointed out that the triad is a special phenomenon because it is the issue of the first six numbers. Consonance theories have been developed based on the nature of the senarius. The musician trusting his ear can proceed with equal right from the quality of the triad. The triad is an eminent musical entity. Therefore the six first numbers possess a particular dignity and must have a particular importance in nature. Such reasoning gave birth to Greek temples and led Kepler to the discovery of his laws on the movement of the planets. The arrangement of proportions in the age-old and yet inexhaustible *Pythagorean Table supplies a basis for all music theory.[1]

(3) We call the relationship of music to meaning *psychogenous* because the processes are wholly enclosed by the mind. Psychic activity produces meaning whether tone is assumed to be the source of meaning or the carrier of induced currents.

When tone is the source of meaning, we deal with relations suggested or imposed by nature. Relevant instances are interval characters, universally acknowledged, such as "octaveness" or "thirdness." Here also belong such more general impressions as high and low, loud and soft, up and down, step and skip, strings and winds. In all these cases, the meaning can be read directly from the score. The notation is expressive—up to a point—of the implied symbolism, for the symbol is produced in the direction that leads from tone to meaning. Thanks to the essential fixation of the relationship, tone and meaning are mutually symbolic.

The established relationship can become disturbed by influences induced to flow in the opposite direction, from psyche to tone. These currents are artificial when understood against the original natural direction. They turn the tone into a symbol of the intended meaning, which can no longer be read from, but rather needs to be "put into," the notation. Music history is full of such secondary symbolism which depends for a meaningful understanding on induced associations. Wagner's leitmotiv technique builds on this kind of connection. If it is successful, the fixed relationship of tone-to-meaning-to-

---

[1]For detailed investigations of tone numbers, see Kayser, *Lehrbuch*, and the authors' *Tone*.

tone supplies the basis. A naturally dissonant tritone might well be associated with the dragon Fafner, and an ascending major triad, played moreover by a trumpet, can easily become identified with a heroic sword. The symbolism in Bach's music actually operates on the same level (nota bene: only the symbolism, not the rest of the music), except that some associations, such as that of a descending second with a sigh, were traditionally known to a German congregation from opera and church, whereas Wagner had to invent his own meanings. The whole doctrine of affections of the eighteenth century uses music to induce currents. To C. P. E. Bach, embellishments were not mere technical devices. "They lend a fitting assistance to make a piece sad, joyful, or otherwise." The meaning is prescribed in such affirmations as that "the portrayal of simplicity or sadness suffers fewer ornaments than other emotions."[1]

The flow in the direction from psyche to tone may so disturb the naturally fixed relationship as to reverse the original meaning. A triad, under special circumstances, may become gignetically understood as a dissonance (see *Ontic-Gignetic).

Our initial clarification of the various symbolic modes helps us gain an insight into their potentialities and limitations—an insight of which the practical importance can hardly be overrated. The musicality of a person may be defined by his instinctive power of grasping musical symbolism. Musical education rests on the possibility of developing this power.

SYMMETRY. See PROPORTION

SYMPHONIC POEM. See PROGRAM MUSIC

SYMPHONY. See SONATA

SYNCOPATION

Syncopation occurs when the actual *rhythm runs counter to the sensible course of rhythmicized meter. This definition presupposes a prior rhythmic organization of meter according to fixed, "natural" laws. We distinguish metric and rhythmic layers. Syncopation is the detachment and subsequent displacement of the rhythmic layer from the metric layer. Our rhythmic sensation splits—an experience appropriately described by the word *syncopation* ("tearing, cutting, into pieces"). Every shift of the accented beat forward or backward effects syncopation.

The earliest definitions of the term, by Philippe de Vitry and Johannes de Muris in the fourteenth century, stress the splitting of a given group of notes by the insertion of larger values and the necessity of completing the original group after the interruption. The normal pattern | ♩ ♩ ♩ ♩. | , for ex-

[1]*Versuch*, Das zweyte Hauptstück, Erste Abtheilung, pars. 1 and 8.

268

ample, may become syncopated by an intruding ♩. after the first or second ♪ ; but in either case, the reestablishment of the full group after the intrusion is necessary:

The situation in crustic rhythm is illuminating. Theoretically in crustic rhythm the form | ♩ ♩ | is normal and the form | ♩ ♩ | , strictly speaking, a syncopation. Practically, however, we do not hear it in this manner but rather accept the form | ♩ ♩ | as normal and the form | ♩ ♩ | as syncopation. Apparently the preponderance of anacrustic rhythm prevails as norm in the rhythmic organization of measures. One can take the anacrustic rhythm as standard while bearing in mind that the crustic rhythm observes the same proportions with reversed breathing phases (exhalation instead of inhalation, and vice versa). The situation presents an analogy to that in *polarity, where in the case of the major and minor modes, for instance, the legitimate, strictly polar interpretation sooner or later bends in favor of major. Although the rhythmic antithesis seems similarly affected by tellurian conditions, the equivalence of both forms is heard through the inevitably imperfect embodiment.

To be properly heard and understood, a syncopation must not totally obliterate the meter from which it is torn; otherwise the syncopated rhythm imposes itself as the new norm and ceases to be heard as syncopation. This error, explicitly avoided by the early medieval explanation, is found all too often in works by Robert Schumann.

Syncopation is a main characteristic of jazz. Herein lies one more proof of the metric rather than rhythmic nature of jazz. The precondition for syncopation is the presence, not of free-flowing complexities, but of regular beats.

TEMPERAMENT

The principle and necessity of temperament, properly understood, present a basic morphological issue; for the forces involved are growth and limitation. The place of the morphological interaction lies before one reaches, so to speak, the musical composition itself.

Two facts are naturally given: the identity of the octave and the otherness of all other intervals. They are irreconcilable except through the compromise of temperament, which permits the formation of closed systems. Octave repetitions set a clear framework but produce no new tones. Projections upward and downward create "cycles of barrenness."[1] Repetitions of any other inter-

---

[1] Plato's phrase, *Republic* viii. 546. Ernest McClain in *The Pythagorean Plato* convincingly demonstrates that the *Republic* throughout employs metaphors related to temperament, for the organization of a state as well as of a tone system demands reconciliation of growth and limitation. Further quotations in this entry all derive from the same source.

val, however, in either direction continue to create new tones. These are "cycles of bearing." For the creation of a tone system, barrenness is as useless as the other extreme of infinite generation. Temperament reconciles the two by adjusting whatever characteristic interval to the octave. The unmanageable cycle of growth by the power of any interval becomes artificially but necessarily limited by the power of the octave.[1]

The inevitable result is a compromise. The particulars of the sacrifice define the kind of temperament used. All tone systems tend toward this initial compromise, although the conscious level of manipulation varies greatly. "The intermixture will engender unlikeness and an unharmonious unevenness, things that always beget war." To Plato, temperament is as original as sin.

The Greek system was built on the integrity of the fifth:

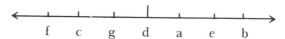

f   c   g   d   a   e   b

Three more "offsprings" in either direction, by "waxing and waning," lead to "enmity and dissension" between G-sharp and A-flat. The temperament of this system sacrificed the natural third to the pure fifth. The acceptance by medieval theorists of the Pythagorean third (larger than the natural by the syntonic comma 80/81) led to the misunderstanding that the third was meant to be a dissonance.

Emergence of the triad as primary unit in the harmonic language of the sixteenth and seventeenth centuries led to "just intonation." Here the victim is the equality of several intervals. The fifth and minor third on the second scale degree are smaller than the norm, and the wholetones are uneven. Meantone temperament, favored at the same time particularly by organists, preserves the major third at the expense of the perfect fifth. Equal temperament, finally, sacrifices all intervals to the octave but thereby also minimizes the "sin" by dividing it equally into twelve parts.

All these and any other possible temperaments are principles of limitation. The "barrenness" of octave identities as well as the endless "bearing" cycles of all other intervals lie in the nature of things. The inner contradiction between the two necessitates a compromise which is a man-made artistic accomplishment. Temperament should be seen in this positive light.

TEMPO

The seemingly straightforward notion of tempo as the pace of music needs to be qualified, for the significance of tempo is variable. Inasmuch as the world of music is a human creation, it reflects the structure of our being. Accordingly music is not all of a single essence but moves in different spheres that appeal to the corresponding spheres of our physical and spiritual consti-

---

[1]For more technical details and mathematical demonstration, cf. the authors' *Tone*, pp. 212–31.

tution. The bearing of these spheres on tempo is considerable. Meaning and significance of tempo in a plainsong melody and in a military march are as different as the concepts of soul and body. The attempt to distinguish and characterize musical spheres of existence stands in danger of being misunderstood. We may distinguish between soul and body: still we are One. Similarly, all music is One. A particular sphere may be at times emphasized. It may come to the fore, even to the near-exclusion of other spheres. Yet they all always coexist. We can never, during our lifetime, be all body or all soul. The distinctions between the spheres are not clear-cut, and the very number of spheres is debatable. For the sake of giving order to the musical phenomenon of tempo, however, we suggest three spheres of experience:

(1) Muscular, which expresses our instinctive life;

(2) Emotive, of which our rational side is the philosophic counterpart; and

(3) Spiritual, which corresponds to our contemplative intellect.

In relation to each other, these three spheres are here presented in the order of an ascending hierarchy.

(1) A typical representative of the muscular sphere is the march. The usual definition of tempo as the pulse or pace of music here assumes its full physical meaning, and the concomitant rules are valid without restriction. The heart is a built-in metronome providing us with a human measure of speed. It beats normally about 60 to 80 times per minute. Tempi at either side of this norm strike us as, respectively, slow or fast.

The speed of walking is connected with that of the heartbeat but, like all peripheral motions, can be varied within wide limits. The normalcy of pace depends, of course, on the physical build of a person; yet average values are discernible. At a step width of 2 feet and a walking speed of 2 miles per hour, the step frequency is 88 per minute (5280×2 divided by 60×2). This is leisurely walking. Even 100 steps per minute (2 1/4 miles per hour) lie within a pace range that may be called normal. The Triumphal March in *Aida* is marked at this speed. The American army prescribes 120 steps as the norm. By comparison, a very quick march (which reportedly is practiced in the French army) is commonly assumed to reach 180 steps per minute.

While both our heartbeat and walking speed are muscular and instinctive, we notice a slight difference in their musical implications. A pulse rate of 100 is decidedly fast, whereas a pace of the same rate is not. On the other side of the norm, however, 50 beats per minute designate a slow heart and also the tempo of a funeral march. We must therefore conclude that whereas the lower limits of heartbeat and walking lie close together, the upper limits do not. The metronome range from 40 to over 200 is thus to be interpreted as referring to the rate of walking rather than to that of the heartbeat (although in the slow region they approximately coincide). Characteristically, the only physiological term among the standard tempo indications is the neutral *andante*, walking.

The *integer valor* of mensural music derives from the muscular-instinctive norm. The idea of a fixed time unit, the tactus, pervades the music of the late Renaissance, whatever the different definitions among theorists and the subsequent modifications by proportion. Franchino Gafori, Leonardo da Vinci's friend in Milan, equates the tactus to the "pulse beat of a quietly

271

breathing man," and other theorists use comparable physiological measuring devices.[1] The literal meaning of tactus, 'touch', connects it with the muscular sphere. We are on safe ground in performing the sixteenth-century semibrevis, the normal form of the tactus, at about 60 to 80 beats per minute (a faster and musically more plausible rate than Willi Apel's somewhat arbitrary suggestion of 48).[2]

In this sphere of muscular tempo experience, meter predominates. Melody and harmony are subordinate to it. The time production is generally binary because related to systole and diastole of the heart and to left and right of walking. March being the archetype of all music that is metric and binary, blurring of the march character becomes desirable in all pieces in duple time which belong to other spheres. This blurring is best achieved, in slow as well as fast pieces, by keeping ambiguous the actual time value to which the tempo refers. In the first movement of Beethoven's Piano Sonata op. 10 no. 3, for example, the rate of the halfnote lies in the neighborhood of 144. Obviously the "real" pace is set by the whole note at 72. Nevertheless, the pulse of the halfnote is ever present and actually operative in a number of places (cf. the themes at mm. 23 ff., 53 ff.). This ambiguity prevents the march sphere from becoming prevalent. The adjustment of the tempo to the ambiguity is even a criterion for the "right" tempo. The situation has been jokingly described in the form of a rule: "The right tempo is the one where you feel like going just a little faster or a little slower in order to be comfortable." What is meant is that the applicability of more than one pulse, that is, the ambiguity itself, marks in certain compositions the point of the right tempo.

(2) In the emotive-rational sphere, the feeling for pace is dimmed or even suppressed in favor of that for breath. Breathing is here the factor destined to produce tempo, and rhythm and harmony are the predominant elements. Breathing is slower than either pulse or step. Although we may consciously influence our breathing to vary within very wide limits, the normal rate of breathing lies between 14 and 18 times per minute. Assuming an average value of 72 for the heartbeat, we note that breathing is about four to five times slower.

The extreme case of the *Tristan* Prelude provides an instructive example. The time signature is 6/8; the tempo indication, "Langsam und schmachtend" ("Slow and languishing"). The conductor beats eighth notes, but this fact is irrelevant to our investigation of tempo because the choice of a conductor's beat is dictated not only by musical considerations but also to a great extent by technical demands. The rate of the eighth notes lies in the 70s—not a slow tempo for either the heart or walking. If we try to tie the tempo indication to some other note value, we also fail; for the opening phrase contains no feeling of pace at all and leads us to suspect that the pace standard is here not valid. The dotted quarter notes, for instance, which supply the inaudible background in each measure, follow each other at a rate lying in the 20s—far below the physiological limits of the heart as well as of pace. Below these

[1] *Practica musicae* (1496), 3:4.

[2] *Notation*, p. 191. In support of our reasoning, see also Sachs, "Some Remarks about Old Notation."

limits, beats can no longer be directly related to each other without suffering subdivision. The tempo indication of the *Tristan* Prelude, in short, can refer to neither value. It must be related to another standard, which in this sphere is breath. The opening phrase spans four measures which, at a rate of about 72 per eighth note, have a duration of about 20 seconds. This breathing tempo (corresponding to only three complete cycles per minute) approaches the lowest threshold of the physically possible but is no doubt the intended one. A good conductor cannot afford to drop below it or the phrase will fall apart by subdivision. Subdivision means a shorter breath; hence a chronologically slower tempo can under these circumstances give the impression of being faster. In the course of the Prelude, the tempo fluctuates. The acceleration toward the climax is accompanied by changes in the rate of breathing. The initial span of four measures is eventually shortened to two measures (46 ff.) and later to one (52 ff.). Both actually and aesthetically, these changes of breath are more important than those of the pulse tempo.

Unfortunately, breathing is not practically usable as a standard of speed because, unlike the heartbeat or step, it cannot be expressed by a formula. It reminds us, however, that metronome marks are a simple convenience of indetermined musical significance because the relation of heart to breath is variable.

(3) The spiritual-contemplative sphere belongs to pure melody (the first sphere was characterized by a preference for meter; the second, for rhythm and harmony). Pure melody is determined as little as is humanly possible by the power of the other elements. In metrical music of this sphere, pace is kept subliminal through its very normalcy, just as the heartbeat remains unnoticed as long as it is normal. Harmony, if present, is made as unobtrusive as possible, and harmonic motion is slow to avoid startling changes. Rhythmic impulses are minimized. The dynamic level remains constant over long stretches, and dynamic variations are inconspicuous.

The enumeration of these postulates show that the spheres, through their correspondences with musical elements, are to a high degree determinants of style. In this spiritual-contemplative sphere, monophonic plainchant comes closest to the intended ideal. Among nonmonophonic compositions, the purest examples of absolute polyphony are most favorable to the style. In a Renaissance motet, for example, the rhythmic impulses cancel each other; and the participation of loudness matters here as little as, to give a later example, in the opening movement of Bach's *St. Matthew Passion*. In both monodic and polyphonic pieces belonging to this sphere, breathing is the tempo standard. Yet in favor of melody, it is kept as unobtrusive as is pace. The Renaissance term *tactus* for pace is inseparable from the notion of normalcy, which indicates an aesthetically inoperative factor. The overall result is spiritualization of melody. Here also lies the explanation for the somewhat puzzling use of a secular cantus firmus in a Mass: a popular, sometimes vulgar, melody is transformed and elevated from its own sphere to this highest one.

The Gloria from the Third Gregorian Mass may serve to give substance to our thoughts.[1] Although the music is in principle nonmetrical, some basic

---

[1]*Liber usualis*, pp. 23 f.

unit has to give a choral performance a certain uniformity of flow from which irrational deviations may then occur. Obviously the notes of the melody are not bearers of a pulse and hence cannot be utilized as representing tempo. The pulse or pace must be sought in groups of notes. The metric principle is here not division or multiplication but rather addition; the basic groups are binary and ternary. The "beats" are therefore irregular, even if one should stipulate a particular length for each note in the melody, and they grow even more irregular through the irrational differences in the duration of each note. In order to escape any muscular impulse, the "beats" lie well below normal walking tempo. In an authoritative performance, the notes follow each other at about 120—the equivalent of 60 for binary groups and of 40 for ternary groups. In this persuasive tempo, the notes flow yet the beats are slow. (The beats, of course, are not at all felt as such: they disappear behind the melodic flow.)

If we measure the tempo of the Gloria by breathing, we first notice that among eighteen phrases sung on one breath (*cantilena*, from double bar to double bar), eleven are relatively long (15 to 28 notes) and seven are relatively short (6 to 10 notes). At the rate of 120 notes per minute, the extremes correspond to, respectively, slightly over four full breaths per minute and twenty breaths per minute; the approximate averages, to, respectively, five and thirteen. The fast breathing in the short phrases (thirteen to twenty times per minute) stays close to normal bounds whereas the slow breathing in the preponderant long phrases (four to five times per minute) approaches a rate that is "superhuman" and can be best felt through "spiritual contemplation." This is eminently *pneumatic music perceived by the listener kinematically. The apparent contradiction is a by-product of the subordination of all elements to pure melody.

In this third sphere, the consciousness of tempo is held to a minimum by two factors: the constant normalcy of the pace, and a breathing rate reaching from normalcy to spans transcending individual physical possibilities.

Our suggested distinction among three spheres makes more readily understandable that the importance of tempo is variable. Tempo is not necessarily identical with pace, although in our motored era one observes a general tendency to determine tempo by pace even when inappropriate. Unless a composition clearly belongs to the first sphere, tempo will be misinterpreted if equated with pace in a crudely physical sense. If in the opening movement of Bach's *St. Matthew Passion* the dotted quarter of the "spiritualized Siciliano" is adjusted to a walking step, the music is dragged down to the muscular sphere. Instead of evolving "contemplatively," the melody becomes a mere filler for a march rhythm. Inversely, an interpretation of Wagner's *Meistersinger* Prelude in two felt beats per measure—regardless of the chronological tempo—moves the piece from a march, which it really is, to a spiritualized sphere, where it does not belong. Understanding of the three spheres should help performers choose the right tempo.

TEXTURE. See **FABRIC**

THEME

Taken literally, *theme* means "proposition," the topic of discourse set before us. In this widest sense, theme need not at all be identical with a melody or musical motive, though it may be. A composition traditionally entitled "theme and variations" illustrates the point. The *Variations sérieuses* by Mendelssohn are based on a melody. The given theme of the Diabelli Variations by Beethoven, however, is a harmonic scheme, determined by ordinary metrics and accompanied by a few motivic fragments; the melody matters little.

Theme and melody coincide in a fugue. The piece is precisely "about" the given theme, in the sense that the proposition is set before us as a task to be worked out. One is led to the conclusion, borne out by music history, that the concept of theme is indebted to that of *imitation (and thereby indirectly also of repetition). When imitation is absent, as in Gregorian chant, the term explains little or nothing. Gregorian melodies are not identified by a theme, although they are obviously "about" something. The famous opening phrase of "Dies irae" is memorable and recurs throughout the piece, but one can hardly claim that it constitutes the theme of the sequence. The same morphological situation exists in all those polyphonic pieces that are structured independently of imitation: there is no "theme" in a Notre Dame organum, a Machaut motet, a Dufay chanson. Nor can a cantus firmus underlying a Mass claim the role of a theme. The concept assumes meaning together with the technique of imitation. Every movement of Josquin's *Missa Pange lingua*, for instance, begins with the first few notes of the Gregorian hymn stated by one voice and imitated by the others. The gestalt of the hymn as a whole has disappeared and yielded to the identification of each movement by the characteristic head theme. Contrapuntal imitation is the essential event, the topic of discourse.

In the subsequent evolution from ricercar to fugue, thematic imitation becomes central. The sections of a ricercar gain identity through different themes. In the final reduction of the manifold ricercar to the monothematic fugue, as best shown in Bach's *Well-tempered Keyboard*, the term reveals most of its nature. The theme of a fugue, where imitation is essential, is the truest representative of its genre. A good fugue theme is clearly defined, memorable, unified in structure, and usable for imitation. A comparison of a fugue by Bach with one of his dance or (nonfugal) concerto movements elucidates the close connection of theme and imitation: without the latter, there is little sense in applying the concept of the former to, let us say, the beginning of the First Brandenburg Concerto.

By reconciling the homophonic language of the gallant period with imitative polyphony, often favoring repetition along with imitation, the Vienna classical style permitted the transfer of the term *theme* to sonata movements. Here common usage has identified theme with a short characteristic melody while pushing the original, more precise, and revealing meaning into the background. One result of the confusion is the exaggerated importance ascribed to a musical theme throughout the last two hundred years. Is the first movement of Beethoven's Fifth Symphony "about" the famous opening four-note motive or about a harmonic movement away from, and back to, an established tonal center? The alternatives lie between recognizing as theme the popular, obvious, foreground "tune" or the ideal, underlying, background proposition. Obviously we are dealing with two different meanings of the word *theme*. Under the impact of pieces like the Beethoven symphony, one is tempted to identify the melodic motive with the contents of the sonata form. Yet there are comparable pieces, like the full-fledged sonata-form finale of the same composer's Piano Sonata op. 54, which have no theme at all in the common meaning. Beethoven's notebooks give some evidence of his deciding on the final form of a main theme often after completing much of the movement. Schubert had finished the composition of the first movement of his big C major Symphony on a first theme that sounded:

The version as we know it was an afterthought and hence could not have served as the basic topic of discourse.

In its narrow definition as melody, theme functions as a marker. It indicates the occurrence of a musical event without being necessarily the event itself. In a fugue, the two qualities coincide, and they are morphologically significant also in those pieces where the character of imitation is lost and mere repetition is left (refrain forms, rondo, da capo aria, etc.). In a *sonata form, theme is merely the carrier of an event. The presence of the first theme at the point of recapitulation is not always obligatory (Scarlatti), but it helps point out the return to the established and then abandoned tonic key. The presence of a second theme at the point of accomplished modulation also is not necessary (Haydn, sometimes Brahms), but the harmonic proposition underlying the form becomes thereby marked and memorable.

The internal structure of a theme often reflects the function it serves. In a fugue, where proposition and melody coincide, the theme is a definite type with a clear beginning and end, inviting imitation. In a sonata form, particularly by Beethoven, the theme is melodically indefinite and open-ended. It tries to find its own end while we are listening. Thus it serves the dramatic exegesis characteristic of a classical development section. The difference between the opening statements of the two Beethoven examples given above (the C minor Symphony and the little F major Sonata) lies in their memorability, not in their technical usefulness; for neither is a melody, and both are indefinite and open-ended. They are initial carriers of the real events of the sonata form.

The formative techniques corresponding to the two types—one a full-grown individuality, the other a seed—necessarily proceed in opposite directions: from the definite to the complex in a fugue, and from the relatively indefinite toward the complete in a classical sonata. The morphology of a particular piece is related to one or the other type.

THOROUGH BASS. See **BASSO CONTINUO**

THROUGH-COMPOSED

By definition, a through-composed piece does not inherently follow or display any laws of musical morphology. It is not primarily a musical form. There is a chance for a through-composed piece to be musically valuable if it admits the play of formative musical forces.

Through-composing is artistically most precarious; for in addition to all other difficulties arising from the relation of *word and tone, it rejects any compromise by letting the music be led by the text. The dangers are similar to those existing in *program music but rendered more acute by the relentless and constant presence of a text which in fact dictates a program. The text, poetic or otherwise, is in any case used as if it were prose. The musical discourse is continuous whether the poem contains stanzas too different in content to allow strophic composition or by itself shows no division into stanzas. The temptation to follow the given text slavishly is strong and pushes the composer into the pitfall of a "compose-as-you-go" plan. The principle involved is that of primitive recitative, in regard to the subservience of music to text akin to the notions of the Florentine Camerata. But a through-composed song of later centuries moves on a more pretentious level, for the music is here expected to come into its own but actually does not. If the composer ignores the poetic guidelines, he faces the purely musical postulates which are inherently contrary to those of words. In short, what to an uncritical mind at first might seem the easiest of all vocal types is in reality the one in which language and music, word and tone, clash most violently.

The formative task for the composer consists above all in discovering any unifying literary elements and transforming them into unifying musical elements. Form elements contained in the text and the innate morphological norms of music must be attuned to each other within the relatively brief duration of a through-composed piece, without the option possible in *opera of dividing the field between recitatives and arias. The ideal is a piece that sounds as if the musical form, though self-contained, had been abstracted from the text which in reality it has molded.

We point here to an anonymous failure of setting Grimm's *Fairy Tales* to music—word by word, and animal by animal. Not far above this level are some of the once popular ballads by Carl Loewe. Stories like the ones told in "Goldschmieds Töchterlein," "Kleiner Haushalt," or "Archibald Douglas" relentlessly dominate the structure and subjugate the musical invention; but whenever the poem played into his hands, as, for example, in "Der Nöck," Loewe succeeded in creating a primarily musical shape. On the borderline are also the famous chansons by Clement Janequin, such as "La Guerre" and "La Chasse," which, like the Loewe ballads, were greatly conditioned by the literary demands of the surrounding society.[1] Only a great admirer of Janequin

---

[1] Both originally published by Attaingnant in 1529 and reprinted in Expert, *Renaissance*, vol. 7.

can argue that the faithful description of blow by blow, and dog by dog, follows the sectional organization of the traditional Franco-Flemish motet. Completely successful, on the other hand, was Heinrich Schütz. Proceeding from a text in all his works, he consistently musicalized it in such a way that the result sounds as if the grammar of both arts had been satisfied and neither violated. His setting (to give an example) of Psalm 8 as a German concerto in the *Symphoniae sacrae* of 1647 skirts the pitfall of rendering the mouths of babes, the moon, the stars, all sheep and oxen, the birds of the heaven and the fish of the sea, and other items listed to illustrate the glory of the Lord.[1] While accepting rhythmic inspiration from the various phrases, Schütz framed them by a huge da capo arch characterized by a meaningful ostinato on "Herr unser Herrscher, wie herrlich ist dein Nam" ("O Lord, our Lord, how glorious is Thy name") and shaped the illustrative middle section by letting cadences produce correspondences and musical cohesion.

TIMBRE

The morphological power inherent in timbre is small. Timbre serves music best by underlining and emphasizing other factors. In a classical symphony, for example, trumpets and timpani usually mark cadential and other structural points, bassoons join the violoncelli when a bass line demands attention, strings and winds divide between themselves the first and second subjects.

The timbre distinction between strings and winds has deep roots. To the Greeks, lyra, the stringed instrument of Apollo, and aulos, the wind instrument of Dionysus, embodied the polarity of two elementary experiences of music. The lyra was invented when Hermes found a dead tortoise on the beach and realized that the shell with guts stretched across it could produce sound. Music on the lyra is not a personal expression of man but a reflection of the sound of the world around him. It is objective. The aulos was invented by Pallas Athena to imitate the wailing clamor of mortals in anguish. The tone of both a wind instrument and the human voice is created by the pulsation of breath. Music on the aulos expresses the feelings of an individual. It is subjective. Greeks heard string timbre in the temple, wind timbre in the theater.

Every society and time have particular sound ideals appropriate to them. By favoring strings, the Renaissance showed its affinity to the Greeks. Castiglione's *Cortegiano*, the ideal courtier, recommends lute and viols because such instruments "are full of harmony . . . and delight a man."[2] The sound of strings is "very sweet and artful." The desired blend produced by a set of viols is in strong contrast to the harsh frictions between instruments of different families that characterize music of the thirteenth century. In general, the structure of the music of various styles demands either unified timbre or distinct separation, but to a small extent the influence may be reciprocal. Fantasias in which four voices carry the same melodic material may have been pop-

[1] *Werke*, 7:16–22.
[2] Here quoted from Strunk, *Source Readings*, p. 284.

ular in the sixteenth century partly because such structures were ideally suited to project the valued blend by a family of similar instruments. Sound ideals change and become part of style. Today brass and percussion seem to prevail.

Structure and timbre appear to be inversely proportional. Pieces in which structure is paramount depend least of all on a specific timbre contribution. The case is most obvious in fugues, which can be played in different instrumentations without real damage. Organ music, almost by definition, leaves timbre undetermined: the organist chooses his registration to serve the structure. In the widest sense, this situation holds true for all polyphony. Hence composers before the rise of homophony, that is, into the sixteenth century, seldom if ever specified timbre. They could count on the strength of the structure which admitted almost any possible or practically available combination of instruments and voices. People of all times, of course, have enjoyed the sensuous experience of timbre, but for many centuries this experience was not a necessary nor intrinsic part of the work.

The use of timbre as an independent morphological means is relatively recent. Specifically prescribed orchestrations initiate the development. Whereas most trio sonatas of the figured-bass period can still be played by a variety of instruments that fit the range, Bach's concern with timbre becomes articulate and defined. One can, but should not, replace an oboe by a violin in his cantatas; and the timbre combinations in his six Brandenburg Concertos are as essential as the structure. Treatises on orchestration which at the beginning of the thorough-bass period had classified instruments according to pitch no longer were of any use to composers who increasingly individualized the participants in their growing orchestras. As never before, timbre was established in the classic symphonies, in which instrumentation may not be tampered with. The program for the new role of timbre was forcefully set out in Berlioz's *Traité d'instrumentation*, of 1844. Ever since, composers have endeavored to add evidence to his claim that timbre alone can under circumstances create a musical morphé. As a characteristic concomitant, concern with structure has receded before the new preoccupation with sound.

The most radical experiments in this direction stem from Arnold Schönberg and his school. At the conclusion of his *Harmonielehre* (1911), he speculates on the possibility of making melody without participation by pitch out of pure timbre: "*Klangfarbenmelodie*! What fine senses, to discriminate, and what highly developed mind, to find delight in such subtle things" (p. 471). He had come close to materializing this idea two years earlier in the third of his *Five Orchestra Pieces*, although after a beginning on one sustained chord pulsating (metrically!) in different tone colors, the pitches, and with them melodies and harmonies, do change. Anton Webern, following his teacher's lead, orchestrated the six-part ricercare from Bach's *Musikalisches Opfer* in order "to reveal the motivic coherence" and "to indicate the way [to] feel the character of the piece" by means of ever-varying timbres.[1] Thus the first statement of the bare subject is shared by trombone, horn, trumpet, harp, and violin in alternation and different combinations. The

[1] In a letter to the conductor Hermann Scherchen, *Die Reihe* 2 (1955):7.

excessive realization of possibly implicit changes of color results in overemphasis on detail at the expense of the unity of the whole.

Theoretically the idea of *Klangfarbenmelodie* can be truly realized only on a single held tone; for if the change of timbre is coupled with anything else (rhythm, harmony, melody), *Klangfarbenmelodie* becomes a coloring of something else and thereby loses its pretended autonomy. Practically the issue depends, as in all music, on the prevalence of this or that element. The idea is therefore more useful as incitement to intensive timbre research than for the creation of an independent aesthetic factor.

TIME AND SPACE

The life sphere of tone suggests a world quite different from that in which we live. If anything connected with tone seems to point toward ordinary physical notions, our experience always turns out, upon examination, to be tainted by our destiny of living in three-dimensional space and subject to gravity—conditions that have shaped our body and permeate our imagination. Whatever we find of gravity in tone space is utterly freakish. At any moment, gravitational direction may be canceled, reversed, or rotated. A tone may appear now to be heavy, now light. It may be felt now to fall, now to dig into something, now to be hovering, now to rise like a balloon. Its ascent in a direction opposite to that of tellurian gravity may sound easy, as if by attraction, or painful, as if against great resistance. A tone gesture might suggest a right-left motion or a circular motion although neither is actually possible. We might receive impressions of depth, of mass, or of volume. All of this is possible, but all of it is vague, inconsistent, and out of conformity with the physical world, by which it is merely colored.

Yet to a musical person, the tone world is self-evident and contains no strangeness. It is a different world. Difficulties arise at the moment we try to talk about music. Although the technical vocabulary in music is more precise than in the other arts, we are all too often forced to supplement it with terms borrowed from everyday language, which are at best analogical and never literal.

Each one of our senses provides us with impressions that are specific and of which the linguistic symbols are essentially untranslatable into those of the other senses. Hot and cold, soft and hard, sweet and bitter, light and dark are such symbols. When speaking of "cold colors," "sweet music," "melodic line," and the like, we use analogical, metaphorical language. The nontechnical, specifically acoustical vocabulary is relatively poor. There is no acoustical English word, for instance, designating the opposite of *loud*; the word *soft* is borrowed from the tactile realm. In dealing with the objective world, we draw heavily on optical terminology. The informatory value of sight is enormous, that of hearing small in comparison. Hearing is in the main restricted to a warning role and, in contrast to seeing, turned more inward than outward. The disadvantage of the ear versus the eye in regard to the physical world is offset by two particular psychic functions. The ear is the organ of communication between the isolated inner lives of individuals. Music, the creation of a specific art of the acoustical sense, is the art of Psyche herself. It is a wholly psychological art that owes nothing to the outside world. It is non-imitative, not only inasmuch as it does not take models from the outer world, but because it does not take them even from the soul. It is produced by Psyche herself—it is Psyche's own language.

Imagining an optical parallel is instructive. Suppose the eye not having been destined to the acquisition of knowledge of the outer world but only to the reception of warning signals from it. The optical experience would be reduced to a world of light in which colors and forms generate a universe *sui generis*. Somebody knowing the outside world through other senses would then receive through the eye suggestions of that world, but the two spheres would remain incommensurable, without reference to each other. The optical universe would stand apart as does now the acoustical one, and visual art would be an art of inside, not outside, vision. In this description, the reader recognizes the aims of nonobjective art. It is an art born, so to speak, out of the painter's and sculptor's aspiration to the state of a musician. Because of the specific destiny of the eye, however, nonobjective art appears not as a necessity but only as a possibility. Whereas the nonobjective is the very realm of music, the trend to explore this possibility in the visual arts lacks indigenousness and universality. Paradoxically, at the same time in which painters and sculptors tend to break away from imitation, composers show symptoms of trying to break away from the nonobjective. The symptoms show in such novel terms as *sound objects, musique concrète*, or in the role assigned to three-dimensional space in some compositions. These, like other contemporary phenomena, are in the last analysis rooted in the general revolt against any sort of hierarchy and in a concomitant, typically romantic longing to deny border lines and to aspire toward the indefinite.

The tone field is entirely *sui generis* and incomparable with our three-dimensional world, of which it sometimes reminds all of us who live in it. Such allusions to space, however, are fundamentally irrelevant, because the musical universe of discourse is complete and orderly in its own way. We call that within which tone exists a "field" because it is something generated by psychic energy manifesting itself in an interplay of forces induced in tone. Our ways of musical thinking evince that tone is only a symptom of these forces and not their cause. Thus we take melody to be a continuum when in fact we hear only separate tones. We are able to experience the same chord now as ontic, now as gignetic. We endow a leading tone with a tendency. Cf. *Alteration.

Time and space elicit from us characteristically different relationships. We seem to enjoy a certain freedom in space that time denies us. We may go to and fro in space; we can, as one says, "conquer" it. To time, however, we are inexorably chained. We may return to our birthplace but not to our birthday. Music is a time art, and musical morphology is a time morphology. Withal musical time is not identical with clock time. We do not use time in music: we create it. Musical time is not objective but subjective (which does not mean arbitrary). As we grow older, time seems to go by ever faster. Indeed our time feeling develops in inverse proportion to the aging process and approxi-mately logarithmically. In broad terms, the time lapse between the ages 5 and

10 corresponds to the subjective time spans from 10 to 20, 20 to 40, 40 to 80 years. The more the life functions are slowed down, the faster time seems to go by. In other words: the less that happens physiologically within a given clock time, the shorter the time span appears to us subjectively.

Something similar occurs in music. Experiments have shown that of two pieces of music of equal clock time, the faster composition is felt to last longer than the slower composition. This result may at first seem puzzling but can be readily explained. Let us assume beats following each other at constant speed. "Constant speed" means that the time lapses between beats are equal. How do we sense they are equal? How do we judge a length of time? Obviously by memory. Memory of what? What is it that the beats enclose? Apparently nothingness, but actually a sort of flowing that we can experience. We call that flow the chronal stream. The beats are but signals on that stream on which they float like corks on a stream of water. When the tempo of the beats changes, actually the chronal stream changes speed. With it, our feeling for the passing of time changes, for that stream *is* time. The faster the flow, the more time goes by subjectively—the more corks float by—in respect to a given clock time. Time is an intrinsic factor of music, but musical time is independent of clock time. Consequently music is measured not by minutes but by musical periods. When we give the example of a sixteen-measure period in metrical music as a satisfactorily complete and self-contained unit, this statement is valid for a fast as well as for a slow piece. The latter will, of course, take up more clock time than the former, which is another way of saying that if we bring both to the same objective length by cutting the slow piece, it will appear shorter than the fast piece. What produces musical time is the density of musical events.

The musical universe is thus removed in every way from the ordinary world. It creates its own space and its own time. It also establishes its own, different relationship of space to time. In everyday life, we act in space but suffer time. The experience of existing is primarily spatial; time awareness develops slowly. A child moves—an event bound to and dictated by space—long before realizing a chronal before-after. His awareness of time probably begins with the periodicity of day and night, feeding, and other recurring events, that is, with oscillatory experiences rather than with the before-after. In it all, he still feels time as a sort of appendage to space without the latter's reality. Later in life, the elusiveness of time is confirmed to us by our measuring it geometrically on our watch. Perhaps only the consciousness of passing, of impending death, strikes us with the full and direct impact of the meaning of time. Even then, however, and as long as we live, space remains the "real" world in which we act, with time attached to it as an inescapable fatality. This, we submit, is our human experience regardless of what the "actual" relationship between time and space may be.

Quite different is our experience in music. Whereas in ordinary life we "live in space," in the musical world we "live in time." Everyday statements such as "this does not move" or "this motion is perpendicular" presuppose the primacy of space and the assumption of a coordinate system in which time is, so to speak, imprisoned. In music, on the contrary, time is the given dimension, which determines the kind of space we shall have. In ordinary life, we experience space as given and time as a variable arising from it. In music, we experience time as given and space as the variable.

This reversal of roles has consequences. In music that consists only of rhythm, space consciousness is almost entirely absent, for the music is all time. Generation of space consciousness begins with our awareness of pitch. Percussion music made with instruments of indefinite but varied pitch stands at the onset of a primitive space feeling, which increases with the introduction of definite and fixed pitches and develops fully with moving tones.

Suppose now that a tone or chord sounds for an indefinite time. The result is a sort of immobility. Our reaction to it, however, differs from the one we experience while looking at a stable object. A painting or sculpture in a state of repose is a normal sight in our physical living space with its seemingly rigid coordinates, but a persisting tone is irritating. It seems to be in an abnormal situation. It seems to contradict hurrying time tugging at it. Because time is foremost in music, there is here no immobility comparable to immobility in three-dimensional space. Musical space exists only as a function of time. The absence of real immobility is the first consequence. Beyond it, all motions in music are deeply affected by the peculiar time-space relationship. Because specific space coordinates—coordinates disregarding time—do not exist in music, vertical motion is not possible. Nor is there any rectilinear horizontal motion; its temporal equivalent is repetition of the same tone, ♩♩♩♩ . Depth as an immediately given dimension does not exist. Above all, there is the impossibility of *retrograde motion; time cannot be turned back. We are left with little in our hands: time and a kind of up-down wave motion. Both are reflected in our notation, in which the x-axis represents time, and the y-axis pitch.

A closer look at this wave motion increases our understanding of the musical space phenomenon. The very words *up* and *down* are inseparably bound up with our earthly condition. They make no sense at all without gravity. Indeed they presuppose both gravity and our own human viewpoint. Music theory has profited from the assumption that tones are originally just different from each other and that the perpendicularity of the "tone ladder" (scale) stems from an adaptation to tellurian gravity.[1] In the present context as well, whatever in "tone space" reminds us of ordinary space is induced by our remembrance of that space. For this reason we should not speak of a tone space but of a tone field of induced forces of which the tones are the carriers. The configuration of these forces is subject to continuous change produced by the musical intentions. Analogical allusions to ordinary space are supervenient. The tone field—an attribute of time—is to be considered as completely autonomous. Efforts tending to integrate it with outside space must fail.

This very autonomy, on the other hand, allows for allusions to, and interpretations of, notions belonging to ordinary space. Foremost among these notions are up-down, mass, and volume. The indebtedness of up-down to tellurian adaptation is responsible for all further suggestions of space motion in music. Being analogical remembrances and no more, they remain forever inadequate, unsatisfactory, fleeting, and essentially unnecessary. What we

[1]Cf. the authors' *Tone*, pp. 192 ff.

call a "melodic line" does not correspond to a graph drawn according to pitches. Is a diatonic scale an oblique straight line or should it show the intermittence of wholetones and halftones? If so, the halftones will be less steep than the wholetones; yet the musical halftone tension, the "steepness," is greater than that of the wholetone. If not, how would the diatonic scale be graphically differentiated from the wholetone scale? Such questions, which remain vague because they are only analogies and which can be continued without end, are actually meaningless, for they bear on naked tones when these are musically intelligible only as carriers of currents. A diatonic scale may or may not be understood as a "straight line" depending on rhythm, speed, or functional interpretation. If it is true that music is made with tones (as poetry, according to Mallarmé, is made with words), the perceived phenomena are fraught with intentions from which they must not be separated. To feel these intentions, to understand the hidden forces present in tones, is to think musically.

As concerns mass and volume, the other prominent space notions in music, one may concede something corporeal, hence spatial, even to a single tone. But the notion is vague like all other space suggestions. We risk the admission of a general feeling of lessening mass and lessening volume with increasing pitch and diminishing loudness, and vice versa. Moreover, the mass-volume feeling evokes an indeterminate depth dimension, often related to the impression of something going away or approaching. The long crescendo on a single tone after the murder scene in Berg's *Wozzeck* eventually fills one's entire head; the desired effect creates a feeling of volume. Although such tone motions are especially suggestive when coupled with changes of loudness, other factors contribute. Does a triad in closed position have more mass than in open? Do mass and volume of the first fugue from Bach's *Well-tempered Keyboard* decrease at the very end, notwithstanding the addition of a fifth voice in the final chord (a situation easily tested on a harpsichord on which loudness remains constant)?

Of vastly greater importance than all such questions is the establishment of musical coordinates in the tone field. To some extent, they are prepared by the morphology of *tone itself (cf. *Pythagorean Table). Based on these natural reference points, "artificial" coordinates can be introduced. The general term for a musical coordinate system is *tonality. It becomes possible through the establishment of a definite gravitational configuration carried through time by memory. We have stated that by nature a tone field can have any sort of configuration and that it permits any speed of change of the configuration. If either the particular configuration or the rate of change remained unregulated, total disorder would result, and the means of expression would be reduced to almost nothing. With the introduction of tonality (in the widest sense), an order is established that immensely multiplies the aesthetic factors at the disposal of the composer. The order, whatever its details, fertilizes imagination which without it finds itself frustrated and sterilized by the indefiniteness of possibilities. Tonality does not exclude any kind of change in the configuration of the tone field, provided the new configuration (for instance, modulation) is capable of being understood as a gravitational sub-configuration relatable to the adopted system.

The role of memory in the definition of tonality contains an apparent paradox that calls for clarification. Although both memory and music are clearly tied to the temporal concepts of "before" and "after," our memory of musical gestalts is spatial. The written form of a composition, notation, belongs entirely to space. The great difficulty and even inability to suppress wholly inner space representations from time feeling emerge in the usage of all languages. Time interval, life cycle, *Zeitraum, espace de temps*—these are all spatial terms. They suggest the infiltration of time concepts by space notions. A month or a year are remembered in a vaguely spatial way: "Christmas comes around again." We may expect something similar in music. A composition remembered as a whole—be it a theme, movement, or entire work— carries the spatial tint of any temporal shape, just as the very words *shape* and *morphé* do. While certainly not generated by notational representation, spatial connotations are doubtless reinforced by our vision of the written work. The score is a sort of spatial symbol for the coexistence of the parts of a work. The work exists in the mind as a whole (cf. *Reality). From the flowing medium, a "time block" is "cut out" and "set apart" as a morphé (note the inevitably spatial expressions!). A trained musician is capable of surveying in his mind and in an instant, as at a glance, the total shape of even a large work. Most people have had similar experiences with literary works or historical periods. Such remembrances are always permeated with strong though vague spatial feelings. No wonder that the tone field, though essentially removed from ordinary space, shares the spatial ingredient with all other time representations. The inextricable intertwining of space and time is lastly to be charged to the impalpable nature of time, yet it is precisely in time that music lives.

TONALITY

Tonality is a harmonic force contained in tone. It is not a human invention, nor is it (as Arnold Schönberg suggested) a "device" (*Kunstgriff*) to produce unity.[1] It is a spiritual potential of tone that can be phenomenalized in a multitude of ways. The history of musical systems is a history of discovery and cultivation of a particular tonal field. Each stage has its own definite value and is not merely superseded by the following stage. Theoretically, the series of possible tonal organizations is infinite. Practically, the history of music exemplifies tonalities realized thus far.

We are used to defining tonality by cadence, but the idea of a center of gravity, which underlies all cadences, is a relatively late development. The earlier, more basic definition derives from scale, which is the arrangement of the selected tones. Even scales need not possess a center of gravity. In many Gregorian chants, for instance, one often does not know the goal till the last note has been sounded. The scale determines here ambitus and finalis, but the latter often varies for the same Psalm tone. We may imagine an early stage in which scale and total available sounds were identical. Such is the case in a pentatonic world in which the five tones are at the same time total resource

---

[1]*Harmonielehre*, p. 28.

and scale, and in which modes are formed (exactly as in our diatonic system) by the selection of a particular pitch as the determinant of the scale. So long as there is no transposition and no perceptible preponderance of one mode over another, identity of scale and total resource is maintained. Their separation is caused by changes introduced into this situation. By such means the chromatic spectrum came into existence.

The chromatic stage (the adjective interpreted in the widest sense) is best understood by reference to the respective roles of fixed and movable tones. The distinction characterizes Greek tonality but probably is reflected by plainchant more than has generally been conceded. The harmonical development of tone here becomes patently audible. One firm principle asserts itself in the definite outline of the octave and its dominant subdivisions, that is, of two juxtaposed tetrachords in Greek terminology and of the steps I-IV-V-I in ours. To this fixed frame, the chromatically movable tones subordinate themselves. In old Greek music, the three genera (diatonic, chromatic, enharmonic) shared the fixed tones and were distinguished from one another by the position of the movable tones. The Church modes can be similarly understood. All Church modes are anchored on the same four tones (the theoretic deviation of Lydian being adjusted in practice more often than not). The second, third, sixth, and seventh degrees of the scale remain movable. Dorian, Phrygian, and eventually Aeolian are characterized by maintaining the minor third while keeping the other tones elastic; Lydian, Mixolydian, and eventually Ionian, by maintaining the major second, major third, and major sixth. The relative rigidity of the major-third modes stamps them as representative of a later concept of tonality. Even in the apparently clear polarity of the *major-minor modes, some movable elements have remained, witness the natural, melodic, and harmonic versions of minor and the frequent occurrence of the minor sixth in major.

The independent life achieved by the chromatic spectrum has led to dodecaphony in which, once again, scale and total resource are identical; but the twelve-tone scale, unlike all earlier ones, is undifferentiated and indifferent. Thus understood, Schönberg's *atonality is really only one particular manifestation of tonality.

All tonalities are based on the natural forces inherent in tone. Each kind of tonality, however, is based on a more or less arbitrary selection of the number of tones chosen from the infinity of possible tones. The best known examples are the numbers 5 for the Chinese scale, 7 for much Western music, and 12 for dodecaphony and other twentieth-century developments. Any other number is theoretically possible, but there seem to be morphological advantages to the favored systems which transcend purely musical considerations. The Chinese seem to be universally oriented toward five. Lao-Tse speaks of 5 colors (red, yellow, blue, white, black) and 5 tastes (salty, bitter, sour, biting, sweet). There are 5 elements (air, water, fire, organic matter, inorganic matter) and 5 directions (East, South, West, North, Up). To a Western mind the rainbow has 7 colors, the week 7 days, the year 12 months, the foot 12 inches. The particular orientation toward certain numbers has also influenced the choice of tones for forming a tonality.

Presiding over the relations among the selected tones are harmonic proportions which apparently correspond to preestablished forms of our spirit in the Platonic sense. Noteworthy is the inability of melody to produce by itself definite tone steps. The organization of discrete pitches within a tonality is accomplished by the intervention of harmonic forces. The scale is the result of the intersection of the melodic principle (exemplified by the wailing of the siren) and the harmonic principle (exemplified by the fifth or the triad). Melodic and harmonic hearing are very different in kind, the former appreciating frequency relationships, the latter their logarithms. One need only think of the vast qualitative difference between a second heard as a distance and heard as a relation.

The harmonic forces clarify, furthermore, the role of *cadence in tonality. The most precise definition is that supplied by the supreme consonance of the triad on the tone of reference in conjunction with the effective dissonance of the triads on the upper and lower dominants. The "sounding apart" (*dissonare*) of these functions permits tonality to unfold.

In continued unfolding lies the potential for the future of tonality, which cannot be solved by denial of its existence. We may fashion music of as many different sounds as we wish; we may select whatever we wish as its tonal center; but we cannot eliminate the idea of tonality. What is wanted is the emergence of new ways of tonality. Tone contains a sonorous world which spreads out, fanwise, to infinity. However far we follow this fanning-out, two factors must be reckoned with: the existence of a primary center, a seed, and a need for a limit to the spread. No limits, no liberty. Freedom is found only within an imposed framework. The crisis in classic tonality was brought about solely by an eruption of the infinite. A further unfolding of tone, under the "sign of the fan," might result in a new organic style, from which simple events would not be excluded, and wherein complexities would not renounce their origins. Such a way of tonality would be truly evolutionary rather than merely functional.

TONE

Tone, the basic building material of music and apparently simple as an isolated phenomenon, contains complex morphological implications both from its origin and for its potential. Musical identification of a tone is the result of a lengthy process of spiritual selection.

Vibration is the given physical event—a particular kind of disturbance of a state of rest or balance. Music follows the fate of vibration inasmuch as it begins by disturbing silence which it finally restores. Of the many possible vibrations, those that cannot be perceived by the senses must first be eliminated. From the remaining sensible vibrations, the musician distills those that he can perceive through the ear. They produce sound, which contains both noise and tone; and although the former is an ingredient, only the latter forms the essential element of music.

Taken as a single event, tone seems to be a final product. It becomes, however, the beginning of a further selection process out of the necessity to establish relations with other tones. The totality of all tones is musically not usable because morphologically unlimited. The continuous pitch variation of a siren has no shape. Discrete pitch variation produced by individuation still includes asystematic chance relations. Only systematic distillation according to some formative principle finally helps us reach musically meaningful tone relations.

In all periods and civilizations, the principle applied is in essence the same although there are significant variations of detail. Proportion governs all systems. Integers being the fundamental principle of organization which man brings to bear on the whole cosmos, division (and inversely multiplication) of the vibrating string by whole numbers identifies all possible tone relations. The simplest operations producing octave and fifth characterize all systems. Variants appear depending on the particular selections among subsequent operations. The number of tones within the octave and the resulting relationships define the morphology of a system. The difference between a pentatonic and heptatonic scale is morphological.

The overtone series, by nature inherent in every tone, is itself a symptom rather than a material cause. It appears as a natural by-product, so to speak, of string division by integers. The series itself has its own shape. The gradual decrease in size of the successive intervals produces an asymptotic curve converging toward infinity.

The morphology of tone has a direct influence on both the practice and theory of music. It conditions the construction of instruments, for instance, as much as that of harmonic systems.[1]

TONE POEM. See PROGRAM MUSIC

TONE ROW

Tone row, also called series, is a term stemming from the theory of dodecaphony but actually identical with what we call *raga. The word *raga* is borrowed from Hindu musical theory and here freely interpreted. Raga, in our parlance, is a tone row based on certain pitch material, the determination of which is not contained in the definition of raga. Accordingly a raga may contain any number of tones from any scale, excluding none. In this light, twelve-tone rows appear to be the one particular case of raga that uses our total tone material. The twelve tones thereby become identified with mode because no selection takes place. The concept of mode is consequently missing from dodecaphonic theory. Cf. *Atonality.

TONIC

The concept is inseparable from that of *tonality in which it is the ultimate unit of reference.

[1]The musical implications arising from the morphology of tone are developed in the authors' book *Tone*.

288

We say "ultimate" rather than "first" or "central" because a work or even style can be imagined in which the actual tonic is never sounded, remaining outside the field of the used tonal relationships. Wagner's treatment of the tonic in *Tristan und Isolde* closely approaches this condition (cf. p. 81). The extrapolation of a postulated but never realized tonic plays a role in more or less extended stretches of existing music.

We chose the word *unit* rather than *point* because the tonic can be defined not only by a single tone, *punctus*, but also by more or less complex units of diverse character, such as chords or scales. The row or series in *atonality functions as a unit.

Reference indicates One, the unit from which all other tones flow and in relation to which they find their particular qualities. Cf. *Pythagorean Table. In this widest sense, the term *tonic* is applicable to the music of all styles and not, as is common usage, only to that of the major-minor orientation of the last four centuries. Every plainchant, for instance, has some ultimate unit of reference, although it need not be the first or last or lowest tone of the melody. The same holds true of all modal polyphonic compositions.

TOPOLOGY

Topos indicates a place. Topology, in the general sense, is the study of modifications caused by space. In music, because of the inversion of the roles of space and time, we shall consider topology the study of aesthetic modifications caused by time.

The chronal stream becomes aesthetically operative through *rhythm and meter. Indefinable without them, it appears immediately structured by groups formed according to rhythmic or metric-rhythmic norms. In a thus organized time span, each moment, by its position, possesses a unique qualification; and a musical entity occupying a certain position will come under the influence of the corresponding moment.

Position is thus actually a primary factor in the determination of musical meaning. As the purest attribute of musical time, position precedes even musical substance. Substance without position is a shapeless raga. Position without musical substance, on the other hand, involves strong morphological powers. A metrical scheme of, let us say, 2 + 2 + 2 + 2 will impose its influence on anything one writes. So also will the metrical scheme of a poem, which is given before the melody adjusts itself to it.

Although the validity of topological influence is universal, it can be most readily demonstrated by metric examples that exhibit identical repetition of a musical entity. The finale of Lalo's *Symphonie espagnole* opens with seventeen repetitions of the following motive:

The repetition produces not a mere additive effect, because it serves at the same time as substance to the rhythmic-metric structure implied by the phrase.

Thus the motive acquires a different meaning at every repetition by virtue of the preestablished quality of the place (topos) where it occurs. The structure is made more easily perceptible by a crescendo toward, and a decrescendo away from, the center (exactly the center if we count the suggestive "empty" four measures at the beginning); they help the listener grasp the build by the maintenance of tension and release over the required period.

In the nonmetrical flow of the Kyrie from the Third Gregorian Mass, the first little phrase (1) is heavy, functioning as thesis; and the second little phrase (2) is light, functioning as arsis, simply by topological virtue:

If we invert the succession, we also invert the significance of both motives:

The roles of thesis and arsis impose themselves by sheer topology on the respective motivic substance.

The entire Kyrie I is a good example of nonmetrical breathing form. It consists of four groups:

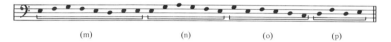

If we now interchange the middle two, the overall process is modified not only through the change of melody but also through topology. Within the total crustic rhythm, (n) becomes stronger by topos, and (o) weaker:

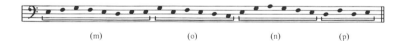

Topology in relatively small forms is closely associated with breathing. It is just as significant in macro-morphology. Although in wide time spans, rhythm and meter in the original, direct, quasi-physiological sense are no longer operative, yet rhythm acts on memory in such a way as to modify the meaning of a remembered event at the re-happening of the same event. A rondo theme, for instance, assumes at each recurrence a different sense. The first statement is a fresh event. The second leads away. The next generally reaffirms. In larger rondos, the effects of the topological differences are even more complex and varied. Any recapitulation, even when literal, obviously takes on a meaning different from the exposition.

Topology is well elucidated by the behavior of a magnet. The particles are not predetermined to belong to either the south pole or north pole; for in a magnetic rod broken in two, they rearrange themselves and regenerate into a newly oriented magnet. What makes the magnetic fragment complete is the changed topology. The musical situation is similar. The last movement of a multipartite takes over finale function even if otherwise not particularly pre-destined for the role. The eighteenth-century *suite illustrates the possibili-ties. The *Adagio lamentoso* of Tchaikovsky's *Pathétique* Symphony, to give a specific example, belongs normally somewhere in the middle of the work; but by virtue of topology alone, it becomes the legitimate finale.

Somewhere along the line from micro- to macro-morphology, the aging process shows its influence. It is patent in very large time spans. When we again hear the same composition or read the same book after twenty years, we are differently impressed. All one has lived through in the interim colors the later experience. Whether the results of the aging process belong in the field of topology is as debatable a question as the inverse formulation: in how small a time lapse is the aging process aesthetically operative? Does it already modify the meaning of the recapitulation in a sonata form? The effect of the finale of a symphony? The problem deserves to be experimentally investigated by physio-psychologists.

The essential role of topology in music permits aleatory experiments. Musical dice games, popular in the late eighteenth century, depended on po-tential topological equality of all phrases. Any order prescribed by the rolling dice had to produce an acceptable melody. Topology was set by the dice. The composer merely had to adjust his invention so that each phrase could play any role in any position. When Haydn or Mozart put minuet phrases on the sides of dice and suggested that players could "compose" these phrases, that is, put them together, according to the way the dice fell, they were concocting a joke. The change of topos due to permutation, even within very narrow limits, could only be funny. Stockhausen (*No. 4 Klavierstück XI pour piano*, 1957) and Boulez (Third Sonata), on the other hand, seem to take the joke seriously. These pieces consist of musical fragments that the performer can play in any order (and even with tempo and loudness variants). The work, continually destroyed and built up again, appears in a new form at each hearing. Playing a game with topological and morphological principles is made possible only by the strong permanence and presence of these principles. The question as to the intrinsic value and seriousness of such games remains open.

TRIAD

Triad is a unified entity, not the superposition of two thirds. By stating that the triad was first introduced into music in the sixteenth century, we do not in the least suggest that coincidences of third and fifth above a root were not heard all along. The change occurred in man's interpretation and use of that sound. In the middle of the century, Zarlino first wrote about it. Compos-ers in the generations around him experimented with it. By the time the new style of *basso continuo came into being around 1600, the triad had been gen-erally recognized, no longer as a conglomerate of three different tones, but as a unit. From this recognition stem all subsequently formulated laws of har-monic function.

The discovery of the triad is intimately tied to that of *major-minor. Projected from the same generator, the *senarius creates the major triad in one direction, the minor triad in the other. This *polarity underlies the basic force of functional *harmony. The two triads on the same generator tend toward each other. In general terms, every major triad acts like a dominant, and every minor triad like a subdominant. The latent force of these two functions is brought into the open by the harmonic unfolding one step beyond the senarius:

The major dominant with the minor seventh, and the minor subdominant with the *sixte ajoutée* represent the strongest and most unambivalent basic functions around a generating tonic.

There are—precisely interpreted—no other but the major and minor triads. The diminished seventh chord, for example, is an even mixture of the two:

The explanation of the minor triad as resulting from the ratios 10 : 12 : 15 (E-G-B) must be rejected for not arising out of the generating One.

The triad, major or minor, magnetizes the current running back and forth in an empty, pretriadic, presexual fifth. The beginning of Beethoven's Ninth Symphony, for instance, projects the character of something occurring "before creation." The decisive creation takes place at the precise moment the triad emerges together with the first theme. The two possibilities (D minor-D major) are fully explored in the course of the movement—witness the gigantic event of the bass step from f_2-sharp to f_2-natural at the entrance of the recapitulation.

Inversion is made possible through octave identity:

The inversions, bracketed above, each appear as a "defective series," cut off from its generator at a certain point. If the root of such a series, though not sounded, is strongly present in the memory, we are not presented with true inversions:

These cases support Rameau's theory of triad identity regardless of bass tone. Only when the bass of the cutoff series asserts itself as fundamental, then the chord is heard as a true inversion and ceases to behave as if it were in root position.

In the scale, the tonic triad sets the standard for *consonance and dissonance. The triadic tones are the only points of rest between which the nontriadic tones act as melodically driving dissonances.

TROPE

Rather than thinking of trope as a particular device popular for a few centuries in the Middle Ages, we submit that it is a basic technique of composition that has contributed to musical morphology at all times under varying names—frequently even implicitly accepted under no name at all. Trope is technically defined as an insert in a given piece. In the Middle Ages, the trope could be literary, or musical, or both; and the piece was a liturgical chant. The standard translation of the Greek word *tropos* as 'turn' reveals less than the connection with 'fashion', 'manner'. The term, originating in performance practice and identified with melody (*modulus*), invited enrichment of the chant in every possible manner.

Morphologically significant is the widespread fashion of tying the trope to the chant by motivic elaboration. Characteristic is the following eleventh-century French example of the beginning of a troped Sanctus:[1]

Here the trope unfolds the succinct melodic cell of the chant and continues to do so for the remainder of the Sanctus. Dramatic implications of this technique have stamped the Christmas trope "Hodie cantandus est" and the Easter trope "Quem queritis in sepulcro"—both of the tenth century—as the sources of all subsequent liturgical plays. Early manuscripts developing polyphony out of monophonic chant are, true to their manner, called *troparia*, among which the Winchester Troper of the eleventh century is the most famous.

The inherent fashion of unfolding a given unit has prompted some musicologists to refer to early motets as "polyphonic tropes" or "vertical tropes," for the new upper line elaborates on the original chant. In all these cases, trope is understood as an enlargement of an initial statement, an exegesis of an accepted "text," musical as much as literary.

From this wide interpretation, trope emerges as a basic principle of composition, contributing to growth by both idiogenesis and heterogenesis. Our six examples in the Discourse profitably illustrate trope influencing musical behavior in most diverse styles. Trope characterizes the entire manner of the

[1]Here quoted from Besseler, *Die Musik des Mittelalters und der Renaissance*, p. 90.

discant melody in relation to the underlying chant. It appears in the mature Franco-Flemish movement as imitation expanding a head theme. It amplifies throughout the Bach chorale the essential outline of the cadence tonic-dominant-tonic. It gives to the Beethoven march, in addition to the same technique, particular shape by the "detour," as we have called it—another term for trope. It transforms the initial thematic rhythm of Schönberg's Piano Piece in subsequent sections.

These examples open the door to our recognizing troping behind many other different forms. All variations, under whatever guise, are tropes. An authoritative expert in the music of the Middle Ages, Friedrich Gennrich, called trope the origin of rondeau when observing the trouvère procedure of an interpolation between the two halves of a refrain.[1] The *motet enté* of the thirteenth century receives similar credit from him, to which we add that the "grafting" of fresh on old material, of a new counterpoint to a cantus firmus, is not restricted to any style. Just as in functional harmony the tonal flow of a piece can rightly be understood as the unfolding of one cadence, so all the foreground material giving shape to an *Urlinie* acts in the fashion of a trope.

In a more specific sense, embellishments of a passage and cadenzas in any spot are tropes, the former explicating the contents of a melody, and the latter bringing to life a fermata. The interrelation of trope, fermata, cadenza, and detour is singularly well elucidated by the third movement of the First Symphony by Brahms. The opening melody in the tonic occurs four times in the course of the movement. Before the initial four-measure phrase of the melody is normally answered, a trope interferes which at first is one measure long (5), then three (23–25), then five (66–70), and finally seven (119–25). The gradual prolongation turns the original fermata into a structurally significant unit.

The purely generative force of trope is so strong that the Roman Catholic Church, afraid of its overrunning the sacred chant like weeds spreading over a garden, set a limit to the practice by prohibiting it explicitly at the Council of Trent.

UNCLEARNESS-CLEARNESS. See CLEARNESS-UNCLEARNESS

UNITY. See pp. 39 ff.

VARIATION

The term *variation* implies something that is being varied, which in turn implies a certain persistence of that "something" within each variation. We postulate a gestalt as the unvarying, constant substratum of variation. A gestalt is a mode of perception impressed by the perceiver upon the phenomenon. Without the assumption of a gestalt, variation is impossible. The concept of variation implies the existence of a gestalt which is not that of the variation.

---

[1]*Rondeaux.*

The first concrete gestalt in the process of musical *phenomenalization is a mode realized on a particular pitch—a key. Earlier steps in the process remain abstract. From this first gestalt—for example, a Mixolydian scale on F—artistic variations may proceed.

*Raga is an appropriate designation for the next step. We define raga as melody minus rhythm, and reach it from key by selection and variation.[1] Understood as filiation from key, raga plays a considerable role in Western music. It is the principle governing *color* in an isorhythmic piece; the use of a cantus firmus in a Netherlands Mass; tone rows like B-A-C-H or A-B-E-G-G; some transformations of folksongs into chorales; etc. In all such cases, the initial gestalt is a succession of tones (melody minus rhythm) which in turn gives birth to various melodies. As a distinct stage in the variation process, the concept of raga clarifies the relation, in melody, of pitch succession to rhythm.

Melos, the next step toward artistic phenomenalization, is a gestalt formed by melodic vectors. As the skeleton of a melody, melos appears as a more or less simplified melody. In a strict sense, melos is an abstraction, for the definition does not specify intervals. This characteristic of melos explains the possibility of our recognizing a melody in which the intervals have been deformed. In *pneumatic music, melos and melody are sometimes identical; in kinematic music, never. Because pneumatic melodies are thus always closer to melos than kinematic melodies, variation of pneumatic melodies proceeds by complication (cf. Beethoven's Op. 109); variation of kinematic melodies, by simplification. This latter concept of variation as a reduction of the given gestalt is contrary to the ordinary experience, and instances are rare. Vincent d'Indy's *Istar* Variations exemplify the possibility, provided one accepts the first statement not as the most densely "veiled" theme but as the gestalt to be varied. The kinematic Paganini theme that has served Brahms and Rachmaninoff also invites melodic simplification rather than extension by variation, although on other levels complications arise.

Melody as variation of melos is the next stage. Examples are legion, for they include just about all variation sets on a chosen theme. The only exception is variation by sheer *ornamentation, although one often is in a quandary to decide when an ornament is literally an expendable, "pasted-on" addition and not a melodic transformation. In all other cases—think of any "theme and variations"—the identity of the gestalt undergoing variation is the melos behind the theme, and not the melody of the theme itself, which is already a variation of the melos. If variation is pushed further back by the replacement of one melos by another with maintenance of the characteristic interval succession, raga becomes the *tertium comparationis*—the idea behind the phenomena that warrants the identity of the gestalt. If the raga itself is varied (through selection and permutation—a technique important in plainchant), the *tertium comparationis* will be the mode that establishes the raga. These observations lead to the significant morphological conclusion that—except in the most primitive kind of ornamentation—variation never pertains to the model proposed for variation but always to something of which the model is

---

[1]This use of the term seems a fair Western interpretation of the Oriental meaning, as explained by Lal Roy, "Hindustani Ragas."

already a variation. The gestalt identity underlying variation is to be sought, not in the thing to which variation is applied, but always in a gestalt lying behind that thing.

The following table summarizes the genetic variation process leading to melody:

Melodic Gestalt on Progressive Levels

1. Concrete Mode (Key)

2. Raga

3. Melos

4. Melody

5. Variation

In this genetic process, variation is the shaping factor. Besides leading from one stage to the next by virtue of its status as variation of something, it also possesses intrinsic value as a final gestalt. Every variation is thus an individual within a species, and its value is comparable to that of a personality within a group. Every variation, in other words, is a melody in its own right.

*Rhythm, as we have seen, is an integral part of melody; for without rhythm, melody is raga. In melos, rhythm is still undefined but certainly implied, even in the most abstract form, by the inherent direction of energy. This vectorial concept is essentially rhythmic and hence permits the application of the principle of variation to rhythm as well as to pitch.

In any specific instance, variation principles can be usefully isolated by analysis of the factors that remain constant and the concomitant possible variants.

In Gregorian chant, for instance, rhythm participates minimally as a variation principle. Singing different psalm verses to the same psalm tone may produce small rhythmic variants conditioned by the changing text, but the melodic experience within the style seems barely affected. In short, one is left with raga. Mensural music of the fifteenth century is, as the name implies, metric but generally knows no periods; raga and rhythm remain as variable elements to be analyzed. One can thus pinpoint the different ways in which a cantus firmus supplies genetic force to various movements based on it. The beginning of the hymn *Pange lingua*, for example, occurs in all sections of Josquin's Mass; the variations apply either to raga or rhythm or both.

The role of variation in the process of musical phenomenalization has been exemplified thus far by its effect on melody, for melody includes all other musical elements except harmony. In Western music since the Renaissance, harmonic variation inevitably refers back to the prime model of the *triad. In a sense, all possible chords are variations of the one archetype. Seventh chords, for instance, are intensifications; diminished triads, fragments; relative functions, representative substitutions. Behind all, the triad stands in its major and minor forms. Even in a nontriadic style, harmonic variation inevitably refers back to some harmonic model. When one chord begins to unfold, the variation acquires melodic behavior and follows melodic rather than harmonic laws. When the model consists of chord relationships, the variations act as realizations of a cadence. The Chaconne from Bach's Partita in D minor for Unaccompanied Violin illustrates the point. The ostinato model underlying the variations consists of a tetrachord descending from tonic to dominant, each note occupying one of the four measures allotted to the *theme. We define *theme* literally as the "given proposition," in this case a stretched I-V cadence. The variations all relate to this idea which, however, is explicit only at the beginning, in the middle, and at the end. Each variation interprets and realizes the cadence in its own particular way. The melodic surface appearance of each variation on a proposed harmonic gestalt lends weight to our initial concentration on melodic variation. Actually every harmonic progression generates a melody by projection in time and by always being reducible to a bass line.

Theoretically a musical gestalt can be produced by any musical factor. The contribution by dynamics or timbre is possible but negligible. The third of Schönberg's *Five Orchestra Pieces* (1909) experiments with the theoretic proposal, expressed at the end of his *Harmonielehre* (p. 471), to make melody out of tone color without benefit of changing pitch: *Klangfarbenmelodie*. If a style warrants the procedure, harmony, dynamics, and timbre can be systematically incorporated in an analytic investigation. Practically, however, rhythm and melody have remained the prime musical factors for determining a concrete gestalt that profitably serves recognizable variations.

Morphologically, we have distinguished all along between principles of extension and principles of shaping—between growth and limitation. In the process of musical phenomenalization, which we have thus far pursued, variation serves as a shaping principle. In the process of musical building, however, it is, along with repetition and juxtaposition, only a means of extension. A chain of variations guided by no other principle does not produce a form. A design based on symmetry, proportion, or other such ideas must participate to shape the otherwise endless chain of variations. The term *variation form* is therefore totally incorrect and should not occur in a precise technical vocabulary. Variation can shape only genetically but not constructionally. For examples, see Appendix A (pp. 322 ff.).

Variation is the most powerful single principle of extension and shaping. It possesses universal meaning. We observe its workings in the inorganic as well as organic realms. If, as the modern physicist puts it, "most matter exists in the form of energy," then the various energy constellations that produce the phenomenal world would make it appear, so to speak, as a gigantic set of variations on an unknown theme.

VIRTUOSITY

The concept is morphologically relevant to the extent that it bears on style. Virtuosity arises from mastery of means coupled with buoyant energy and playfulness. It is not to be condemned, for a virtuoso performance—be it that of a brilliant thinker, orator, writer, composer, singer, or instrumentalist —can indeed be very enjoyable. There are also virtuoso works in painting, sculpture, and architecture that generate intoxicating enthusiasm. But virtuosity eventually destroys the field on which it grew because the means become divorced from the meaning. Technique begins to substitute its own goals for those it was originally created to serve. Art degenerates into circus. It ceases to be significant, and the results are decay and death of a style.

The two towers of the cathedral in Chartres show at one glance the diametrically opposite possibilities. The South tower, built in the twelfth century, visualizes the early triumph of medieval aspiration over heavy materiality. The effort is noticeable and evokes admiration. The higher North tower was completed over three hundred years later when engineering techniques had assumed supremacy over artistic intentions. The easy ornamentation and flamboyant virtuosity lose the beholder's attention much more quickly than the stark simplicity of its counterpart.

The great moments in the history of any art are those when a delicate balance prevails between urge and means. They are the moments when mastery has been reached but the struggle can still be felt. Within any single style period, the one right moment occurs usually toward the end of that period when the masters are old and established, and both the virtuoso state and the virtuosos still young. The appearance of virtuosity is a fairly reliable symptom indicating that the end of a style period is at hand. Increasing virtuosity, which inevitably takes over, generates a reaction bringing about a change of style that more often than not assumes at first a primitive character. Thereby new problems are created, new difficulties arise in their wake, and the struggle begins anew and reestablishes a more favorable proportion between effort and mastery.

Music history affords countless examples of this cycle. Think of the Franco-Flemish schools and measure the totally integrated perfection of Josquin des Prez against the masterful exertion of the generation before him and the smooth, almost slick polyphony of his epigonists. The eventual primitivism of the composers around 1600 heralds the arrival of a new style. In the baroque of the early eighteenth century, the many treatises on "how to compose," and the many "recipes" for producing almost anything up to operas, clearly indicate that a style period was coming to an end. The virtuosity of a Vivaldi or Telemann invites some respect. In Franz Liszt's Piano Sonata, of 1854, the balance between idea and execution seems still right; but his many transcriptions from Verdi operas, most of them belonging to the next decade, seem to have transgressed the critical point. At the same time, the orchestra, which had served to clarify the total structure in a classical symphony, becomes a means for its own sake. In the hands of Debussy and Richard Strauss it attains virtuosity that forebodes the end of an entire style.

It is difficult not to draw parallels with the general contemporary situation. Technology was rather beneficial as long as the proportion between its goals and means remained favorable. But since entering its period of virtuosity, it has become threatening to us—that is to say, to the field from which it arose. Moreover, as a consequence of our affluent, materialistic society, a certain "virtuosity of living" has developed that favors the generation of violence and crime.

In art as in life, too much facility appears to have undesirable and unhealthy effects. A modicum of tightness, of resistance, seems necessary for achievement and happiness—notions that are both inevitably associated with effort and struggle. The hidden reasons lie in polarity and proportion.

VOCAL MUSIC

In consequence of the morphological antipathies between language and music (cf. *Word and Tone; *Opera), a long array of types exists in vocal music which differ according to the relative importance conceded to either factor. At each end of the array the proportion is so disparate that it practically amounts to absolute ascendancy of one factor over the other. The following tabulation of types of vocal music suggests an order proceeding from supreme authority of language to that of music:

(1) Monotone
(2) Recitativo secco
(3) Recitativo accompagnato, arioso, chant
(4) Through-composed
(5) Strophic, strophic-varied, aria
(6) Textually conditioned polyphony
(7) Vocalization
(8) Absolute polyphony

In practice, the types are readily identified; but one must never forget that any classification is an abstraction and cannot do justice to intermediate types. Moreover, changes from one type to another may occur in one and the same piece.

(1) Monotone is recitation on one pitch with occasional inflections. The music is signally subordinate to the text. As a result, the contribution to musical morphology is minimal. One hears monotone in situations in which the intelligibility of the words remains paramount, such as the recitation of prayers, lessons, and passages from the Scriptures in a liturgical service. The eight Gregorian psalm tones, which articulate beginning, middle, and end of a phrase by a few ascending or descending tones, have been called "inflected monotone."

(2) Recitativo secco maintains the authority of the word, but the recitation is more inflected and the musical factor strengthened, particularly if the recitative is imaginatively harmonized. This was the exclusive style adopted by the Camerata composers for their operas. It became relegated to the dramatic-literary sections between musical numbers in the compromise be-

tween word and tone worked out primarily in the eighteenth century in operas, oratorios, and cantatas.

(3) Recitativo accompagnato markedly increases the share of music, though mainly by the nature of the instrumental accompaniment rather than the vocal treatment. If the latter also contributes, by occasional melismas or motivic repetition, the mere change of terminology to arioso indicates the growing role of music. In terms of balance between word and tone, Gregorian chant might also find its place at this level.

(4) About the middle of the spectrum, we find the type called through-composed. It includes many varieties. Settings of the Credo belong here as do narrative songs. The latter may exhibit a subtle and excellent balance between the exigencies of word and tone; Schubert's "Der Erlkönig" remains exemplary. Other specimens may be counted among the worst in vocal music if the composer follows what may be characterized as a "compose as you go" plan.

(5) Strophic pieces, as also the two preceding types, are primarily homophonic—a texture that by its nature favors equilibrium of music and text. The absence of an extreme position accounts for the wide popular appeal of this type. It embraces both choral and solo pieces, such as a Protestant chorale sung by a congregation or a lied of the kind Schubert placed at the beginning and end of *Die schöne Müllerin*.

(6) Polyphony of any kind negates the intelligibility of words and hence by definition tips the balance toward music. Among the vast literature in this category, the French polyphonic chanson of the sixteenth century most clearly demonstrates the composer's concession to a strong literary orientation. Although really polyphonic, the writing is to some degree determined by the text. In this respect, Handel straddles the fence very successfully (think particularly of *Israel in Egypt*), and Brahms approaches it in the organ-point fugue of his *Deutsches Requiem*.

(7) Vocalization is the monophonic counterpart, so to speak, of absolute polyphony. Because only one line is involved, the text has a chance to be understood although the music makes no effort to honor it. Melismas on words like "Amen" or "Hallelujah" are entirely musical events. The attempt to reduce the latter by a text underlay, which produced the Gregorian sequences, appears as a literary reaction against the overpowering flow of pure music. Extended coloratura passages in opera arias are equally "nonsensical" and hence most appropriate in Lucia's mad scene. An Alpine yodel is a natural, Ravel's "Vocalise en forme d'Habanera" a self-conscious, expression of sensual musical behavior. Glière wrote a textless Concerto for Soprano and Orchestra.

(8) Absolute polyphony establishes the musical structure with hardly any consideration of textual exigencies. The Netherlands masters, it is well known, composed their superior polyphonic settings of the Mass text without bothering to place the words under the corresponding notes. The problem of text underlay thus finds itself relegated to a secondary role at the mercy of the improvising singer or modern editor. Along the same tradition, a choral fugue is little concerned with the words except in the opening statement of the theme. The piece is generally worked out without much regard for the text which the composer fits afterwards to the notes.

All types are admirably represented in the passions and oratorios by Heinrich Schütz. The recitation often approaches monotone, particularly in the unaccompanied passions. The opening and closing numbers are generally of the best polyphonic texture of the period. The singing characters within the story employ vocal devices in all gradations, from recitativo secco to textually conditioned polyphony.

VOICE

The human voice, a given natural phenomenon, exerts a strong influence on various aspects of musical morphology. Singing is the primary musical activity. Instruments are at first merely "tools" extending the voice. Instrumental music, for millennia before gaining autonomy, intensified or emulated vocal music by doubling. Even in its present state of apparently absolute supremacy, instrumental music can be judged by its relation to the vocal model, that is, the degree and kind of transformation of the norm.

The human voice bears on both growth and limitation. The contribution to growth is fundamental; for breathing, the activity underlying singing, is in effect the physiological symbol of the primordial form of an energetic process. The breathing cycle, in-out-rest, tension-relaxation-balance, is the archetype of all musical morphology. It is the vital form of music found in the details as much as in the whole, in a short melody as well as in a huge symphonic movement. Breathing is an image of life; and just as the life process is composed of ever longer cycles starting with the first inhalation and the following exhalation, so also the morphology of a musical work results from superimposed cycles with ever longer breath. Musical form which does not breathe has no life. Once again our morphological inquiry has led us back to rhythm, of which breathing, made audible and musical by the human voice, is the primary physiological expression.

In a less significant way, the human voice may help mold the timbre ideal of a society. Chinese instruments seem to emulate the guttural tone production characteristic of the Far East; Arabic instruments, the nasal quality of near-Eastern speech; our own violin family, the open projection of bel canto. Because the predilections of Western musicians for various types of instruments have changed through the centuries, one might well draw tentative conclusions as to the particular voice production popular at the time. The instruments, unlike the voices, have been preserved and make us wonder whether the desired vocal quality in the Middle Ages was as raucous as krummhorn and zinc; in the Renaissance, as gentle as lute and viol; in the eighteenth century, as clearly articulated as harpsichord and violin; at present, as aggressive as a brass band.

As an expression of human measure, the voice sets meaningful musical limitations. They all pertain directly to melody, the natural issue of a single voice, but might be applied to wider concepts. Foremost is the length of one breath. It defines the length of a musical event heard as one unit. A melody may be sung on one breath. If it requires more, it is a composite. A melody normally progresses by step, for the vocal cords naturally tighten and relax gradually and not possibly by jumps. In reference to this norm, any melodic skip becomes a particular event. A melody falls within the range of a human voice, that is, a maximum of two octaves but generally an average of a twelfth. By transgressing this range, it risks losing cohesion.

Range, one notes with interest, is heard both relatively and absolutely. Each voice, from soprano down to bass, has its own high, middle, and low regions. Low *c* sung by a soprano will strike us as lying at the bottom; the same absolute pitch sung by a bass, as relatively high. (Munich feels more "southern" in atmosphere than "northern" Milano, though Germany as a whole lies north of Italy.) The four human voices together span a range of about four octaves, equally distributed on either side of middle *c*, which they share. This total area, with its own determination of high and low, is the normal playground of all music, vocal and instrumental, of all styles.

WORD AND TONE

At an early stage of civilization, word and tone were united. The precarious relationship existing today results from their progressive separation. The morphological implications all derive from artistic attempts at reunification.

Evidence of the original union is scant but persuasive. Classical Greek writers, Plato among them, refer to a much earlier, unrecorded stage in which *musiké* designated both music and spoken language because they were one. Homer was still chanted. The dramas by Aeschylus and Sophocles were already relatively late efforts to combine again in a work of art what daily life had cut in two. In this respect, the Greek dramas are actually no different from all later operatic ventures. The influence of melodic inflection on the meaning of words and phrases has stayed alive in the Chinese language in which the tone assigned to a word (*lü*) is one of the determinants of the interpretation. Under circumstances, all modern languages still resort to a similar technique. The difference in meaning among the following four sentences is projected entirely and exclusively by musical devices: "*What* do you mean?" "What *do* you mean?" "What do *you* mean?" "What do you *mean*?" We apply musical intonation to speech in order to emphasize: "Graaaacious meee!" "How daaaare you?" Shakespeare's "Hey nonny, nonny" and "Hey ding a ding, ding," yodel syllables, and many children's chants may be grammatical nonsense; but because of their musical quality they carry meaning and general appeal. When we consider that some words with a clear literary sense like *Hallelujah* ("praise the Lord") and *Amen* ("truth") are generally being used as if they were nonsense syllables, the speculation is tempting that at the beginning of human language all words, in a grammatical sense, were "nonsense" words which established communication only through intonation.

The tradition of the union of word and tone has been well maintained, outside art, by children and by members of Mediterranean cultures (Greek, Sicilian, Spanish, Jewish) whose singsong makes them conspicuous in a sober Anglo-Saxon society. When language separated from music, it became increasingly conceptualized, evolving its own grammatical forms, with the sole object of conveying thought.[1] The high conceptual accomplishments of the English are in inverse proportion to their musical propensities, which are relatively small in the history of composition and almost nonexistent in the monotone inflection of daily speech. An Englishman would be inclined to characterize both the children's chant and the Mediterranean bend as "primitive," thereby unknowingly pointing back to the original ideal state of the united *musiké*.

The act of using a vocable for denotation was probably the initial divider of word and tone. By this act, words per se came into separate existence, and words as sounds became extrinsic to the significance for which we use them. The contents of speech are propositions, expressed according to rules of linguistic grammar and governed by laws of conceptual logic and dialectics. While grammars of different languages reflect specific turns of mind, they are not by themselves a creative force. Linguistic grammar is in a way an extrinsic element. Scholars agree that as long as the objective of conveying a thought is achieved, the machinery of attaining it is of comparatively slight importance.

Musical grammar, on the other hand, is intrinsic. The morphology of music is identical with its grammar. Grammar and expression coincide, are inseparable, and are therefore untranslatable. Music cannot make statements about the outside world. Musical morphology evolves from polarity: generation and limitation of matter. The first concerns principles of continuation; the second, of form proper. These principles show by their very nature their remoteness from principles governing any literary grammar. A cadence (to give an example) in the form of tonic-dominant-tonic is a musical notion of which the acoustical manifestation could be the equivalent of some poetic piece. Whereas, however, in music the acoustical event is identical with its meaning, in poetry the event would have to be expressed by some parallel conceptual construction, essentially divorced from the acoustical aspect notwithstanding the presence of musical elements in the poetry.

Among these elements, rhythm and meter have the same meaning in poetry as in music but different roles. In music they are an intrinsic ingredient of the main happening. In a poetic phrase they are background factors, however noticeable. Melody, too, seems to be shared by speech and music, but speech melody is very remote from musical melody. It is not an artistic accomplishment but, being a continuum, rather raw material of the first order. Speech melody, moreover, is subservient to conceptual meaning, which it may modify but not transgress. Made independent, it produces a comical effect. Musical melody, quite to the contrary, follows inherent artistic laws. Hence the composer's task is not to bring out the stylized speech inflection but rather—not in any material sense—the inner melody of the poem. Made independent of speech melody, musical melody is not comical.

Assonance, alliteration, rhyme, and repetition in language are all musical residues. In Italian (which has remained far more musical than English), intensification of an expression is normally produced, not by the intellectual accomplishment of an adverb or superlative form, but by the musical repeti-

---

[1]Susanne K. Langer treats this question extensively in *New Key*.

tion of the same word: "Piano piano!" "Poco poco!" "Sono convinto convinto!" Repetition and its derivatives variation and transformation, which are structurally fundamental in music, have otherwise no parallels in language. Speech exhibits no tendency to return to its starting point, whereas music favors recurrence and recapitulation. Conceptual discourse appears *"open" and straight compared to musical discourse, which appears "closed" and cyclic. In this regard, as in others, music is closer to architecture than to language.

The reunion of music and language has been the goal of many efforts proper to both arts. In relation to musical morphology, we can distinguish three stages of word-tone combinations, here arranged in the direction of increasing unification. Word and tone may be (1) separate in regard to both time and level; (2) synchronous but on separate levels; or (3) synchronous and on the same level.

To the first class belong instrumental works written on a piece of prose or poetry, provided the literary contribution is an integral artistic part of the whole. Such is the case only if the text is read as part of the performance before or after the music. Concert performances of Mendelssohn's music to *A Midsummer-Night's Dream* with oral reading from the play leading into each number have provided infrequent experiences of this type. Here also belong brief alternations of dialogue and orchestral music, as between Leonore and Rocco in the prison scene of *Fidelio*. When the literary part of the program is not actually recited, the result is *program music as exemplified by the *tone poems of Liszt and Strauss.

The second class produces melodrama, that is, a text spoken to instrumental accompaniment. This is actually the name given by Beethoven to the *Fidelio* scene referred to above, for a few times the characters talk into the music. The history of melodrama has little morphological success to its credit, but the recurrence of such works testifies to the temptation offered by this kind of union—be it Georg Benda's idea in the eighteenth century of writing a whole music drama with spoken words to orchestral accompaniment, Weber's romantic setting of magical incantation in *Der Freischütz*, or Honegger's modern projection of *Jeanne d'Arc au bûcher*.

The third class includes all *vocal music. Here the union of word and tone, from monotone to absolute polyphony, should be regarded as a reinstatement of the pristine unity on the different plane of organized tone, of music. In this respect, vocal music is the most significant of the three stages, just as within the category itself an aria seems a more accomplished union than a dry recitative. Characteristically, the reverse view, which prevailed for a brief moment at the inception of modern *opera, was soon abandoned; and the subsequent triumphant resistance of opera to recurring reproaches of harboring "unnatural" speech confirms our hypothesis that it is the separation of word and tone rather than the union that is fundamentally "unnatural."

The existence of the various types of vocal music can best be tested by empathy with the composer's task. He has to decide a priori whether to dissolve a piece of poetry into prose; write a monophonic or polyphonic composition; etc. By reciting a given text, we can fix the rhythm and then compare it together with the speech melody to the actual setting of the text by a master composer. The transition from monotone to cantillation reveals a great deal. If, for instance, people gather and speak together the same text, as in prayer, they soon strive to unite on a tone. Conditions of phrasing and breathing produce inflections. As soon as melodic bits assert themselves, the relation of purely musical laws to those of logical grammar creates a new situation. Plainchant supplies a wealth of examples on various levels—from simple psalm tones to complex graduals and alleluias.

Vocal music has dealt with the incompatibilities of word and tone by way of compromise. In a *lied* with undisputed supremacy of music over poetry, the compromise is small. The history of opera and oratorio, on the other hand, basically one of a competition for ascendancy, bears witness to all possible proportions compromise may achieve.

In a famous essay on the Laocoön statue, Gotthold Ephraim Lessing has investigated the relation of poetry to the visual arts. One of the legitimate questions he asked and answered concerned the possibility of one art behaving in terms of the other. How can a picture tell a story in time? How can words describe an object in space? We may similarly ask: how does a writer proceed when he desires to express musical experiences? What can a musician do to convey intellectual concepts? There are examples in answer to both questions. Walter Pater has stipulated that all arts aspire to the state of music. James Joyce carried this aspiration to an extreme, notably in *Finnegans Wake*, by destroying, or at least violating, the logic of linguistic grammar and syntax. Richard Wagner developed his leitmotiv technique by conditioning his listener to associate certain ideas with certain musical phrases so that the latter eventually seemed to become independent carriers of the former. Yet no musical forms can be built through the literary logic of leitmotivs. Whatever Wagner's theories about the reunion in his operas of word and tone, his music flourishes in the concert hall, whereas attempts to perform his libretti as spoken plays have failed. His operas may thus be one-way affairs. Wagner's life work, however, must be properly evaluated as one more serious effort in the perennial artistic desire to return to the perfect union of word and tone in the magical *musiké*.

Cf. *Aria, *Matter and Form, *Opera, *Oratorio, *Program Music, *Strophe, *Through-Composed, *Vocal Music.

APPENDIXES

A. Illustrations

MELODY

Mozart, Piano Sonata, A major, K. 331, first movement, theme.

Only the melody is under consideration. For our special purpose, we shall refer to the harmonic accompaniment as supporting, but not as primary, evidence. Every melodic analysis can proceed from an ontic or gignetic viewpoint. We shall attempt to do justice to both, one after the other. Far from contradicting each other, the two methods are complementary and occasionally may overlap.

Considered ontically, the melody unfolds in time the tonic scale of A major. The first half of the melody deals with the stretch from dominant down to tonic; the middle section, with the inversion from dominant up to tonic; and the recapitulation together with the two-measure coda combines and summarizes all preceding drives.

The tonic triad as unfolded by the melody is a main shaping factor. It supplies structural strong points between which the melody has free play. Third and fifth of the triad define the initial level of operation (m. 1). The arrival of the prime at the end of the antecedent is tentative (mm. 3 and 4), that at the end of the consequent more conclusive (mm. 7 and 8). The middle section supplies the missing octave; the accomplishment is marked by the only grace notes in the entire melody (m. 10). The following sforzato phrases prepare the recapitulation by insisting on the pitch level of the beginning. The recapitulation itself arrives at an imperfect cadence (m. 16) which thereby makes possible the brief coda (mm. 17 and 18). The coda summarizes and completes the whole melodic experience. It contains the entire tonic scale anchored by the favored tones of the triad.

Considered gignetically, the melody grows as we hear it from beginning to end. The limitation is built in by the rules and conditions of the given style, which is presupposed to be known. The hearer follows the drive of two parallel lines—one starting on the third degree of the scale, the other on the fifth—down to the tonic. The goal, always before one's ears, is satisfactorily reached only at the very end.

The opening c^1-sharp "quivers" in a rhythmic mordent; the neighboring dissonance d^1 suffices to push the line up to e^1. The melodic "plot" of the theme consists of the attraction exercised by the fundamental a on the starting c^1-sharp. The forceful turn toward e^1 in the first measure widens the field and creates a secondary drive from e^1 down to a.

By sequence, the two lines move toward the tonic (m. 2). The accomplishment of reaching a is only partial (m. 3)—the deceptive cadence corroborating the incompleteness—for the upper line, abandoned on d^1, has to be retrieved. The remainder of the phrase does so and, reiterating more rapidly the original descents, falls one step short of the final resolution. Metrically, the first major punctuation is reached; harmonically, the dominant.

The next four-measure phrase repeats the effort, out of rhythmic rather than melodic necessity. A final A major chord after the first phrase might answer the melodic, but certainly not the rhythmic, play of forces. The respective first two measures are identical. The retrieving of the dangling d^1 is now attempted with the greater urgency of an acceleration; and the time gain is used to end the line by a perfect authentic cadence. But the force away from the center (m. 7) has left d^1, by retrieving it, dangling on a dissonant and accented fourth against the tonic, so that the secondary resolution toward e^1 is missing at the end of the period. Here is more proof for the prevalent role of rhythm in determining the shape of the piece. Melodically, an appoggiatura e^1 before d^1, as at the end of the first four-measure phrase, would satisfy the drives of both lines to the tonic. The omission of e^1 and the resulting "shock" on d^1 at the end of the second four-measure phrase are obviously deliberate and ancillary to the rhythmic need for continuation. The two quasi-parallel strophes of the first half, like thesis and antithesis, demand a rhythmically equivalent synthesis.

The four measures after the double bar—a contrasting middle section before the recapitulation—amply supply the omitted e^1 in a kind of pedal. The curve of the first two measures reflects the main task of leading e^1 by step to the tonic, but it does so away from the actual center of gravity to the upper octave a^1. The ambitus of a fifth outlined by the first half of the theme is thus widened to the octave. Together with the starting point on the major third, these three delimitative tones derive from the harmonic force of the triad, which thus appears unfolded in time. Below the pedal e^1, the middle voice, in the guise of an arpeggio, harks back to the initial motive ($c^1\sharp$-d^1-$c^1\sharp$-b in mm. 11–12) and thereby skillfully prepares the recapitulation.

The recapitulation follows the path of the antistrophe (mm. 5–8) rather than that of the opening strophe in order to leave an opening for the two-measure coda. This task is strengthened by the turn back to an imperfect cadence (m. 16) in addition to the abrupt marking of d^1 (m. 15).

The length of the coda is determined by the metric unit pervading the whole piece. The new dynamic level (*forte*) distinguishes the emphatic summary statement from the main body. The summary is precise. The tone c^1-sharp yields to the attraction of the tonic a first by the detour to the higher octave and finally by reconciling the ascending and descending drives in the octave outline of the tonal field. The last three notes, like a coda to the coda, present the essence of the whole melody in its most concise form.

Gregorian Chant: Missa III, Kyrie I.

In contrast to the classic melody by Mozart, characterized by a highly individual head motive, here continuation technique proceeds from a relatively indefinite seed. The permanent element in the chant lies in a raga behind the apparent forms. The raga continues to bring forth new melodic motives which, however, never reach the definiteness of the classic theme. In the following table, which concerns the first Kyrie exclamation, letters refer to the parentage and kinship of motives:

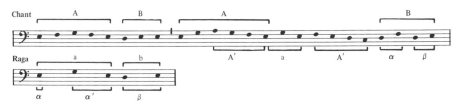

Relation	Constant Element	Variant
A-A	Gesture	Intensity (amplitude)
B-B	Gesture	Intensity (amplitude plus combination $\alpha\beta$)
A'-A'	Gesture	Pitch
A-a	Gesture	Reduction to raga, dovetailing A'α'
B-β	Gesture	Reduction to raga

MULTIPARTITE

Schubert's *Die schöne Müllerin* is a unified entity formed of twenty songs. It has a plot with a definite beginning and end. It has a basic key generating unity and cohesion, although the tonic, by a legitimate device of romantic suggestiveness, is at first obscured. If we recognize the first song in B-flat major as a prelude, and the last song in E major as a postlude, the closed tonality of G major becomes apparent. The two songs on the outside (nos. 1 and 20) contain and share certain qualities that justify their somewhat detached position. Each is built in five strophes; the quintuple repetition of exactly the same melody to changing words minimizes the effect of personal involvement. The only reference in the prelude to the hero is confined to an incidental sentence in the last strophe which serves as an introductory link to the main plot. In the postlude, the impersonal character is even more pronounced, for the hero is dead and no longer the narrator as before. The analogous roles of prelude and postlude are precisely expressed by their key relationships, for B-flat major is as far below the tonic of G major as E major is above it. The crossing of modes, symptomatic of romantic harmony, permits the interpretation of these two apparently distant keys as tonic substitutes (B-flat major = tR of G minor; E major = TrP of G major).

The main structure of the whole work now emerges as a double arc, stretching from the beginning of the hero's journey (no. 2, in the tonic) across the central triumph (no. 11, in the dominant) to the hero's tragic end (no. 19, back in the tonic). The central song is the only one in the dominant, and it is the climax of the plot ("Mein!").[1]

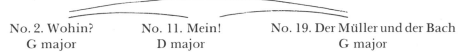

No. 2. Wohin?	No. 11. Mein!	No. 19. Der Müller und der Bach
G major	D major	G major

[1]Most performers, instinctively, make a short intermission after this song. The title of the following song, "Pause," bears them out.

Each half can again be architecturally subdivided, as shown in the following table:

No.	Title	Key	Harmonic Function	
			Specific	*General*
2.	Wohin?	G	T	T
3.	Halt!	C	S	S
4.	Danksagung an den Bach	G	T	T
5.	Am Feierabend	a	Sr	S
6.	Der Neugierige	B	(D)Tr	D
7.	Ungeduld	A	DD (or SrP)	S
8.	Morgengruss	C	S	S
9.	Des Müllers Blumen	A	DD (or SrP)	S
10.	Tränenregen	A-a	DD (or SrP)-Sr	S
11.	Mein!	D	D	D
12.	Pause	B-flat	tR	T
13.	Mit dem grünen Lautenbande	B-flat	tR	T
14.	Der Jäger	c	s	S
15.	Eifersucht und Stolz	g-G	t-T	T
16.	Die liebe Farbe	b	Dr	D
17.	Die böse Farbe	B-b	(D)Tr-Dr	D
18.	Trockne Blumen	e-E	Tr-TrP	T
19.	Der Müller und der Bach	g-G	t-T	T

The indicated caesuras are produced tonally as well as dramatically. The harmonic flow breaks after "Der Neugierige"; there is no direct link from the vicarious dominant function of the high, isolated B major to the fresh subdominant start of the following song. At the same time, the plot, too, turns from the hero's introspective desires and his dialogues with the brook to an outgoing pursuit and eventual conquest of the beloved. The case is clearer still in the second half where after the single cadence in the tonic proper ("Eifersucht und Stolz") the hero, yielding to the rival hunter, relinquishes his hold on the girl and falls back into self-destructive introversion.

The four sections, which thus form the substructure of the large vault across the composition, reveal an internal architecture of their own. Each section is in barform, the general principle executed with fine differentiation at each occurrence.

In the first section, the analogy of strophe (nos. 2, 3) and antistrophe (nos. 4, 5) is given by the reiterated drive from tonic to subdominant, crowned only in the epode (no. 6) by the intensifying cadential step to the dominant. The tonal structure reflects that of the plot. Strophe and antistrophe each turn from an idealized conversation with the brook to an actual encounter with a concrete object. The advanced complexity of the antistrophe is manifested by the vicarious use of the minor subdominant relative for the clear and major subdominant as well as by the hero's promotion from beholding the mill to beholding the maid of the mill. The epode of the whole section gains its weight from the isolated dominant function of the five sharps and from the crucial tension of the poetic situation.

The architecture of the second section follows similar lines. Strophe (nos. 7, 8) and antistrophe (nos. 9, 10) move in parallel from the second dominant to the subdominant (C major) and its relative (A minor). Simultaneously the plot drives the hero, within each strophe, from a romantic message transmitted by nature to his beloved toward a personal conversation with the girl. The antistrophe shows progress against the strophe by the same modal relationship as encountered in the first section (cf. nos. 3 and 5 with 8 and 10) and by the hero's coincident change from a serenader standing beneath a window to a lover sitting with his sweetheart under a tree. The epode (no. 11) cannot be missed: the climactic exaltation at the conquest is obvious.

The parallelism between these first two sections makes them act on each other like strophe and antistrophe:

STROPHE (NOS. 2–6)   ANTISTROPHE (NOS. 7–11)

Strophe   *Strophe*
  2. Guide me, brook . . . . . . T   7. Help me, nature . . . . . DD
  3. I see the mill . . . . S   8. I greet the girl . . . . S

Antistrophe   *Antistrophe*
  4. Thank you, brook . . . . T   9. Help me, flowers . . . . DD
  5. I see the girl . . . . Sr   10. I hold the girl . . . . Sr

Epode   *Epode*
  6. Does she love me? . . (D)Tr   11. She is mine . . . . D

The flow of tonality in the first large strophe (nos. 2–6) can best be grasped as a cadence T-S-D. It serves primarily the clear establishment of the tonic or, in poetic terms, of the basic mood. Any ambiguity that may have arisen from the romantically veiled function of the prelude (no. 1) is dispelled by the emphatic reiteration of the first half of the cadence, which contains the tonic proper. The whole section breaks off on a half-cadence, the dominant question (no. 6) leaving an opening for the continuation of the plot.

The large antistrophe (nos. 7–11) develops the dissonant elements of the cadence. The tonic is completely absent, and the polar step S-D is fully exploited by a lingering in the subdominant realm. What the subdominant means in the poetic context of the whole work can perhaps be educed from the fact that precisely the songs in the subdominant and its relative (nos. 3, 5, 8, and 10) deal with the maid of the mill, whereas all other songs refer to her at best indirectly in the hero's dialogues with nature. The single recurrence of the subdominant together with the rival hunter (no. 14, "Der Jäger") in the second half of the work reinforces the particular emotional impact of this group of keys. They lead to the greatest tension of the dominant "Mein!" on which the antistrophe ends.

In relation to these two large strophes, the second half (nos. 12–19) acts as a balancing epode and thus helps us hear the whole as a perfect barform. The epode matches the combined strophes not merely in length: it contains the development—commencing exactly with the change of fortune—of the initial complication. Harmonically, the epode initiates the return to the tonic, which the hero had forsaken in his dissonant pursuit of love. The restfulness of the tonic is what he now strives for: first in vicarious keys (nos. 12, 13), and then—after a taste of it in his first acute loneliness (no. 15, G)—ever closer, through the last colorful flickering of former emotions (nos. 16, 17, dominant) toward the final resolution and death (nos. 18 ff.).

In the architecture of the epode, the two distinguishable sections (nos. 12–15 and 16–19) divide the cadential burden among themselves. The subdominant is discharged in the first (no. 14), and the dominant in the second (nos. 16, 17). Barform influences the internal structure of each section, as shown below:

Strophe
12. The silent lute hangs on the wall. } same keys, similar ideas

Antistrophe
13. She wants the green ribbon of the lute. }

Epode
14. The hunter is pursuing her. } new keys, new situation
15. The hunter has won her. }

From here on, the subdominant realm is forever abandoned:

Strophe
16. Green is a good color. } same keys, similar ideas

Antistrophe
17. Green is a bad color. }

Epode
18. Death appears desirable. } new keys, new situation
19. Suicide. }

POLYPHONY

A polyphonic piece is such a complex creation that one may be allowed to speculate on the manner in which the morphé of a polyphonic piece may come to life in the hearer. What does a musical person of average perceptivity and knowledge experience when hearing, for example, for the first time a piece like the "Confiteor" from Bach's Mass in B minor?

Like the composer, the hearer must know the text before dealing with the music. This sentence of the Credo (and we need pursue our inquiry only through the first sentence, that is, until the new "Et expecto" section) is neither lyric nor dramatic. Musically rather uninspiring, it states a particular dogma. A composer can treat such an unpromising text by relying on the virtue of musical structure and its symbolism. Bach chose polyphonic fabric as particularly well suited for symbolizing the ontic quality conveyed by the "Confiteor" sentence.

As the hearer follows the music, he is likely to notice and distinguish two melodies or at least their characteristic inceptions. They are introduced separately of each other, one at the very beginning (mm. 1–3) and the other at the first waning of sound (mm. 16–17). In their frequent returns thereafter (which the hearer should try to spot), both melodies are always coupled and projected simultaneously. Little by little the hearer will come to recognize that these two melodies are "what the piece is about." They are used as "themes" or "subjects." If he presently notices that the themes always enter successively in different voices, the piece might remind him of a fugue (of which he need not know more than that it is an imitative structure characterized by one or more than one subject).

One more feature may become perceptible at first hearing, but much depends on the clarity of the performance and the listener's prior knowledge of Gregorian melody. A cantus firmus appears, first in canon between bass and alto (mm. 73–88) and then in duple augmentation in the tenor (mm. 92–118). This is about as much as a fresh listener of average training and knowledge will be able to follow.

In retrospect, the listener will be left with an impression of unity, disturbed only by an occasional waning and waxing of sound due to the reduction and increase of the number of parts sung simultaneously. The oscillation is particularly apparent at the first rarefactions (mm. 16 and 32). The simultaneity of events has made it very difficult for the listener to perceive and comprehend the inner polyphonic happenings. He therefore holds on to, or takes refuge in, the simplest aspect, the musical "skin." The surface tension generated by the "Confiteor" hides the basic multiplicity from the listener, who perceives instead a "Oneness," at least as a spontaneous impression.

How much more will he perceive at a second hearing? At a third? Does study of the score become necessary? The answers to such questions fall into place when we realize that perception in musical morphology is to be treated, not in behavioristic terms (as it is in psychology), but rather in teleological. The objective, the *telos*, is personal identification with the composer's intentions. Such sympathy and resonance demand, sooner or later, understanding of grammar and technical implications. The conditions for this kind of perception cannot always be met by "naïve" hearing, least of all in the case of a dense polyphonic fabric. The need for perception by study explains the immense importance of notation in the whole history of Western music. But whereas elsewhere the intellectual pleasure of discovery is the last term of the process, in music it is only preparatory to the experience of hearing. Knowledge and insight must be transferred to musical instinct. They must serve as nourishment and education of musicality, transforming everything we learn about music into processes and states of the musical mind. To achieve true musical understanding, we must try to hear what we know is there.

Pursuing the "Confiteor," our hearer perceives next—through repeated hearing and study—the contrapuntal relationship of the two subjects. Their respective expositions stretch in succession over a period of 32 measures, the second subject entering at the halfway point. It exhibits two notable features. First, it is a countersubject, as one learns from the consistently recurring contrapuntal combinations of both subjects after the initial separate exposition. Second, it is the second half of a larger melody which emerges as a whole when both subjects are heard in succession.

Subject and countersubject thus belong to each other in space as well as in time. The morphology of polyphony is spatial, manifested through the simultaneity of happenings. The morphology of homophony is temporal, manifested through the succession of happenings. The contrapuntal combination of both subjects is a polyphonic phenomenon. The separate exposition of both subjects is a homophonic phenomenon. Multiplicity and unity are here perfectly interwoven.

In polyphonic compositions, metric organization is aesthetically far less important than spatial organization; for meter belongs primarily to homophony. One nevertheless becomes aware of main temporal divisions, especially as they concern the harmonic flow. A noticeable signpost is the interruption of the heretofore steady bass motion by an organ point (mm. 69–72). It indicates an important structural point, for immediately afterward the cantus firmus sets in. The next significant and obvious metric event is a change of tempo that marks the end of the section under consideration (Adagio, m. 121). Regularity of metrically determined periods is observable only at the beginning of the piece, in the double exposition of 2×16 measures. Elsewhere the length of periods is blurred and modified by imitative polyphony, which cancels them as relevant aesthetic factors. Duration is determined by what happens in the voices of the polyphonic texture. Consider, for instance, the time spent on one complete entrance by all voices. At the very beginning, soprano II and tenor enter in narrow stretto; alto and bass, in wider stretto. All voices have appeared after seven measures. At the beginning of the section in double counterpoint (mm. 31 ff.), the entrances of the first subject follow each other at equal time spans but only in four out of the five voices. All voices have appeared after ten measures. Evidently the particular technique of imitation accounts for these durations. The length of the cantus firmus section (mm. 73 ff.) is determined by the cantus firmus itself and by the pauses separating the phrases. The pauses allow the development of the two-part canon while safeguarding the clarity of the melody fragments. Later (mm. 92 ff.) the cantus firmus—this time without canon—is sung by the tenor in duple augmentation, the pauses less affected than the notes. Again the polyphonic procedure, not the meter, determines the length of the section.

In a few instances in which four-measure periods assert themselves, polyphony submits to the metric force by assuming a more blocklike aspect. The organ point mentioned earlier (mm. 69–72) and the four-measure unit leading into it (mm. 65–68) illustrate the situation, as does the passage between the two cantus firmus sections (mm. 88–91). In each case, the metric surge heralds an important structural change.

Harmonically the "Confiteor" section under discussion maintains the key of F-sharp minor throughout. No real modulation occurs. The unified key contributes greatly toward the impression of "motionless strength." Only in the first measure of the Adagio section, the music begins to modulate toward D major, the key of the following "Et expecto" section (Vivace ed allegro). Within the overall harmonic immobility, however, there is relentless motion and continued variety—a conjunction of opposites as fascinating as sea waves rolling onto the shore or flames playing in a fireplace. In all these instances, one perceives movement within an overall permanency.

The instrumental bass conveys a similar impression. Within the polyphony of the piece, it is the lowest voice. While in this regard identical with the choral bass, it differs from it in the following significant details. As a true basso continuo, the instrumental bass continues through the pauses of the vocal bass. It moves in a steady quarter-note pulse and consequently presents a variation on the underlying, more slowly moving harmonic bass. In relation to the choral bass, this variation by the instrumental bass frequently assumes the character of heterophony. The changing relationship between the two basses—now diverging, now converging, now reinforcing each other by identification—produces a great variety of energy constellations. A comparison of parallel passages provides an inkling of these shadings (cf. mm. 1–5 and 31–35; 7–11 and 57–61; 16–18 and 31–33; etc.).

A study of the fugal structure itself would overstep the limits we have assigned ourselves. Within these limits, the cantus firmus attracts further attention. The leading voice in the canon is the vocal bass (mm. 73 ff.). During the canon, the instrumental bass is independent to the point of forming a sixth voice. The sole brief unison of the two basses (mm. 82–83) emphasizes the culmination of the cantus firmus melody. Otherwise the cantus firmus remains isolated from the orchestra bass. The notion of isolation illuminates a general characteristic of cantus firmus technique. The cantus firmus, here as in other pieces, is isolated from the rest of the structure by solemnly slow and regular motion; by pauses that seem to divide the melody in phrases but actually increase cohesion by generating suspense; and by the newness of material not heard earlier within the composition. The introduction of a traditional melody supposed to be known by the listener renders the newness within a piece all the more striking. (The "Confiteor" melody is taken from the second Gregorian Credo.) The isolation of the cantus firmus divides the polyphonic fabric in two contrasting layers: one in which the Gregorian chant is used, and one in which it is not. Multiplicity results from this absence of material unity. The impression of artistic unity nonetheless gained by the hearer arises from several factors. The cantus firmus fills the last portion of the piece, stopping just before the Adagio. It begins just at the moment after which monotony might threaten, which it prevents by being new. It contains an increase of intensity on its path from canon to augmentation, from multiplicity to unity. The augmentation by a single voice also shifts the focus to the Gregorian melody so that the fugal polyphony, though unabated, recedes into the background. The cantus firmus is thus felt to be a hymnic conclusion and a kind of hieratic confirmation of a text entirely subordinated to the word "Confiteor," "I confess." The unity of the fugal structure and that of the cantus firmus merge on the higher level of signification.

PROGRAM MUSIC

Les Préludes by Liszt was inspired by a piece of poetically meditative prose by Lamartine. Life is regarded as "a series of preludes to that unknown chant of which death sounds the first solemn note." The thought, apart from setting a general mood of seriousness, is musically barren. Subsequent text phrases, however, denoting a life pattern of man, admit of analogical treatment. They pertain to love at the dawn of youth; storms and blows of destiny interrupting and destroying the enchantment; man seeking to heal his wounds in pastoral surroundings; and the call to life's battles which alone enable him to develop fully the consciousness of his power and to realize his potentialities. In Liszt's version, this succession of love, storms, pastoral, and struggle for self-realization is preceded by the introduction of the "self," the subject of the inner biography. The dramatic sections, "storms" and "life's battles," correspond to the nineteenth-century notion of development. The two other elements, "love" and "pastoral," contribute lyrical contrasts.

We are presented with a sonata in one movement. The layout is less complex than that of the B minor Sonata (cf. pp. 321 f.) but the idea is the same. One hears a purely musical sonata structure of which the contrasting middle movements are embedded in an all-pervasive development, and of which the finale coincides with the recapitulation. The slow movement proper is missing but adequately intimated (Un poco più moderato) just before the scherzo (Allegretto pastorale). The following table outlines the structure:

Introduction	"Seed" motive: Andante.
Exposition	Theme Ia (first shape): Andante maestoso.
	Theme Ib (second shape): L'istesso tempo.
	Theme II (E major): Espressivo ma tranquillo.
Development	Allegro ma non troppo.
Scherzo	Allegretto pastorale.
Recapitulation	Reentry of Theme II (m. 260).
	Theme Ia: Allegro maestoso.

The introduction lets us witness the birth of musical shapes from a seed. Even the seemingly new brass theme in the development (mm. 161 ff.) is the result of transformation:

The pastoral section assumes development character when Theme II joins it. The recapitulation, taking the place of the finale, also continues the development. The rising tension and excitement presage an impending climax, reached when Themes Ib and II return transformed as martial tunes (Allegro marziale animato). The final apotheosis sounds a varied recapitulation of Theme Ia (Allegro maestoso).

RHYTHM AND METER

Schubert, Moment musical op. 94 no. 5.

The piece follows almost throughout the crustic rhythm inhalation-exhalation, ♩ ♪♪ . It is a bouncing, not a striking, rhythm. In order to project the meaning and not to sound pedestrian, one should play the quarter note staccato rather than tenuto.

After the metric regularity of the first eight measures, the next phrase contains six measures (9–14). They may be interpreted either gignetically as a psychological prolongation (metric ritardando) or ontically as a structural *ritmo di tre battute* (metric ritenuto). This latter alternative gains support by the following seven-measure phrase (15–21) which obeys a *ritmo di tre battute*; a metric ritardando prolongs the last two measures to three.

In the coda, rhythm conflicts with dynamics. The *fortissimo* explosions all fall on weak measures. The last of these (m. 110) in addition performs a leap realizing the potential suggested by the earlier outbursts. The result sounds humorous. The two-times-four measures opening the coda (99–106) are subsequently reduced to twice two measures—a metric accelerato. The silent measure added to the final two-measure phrase suggests a metrical ritenuto.

In the course of the piece, the otherwise persisting rhythm undergoes two sorts of change. The first occurs together with the first *fortissimo* (mm. 15 ff.). The quarter notes are to be understood in the sense of exhalations (E). The new rhythm, implicitly anacrustic, reverses the main rhythm. The second change takes place in the middle section (mm. 34 ff.). The rhythm here is levelled and reduced to neutrality. The preceding rhythmic persistence produces an "afterimage" that the listener superimposes on the neutral motion. Accordingly perception turns from pneumatic to kinetic experience as actual rhythm is transformed into potential rhythm.

Johann Strauss, Frühlingsstimmen-Walzer.

Whereas in the preceding example by Schubert melody is subordinated to rhythm, here the melody is largely independent of the main waltz rhythm. The melody dominates the hearer's conscious attention, which seldom needs to focus upon the underlying continuity of the rhythm.

Phrasing emerges from the breathing patterns of the various melodic periods. One distinguishes several layers:

(a) Actual breathing rhythm: unconscious, quiet, regular, dissociated.

(b) Macro-rhythm: conscious mental breathing, in focus.

(c) Micro-rhythms: out of focus, subordinated.

(d) Meter: almost subconscious.

The following analysis deals with characteristic passages.[1]

Measures

1–4 (1–4)   ♩ 𝄾 ♫ | ♩ 𝄾 etc.   Crustic. The last eighth note in the measure is an anticipation of I.

5–8 (5–8)   ♪ | ♩ 𝄾 𝄾 | etc.   Anacrustic waltz rhythm. On a "vulgar" level, purely metrical: | ♩ ♩ ♩ | etc. The intended "refined" meaning: | ♩ ♩ ♩ ♩ ♩ ♩ | etc. This true waltz rhythm is coupled with a slight agogic shortening of the first beat and a concomitant lengthening of the second beat. It may become more neutral when the foreground is occupied by an independent melody, as in measures 9–10.

9–16 (9–16)   ♫ | | | ♩ 𝄾 ♪ | | | ♩. | ♩ 𝄾 ♫ | The rhythm is almost neutral, with only a slight tendency toward accentuation of I at the beginning of measure 11 (= C). Note the approximate proportion of I : E (+ R) = 3 : 5.

33–35 (33–35)   ♩. 𝄾 𝄾 ♪ | ♩. 𝄾 𝄾 ♪ | ♩   Anacrustic micro-rhythm.

37–39 (37–39)   ♩ ♪ 𝄾 ♪ 𝄾 | ♪ 𝄾 𝄾 ♪ 𝄾 | ♩   Confirmation of the preceding change from crustic to anacrustic rhythm.

40–44 (40–44)   ♩ 𝄾 ♩ | ♩ ♩ | etc.   Crustic.

[1] The first set of measure numbers refers to the piano version dedicated to Alfred Grünfeld by Johann Strauss; the second, to the orchestra version published by Eulenburg. AC = Anacrustic. C = Crustic. E = Exhalation. I = Inhalation. R = Rest.

45–47 (45–47)

53–56 (53–56)   changes to —an inversion of micro-rhythm AC to C. Against the metrical behavior of the actual anacrustic rhythm: the hemiola syncopation should be accentuated:

.

93–102 (127–36)

125–31 (165–71)   sim.

160–67 (186–93)   etc.

173 ff. (198 ff.)   etc.

201–6 (226–31)

SONATA

Franz Liszt's Piano Sonata in B minor, of 1853, is a continuous piece lacking the usual division by movements. The result is transformation of the model set by Beethoven. In attitude, the structure remains classic; in detail, it sounds romantic. The inherent dramatism of sonata form had admitted a dialectical principle. Beethoven still distributed this dramatism across a number of separate movements. Liszt took the next step by treating the movements as stations in a continuous dialectical process.

In his Piano Sonata, the dramatic idea has taken hold of the whole work. Sonata form, once restricted to one movement, now identifies the overall structure. One hears one huge development in which the lyrical parts lie embedded. In this "drama played without interruption," the finale becomes identical with the recapitulation. This arrangement provides the possibility of letting the slow movement and the scherzo become functions of the development section. In fact, all parts of the sonata have become functions of development, which begins immediately in the exposition and extends through the recapitulation. The climax coincides with the beginning of the recapitulation (as in many Beethoven works). The overall plan is outlined in the following diagram:

Exposition	Theme Ia (motto): Lento assai.
	Theme I: Allegro energico.
	Theme Ib: Grandioso.
	Theme II (transformation of part of Theme I):
	Cantando espressivo.
Development	Fortissimo after cadenza.
Slow Movement	Andante sostenuto—Quasi Adagio.
Scherzo	Allegro energico (fugato).
Recapitulation	Theme I: First fortissimo after fugato.
	Theme Ib: 3/2 accentuato il Canto.
	Theme II: Cantando espressivo.
Stretta	Quasi Presto—Presto—Prestissimo.
"Catastrophe"	Theme Ib: 3/2 fff.
Conclusion	Andante sostenuto (material from slow movement).
	Allegro moderato (material from Theme I).
	Lento assai (motto).

The sections are interrelated by variation technique. In the place of the second theme, for instance, one hears a transformation of part of the first theme. This shift of emphasis from being to becoming makes one perceive themes, not as immutable personalities, but as fleeting appearances of hidden shaping forces.

VARIATION

In order to become a form, an otherwise loose set of variations must be limited by some governing principle. The following five variation works by Beethoven exemplify various procedures.

Six Easy Variations on a Swiss Song, WoO 64.

Even the simplest set obeys a formative principle. The exact center is marked by a turn to the minor mode. This particular variation, moreover, is the only one repeating a section; it thereby exceeds all others in length. Around the center, the theme and remaining variations group themselves in obvious symmetry.

Fifteen Variations (with Fugue) for Piano, E-flat major, op. 35.

After the introduction, obvious caesuras marking off three sections occur

322

before the turn to the minor mode in Variation 14 and before the closing fugue. The resulting structure can be interpreted as a three-movement sonata according to the following diagram:

Introduction	Introduzione col Basso del Tema.
First Movement	Tema. Variations 1–14.
Middle Movement	Minore—Maggiore. Largo.
Finale	Alla Fuga.

By hearing subdivisions in the long "first movement" after Variation 3 (the temporary goal of a steadily increasing momentum) and Variation 7 (canonic climax), one may be tempted to distinguish a sonata-form exposition (Variations 1–3), development section (4–7), transition (8), and recapitulation (9–13).[1]

One may also speculate that the entire work suggests the possibility of a one-movement sonata (as later realized by Liszt; cf. pp 321 f.). In such a structure, the two middle movements take the place of the development:

Exposition	Theme I: Basso del Tema.
	Theme II: Tema. Variations 1–7.
Development	Transition: Variation 8.
	Scherzo: Variations 9–13.
	Slow Movement: Minore—Maggiore. Largo.
Recapitulation	Finale. Alla Fuga.
	Theme I: Allegro con brio.
	Theme II: Andante con moto.

Symphony No. 3, finale.

These variations are a slightly later version of the Fifteen Variations for Piano just discussed. The themes are identical. The symphonic movement, now avowedly continuous, limits the variation set most audibly by symmetry:

Introduction. G minor runs.
   Theme and Variations. E-flat major.
      Fugato.
         Center. G minor march.
      Fugato.
   Theme and Variations. E-flat major.
Coda. G minor runs.

This structure approaches sonata form if one hears the first fugato as initiating the development section, and the climactic statement of the melodic theme in the bass (mm. 381 ff.) as marking the recapitulation.

---

[1]Fischer, "Eroica-Variationen."

33 Variations on a Waltz by Diabelli, op. 120.

Just as in each of the three poems of thirty-three cantos that describe, in turn, Hell, Purgatory, and Paradise, Dante endows with special significance the central position of the seventeenth canto, so Beethoven clearly marks no. 17 of his 33 Diabelli Variations as the fulcrum about which the entire variation set moves. Overall symmetry is projected by balance between the first ten and the last ten variations, and between the remaining two inner groups:

10 Variations——7 Variations	‖	6 Variations——10 Variations
(1–10)　　　　(11–17)		(18–23)　　　　(24–33)

The correspondence is not merely numerical; there are strong parallelisms between the groups.[1] Each of the outer sets (1–10 and 24–33) moves with increasing momentum toward a climax, which is preceded by a deviation into a different key (9 and 29–32). The parallelism between the two inner two sets is outlined in the following diagram:

11 ⎫	slow	
12 ⎬	similar mood	18
13	very fast	19
14	slow, subdued, imitative	20
15 ⎫		⎧ 21
16 ⎬	scherzo leading to virtuoso climax	⎨ 22
17 ⎭		⎩ 23

Symphony No. 9, finale

The complexity of this movement as well as of the literature about it serves us to make one single point: there are different, but not necessarily mutually exclusive, possibilities of interpreting the morphological limitations of a piece. The presence of a structure in the finale of the Ninth Symphony is beyond need of proof or discussion. The kind of structure one hears depends on one's recognition of the limiting principles.

(1)　Under the impact of the human voice, one may consider the opening, purely instrumental section (mm. 1–207) as a transition from the third to the last movement and a dramatic anticipation of the main vocal structure. Disregarding this introductory section, one hears the five following vocal variations (until m. 594) as a unit comparable to sonata form:

Exposition
3 variations, D major (mm. 241–330)	Tonic key area
Turkish March, B-flat major (mm. 331–431)	Foreign key area

Development
Orchestral fugato (mm. 431–542)	Return modulation

[1]Cf. Porter, "Diabelli Variations." An excellent bibliography on the topic can be found in Geiringer, "Diabelli Variations."

Recapitulation
   Choral variation, D major, fortissimo
    (mm. 545–94)   Tonic key area

Such an interpretation, far from being the only one, is entirely licit. Every historic period is characterized by a particular notion of form to which each individual form relates. In the finale under discussion, sonata form, the ruling concept in Beethoven's time, is not actually present, but its contours are. To become aware of it one need only imagine the totally different entelechy a comparable composition born a hundred years earlier would have presented.

In a symphonic perspective, one then hears the following Andante maestoso ("Seid umschlungen"), set off by tempo and key, as a second, slow movement. The return to D major and to the first theme (mm. 655 ff.) initiates the symphonic finale. These three sections (or "movements" in the terms of this particular interpretation) are so obvious that nobody giving the whole finale any thought can miss them. Differences arise only from the assumptions which lead one to establish relationships.

(2) Against the background of sonata form and sonata, one may also hear these same three sections as a continuous one-movement symphony—an organization later followed by Liszt in his Piano Sonata in B minor (cf. Appendix A, pp. 321 f.). Guided by the principle of "continuous development," one accepts the first three choral variations as the exposition; the Turkish March, as the scherzo; the Andante maestoso, as the slow movement; and the return to D major, as the overall recapitulation and synthesis. With this solution in mind, one recognizes morphologically parallel functions for the two fugal sections—one instrumental (mm. 431–542) and the other choral (mm. 655–762)—featuring classical development techniques.

Such an interpretation is worth considering if only to provide a perspective by no means foreign to the whole. The perspective brings to light the real ambiguities in the functions of the various sections—ambiguities that are due to simultaneous influences of the principles of strophe, sonata form, and sonata. Other principles also intrude, among which that of rondo is most conspicuous because of the literal and varied recurrences of the tune.

(3) Contrary to the two preceding solutions, one may just as readily hear the opening instrumental section (mm. 1–207) as an integral part of the whole structure. One now deals with a total of eight variations before the new tempo and new theme of the Andante maestoso. The orchestra alone plays three variations; the chorus joins the orchestra for the following five. Yet the apparent numerical discrepancy disappears before the strong impression of parallelism made by the two subsections. Each begins with the shocking "Schreckensfanfare" ("terror fanfare"), each then introduces by way of a recitative the single statement of the theme, and each subsequently embarks on strophic variations of the theme. The repetition of the instrumental by the choral section creates the impression of two parallel units—a gigantic strophe followed by a gigantic antistrophe.

The following Andante maestoso contains all the qualities expected of an epode. Text, melody, tempo, key, and fabric are all new. The double fugue (mm. 655 ff.) confirms the behavior of a recapitulation barform; for the new elements of the epode continue while recapturing the original theme. The end of the epode presents characteristic cadenzas (mm. 832–42) and a stretta.

> *Strophe* (instrumental)
>> Fanfare, recitative, theme, variations
>
> *Antistrophe* (vocal)
>> Fanfare, recitative, theme, variations
>
> *Epode*
>> New theme ("Seid umschlungen")
>> Recapitulation (double fugue on both themes)
>> Coda

Remembering the close original relationship of *barform and *sonata form, one can reconcile this interpretation with the ones given earlier, different as they all may appear. A reader expecting clear-cut answers and used to thinking in fixed patterns should compare the paucity of form principles with the inexhaustible wealth of actually living forms. Extended masterworks are always really, not apparently, complex. The task of the analyst consists, not in the reduction of an individual organism to an abstract pattern, but in the discovery of the sources of the vital complexity.

B. Quotations

FUNDAMENTALS AND METHODS

After you have learned how to measure and have acquired understanding as well as skill, so that you can now make a thing in free certitude, and know how to do justice to each thing, then it will no longer be necessary to measure each thing, for the art you have acquired will provide you with a just eye, and the trained hand will be obedient.

> Albrecht Dürer
> *Von menschlicher Proportion*

The secret of progress is the speculative interest in abstract schemes of morphology. It is hardly realized for how long a time such abstract schemes can grow in the minds of men before contact with practical interests. . . . [Mathematics] is . . . the greatest example of a science of abstract forms.

The abstract theory of music is another such science. . . . The point is that the development of abstract theory precedes the understanding of fact.

> Alfred North Whitehead
> *The Function of Reason*, pp. 73ff.

For many years I have been trying to develop, in cooperation with others, a morphological way of thinking, using the idea of "dynamic" form to unify knowledge and to strengthen our conception of human nature. I have no doubt of the human and scientific importance of the widespread—though, until recently, rather neglected by philosophers and scientists—*tendency toward form*. This is evident in the inorganic world in the genesis of spiral nebulae, of our solar system, of crystals, of molecules, and of much else. It also pervades the organic realm, and in a different sense the ordering processes of the human brain-mind. If the universe was "originally" a vast chaos or a sea of hydrogen, all the forms that have ever existed, or do so now, must have been formed sometime. The cosmos we know is the product of formative processes.

Aristotle thought a great deal about the process of things coming into existence, but not in the sense in which we now mean it. Kepler called this tendency the *facultas formatrix*, Goethe called it *Gestaltung*, and the biologists speak of it in their realm as morphogenesis. I use *formative process* as an inclusive term for all processes in which visual three-dimensional forms are produced. This is a wide class of phenomena, some of which physics and biophysics have only begun to study seriously during the last decade or two. These processes involve a local increase of order, but the precise conditions under which this occurs are as yet known only in some of the simpler cases (e.g., formation of atomic nuclei, of simple molecules, and of crystals).

But if this tendency is widespread, why were the teachers of architecture the first professional group to spot the value of this emphasis on form and formative process? Because architects—unlike physicists, engineers, etc., who are guided by accepted principles and standard textbooks—possess no body of systematic thought expressed in reliable books to assist them in designing things. So they have been glad to follow my explorations of the world of form, philosophical and *pre*-scientific as they are.

It goes deeper than that. Is the architect an imaginative creator of beautiful buildings, a calculating engineer of structures, or a planner of homes enhancing family life? Some claim he is all this and more: a humanist unifying all aspects of life in a manner suited to, say, ten or twenty years hence! Thus they welcome a philosopher of form who tries to make his thinking integral with science and is looking ahead.

The response began with American architects and humanists. Now it comes from biology as well. At this stage the physicists, whose standards are necessarily strict, cannot see much value in philosophical ideas about form. For they still rely on using atomic properties (such as electric charge, spin, etc.) as well as morphological ones (wave patterns, groups). Schrödinger's waves represent *stationary* states, and no one as yet has produced a dynamical theory using only morphological properties. Thus, in the physicist's image of the world, form has not yet been given the central position which it has in the real world. This means that a doctrine of form has gradually to win its way across the spectrum of knowledge, starting with the humanists and perhaps reaching the physicists last.

Lancelot Law Whyte
"Age of Separatism"

The unifying natural philosophy of the coming period may be a morphology, a doctrine of form viewed as structure.

Lancelot Law Whyte
Structure, p. 20

GROWTH AND LIMITATION

Form is both deeply material and highly spiritual. It cannot exist without a material support; it cannot be properly expressed without invoking some supra-material principle. . . . In our western methods of education, the acquisition of a sense of abstract form is based on literary, mathematical, and aesthetic teaching. By studying verse and prose, geometrical relations, sculptural canons, and musical rhythms, sufficiently gifted minds gradually acquire a growing sense of form. Later, if their mental development attains its full maturity, they may become capable of penetrating the modern views on the structure of the universe, or, conversely, on the intimate structure of matter and energy, and thereby recognize that, at both levels, form rejoins order and is best translated by mathematical relations.

. . . No formulation of reality can be satisfactory if it does not imply some concept related to form.

. . .Whatever aspect of form is examined, be it in the most general sense, or in morphogenesis, in evolution, or in mental achievements, the primacy of an Order, of an Idea, can always be asserted.

Albert M. Dalcq
Aspects of Form, pp. 91 ff.

The most obvious function of the plant . . . is growth. . . . The final form of the plant . . . [arises] by a continual production of appendages within growing points. Multiplication of cells . . . goes on without intermission. . . . It is clear therefore that "regulating factors" must exist in the intact organ maintaining an equilibrium between the various cells and inhibiting further division.

F. G. Gregory
Aspects of Form, pp. 58 f.

Here we are investigating the limiting factors which, as it were, select the actual from the row of candidate possibles.

Thus to ask how living organisms come to have the properties they do have is to ask what other properties they could have had.

Joseph Needham
Order and Life, pp. 14 f.

The whole science of biology has its origin in the study of form. . . . Organic forms develop. The flow of time is an essential component of their full nature. . . .

The quality which we recognize as organic wholeness—individuation—is the symptom and expression of an underlying order; an internal order which endows the organ with such unity as it possesses and an external order which relates it to the rest of the organism. . . .

Organic form is, then, the resultant of the interaction of many different forces. The wholeness of the form indicates that this resultant is always in some sense an equilibrium. The internal tensions are balanced against one another into a stable configuration—or rather, nearly balanced, since the configuration is destined slowly to change as development proceeds.

But it is not this slight degree of ill-balance which strikes us, not the remaining elements of arbitrary and unresolved peculiarity, but rather the connectedness and unity. It is instructive to compare the character of the variations from the ideal form in an organic and in human creation. . . .

We come then to conceive of organic form as something which is produced by the interaction of numerous forces which are balanced against one another in a near-equilibrium that has the character not of a precisely definable pattern but rather of a slightly fluid one, a rhythm. It is perhaps easiest to appreciate the character of forms of this kind by considering some of the variations which may be produced when the normal balance of forces is upset.

C. H. Waddington
Aspects of Form, pp. 43 ff.

If this fitting together were too good, the system would jam and could not continue pulsating. Thus biological organization is from one point of view necessarily imperfect, incomplete, and unstable, though in the healthy organism it is always tending to improve and to restore itself after any disturbance.

Lancelot Law Whyte
Accent on Form, pp. 115 f.

Imperfection symbolizes the incompleteness of everything that is alive and can attract things to itself in seeking completion.

. . . The facts of process, of nuclear and atomic chemistry and of life, of necessity involve incomplete patterns trying to become complete. . . . This sets going the whole machinery of process, the valencies of chemistry, and the attractions and repulsions of life.

. . . Incomplete patterns possess their own inherent *élan*. The mathematical symbolism of patterns displays a tendency and movement of its own: toward completion. . . .

Along the main path of structural advance simpler structures must have *preceded* their more complex variants. . . . Structure is not a thing which comes into being arbitrarily, it must grow from simpler to more complex forms by a series of connected steps.

Lancelot Law Whyte
Accent on Form, pp. 96 ff.

MULTIPLICITY AND UNITY

Emergent Evolutionism seems to hold that the specific properties of wholes are conferred on them over and above the specific properties of their parts by a continuous Creativity acting from outside. Dialectical Materialism . . . seems to hold that the specific properties of wholes result from properties of the parts which are invisible or latent in isolation. The former view, which is not dissimilar to the deist conception of the "general concourse" whereby God continuously upholds his creation, seems suited to a religious world-outlook. The latter view seems equally suited to a scientific world-outlook. The problem of which view is correct, if it is a problem, appears to be extra-scientific and quite insoluble.

Joseph Needham
Order and Life, p. 166 n. 91

The universe is dual because, in the fullest sense, it is both transient and eternal. The universe is dual because each final actuality is both physical and mental. The universe is dual because each actuality requires abstract character. The universe is dual because each occasion unites its formal immediacy with objective otherness. The universe is *many* because it is wholly and completely to be analysed into many final actualities—or in Cartesian language, into many *res verae*. The Universe is *one*, because of the universal immanence. There is thus a dualism in this contrast between the unity and multiplicity. Throughout the universe there reigns the union of opposites which is the ground of dualism.

> Alfred North Whitehead
> *Adventures of Ideas*, p. 190

BALANCE

Development, then, consists of a progressive restriction of potencies by determination of parts to pursue fixed fates. It is the conviction of many that this state of affairs can best be pictured in the manner of a series of equilibrium states.

> Joseph Needham
> *Order and Life*, p. 58

BEGINNING, MIDDLE, AND END

The merit of Art in its service to civilization lies in its artificiality and its finiteness. It exhibits for consciousness a finite fragment of human effort achieving its own perfection within its own limits. Thus the mere toil for the slavish purpose of prolonging life for more toil or for mere bodily gratification, is transformed into the conscious realization of a self-contained end, timeless within time. The work of Art is a fragment of nature with the mark on it of a finite creative effort, so that it stands alone, an individual thing detailed from the vague infinity of its background. Thus Art heightens the sense of humanity. It gives an elation of feeling which is supernatural. A sunset is glorious, but it dwarfs humanity and belongs to the general flow of nature. A million sunsets will not spur on men towards civilization. It requires Art to evoke into consciousness the finite perfections which lie ready for human achievement.

> Alfred North Whitehead
> *Adventures of Ideas*, pp. 270 f.

CADENCE

The processes of living systems always display two aspects: a periodic or cyclic aspect which restores the normal state and leaves no net change and a progressive or one-way aspect which results in the cumulative extension or multiplication of the organic patterns. . . .

The heart in pulsating returns to its original state, or very nearly, but it maintains the circulation of the blood. The lungs undergo cycles, and in so doing maintain a perpetual intake of oxygen and discharge of carbon dioxide. . . . There is a systole and diastole, an up-phase and a down-phase in the operation of every organ and structure, yet these cycles take place in a wider system where they produce a cumulative result.

Lancelot Law Whyte
Accent on Form, pp. 114 f.

END

Such old antitheses as that of form and function need not, indeed, detain us, for . . . form is simply a short time-slide of a single spatio-temporal entity. . . . The concrete organism is a spatio-temporal structure and . . . this spatio-temporal structure is the activity itself.

Joseph Needham
Order and Life, p. 6

EXPRESSION

The belief that music is essentially a form of self-expression meets with paradox in very short order; philosophically it comes to a stop almost at its very beginning. For the history of music has been a history of more and more integrated, disciplined, and articulated *forms*. . . . The laws of emotional catharsis are natural laws, not artistic.

Susanne K. Langer
Philosophy in a New Key, p. 175

OPEN-CLOSED

A work of art is a house. A house is much more than a shelter, though shelter is a good symbol for certain nonphysical properties of the house. Among other things, the house is a reflector for our form, our senses, and our thoughts. Interior acoustics is part of the situation. There is something like metaphysical acoustics: curved surfaces are risky, and we do not feel quite right in a circular house. Closedness of form is the highest term in the process of creation because it signifies complete individuation. Hence squares and cubes, delimiting an object on our circular earth and in our spherical cosmos, are perfect enclosures. They provide artistic shelters amidst natural openness. The strong connection of circular houses with the cosmos shows in the emphasis on the vertical axis given by a central smoke hole.

Ernst Levy

PHENOMENALIZATION

Creation means change. Change means form. Any change that may occur in chaos eventuates in nonchaos. Chaos is not perceptible, because the unlimited is not perceptible. Change means phenomenalization. The phenomenalized world is a world of forms.

The higher the degree of indetermination in a phenomeno the less created it appears. The character of a highly indeterminate phenomenon suggests infinity; the form value is small. We imagine infinity only against the foreground of form. A straight line has very little form value by itself. A single tone held indefinitely and devoid of change has no more form value than a single straight line.

Chaos and disorder are not the same. Chaos is no phenomenon at all since the world has come into being. Disorder, however, is constantly threatening us. Entropy is disorder, not chaos, because it is a state of being of phenomena. Disorder exhibits essentially the character of indifference, and in human affairs (even small ones) it is also caused by indifference.

An average level of orderliness is part of style. We evaluate Haydn's composition of "chaos" retrospectively against the fiat of the C major chord. In another context, the piece might assume another significance. Changes in plainsong are very subtle, occurring on the basis of a single tone, or of two tones, and within a restricted ambitus.

In art, infinity cannot be suggested quantitatively (as by a great number of repetitions or by a single held tone) but only qualitatively and symbolically (as by the painting of an open door or by silence within the flow of a composition).

Ernst Levy

PROPORTION

The appearance of symmetry is an invariable characteristic of growth whether it be of a living or non-living system; this is true both of the simpler organisms consisting of single cells and of higher organisms composed of multitudes of such cells. We recognize this symmetry as the characteristic shape of the living organism, and this feature is so constant that it enables us to classify the myriads of living organisms into a comparatively few species; and so enduring is the shape that successive generations of individuals covering vast periods of time may remain substantially unchanged. It must be stressed that the external form of the organism bears no relation to the form of the individual cell, but is dependent upon the mode of aggregation of cells in the tissues and organs.

The study of form in organisms goes by the name of Morphology, a term introduced into biology by Goethe in 1827. He regarded plants as variants of an "archetypical" form.

F. G. Gregory
Aspects of Form, p. 57

The increasing significance given to *form* or *pattern* in various branches of science has suggested the possibility of a certain parallelism, if not identity, in the structures of natural phenomena and of authentic works of art. That the work of art has a formal structure of a rhythmical, even of a precisely geometrical kind, has for centuries been recognized by all but a few nihilists (the Dadaists, for example). That some at any rate of these structures or proportions—notably the Golden Section—have correspondences in nature has also been recognized for many years. The assumption, except on the part of a few mystics, was that nature, in these rare instances, was paying an unconscious tribute to art; or that the artist was unconsciously imitating nature. But now the revelation that perception itself is essentially a pattern-selecting and pattern-making function (a Gestalt formation); that pattern is inherent in the physical structure or in the functioning of the nervous system; that matter itself analyses into coherent patterns or arrangements of molecules; and the gradual realisation that all these patterns are effective and ontologically significant by virtue of an organisation of their parts which can only be characterised as *aesthetic*—all this development has brought works of art and natural phenomena on to an identical plane of enquiry. Aesthetics is no longer an isolated science of beauty; science can no longer neglect aesthetic factors.

Herbert Read
Aspects of Form, Preface

This historical and formative bias, which leads us to look for a past process of formation when we perceive any definite form, has a philosophical justification . . . : asymmetries can disappear and symmetry can develop spontaneously, but existing symmetries cannot disappear without a cause.

Lancelot Law Whyte
Accent on Form, p. 71 n

TIME AND SPACE

The essence of form as being is geometrical. The essence of form as becoming is respiratory (rhythmic). The shape of a tree pertains to geometry. The growth of a tree pertains to breathing. In the arts of space, emphasis is on being. In the arts of time, emphasis is on becoming. The painter or sculptor starts with the idea of a form. The composer starts with the idea of a motion.

But the musical work as a finished product shows a form of which the essence is geometrical, and the form of the painting suggests a movement. Closest to the true essence of music are monody and polyphony, for here geometry is secondary. The listener participates in events of expansion and contraction, of which the layers produce an almost pure time form.

Ernst Levy

TRIAD

We now stand before a problem which the supporters of the Gestalt-theory have hardly yet answered, namely, how is the origin of pattern (*Gestaltcharacter*) in material objects in general and living things in particular, to be explained? Is it not indeed inconceivable that properties should be found in a material complex, which are *not* the result of the summation of the properties of the components? Are we really forced to the assumption of some supra-material, hyper-individual, factors, in order to account for the appearance of the qualitatively new in the organised patterns? In my view there is only one way to picture the organisation of a material complex without having recourse to such assumptions; and that is to assume that the qualitatively new in the pattern derives from the properties of the elements involved, but certain of these properties can only come into operation in connection with certain specific stages of complexity. There is of course no proof available for demonstrating the rightness of this viewpoint. But it will not be denied that it describes the facts in the simplest way and has the advantage of agreeing with the analogy from the social life of man [e.g., combination of musicians in an orchestra, etc.]. If one disagrees with it, one has the choice, *either* of seeking to contest the facts of the existence of non-additive properties in complex patterns, *or* of regarding them as fundamentally inexplicable and unintelligible.

Karl Sapper
Philosophie des Organischen, pp. 85 ff.

VALUE

The most comprehensive natural law expresses a formative tendency.

This universal tendency finds one of its expressions in organisms, which display a tendency both toward the development and extension of a specific stabilized form and toward the development of new forms. . . .

The aesthetic sense, or surprised delight in the products of the formative processes, underlies all human affections, faculties, and judgments, whether these judgments are seen as aesthetic, intellectual, ethical, or practical. . . .

The source of all value is recognized in the *tendency toward* order and harmony.

Lancelot Law Whyte
Accent on Form, pp. 137 f.

Bibliography

Adam de la Halle. *Oeuvres complètes*. Edited by E. de Coussemaker. Paris, 1872. Reprint. Farnborough, England: Gregg Press, 1966.

Adler, Guido. *Handbuch der Musikgeschichte*. Frankfurt: Frankfurter Verlags-Anstalt, 1924.

Anglès, Higini. *El Còdex Musical de las Huelgas*. Barcelona: Institut d'estudis Catalans: Biblioteca de Catalunya, 1931.

Apel, Willi. *The Notation of Polyphonic Music 900–1600*. Cambridge, Massachusetts: The Mediaeval Academy of America, 1953.

Bach, Carl Philipp Emanuel. *Versuch über die wahre Art das Clavier zu spielen*. Berlin, 1753.

──────. *Kurze und leichte Klavierstücke mit veränderten Reprisen*. Edited by Oswald Jonas. Wien: Universal Edition, 1962.

Beethoven, Ludwig van. *Werke*. Vol. 9/2. Reprint. Ann Arbor, Michigan: J. W. Edwards, 1949.

Bergson, Henri. *An Introduction to Metaphysics*. Translated by T. E. Hulme. New York: Liberal Arts Press, 1949.

Besseler, Heinrich. *Die Musik des Mittelalters und der Renaissance*. Potsdam: Athenaion, 1937.

Brahms, Johannes. *Oktaven und Quinten u. A.* Edited by Heinrich Schenker. Wien: Universal-Edition, 1933.

Brossard, Sébastien de. *Dictionnaire de musique*. Paris: Christophe Ballard, 1703.

Buber, Martin. *Daniel: Gespräche von der Verwirklichung*. Leipzig: Insel-Verlag, 1913.

Burckhardt, Jacob. *Der Cicerone*. Stuttgart: Alfred Kröner, 1964.

Busoni, Ferruccio. *Entwurf einer neuen Ästhetik der Tonkunst*. Leipzig: Insel-Verlag, n. d.

Buttree, Julia M. *The Rhythm of the Redman; in Song, Dance and Decoration*. New York: A. S. Barnes, 1930.

Cherubini, Luigi. *Cours de contrepoint et de fugue*. Paris: M. Schlesinger, 1835.

Cole, Malcolm S. "The Vogue of the Instrumental Rondo in the Late 18th Century." *Journal of the American Musicological Society* 22 (1969): 425–55.

Coomaraswamy, Ananda K. *Christian and Oriental Philosophy of Art*. New York: Dover Publications, 1956.

──────. *The Transformation of Nature in Art*. New York: Dover Publications, 1956.

Cooper, Grosvenor W., and Meyer, Leonard B. *The Rhythmic Structure of Music*. Chicago: University of Chicago Press, 1960.

Coussemaker, Edmond de, ed. *Scriptorum de musica medii aevi*. Paris: A. Durand, 1864–76.

Cusanus, Nicolaus. See Kues, Nikolaus von.

Dalcq, Albert M. "Form and Modern Embryology." In *Aspects of Form*, edited by Lancelot Law Whyte, 91–102. Bloomington: Indiana University Press, 1966.

Davison, Archibald T., and Apel, Willi, eds. *Historical Anthology of Music*. Vol. 1. Cambridge, Massachusetts: Harvard University Press, 1970.

Denkmäler der Tonkunst in Oesterreich. Vol. 61. Graz: Akademische Druck- und Verlagsanstalt, 1960.

Des Prez, Josquin. *Werken.* Edited by A. Smijers. Vol. 1. Amsterdam: G. Alsbach, 1925.

Dessoir, Max. *Aesthetik und allgemeine Kunstwissenschaft.* Stuttgart, 1906.

Dürer, Albrecht. *Vier bücher von menschlicher Proportion.* Aus dem ästhetischen Exkurs am Ende des dritten Buches. Nürenberg, 1528.

Expert, Henry, ed. *Les Maîtres Musiciens de la Renaissance Française.* Vol. 7. New York: Broude Brothers, n. d.

Ficker, Rudolf. "Primäre Klangformen." *Jahrbuch der Musikbibliothek Peters für 1929,* vol. 36, pp. 21–34. Leipzig: C. F. Peters, 1930.

Fischer, Kurt von. "Eroica-Variationen op. 35 und Eroica-Finale." *Schweizerische Musikzeitung* 89 (1949): 282–86.

Fitzwilliam Virginal Book. Edited by J. A. Fuller Maitland and W. Barclay Squire. 2 vols. 1899. Reprint. New York: Dover Publications, 1963.

Fux, Johann Joseph. *Gradus ad Parnassum.* Translated by Alfred Mann, *Steps to Parnassus.* New York: W. W. Norton, 1943.

Geiringer, Karl. "The Structure of Beethoven's Diabelli Variations." *The Musical Quarterly* 50 (1964): 496–503.

Gennrich, Friedrich. *Rondeaux, Virelais und Balladen.* 3 vols. Dresden: Gesellschaft für romanische Literatur, 1921–63.

Gerbert, Martin, ed. *Scriptores ecclesiastici de musica.* St. Blasius, 1784.

Giraldus Cambrensis. *The Itinerary through Wales.* Everyman's Library. London: J. M. Dent & Sons, 1935.

Goethe, Johann Wolfgang. "Zur Morphologie" (1817). *Naturwissenschaftliche Schriften.* Hamburger Goethe-Ausgabe. Vol. 13. Hamburg: Christian Wegner, 1955.

Gregory, F. G. "Form in Plants." In *Aspects of Form,* edited by Lancelot Law Whyte, 57–76. Bloomington: Indiana University Press, 1966.

Guthrie, Kenneth Sylvan. *Pythagoras: Source-book and Library.* North Yonkers, N. Y.: Platonist Press, 1920.

Harvard Dictionary of Music. Edited by Willi Apel. Cambridge, Massachusetts: Harvard University Press, 1946.

Hornbostel, Erich von. "Ueber Mehrstimmigkeit in der aussereuropäischen Musik." In *Kongressbericht der Haydn-Zentenarfeier,* 298–303. Wien, 1909.

Huizinga, J. *The Waning of the Middle Ages.* Garden City, N.Y.: Doubleday, 1954.

Huygens, Christian. *Treatise on Light.* 1690. New English edition. New York: Dover Publications, 1962.

Jacobsthal, Gustav. *Die chromatische Alteration im liturgischen Gesang der abendländischen Kirche.* Berlin: J. Springer, 1897.

Jonas, Oswald. *Das Wesen des musikalischen Kunstwerks.* Wien: Saturn Verlag, 1934.

Kauder, Hugo. *Counterpoint: An Introduction to Polyphonic Composition.* New York: Macmillan, 1960.

Kayser, Hans. "Pythagoras." In *Abhandlungen zur Ektypik Harmonikaler Wertformen.* Zürich und Leipzig: Max Niehans, 1938.

———. *Lehrbuch der Harmonik.* Zürich: Occident Verlag, 1950.

Kepes, Gyorgy, ed. *Structure in Art and in Science.* New York: George Braziller, 1965.

Kirkpatrick, Ralph. *Domenico Scarlatti.* Princeton: Princeton University Press, 1953.

Kues, Nikolaus von. *Philosophisch-Theologische Schriften.* Edited by Leo Gabriel. 3 vols. Wien: Verlag Herder, 1966.

Kuhnau, Johann. *Klavierwerke.* Denkmäler deutscher Tonkunst. Vol. 4. Wiesbaden: Breitkopf und Härtel, 1958.

Kurth, Ernst. *Romantische Harmonik und ihre Krise in Wagners "Tristan."* Berlin: Max Hesse, 1920.

Lach, Robert. *Das Konstruktionsprinzip der Wiederholung in Musik, Sprache und Literatur.* Wien: Hölder-Pichler-Tempsky, 1925.

Lal Roy, Robindra. "Hindustani Ragas." *Musical Quarterly* 3 (1934): 320–33.

Langer, Susanne K. *Philosophy in a New Key: A Study in the Symbolism of Reason, Rite, and Art.* New York: Penguin Books, 1948.

Levarie, Siegmund. *Fugue and Form.* Chicago, 1941.

————. "An Application of a Historical Principle to Early Opera." *Chicago Review* 5 (1951): 38–43. Abstract in *Journal of the American Musicological Society* 2 (1949): 98–99.

————. *Mozart's "Le nozze di Figaro": A Critical Analysis.* Chicago: University of Chicago Press, 1952. Reprint New York: Da Capo Press, 1977.

————. *Guillaume de Machaut.* New York: Sheed & Ward, 1954. Reprint New York: Da Capo Press, 1970.

————. "Noise." *Critical Inquiry* 4 (1977): 21–31.

————. "Once More: The Slow Introduction to Beethoven's First Symphony." *The Music Review* 40 (1979): 168–75.

————. "Music as a Structural Model." *Journal of Social and Biological Structures* 3 (1980): 237–45.

Levarie, Siegmund, and Levy, Ernst. *Tone: A Study in Musical Acoustics.* Kent, Ohio: Kent State University Press, 1968. Second, revised edition 1980. Reprint Westport, Connecticut: Greenwood Press, 1981.

Levy, Ernst. "Essay sur la dodécaphonie." *Schweizerische Musikzeitung* 106 (1966): 355–60.

————. *Des rapports entre la musique et la société. Réflexions.* Neuchâtel: Baconnière, 1979.

Liber usualis. Paris, Tournai, and Rome: Desclée & Socii, 1937.

Lorenz, Alfred. *Der musikalische Aufbau des Bühnenfestspieles "Der Ring des Nibelungen." Das Geheimnis der Form bei Richard Wagner.* Vol. 1. Berlin: Max Hesse, 1924.

————. *Der musikalische Aufbau von Richard Wagners "Tristan und Isolde." Das Geheimnis der Form bei Richard Wagner.* Vol. 2. Berlin: Max Hesse, 1926.

————. *Abendländische Musikgeschichte im Rhythmus der Generationen.* Berlin: Max Hesse, 1928.

Lowinsky, Edward E. *Secret Chromatic Art in the Netherlands Motet.* New York: Columbia University Press, 1946.

Machaut, Guillaume de. *La Prise d'Alexandrie.* Edited by L. de Mas Latrie. Geneva, 1877.

————. *Musikalische Werke.* Vols. 1 and 3. Edited by Friedrich Ludwig. Leipzig: Breitkopf & Härtel, 1926 and 1929.

McClain, Ernest G. *The Myth of Invariance: The Origin of the Gods, Mathematics, and Music.* New York: Nicolas Hays, 1976.

————. *The Pythagorean Plato: Prelude to the Song Itself.* Stony Brook, New York: Nicolas Hays, 1978.

Marco, Guy. "A Musical Task in the 'Surprise' Symphony." *Journal of the American Musicological Society* 11 (1958): 41–44.

Motu Proprio on Sacred Music. Vatican City, 1903.

Needham, Joseph. *Order and Life.* New Haven: Yale University Press, 1936.

————. *Biochemistry and Morphogenesis.* 3d ed. Cambridge: Cambridge University Press, 1966.

Obrecht, Jacobus. *Opera omnia.* Vol. 6, *Missa Sub tuum praesidium.* Vol. 7, *Missa Maria zart.* Edited by Max Van Crevel. Amsterdam: Vereniging voor nederlandse Musiekgeschiedenis, 1959–64.

Orenstein, Herta. *Die Refrainformen im Chansonnier de l'Arsenal.* Brooklyn: Institute of Mediaeval Music, 1970.

Pannwitz, Rudolf. *Kosmos Atheos: Renaissance der Vokalmusik aus dem Geiste und als Schöpfung des Kosmos Atheos.* München: Hans Carl, 1926.

Plotinus. *The Enneads.* Translated by Stephen MacKenna. 4th ed. Revised by B. S. Page. London: Faber and Faber Limited, 1969.

Porter, David H. "The Structure of Beethoven's Diabelli Variations, op. 120." *The Music Review* 31 (1970): 295–301.

Ratner, Leonard G. "Harmonic Aspects of Classic Form." *Journal of the American Musicological Society* 2 (1949): 159–68.

———. "Eighteenth-Century Theories of Musical Period Structure." *Musical Quarterly* 42 (1956): 439–54.

Read, Herbert. "Preface." In *Aspects of Form*, edited by Lancelot Law Whyte, v–vi. Bloomington: Indiana University Press, 1966.

Riemann, Hugo. *Musikalische Dynamik und Agogik.* Hamburg & St. Petersburg: D. Rahter, 1884.

Rokseth, Yvonne. *Polyphonies du xiii᷎ siècle.* 4 vols. Paris: Éditions de l'Oiseau lyre, 1935–39.

Sachs, Curt. "Some Remarks about Old Notation." *The Musical Quarterly* 34 (1948): 365–70.

Sapper, Karl. *Philosophie des Organischen.* Breslau: Hirt, 1928.

Schenker, Heinrich. *Kontrapunkt: Cantus Firmus und zweistimmiger Satz.* Neue musikalische Theorien und Phantasien. Vol. 2/1. Wien-Leipzig: Universal-Edition, 1910.

Schneider, Marius. *Geschichte der Mehrstimmigkeit.* 2 vols. Berlin: Julius Bard Verlag, 1934–35.

Schönberg, Arnold. *Harmonielehre.* Leipzig-Wien: Universal-Edition, 1911.

Schrödinger, Erwin. "Heredity and the Quantum Theory." In *The World of Mathematics*, edited by James R. Newman. New York: Simon and Schuster, 1956.

Schumann, Robert. *Gesammelte Schriften über Musik und Musiker.* Leipzig: Breitkopf & Härtel, 1914.

Schütz, Heinrich. *Sämmtliche Werke.* Vol. 7. Edited by Philipp Spitta. Leipzig: Breitkopf & Härtel, 1888.

Speiser, Andreas. "Ueber die Freiheit." *Basler Universitätsreden.* Vol. 28. Rektoratsrede, gehalten am 24. November 1950. Basel: Helbing und Lichtenhahn, 1950.

Strunk, Oliver, ed. *Source Readings in Music History.* New York: W. W. Norton & Company, 1950.

Thimus, Albert von. *Die harmonikale Symbolik des Alterthums.* Köln: DuMont-Schauberg, 1868–76.

Thompson, D'Arcy. *On Growth and Form.* Cambridge: Cambridge University Press, 1966.

Travis, James. *Miscellanea Musica Celtica.* Brooklyn: The Institute of Mediaeval Music, 1968.

Vecchi, Orazio. *Convito Musicale.* Rome: De Santis, 1966.

Vermeulen, Matthijs. "Seventh Symphony: Dithyrambes pour les temps à venir." *Sonorum Speculum* 29 (1966): 24–36.

Vitruvius. *The Ten Books on Architecture.* Translated by Morris H. Morgan. New York: Dover Publications, 1960.

Waddington, C. H. "The Character of Biological Form." In *Aspects of Form*, edited by Lancelot Law Whyte, 43–56. Bloomington: Indiana University Press, 1966.

Walker, Thomas. "Ciaccona and Passacaglia: Remarks on their Origin and Early History." *Journal of the American Musicological Society* 21 (1968): 300–320.

Bibliography

Warrain, Francis. *Essai sur L'Harmonices Mundi ou Musique du Monde de Johann Kepler*. Fondements Mathématiques de L'Harmonie. Tome I. Paris: Hermann & Cie., 1942.

Weingartner, Felix. *Ratschläge für Aufführungen der Symphonien Beethovens*. Leipzig: Breitkopf & Härtel, 1916.

Weyl, Hermann. *Symmetry*. Princeton: Princeton University Press, 1952.

Whitehead, Alfred North. *An Enquiry concerning the Principles of Natural Knowledge*. Cambridge: University Press, 1919.

————. *Adventures of Ideas*. New York: Free Press, 1967.

————. *The Function of Reason*. Boston: Beacon Press, 1967.

————. *Modes of Thought*. New York: Free Press, 1968.

Whyte, Lancelot Law. *Accent on Form: An Anticipation of the Science of Tomorrow*. World Perspectives. Vol. 2. New York: Harper and Brothers, 1954.

————. "Atomism, Structure and Form." In *Structure in Art and in Science*, edited by Gyorgy Kepes, 20–28. New York: George Braziller, 1965.

————, ed. *Aspects of Form: A Symposium on Form in Nature and Art*. Bloomington: Indiana University Press, 1966.

————. "The End of the Age of Separatism." *Saturday Review*, 18 May 1968.

Wölfflin, Heinrich. *Kunstgeschichtliche Grundbegriffe*. München: F. Bruckmann, 1915.

Yasser, Joseph. *A Theory of Evolving Tonality*. New York: American Library of Musicology, 1932.

Index of Composers and Compositions

Siegmund Levarie, Professor of Music at Brooklyn College, CUNY, has taught at the University of Chicago, was dean of the Chicago Musical College, and executive director of the Fromm Music Foundation. He has served on the National Council of the American Musicological Society, the National Fulbright Committee on Musicology, and is a regular member of the Metropolitan Opera Texaco Quiz panel. The late Ernst Levy was well known on both sides of the Atlantic as a concert pianist and a prolific composer. He founded the Philharmonic Choir in Paris and directed the first concerts of requiems of Brahms, Verdi, Liszt, and Kodály. He taught at the New England Conservatory of Music, the University of Vermont, the University of Chicago, M.I.T., and Brooklyn College, CUNY. Both authors have lectured and written widely on musical subjects; their previous book collaboration was *Tone: A Study in Musical Acoustics*, also published by the Kent State University Press.